John Adolphus

Biographical Memoirs of the French Revolution

John Adolphus

Biographical Memoirs of the French Revolution

ISBN/EAN: 9783743313453

Manufactured in Europe, USA, Canada, Australia, Japa

Cover: Foto ©ninafisch / pixelio.de

Manufactured and distributed by brebook publishing software (www.brebook.com)

John Adolphus

Biographical Memoirs of the French Revolution

BIOGRAPHICAL

MEMOIRS

OF

THE FRENCH REVOLUTION.

By JOHN ADOLPHUS, F.S.A.

IN TWO VOLUMES.

VOL. II.

LONDON:

PRINTED FOR T. CADELL, JUN. AND W. DAVIES,
IN THE STRAND.

1799.

MICHEL LEPELLETIER DE SAINT FARGEAU.

THE family of Lepelletier was originally of Mans, where records of its establishment were preserved as far back as the year 1508. His father was a judge, and filled that office with remarkable severity. *His family.*

The subject of these memoirs was bred to the profession of the law, and attained the important and honorable office of *président à Mortier*, in the parliament of Paris [a]. *Birth and profession.*

Before the revolution, Lepelletier was remarkably unobtrusive; he forbore interfering in the disputes between his body and the crown [b]; would not assume titles of nobility, though he possessed several counties and marquisates in his own right [c]; and principally employed himself in the improvement of the very large property he derived from his father. His great wealth procured him the reputation of being proud and avaricious, and his making so unimportant a figure with so many advantages, gave rise to an opinion very derogatory to his talents [d]. He was, however, a member of the society *des Amis des Noirs*, and *Conduct previous to the revolution,*

---

[a] Dictionnaire de la Noblesse. Conjuration de d'Orleans, vol. iii. p. 232.
[b] Apologie des Projets, &c. p. 226.
[c] Impartial History, vol. i. p. 347.
[d] Madame Roland calls him "a poor rich man," *homme foible et riche.* Appel. vol. ii. p. 72. But the author of the *Apologie des Projets*, &c. who is not to be suspected of partiality towards Lepelletier, allows him to have possessed wit, learning, and vigor of intellect, p. 220.

considered of importance sufficient to be one of the regulating committee [e].

in the constituent assembly. He was a member of the constituent assembly, where his eloquence procured him no admiration, but from the beginning of the revolution he attached himself to Orleans, and never deserted his party. In this he was influenced by the timidity of avarice, and the desire of increasing his store; he was persuaded that nothing but the friendship of the predominating party could rescue him from proscription, and was amused with expectations, which applied to his prevailing and insatiable passion, and produced a firm adherence to men, from whose conduct the purity *4th August 1789.* of his mind might have led him to revolt [f]. He was president of the assembly at that famous sitting when an inconsiderate emulation led the nobility and clergy to sacrifice all their rights and privileges, and spoke *19th June 1790.* with some effect on the question concerning the abolition of titles [g].

Forms the penal code. His principal labor was the formation of the penal code in the new constitution, which gave rise to many debates. His mind was by nature disposed to mercy and gentleness, and though the grafting of modern philosophy on a student of the old jurisprudence, sometimes produced a grotesque, sometimes an immoral effect; yet all his notions were derived from laudable sources, and many of them had an appearance of rectitude and propriety. He was, at first, for abolishing pains of death, confining the punishment of crimes to civic degradation, public exposure, solitary imprisonment, chains, or hard labor, according to the magnitude of the offence. This innovation was too great for him to carry, but he succeeded in obtaining a suppression of all tortures or superadded punishments, or, to use his own phrase, "re-

---

[e] Memoire du Jacobinisme, par Barruel, vol. ii. p. 447.
[f] Conjuration de d'Orleans, vol. i. p. 295. Apologie, &c. ubi supra.
[g] Impartial History, vol. i. p. 185. 347. Debates.

"duced

" duced the sentence of death, to the privation of life."
In other parts of his code he betrayed great want of judgment, and shewed himself completely bewildered in the labyrinths of pretended philosophy. He attempted, with a correctness truly ridiculous, to fix the proportions of punishment to be inflicted on an unnatural son, who maimed his parent, so as to make the extent of the penalty, exactly commensurate to the nature of the injury. He endeavoured to obtain for malefactors a period of three days to appeal against their sentence, or move in arrest of judgment; he abolished whipping and branding of criminals, but, on the other hand, he gave to primary assemblies an undefined power of correctional punishment, and inflicted four years imprisonment on the person who should strike a public functionary. He was the parent of two monsters in the jurisprudential system, which frustrated all the humanity of his intentions; namely, that juries should decide on the law, the fact, and the intention of the parties, and should apply the punishment; and that the crown should be deprived of the power of pardoning. He was the first who introduced the practice of the president putting on his hat in cases of tumult which his authority was insufficient to restrain [h]. *26th June 1790.*

From the dissolution of the constituent assembly, he remained in obscurity; he made no figure at the Jacobin club, and I find no trace of him in any public transaction, except an address, which, as president of the department of Yonne, he presented to the legislative assembly, on the subject of the war, and which was ordered to be printed, and procured him the honors of the sitting [i]. *Presents an address to the legislative assembly, 20th December 1791.*

He was returned to the national convention for the department of Yonne, but was as little distin- *Member of the convention.*

[h] See the Debates of the Constituent Assembly, from the 23d of May 1791 to its dissolution; and for the last fact, Anecdotes du Regne de Louis XVI. vol. vi. p. 153.
[i] Debates.

B 2 guished,

guished, as in the preceding part of his career. He shewed his attachment to the Mountain, and more particularly to Orleans, by voting against the Brissotine motion for a law against the instigators of murder, alleging as a reason, that it would be a restraint on the liberty of the press. His conduct respecting the king's trial is involved in much doubt and uncertainty. It is said, on one hand, that he had made an oath never to vote for the death of any person, but that Orleans, fearing the question of the king's condemnation would be lost, partly by terror, and partly by promises, influenced him to change his determination, and to bring over twenty-five members who had resolved to vote as he did [k]. In support of this assertion, Brissot says, that Lepelletier, at the committee of legislation, in the presence of twenty witnesses, defended the propriety of an appeal to the people, and said, if the appeal was not carried, it would be most advisable to vote for the imprisonment of the king [l]. But I do not consider it at all certain, that he ever intended to shew any mercy to the imprisoned sovereign, or to vote otherwise than as the faction to whom he had attached himself should direct. Long before the period alluded to by Brissot, he brought up an address from the friends of the republic at Auxerre, in which were these expressions: "Nations wait with anxiety for the sentence you are about to pass on Louis XVI. Let it be *terrible and speedy;* let it make the tyrants of the earth tremble.—Let the blood of the most worthless of conspirators expiate his crimes *without delay* [m]." It is very improbable that a man who favoured such an address, should be an advocate for an appeal to the people, or for any other measure tending to save the king. But a stronger proof arises from the opinion on this business, which he, like

---

[k] Conjuration de d'Orleans, vol. iii. p. 232. Pagès Histoire Secrete, vol ii. p. 255.
[l] Brissot à ses Commettans, p. 18. n.   [m] Debates.

many

LEPELLETIER.

many others, had publiſhed pending the trial; in which he ſaid, that, " if the repreſentatives of the " people openly betrayed their cauſe, by pronoun- " cing againſt their conſcience, the acquittal of the " tyrant, then the people would have a right of inſur- " rection; that is to ſay, a right of withdrawing their " confidence from their treacherous deputies." He was afterwards reproached by Petion in the conven- tion for this very declaration ⁿ. *5th January 1793.*

He voted for the ſentence of death, and againſt the appeal to the people. The day of the king's ex- ecution, he went to dine at a coffee-houſe in the *Jardin de l'Egalité*. Six perſons came from an ad- joining apartment, and one of them ſaid, " There is " that ſcoundrel Lepelletier."—" My name is Le- pelletier," he anſwered; " but I am no ſcoundrel."— " Did you not vote for the death of the king?" ſaid the aſſaſſin. " I did," anſwered the deputy; " but " that was a duty impoſed on me by my conſcience." Hardly had he uttered theſe words, when the perſon to whom they were addreſſed, plunged a ſabre in his body, and made his eſcape. The wounded deputy was taken home, and expired at one o'clock the next morning. *His death.* *21ſt January.*

Such is the account of this event given in the con- vention, and publiſhed by their authority. The Mountain availed themſelves of the pretended cir- cumſtances, to impute the fact to their political anta- goniſts; their declamations in the convention, the addreſs of the Jacobin club to the affiliated ſocieties and to the legiſlative body, dwell ſtrongly on this fact, and it tended very much to deſtroy the popularity of the Briſſotines ᵒ. But there are many improbabilities in the narrative; particularly that ſo long a converſa- tion, and ſo deliberate a murder, ſhould take place *Obſervations on its effects.*

ⁿ Robeſpierre à ſes Commettans, vol. ii. p. 194.

ᵒ See Debates in the Convention, 21ſt January, 8th and 25th Fe- bruary, 1793. See alſo Robeſpierre à ſes Commettans, vol. ii. p. 130. 241. 346. Briſſot à ſes Commettans, p. 27. n.

in a public coffee-house, in the most frequented part of Paris, and yet the assassin escape, without any effort being made to detain him. It is said, on the other side, that the man who murdered him, uttered a few hasty reproaches, and then perpetrated the deed; that St. Fargeau fell, and immediately expired, uttering only the words, "*J'ai froid,*" *I am cold*[p]. We are told, that the deceased, at the moment of expiring, uttered a fine sentence, which was engraved on his tomb; but this is very improbable. No mention was made of it in the first report of the affair to the convention, and the fiction was obviously calculated to answer two views; to counteract the impression of the last words of the monarch, and to excite suspicions of the Brissotines, by the hope they contain, that the death of the speaker would *unmask the enemies of the republic.*

31st January 1793.
Death of Paris, his supposed murderer.

Ten days after Lepelletier's death, his presumed assassin was discovered, at Forges les Eaux. He was an ex-guard of the king, named Paris. After the death of Lepelletier, a search had been directed, which took place the 29th, on which day Paris is supposed to have made his escape; he pursued his way to Forges, where he arrived the 31st. The manner in which he behaved at the inn exciting some suspicions, a guard was sent for; and while they were putting some questions to him, he blew out his brains, *with a double-barrelled pistol, loaded with two chewed bullets*[q]. When he was stripped, two papers were found next his stomach; the *tender-hearted* Tallien declined shewing them to the convention, because, being stained with blood, they were a disgusting spectacle; but, on his word, one of them contained these expressions: " MY BREVET OF HONOR."— " Let no one be molested. No one was my accom- " plice in the fortunate execution of the villain St.

[p] Conjuration de d'Orleans, vol. iii. p. 241. Pagès Histoire Secrete, vol. ii. p. 70.
[q] Tallien's Report to the Convention, February 5th.

" Fargeau.

"Fargeau. If he had not fallen, I would have done a more praise-worthy action, I would have purged the country of the regicide, the patricide, the parricide, Orleans.—Let no one be molested.—The French are a nation of dastards, to whom I leave these words:

"Peuple, dont les forfaits jettent partout l'effroi,
"Avec calme et plaisir j'abandonne la vie,
"Ce n'est que par la mort qu'on peut fuir l'infamie
"Qu'imprime sur nos fronts le sang de notre roi."

Frenchmen, whose crimes, the universe affright,
Life I resign, with calmness and delight;
By death alone I shun the dire disgrace,
Which our king's blood, stamps on each Frenchman's face.

On this absurd narrative I shall make no comment. The following extract from madame Roland, will enable the reader to form his own conjectures:

"The assassination of Lepelletier is still a kind of mystery; but I shall never forget two circumstances, which I will relate in this place: 1st, That I saw all the persons who are at this day proscribed, in despair at the event; I saw Buzot and Louvet sighing, and shedding tears of anger, under a persuasion *that some bold mountaineer had perpetrated this action, to attribute it to the right side, and to make it the means of exciting the popular fanaticism against them.* 2d, That Gorsas, declaring pretty plainly the same opinion, adds, that in all probability *the assassin would never be discovered, or would not be brought forward alive.* It is true that a Parisian mountaineer, employed with another to search after the assassin, met with Paris in Normandy, in a public house, where they said he blew out his brains. It is also true that the Mountain made a kind of saint of Lepelletier, a silly, "rich

8 LEPELLETIER.

"rich man, who certainly never expected any such thing, having joined them through fear; the only essential service he ever rendered them was, in dying as he did'."

Funeral and posthumous honors.

The honors paid to St. Fargeau, after his decease, form an extraordinary contrast with the insignificance of his life. Robespierre himself made the motion, that his body should be deposited in the Pantheon, and that the convention should attend his funeral.

24th January.

The ceremony was performed with the utmost grandeur and solemnity. The pedestal in the *place Vendôme*, on which the statue of Louis XIV. formerly stood, was adorned with a drapery of white crape, with festoons of oak and cypress. On each side were placed vases with frankincense, and on two of its faces were written, in letters of gold, the supposed last words of Lepelletier: "I am content to shed my blood for my country; I hope it will consolidate liberty and equality, and unmask our enemies." At eight o'clock in the morning, detachments of volunteers and national guards, with fifes and muffled drums, were on the ground. At eleven, the body of Lepelletier, stark naked to shew his wound, was brought from his brother's house, and deposited on the pedestal. The members of the convention arrived at twelve; the president placed a civic garland on the head of the deceased; a funeral oration was pronounced, after which a procession set out from the *place Vendôme*, to the *Pantheon*, in the following order:

A Company of Miners.
A Banner.
A Troop of Horse.
A Body of Pikemen.
The Tables of the Law.
A Body of Horse.

' Appel à l'impartiale Posterité, vol. ii. p. 71.

A Ban-

LEPELLETIER.

A Banner.
The Declaration of the Rights of Man.
A Corps of Cannoneers.
The Statue of Liberty.
Detachment of Federates.
The *Fasces* of the 84 Departments, carried by Federates.
Muffled Drums and Fifes.
The Banner of the Republic.
Twelve Huissiers.
The President of the Convention, surrounded by the Honorary Secretaries.
The Members of the National Convention two and two

THE BODY OF LEPELLETIER.

This was reclining on the bed on which he died, the sheets of which were drenched with his blood.
The Corpse was naked, in order to display his ghastly wound.
On one side of the Corpse,
The Sabre of the Assassin suspended from a Pike;
On the other,
The Clothes which he had on when he was murdered.
The Family and Relations of the Deceased.
A Banner, with the dying Deputy's last Words inscribed upon it.
Warlike Music. [The Drums and Fifes, &c. muffled.]
The Provisional Executive Council.
A Body of Pikemen.
The Directory of the Department.
A Body of Horse.
The Municipality of Paris.
A Detachment of Cannoneers.
A Number of Mothers with their Children.
A Band of Pikemen.
The Electoral Body of Paris.
Eight Huissiers.
The Members of the Courts of Justice.
A Body of Federates.

A Scar-

LEPELLETIER.

A Scarlet Bonnet.
The Jacobin Society.
A Body of Federates.
A Body of Horse.
A Company of Pioneers.

This procession lasted two hours, during which, the music of the national guards performed a funeral dirge. The remains of Lepelletier were deposited in the Pantheon, in a niche between those of Voltaire and Mirabeau. The music played several airs; the brother of the deceased delivered an oration in his praise; the members of the convention swore to preserve union and confraternity, and to save the country; and the ceremony concluded with a grand chorus to Liberty [s].

But this was not the only step taken to perpetuate his memory; the section *des filles St. Thomas* took his name, and one of the ships of the republic was called after him. Forty-eight feasts were given in honor of him and Marat; mausoleums were erected to him in every commune; his bust was in all the temples, and theatres, and, throughout the departments, was to be seen in almost every house; Robespierre himself placed it on the altar of the Supreme Being, the day he made his absurd and sacrilegious feast.[t]

Lepelletier, at the time of his death, was on the point of forming a matrimonial engagement with Madame de Fontenay, daughter of the famous Gabarus, who was so long persecuted by the inquisition [u]. His property was inherited by his brother, of whom M. de Montgaillard speaks with great severity [x].

[s] See the French journals and English newspapers of the time.
[t] Etat de la France, par M. le Comte de Montgaillard, p. 70. Suite du même, p. 36.
[u] Political State of Europe, vol. iii. p. 179.
[x] Suite de l'Etat de la France, p. 73.

The

The day after the performance of Lepelletier's funeral ceremony, his two brothers attended at the bar of the convention, with his infant daughter, and one of them holding her up, exclaimed with sobs, "People, behold your child!" The convention immediately passed a decree, that she was adopted by the nation[y].

25th January. His daughter adopted by the nation.

[y] Robespierre à ses Commettans, vol. ii. p. 352.

PIERRE MANUEL.

Birth and education. MANUEL was son of a linen-draper [a] at Montargis; he received a liberal education, and, early in life, went to Paris, without money, and almost without recommendation, to improve his fortune by the exercise of his abilities. He commenced author, and produced a few works, the names of which are now no longer remembered. His literary efforts were so ill recompensed, that he hired himself to a banker in Paris, as tutor to his children, for which he was allowed a thousand livres (43 *l.* 15 *s.*) a-year. He was afterwards retained by M. de Sartines, as a spy for the police, in the department of publications [b], but **Writes libels.** being of a disposition rather to disseminate scandal than to suppress it, he turned his pen against the court, and wrote a pamphlet respecting the famous affair of the necklace, intitled " *Lettre d'un Garde* **Is imprisoned.** *du Roi.*" This publication, together with the suspicion of his being engaged in selling prohibited **3d February 1786.** works, occasioned his imprisonment. He says he was confined in the Bastille [c], but his enemies affect to deprive him of that honor, and say that the place of **7th April 1786. Discharged.** his retreat was the *Bicêtre*. He was soon enlarged, and returned to Montargis, where he supported himself by hawking about prohibited and indecent books [d].

[a] Bastille dévoillée, 3ᵉ livraison, p. 105. Many persons have said that Manuel's father was a potter.
[b] Conspiracy of Robespierre, p. 45.
[c] Bastille dévoillée, 3ᵉ livraison, p. 105.
[d] Peltier's late Picture of Paris, vol. ii. p. 240.

This livelihood, thus obtained, was scanty and precarious; he therefore, once again, repaired to Paris, and resumed his labors as an author, by a publication called *L'Année Françoise*, intended as a course of juvenile biography, in which he applied to every day in the year the life of some illustrious Frenchman. Manuel's style is disgusting from affectation and pedantry; his work was unfavorably treated by the critics, and the author was reduced to the situation of a newsman and bill-sticker [e].

<small>His poverty.</small>

While he was thus struggling against poverty, the revolution commenced, and promised more advantageous employment. After the destruction of the Bastille, he became a Jacobin, and was taken into the protection of the duke of Orleans, but did not receive from him any effectual supply [f]. He was, however, named provisionally to the administration of the police, in the department of Paris. In this situation, he obtained access to many original papers, and selected from them such as he thought he could afterwards advantageously dispose of to the booksellers [g]. The formation of a more permanent body of police occasioned Manuel's dismission, before he had time to gain any considerable advantages from his employ. He occupied himself for some time in preparing for the press these papers he had so unfairly obtained, and, in about a year, produced in two octavo volumes *La Police de Paris dévoillée*. This work affords a copious collection of all the abuses, real and pretended, which were attributed to the old government. It gave the compiler an opportunity of gratifying his habitual rancor against priests, and against religion; he has abused both in the coarsest and most unqualified terms. It had considerable success, which was probably much increased by exaggerated accounts of the misery of

<small>1789. Conduct at the revolution.</small>

<small>1791. Publishes La Police dévoillée.</small>

---

[e] Peltier's late Picture of Paris, vol. ii. p. 240.
[f] Conjuration de d'Orleans, vol. iii. p. 146.
[g] Mercure Françoise, No. du 19 Mai 1792, p. 209.

the

the lower class of people in England, and by the suggestions of an approaching revolution [h].

December 1791.
Publishes Mirabeau's letters.

At the dissolution of the constituent assembly, he was looked upon as a republican, but he was for some time afterwards attached to the interests of the duke of Orleans [i]. Still Manuel was not opulent, he lived in a garret, at the house of Garnery the bookseller, where he employed himself in decyphering, preparing for the press, and correcting the proofs of another book, which his breach of trust enabled him to publish. It was intitled, *Lettres originales de Mirabeau, ecrites du Donjon de Vincennes, pendent les Années* 1777, 78, 79, *et* 80; *contenant tous les details sur sa vie privée, ses malheurs, et ses amours avec Sophie Ruffei marquise de Monnier.* The interest excited by every thing relating to Mirabeau, promised an extensive and rapid sale; Manuel received from the booksellers two thousand crowns (250 *l.*) for the copy [k]. But the creditors of Mirabeau, who considered themselves better entitled to the produce of this publication than any other person, obtained an order from an administrator of the police, named Maugis, authorizing them to seize the original letters, and prevent a continuation of the impression. Manuel exclaimed loudly against this proceeding, which, for violence and suddenness, was open to the imputation of illegality; he had the address to put himself on the footing of Chamfort, and other honest proprietors of Mirabeau's letters, and by clamorous appeals to the people, by abuse, and threats, silenced all opposition. The public expectation was grievously disappointed; the letters added nothing to Mirabeau's fame, nor was the transaction which procured, or the preface which

---

[h] See the work itself, published by De Boffe, London; also Mercure François Litteraire, du 23 Juillet 1791.
[i] Moore's View, vol. ii. p. 474. Conjuration de d'Orleans, vol. iii. p. 131. 146. Eloge Funebre, &c. par M. Montjoye, p. 106.
[k] Peltier's late Picture of Paris, vol. ii. p. 240.

ushered them into notice, at all advantageous to Manuel [1].

Previous to this publication, he was named *procureur syndique* to the *commune* of Paris. He owed this elevation to his connection with the Jacobins, but did not obtain it without a struggle. M. Bosquillon, a justice of peace, of the most amiable and virtuous character, opposed his election, alleging several circumstances tending to disqualify him. Manuel surmounted this opposition by the same means he employed against Mirabeau's creditors, but he never forgave Bosquillon, and, in the end, sacrificed him to his revenge [m]. This appointment put Manuel in possession of fifteen thousand livres (656*l*. 5*s*.) a-year, besides an extensive patronage [n].

In this situation he gave so many proofs of personal disrespect, and behaved with so much insolence to the king, that he obtained the nickname of *l'anti Roi*, a name with which he was not displeased [o]. His brutality was displayed on every occasion, and he omitted no endeavour to render the king's situation irksome and insupportable. His principal motive for this conduct is said to have been the hope of inducing or compelling the king to a second flight, which would have amounted to an abdication of the throne, and paved a way for the advancement of Orleans [p]. This project, worthy the pitiful machiavelism of Petion and Manuel, being frustrated by the king's resolute adherence to the constitution, it was resolved by the Rolandist faction to abridge his power, and secure their own, by a popular commotion. To effect this, Manuel placarded the walls with libel-

margin notes: November 1791. 1742. Made procureur to the commune.

1792. Treatment of the royal family.

---

[1] See the postscript to the preface, Lettres Originales, vol. i. p. 43. Peltier's late Picture, vol. ii. p. 240. and the letters themselves.

[m] Peltier's late Picture, vol. ii. p. 139. See also Mercure François, No. du 10 Decembre 1791.

[n] Mercure François, No. du 19 Mai 1792.

[o] Idem, No. du 9 Juin 1792, p. 131.

[p] Conjuration de d'Orleans, vol. iii. p. 170. 173. 187. Eloge Funebre, &c. p. 176.

lous invectives against the royal family, and assisted with all his power in exciting the commotions of the twentieth of June [q]. He was, on that day, in the garden of the Tuilleries, without his municipal scarf, laughing, clapping his hands, encouraging the mob to persist in their outrages, and assisting to take away the barrier of tri-colored riband, which alone protected the persons of the royal prisoners [r].

His misconduct was so notorious, that he was provisionally suspended from his office [s], but the influence of the Jacobins was exerted in his favour. The moment the decree made by the directory of the department of Paris was read to the council-general of the commune, Petion, who was suspended as well as Manuel, withdrew; Danton rose, and exclaimed, "Let all good citizens follow the mayor to the national assembly!" He and some of his party accordingly went out, but the majority of the council continued their deliberations [t]. Frequent applications were made to the assembly in behalf of the suspended officers; the journalists repeatedly asserted that the true reason of their disgrace was, that they had refused to obey the court in shedding the blood of citizens, and commencing a civil war [u]. The king wrote to the assembly, declining all interference in the business, on account of its personal reference to himself. Manuel either was, or pretended to be, ill of a fever, but he wrote to the assembly to caution them against giving ear to the calumnies of his enemies, who, he assured them, were enemies of the people. The influence of the Jacobins was so great, that the assembly, without examination, pronounced

(marginal dates: 20th June, 6th July suspended, 7th July, 13th July)

---

[q] Conjuration de d'Orleans, vol. iii. p. 175.
[r] Mercure François, No. du 21 Juillet 1792, p. 195. Peltier's late Picture, vol. ii. p. 241. See also Manuel's Examination on the Queen's Trial, in Jordan's Political State of Europe, vol. v. p. 166.
[s] Impartial History, vol. ii. p. 57.
[t] Mercure François, No. du 7 Juillet 1792, p. 135.
[u] Ibid. See also Le Défenseur de la Constitution, par M. Robespierre, p. 431.

him

him not guilty, and he was restored to his office. On the day when this decree passed in his favour, he went to the assembly and made a violent speech, replete with insolence and false accusations against the king, which was received with the greatest applauses, and procured him the honors of the fitting[x].

16th. Restored.

With so much popularity, and with such principles as he had constantly displayed, it is impossible to suppose that Manuel would not take an active share in the revolution of the 10th of August. He was one of the triumvirate of the *commune*, who retained their seats when the old members were forcibly expelled, and remained all night in the hall of the *commune*, executing the plots of those who had projected the insurrection[y]. He was now gratified with an opportunity of displaying all his malignity against the unfortunate royal family. A decree had passed the legislature, ordering that they should be confined in the hotel of the minister of justice, but Manuel, thinking this degradation insufficient, attended at the bar, and alleged that the *commune* could not be responsible for their detention, unless they were confined in a place of greater security; he did not leave the matter to the judgment of the assembly, but proposed the Temple, which was acceded to[z]. The malicious activity he displayed on this occasion raised his popularity to the greatest height; but he little thought that, under a republican government, his want of energy in the destruction of royalty would be made an article of reproach and accusation against him[a]. He was par-

10th August. His exertions.

---

[x] Debates and Histories.
[y] See his evidence on the queen's trial, Jordan's Political State of Europe, vol. v. p. 167. An Historical and Political Account of the Events of the 9th and 10th of August, by a National Guard, p. 32. Moore's Journal, vol. i. p. 53. 148, &c. &c.
[z] Debates and Histories. See also Eloge Funebre, &c. par M. Montjoye, p. 199. 207.
[a] See Hebert's observations on his evidence against the queen, Jordan's Political State of Europe, vol. v. p. 193.

ticularly

ticularly active in forming the tribunal to try the pretended criminals, and caused a permanent guillotine to be erected in the Carousel, under pretence, that, as that spot had been the theatre of guilt, it ought also to be the place of punishment[b].

<small>2d September. Principal promoter of the massacres.</small>

It has been attempted to vindicate him from the charge of having been concerned in the massacres of September, but his exculpation rests on very slight grounds[c]. For some time before the event he was very active in pointing out proper persons to be arrested; he visited the prisons daily, and numbered the persons confined with the most scrupulous exactness; he told many of them, with a smile, conveying a latent meaning, that they would be liberated the second of September; and intimated to several that they would be shipped off to the coast of Africa, in order to induce them to collect as many of their valuables as possible[d]. It is certain, from the melancholy expression made use of by Chantereine when he stabbed himself, so early as the twenty-second of August, that their projected murder was known[e]; and if Manuel had not known of it by a culpable participation, he must have been apprized officially, and in either case he is highly culpable. But of him it is positively asserted, that he received money of many prisoners to procure

---

[b] Peltier's late Picture, vol. ii. p. 220.
[c] See Garat's Memoirs, p. 27.
[d] Pages, vol. i. p. 479. Peltier's late Picture, vol. ii. p. 230, 279. Conjuration de d'Orleans, vol. iii. p. 206. Conspiracy of Robespierre, p. 74. Gibbon's Miscellaneous Works, vol. i. p. 261. Amongst the instances of individuals sacrificed to his personal hatred is Bosquillon, the justice of peace who opposed his election as procureur de la commune. See Peltier's late Picture, vol. ii. p. 240.
[e] CHANTEREINE was colonel of the constitutional guard of the king's household, on the tenth of August 1792. He was, between that day and the second of September, arrested by order of the commune, and confined in the prison of the Abbaye. Being informed, from sources he considered infallible, of the projected murder of the prisoners, as they were sitting down to dinner on the 22d of August, he suddenly stabbed himself three times with a knife, exclaiming, "We are all doomed to be massacred;—My God, receive me!" and expired almost instantaneously. St. Meard's Agony, p. 10.

their

their acquittal and safety, and particularly fifty thousand crowns (6250 *l.*) of the princesse de Lamballe. A saying of his own, that he would have preserved that lady if she had not lost her presence of mind, corroborates the suggestion. Her murder has been deemed an unpremeditated act of fury; the fact, however, is this: Manuel had agreed to save her, but the duke of Orleans expressly commanded her destruction, and Manuel had not time to counteract the execution of his orders, which were given with secrecy, and performed with diabolical fidelity[f]. The massacres of this and the following days enriched Manuel, but from that period he renounced all connexion with Orleans[g].

He was elected member of the convention for Paris, and attached himself to the party which opposed the views of his late patron. His conduct while he retained a seat in this assembly, except in such parts of it as were produced by his desire of thwarting Orleans and the Mountain, exhibits very little worthy of notice for virtue or consistency. At the opening of the sittings, he made a motion which did some honour to his discernment, namely, that the president of the convention should have apartments in the Tuilleries, and a guard; that he should be styled president of France, and that certain marks of respect should be shewn him in public; but this was negatived. He moved, but unsuccessfully, for the abolition of the order of priesthood, expressing his surprise, not that bishops were paid, but that they were permitted to exist; an expression worthy a Septembrizer[h]. He defended general Montesquiou against the attacks of the Mountain, and, in general, opposed all their proceedings respecting the king.

Member of the convention.

21st September.

27th September and 19th October.

[f] Pagès, vol. i. p. 480, 481. Conjuration de d'Orleans, vol. iii. p. 210.
[g] Conjuration de d'Orleans, vol. iii. p. 210. Pagès, vol. i. p. 486.
[h] Debates.

Conduct respecting the king's trial.

That Manuel should have exerted himself so much to save the life of the king is a subject of surprise, and has given rise to various conjectures. It has been said that he felt a desire to re-establish royalty, which report is countenanced by his observation at the Jacobins, that liberty was better in prospect than in possession, and by some expressions which he dropped, importing a wish to place the duke of York or the duke of Brunswick on the throne[i].

16th October.

It is further strengthened by his motion to submit the question of abolishing royalty, which had passed in the convention by acclamation, to the people in primary assemblies; this motion was speedily over-ruled, Danton and Brissot joined to argue against it. Notwithstanding these facts, I think his conduct can only be ascribed to his disgust against Orleans. He does not appear ever to have become a royalist: he was always ready to forward every measure, and even to extend every suggestion which had a tendency to degrade or harass the king and his family, to whom in his visits to the Temple he behaved with extreme rudeness[k]. He proposed the sale of the chateau of Versailles, as an amendment of an original motion, which only recommended the sale of the furniture. He treated the cross of Saint Louis with scorn, as a stain on the coat of a soldier, and carried his absurd prejudice so far as to move the abolition of Twelfth-Day, (*le Jour des Rois*,) merely on account of its name[l]. He was accused by Hebert of having opposed a reduction of expence in the table of the royal prisoners, but kindness to them was not the motive[m], and a suggestion has been thrown out personally relating to the queen, which could only originate in the most

19th October.

15th October.

30th December.

---

i Conjuration de d'Orleans, vol. iii. p. 203.
k See Journal de Clery, p. 100.
l Debates.
m See trial of the queen, Jordan's Political State of Europe, vol. v. p. 193.

rancorous

rancorous malignity, and merits no notice except contempt[o]. His oppofition, by whatever motive it might be produced, was bold and well combined; he aimed a blow at the influence of the terrorifts, which, had it effectually taken place, would, in all probability, have faved the life of the monarch; this was when he moved that a certain number of tickets of admiffion to the tribunes fhould be fent every day to the fections, to be diftributed amongft the real citizens, which would operate to the exclufion of thofe hired ruffians, who by their interference degraded the national reprefentation, and prejudiced the difcuffion of every queftion. This motion failed, through the influence of the Mountain, and of thofe very galleries againft whom it was intended. After the king's defence had been made, he propofed that it fhould be printed, and fent to the departments, and that the difcuffions of the convention on the fubject fhould be fufpended for three days; but this motion was rejected, and being reported at the Jacobin club, occafioned his expulfion from that fociety[o]. In voting on the queftion refpecting the reference of the fentence againft the king to the primary affemblies, he made fome pointed obfervations on the general conduct of the members of the convention, and on the duke of Orleans. "Judges," he faid, "do not murmur
" at the opinions of their brethren, though different
" from their own: they do not openly abufe and
" calumniate each other; they are cold as the law,
" of which they are the organs. If the convention

Expelled the Jacobin club.

[p] I will not infult the reader by a reference to the publication in which this infinuation is contained—I appeal to the author's fenfe of fhame who could commit fuch an accufation to paper, when he might have been convinced of its impoffibility by the following extract from the queen's trial. *Q. The Prefident, (to Manuel)*—" Why did you
" take it upon you to enter alone into the Temple, and particularly
" into the apartments called Royal?" *Witnefs*—" I never allowed
" myfelf to enter alone into the apartments of the prifoners; I, on the contrary, took
" care always to be accompanied by feveral of the commiffioners who were on duty
" there." Jordan's Political State of Europe, vol. v. p. 168.

[o] Debates. Moore's Journal, vol. ii. p. 534. 538. 566.

" had

" had been a tribunal of law, a near relation of the
" king, who has not been restrained either by a
" sense of shame or by his conscience, would not
" have been permitted to vote on this occasion."
He was proceeding with his observations, when the
president called him to order. When the last *appel
nominal* was made, on the question of punishment,
Manuel was secretary, and indignant at finding the
decision of death carried by so small a majority, he
rose from his place, exclaiming, " I must leave this
" place to seek a purer air." He rushed towards
the door, but some of the Mountain fearing that he
was carrying away the lists of the scrutiny attempted
to stop him. He escaped, however, out of their
hands, and made his retreat, but was followed by
Duhem, who succeeded in making him resume his
seat. This transaction threw the convention into
great confusion, but it is not certain that Manuel
had any intention of carrying off the list [q].

19th January 1793.
Resigns his seat.

When the questions were all decided, he sent a
letter to the convention full of complaints and reproaches, which he concluded by resigning his seat.
The motive he alleged then and afterwards, on the
queen's trial, was, that he despaired of the establishment of liberty from such a body, divided by faction,
and over-ruled by clamour [r]. He also wrote a letter on
the question of an appeal to the people, which was
published in Condorcet's paper, and is esteemed one
of his best productions.

Retires to the country. March 1793.

While the trial was in agitation, Manuel had offered himself to succeed Petion in the mayoralty of Paris,
and was third on the list, having 868 votes [s]. He
retired to his native town, where he was desirous to
remain, and end his days in obscurity. Sensible of
the dangers which awaited him from the increasing

[p] Debates. Moore's Journal, vol. ii. p. 579.
[q] Robespierre à ses Commettans, vol. ii. p. 222.
[r] Debates. Queen's trial, in Jordan's Political State of Europe, vol. v. p. 167.
[s] Mercure François, N° du 3 Novembre 1792.

influence

influence of the Mountain, he caused it to be reported that he was killed in a popular commotion at Montargis. This fallacy was soon detected, he was arrested and brought to Paris, where, after having been examined on the trial of the queen, he was himself accused of a confederacy with Brissot and Petion, tried and executed. When he was put into the Conciergerie, he experienced from the prisoners none of the consolatory kindnesses they generally displayed towards each other; they reproached and detested him as author of the massacres of September; and when he was going to his trial, they thrust him against a pillar still stained with blood shed on that day, exclaiming that it was spilt by his means¹.

Brought to Paris. 16th Nov. 1793. Executed.

In Manuel's character, there appears very little virtue or consistency. His outset in life was marked by ingratitude, his progress by profligacy and instability of principle. As an author he produced nothing worthy of criticism, or likely to reach posterity. His style is disfigured by affectation and clumsy pedantry. He was celebrated as a wit; two instances will prove the foundation of his claims. In the *commune*, he moved that the statue of Louis XIV. might be cast into cannon, that the monarch might continue to *make a noise* to the last". In the convention, in the course of the debates on the king's trial, Manuel having moved something which clashed with the wishes of the Mountain, Legendre, the butcher, said, the assembly had better *decree, that Manuel is a wit.*—" I am " glad," said Manuel, " they are not required to " decree *que je suis bête,* for then Legendre would " think he had a right to kill me." There is some smartness in this repartee, which lies in the word *bête,* being used equivocally to signify a beast, or a fool*.

His character.

25th June 1792.

ᵗ Tableau des Prisons sous Robespierre.
ᵘ Journals.
ˣ Miss Williams's first Collection of Letters on France.

JEAN PAUL MARAT.

MARAT was one of those men whom extraordinary commotions or convulsions in the body politic have exalted to a degree of eminence, from which they are contemplated by succeeding generarations with horror, disgust, and wonder bordering on incredulity. This miscreant verified the narratives of poets and romance writers, who represent souls devoid of every laudable principle, and deformed by every vice, inhabiting bodies of corresponding conformation, equally calculated to inspire abhorrence by the first impression on the senses.

<small>Birth and education.</small> Marat was born at Beaudry, a small hamlet in the Canton of Neufchatel in Switzerland, where his father was public schoolmaster. He did not, however, undertake his son's instruction, but sent him to Geneva. His education, though not finished, was above the common level; and he was distinguished, in that part of his life which preceded the revolution, by an attachment to literature and philosophy. Probably his apparent debility of person, which precluded the possibility of much corporeal exertion, induced his parents to bestow that expence on the cultivation of his mind, which enabled him to signalise himself in the lists of atrocity [y].

[y] Corjuration d'Orleans, vol. ii. p. 153. Pagès, vol. ii. p. 19. There is some doubt about the place of his birth, which some have stated to be Sardinia, others Corsica; but in his lifetime he was generally understood to have been born in the Canton of Neufchatel, part of the dominions of the king of Prussia. See Peltier's Picture of Paris, vol. ii. p. 527.

Poverty, and the difficulty of supporting him- *Goes to* self in his own country, induced him to go to *Paris.* Paris, where he commenced physician. Of the *Practices* profits of his practice there is no certain account, *physic.* though he boasted of it as very extensive, and asserted, that on his arrival in Paris he received thirty-six livres (1 *l*. 11 *s*. 6 *d*.) a visit [a]. He subsisted principally by the sale of a quack medicine, which did woful execution on those who placed confidence in it, though, to screen himself from the laws, he purchased a diploma, and the appointment of physician to the count d'Artois's stables. This medicine was a specific, appearing like a very limpid water, for which he charged two louis-d'ors a bottle [a].

His attention was chiefly engaged by experiments *His philo-* in natural philosophy, and in this pursuit he dis- *sophical* played that envy and malignity which always mark- *ments;* ed his character. He had studied light and electricity; in the former he had discovered many novelties, and made some improvement on the prism, which are well spoken of; in the latter, he does not appear to have been equally successful, but perhaps his envious disposition prevented his greater success in both, since he was more desirous to overturn the systems of Newton, and to deprive Franklin of his celebrity than to profit by their discoveries [b].

He published a book, called "*Recherches physiques* *and p* "*sur le feu*;" and another, in which he affected to *licati* confute the system of Helvetius, under the title of *17* "*A Philosophical Essay on Man*." The former treatise I have seen, but from not sufficiently understanding the subject, can give no opinion respecting

---

[a] Brissot. When, in the Life of Marat, Brissot is quoted without specific reference to his work, I allude to a fragment of his inserted in Miss Williams's Letters in 1794, vol. iii. Appendix II. p. 210.
[a] Conjuration de d'Orleans, vol. ii. p. 152. Brissot.
[b] Brissot.

it.

it. The latter displays a presumption and vanity, which the talents of the author by no means justify. He pronounces dogmatically on the most abstruse questions of the animal economy, and shews the utmost contempt for the judgment of the reader. Voltaire, in his questions on the Encyclopœdia, treats this work with a greater degree of severity than it merited, if we may believe Briffot; but if he committed any mistake with respect to the book, he made none as to the author, when he declared him *more fit to libel men than to analyse them* [c].

Goes to London. He went to England about the same year, and published an essay, called "*The Chains of Slavery*;" of which he afterwards boasted, that it procured him great patronage and honor; but the oblivion in which the book is shrouded, which, even the infamous celebrity of the author has not been able to dispel, aids his known character for mendacity in discrediting the assertion.

Returns to Paris. When he returned to Paris, he resumed his philosophical pursuits, but the academy was so prejudiced against him, it did not condescend to criticise his production, or even to mention his name. His desire to destroy the fame of Newton still pursued him, and he took a singular method to effect it; he translated his *Principia* into French, and falsified the text, to bring disgrace on the author. To smuggle the book into notice, and to escape the severe examination he apprehended the academy would bestow on a production of his, which the reputation of the original would compel them to examine; he prevailed on a grammarian, called Bauffée, to print his name in the title-page as translator; but though this manœuvre succeeded so far as to obtain from the academy a negligent approbation; yet the work fell into disrepute, and was soon forgot [d]. He continued to support himself by the sale of quack medicines, protected by his place

[c] Briffot.   [d] Ibid.

in the household of the comte d'Artois, and the purchased diploma. It is not the least wonderful circumstance of his life, that he was able to obtain the favour, and live in habits of intimacy with a young and beautiful lady of quality, separated from her husband; he had been called in as medical assistant, and had succeeded in inspiring her with a passion for him, which she always retained, in spite of the deformity of his person, the filthiness of his appearance, and the brutality of his behaviour[e].

His amour.

At the time of the revolution he was poor and obscure; the prevailing passion for politics, and the activity of intrigue, were not to be suspended by philosophical curiosity, and he was so little prepared for the events about to take place, that he declared his opinion that the nation was not ripe for a revolution, and declined being concerned in it. When the Bastille was destroyed, however, he came forward, and with his accustomed neglect of truth, sent a pompous account of a pretended valiant exploit to be inserted in the journal of his friend Brissot[f]. Finding he had no chance of advancing himself but by assuming the reigning profession of a journalist, he commenced editor, called his paper *The Publiciste François*, and began, in the usual style, to decry the court, and compliment the popular favorites. In this career he had so many competitors, his superiors in information and eloquence, that his want of success was sufficient to have dispirited any man less sanguine or less persevering[g]. Whether his better genius suggested the plan, or whether some of the agents of the Palais Royal pointed it out to him, cannot be determined, but from his never-failing rancour against eminent persons, the former is extremely probable; he speedily

1789.
His situation.

Commences journalist.

---

[e] Brissot. Conjuration de d'Orleans, vol. ii. p. 155.
[f] Brissot.
[g] Conjuration de d'Orleans, vol. ii. p. 156. Pagès, v. ii. p. 41.

altered

'altered the title and style of his paper; he called it *L'Ami du Peuple*, and commenced a violent attack on Bailly and La Fayette. This brought his publication at once into notice, and as he rather aspired to the favour of the lower than of the superior classes, he constantly adapted his style to their system of rhetoric; his tropes and figures were execrations and obscenities, his argument was ribaldry and abuse, and his patriotism a firm belief in all the rancorous falsehoods of the day[h]. His paper was sold for only two liards (a farthing)[i]; the motto he chose for it, " Ut redeat miseris, " abeat fortuna superbis," plainly pointed to an agrarian law; and the manner in which he recommended blood and slaughter, greatly contributed to take off the restraints, custom, and education imposed on the ferocious disposition of the French populace[k]. La Fayette was so hurt at his insults, combined with others he sustained from Danton, St. Huruge, &c. that he surrounded his house, and blocked up the avenues with a guard; but was prevented, by the threats of Danton, from prosecuting a revenge, which would, if followed with effect, have relieved the country from one of its greatest pests, then in a state of comparative innocency[l].

1790. Attacked by la Fayette.

Becomes a Jacobin.

Marat, having obtained notice, began to enlarge the scope of his ambition; his vanity, of which he had a singular share, led him to suppose that nothing was too high or too arduous for him to undertake. He became a member of the Jacobins, and though his croaking voice and faulty delivery made the task of oratory an insurmountable difficulty, he persevered in ascending the tribune and delivering his opinions whenever he could obtain an

---
[h] Conjuration de d'Orleans, vol. ii. p 157.
[i] Miles's Conduct of France towards Great Britain, p. 227.
[k] Moore's Journal, vol. ii. p. 399.
[l] Miles, ubi supra. Conjuration de d'Orleans, vol. ii. p. 157.

hearing.

hearing. That club, during the sittings of the *and Cor-*
constituent assembly, though disgraced by the re- *delier.*
ception of him, and an indiscriminate rabble beside,
was not a region sufficiently fervent for the propagation of his principles. The *Société fraternelle*, afterwards called the club of Cordeliers, was the scene
where he most frequently displayed himself, and
from the congenial dispositions and similarity of
attainments in most of the members, to the greatest
effect [m]. He now became acquainted with Robespierre, member of the assembly, employed in
some of the inferior agencies of the duke of Orleans, and was of great service to him in gaining
the favour of the inhabitants of the *fauxbourgs*, and
training the galleries of the assembly; his journal
too obtained the protection of the duke, and he, as
editor, partook of his bounty [n]. The easiness of
his circumstances increased his insolence, and gave
full scope to the exercise of his ruling passion,
malice. To this may be ascribed his continual invectives against the king and royal family, against
la Fayette, and every one who possessed any share
of the public esteem [o]. To this may be also attri- *18th April*
buted his rancorous reflections on the king's in- *1791.*
tended journey to Saint Cloud [p], and his extreme
earnestness in promoting the petition signed in the
Champ de Mars. On this occasion his conduct ex- *July.*
posed him to the resentment of the ruling powers. *His press*
He had before excited the disgust of the constituent *seized.*
assembly, by his audacious invitations to murder,
and by exhorting the mob to hang up eight hundred of the deputies on the trees of the Tuilleries [q]. They rejoiced at this opportunity of making *Himself*
him feel the severity of the law; a decree was issued *imprison-*
ed.

[m] Pagès, vol. i. p 458. Louvet's Narrative, p. 9.
[n] Conjuration de d'Orleans, vol. iii. p. 147.
[o] Idem, vol. ii. p. 283.
[p] See Moore's View, vol. ii. p. 231. 247. 249.
[q] Garat's Memoirs, p. 145.

against him, his presses and papers were seized, and he, and a *mademoiselle Colombe*, directress of his journal, put in prison. An order was made, that no hawker should presume to cry his journal on pain of punishment[r]. These exertions, however, were of little consequence; he was soon liberated, either in compliment to the mob, or because doubts were entertained of the legality of his detention. He retired to a vault, in the church of the Cordeliers, prepared for him by Legendre the butcher, from which place, in contempt of authority, he continued to issue his lucubrations[s].

Comparison between him and the Brissotines. At this period, with whatever fastidiousness they afterwards denied it, Brissot and his party were, at least, on good terms with Marat[t]; they laboured in a common cause, and used at first the same means; they were, like him, first Orleanists, afterwards republicans; and though the different degrees of favour obtained by the two parties in the estimation of their common patron caused dissensions in principles and in politics, there was little difference between them, though they afterwards varied in their conduct. In fact, though the Brissotines, and the writers in their interest, attribute to them all the credit of being the *founders of the French Republic*, the incendiary Marat did more service to the cause than they. Their sincerity was about *par*; they and he cared equally for the people, they were willing to risk the happiness of the majority, or even to make indiscriminate sacrifices to establish their theories, or confirm the ascendancy they once acquired. Marat, whose ambition

[r] Mercure François, No. du 30 Juillet 1791, p. 399. et du 6 Août, p. 82.
[s] Marat lived in the *Rue des Cordeliers*, No. 30; this retreat, therefore, was no great inconvenience to him. See Moore's View, vol. ii. p. 415. Etat de la France, par M. le Comte de Montgaillard, p. 66.
[t] Pagès, vol. ii. p. 39. Conjuration de d'Orleans, vol. iii. p. 131. Peltier's late Picture of Paris, vol. ii. p. 269.

extended

extended no farther than to head an outrageous rabble, and whose vanity led him to believe no person so well qualified for the task as himself, was desirous to resolve the whole kingdom into an immense and lawless mob, that by his influence he might perpetuate anarchy. Both aimed at the same object, the degradation of the constituted authorities, the plunder of the wealthy, and the destruction of the loyal, but they pursued it differently. The Brissotines, vain in the stores of book-learning, confident in their eloquence, and wrapt up in their metaphysical speculations, thought they might succeed by establishing theories in favour of a republic, in inducing the people to consent to the elevation of their instigator Orleans, or to their own assumption of all the power of the state. Their attempt had a success proportioned to its sagacity; to read their writings, to hear their speeches, they seemed to possess all the wisdom, all the virtue, all the disinterestedness of those sages and heroes of antiquity, whom they affected to regard as models; but to inspect their web of flimsy, though pernicious, intrigues, to hear of their treacheries, their jealousies, their want of mutual confidence, and their solicitude to secure a share of power by the most flagitious means, it became obvious that they had no real virtue, wisdom, disinterestedness, or patriotism, but that the sentiments analogous to those qualities, with which a laboured eloquence supplied their speeches and writings, proceeded merely from the head, while the heart remained cold, malignant, and selfish. The mob adored them for a short period, then despised, detested, and sacrificed them. Marat, on the other hand, did not make an affected display of wisdom, virtue, or sententiousness; to gain the populace, he adapted himself to their taste, and succeeded to the utmost extent of his wishes.

The attempt to pull down the king, that a regency of learned men might govern, presented no

very

very favourable prospect to the mob, but to tell them of plunder, of an agrarian law, an exemption from restraint, and a possession in common of all authority and all property, was an irresistible allurement. The Brissotines laboured to prove, that the world was made for the *wise*; Marat persuaded them that it was made for the *poor*. It is true, that at this period he was in the pay of Orleans, but with his total want of honour, principle, and veracity, it is very improbable that a tie so weak as gratitude should bind him to a man he despised. His vanity taught him that his talents and support could never be purchased at an adequate price, and his carelessness about money prevented his considering it possible that he should be bought by so vile a mean.

<small>Increases in ferocity.</small> The flagitious conduct of the legislative assembly gave fresh spring to the energy of Marat, and the increasing ascendancy of his friends Danton and Robespierre in the public estimation, enabled him to become additionally conspicuous and obnoxious. His publications became more atrocious and sanguinary; he made no scruple to recommend the destruction of three hundred thousand persons, as <small>3d May 1792. Denounced.</small> aristocrats[a]. He was, at length, denounced to the assembly by M. Beugnot, for having, in one of his Journals, instigated the soldiery *to sacrifice their generals to the public welfare*. Beugnot complained that these writings had been presented to the minister, Duranton, who had not taken proper measures to have the publisher punished. M. de Vaublanc enforced this accusation by producing another of Marat's papers, in which he recommended to the people *to destroy, with fire and sword, the rotten majority of the assembly*. The incendiary was defended by his congenial friends, Bazire, Chabot, and Merlin; a long and tumultuous debate ensued, at the close of which, a decree of accusation was issued against him, but its effect was reduced by a similar

---

[a] Peltier's late Picture of Paris, vol. ii. p. 269.

one, obtained by Briffot and his faction, at the same time againſt the abbé Royou, editor of *l'Ami du Roi*. Seals were ordered to be placed on the houſes and preſſes of both[x].

But, at this period, the regicide faction was ſo ſtrong, and their aſcendancy ſo confirmed, that Marat entertained no fears. Decrees of arreſt were iſſued againſt him, but never executed; and previous to the 20th of June he was as audacious as ever, inſtigating inſurrection, and inforcing the murder of the king[y]. Notwithſtanding the ſucceſs which attended that diſgraceful day, and the meaſures which were purſued to inſure more extenſive conſequences to that perfidious plot which, after ſome delays, was executed on the 10th of Auguſt, he is ſaid by Briſſot to have been ſo deficient in courage, that he requeſted Barbaroux to convey him to Marſeilles as a place of ſafety[z]. He was appointed one of the new council general of the *commune*, who declared themſelves independent of the legiſlature, and determined to render an account of their conduct to none but the *ſovereign people*, in their primary aſſemblies[a].

Soon after the deſtruction of royalty, jealouſies began to manifeſt themſelves amongſt the miniſtry who had obtained their places by ſuch culpable violence. Danton, reſolved on the deſtruction of his pedantic colleagues, employed Marat to inſult, and make them odious to the people. The incendiary, convinced that in a conteſt before the populace, he would be ſecure of ſucceſs, commenced his attack in a manner truly characteriſtic. Firſt, by

June. Excites inſurrection.

Behaviour on the 9th and 10th of Auguſt.

Quarrels with the miniſtry.

---

[x] Mercure François, No. du 12 Mai 1792, p. 118—120.
[y] See Impartial Hiſtory, vol. ii. p. 39.
[z] Briſſot à tous les Republicains, London edition, p. 178. I confeſs I do not believe the ſtory. Briſſot ſays this ſupplication was made on the eve of the 10th of Auguſt, a day too buſy for Barbaroux to have incumbered himſelf with Marat, and Marat was that very day made one of the new commune.
[a] Impartial Hiſtory, vol. ii. p. 129. Peltier's late Picture, vol. ii. p. 213. Moore's Journal, vol. i. p. 335 to 338.

his own authority, he seized four presses from the king's printing-office to indemnify himself for a similar number which had been taken from him[b], this the ministry dared not resist or resent. As soon as the assembly had decreed a sum to be at the disposal of the administration for the purpose of dispersing useful publications, he applied to them for 15,000 livres (656 *l*. 5 *s*.) to enable him to publish some of his works. Roland, to whom the application was made, refused to give the sum without knowing what was to be published; Marat sent him a large bundle of manuscripts about *the Chains of Slavery* which he laid before the council, and they referred the matter to Danton; the event was, that Marat demanded and obtained the required sum from Orleans, posted placards against the incivism of Roland, and published libels against his wife[c]. This was the beginning of a contest which in about nine months overthrew the faction of Brissotines.

2d September.
Conduct of Marat.

A greater scene of horrors was now to be acted, and the part assigned to Marat was congenial to his abilities. He was appointed one of the committee of inspection (*Surveillance*) by the *commune*, in which capacity he assisted in filling the prisons, and by his sanguinary journals and placards inflamed the populace[d]. He even went so far as to obtain from the *commune* an order for the arrestation of Roland, and many of his friends, but this step was too daring even for Danton, he suppressed the execution of it, but it became obvious that no farther measures were to be kept between him and his colleagues, whom Marat began to proscribe and denounce with great fury[e]. On the horrible days of massacres he

---

[b] Roland's Appeal, vol. i. p. 111. Peltier's late Picture, vol. ii. p. 83.
[c] See Roland's Appeal, vol. i. p. 111, 112. Peltier's late Picture, vol. ii. p. 385. Conjuration de d'Orleans, vol. iii. p. 213.
[d] Peltier's late Picture, vol. ii. p. 289. Moore's Journal, vol. i. p. 256.
[e] Roland's Appeal, vol. i. p. 100.

was constantly engaged; Panis and he were alternately presidents of a committee which directed and encouraged the proceedings of the assassins, in the previous arrangement of which he had materially assisted[f]. His conduct on this and other occasions was so ferocious as almost to justify the hyperbolical assertion, that he would have drunk the blood of his mother out of the cranium of his father[g].

Meanwhile, the election for the national convention were proceeding, the friends of Marat were determined to obtain him a seat; and for what place! not for an obscure department, where his name was little known, and his vices only appeared in general details, but for PARIS, the capital of the state, the centre of his crimes, the scene of all his atrocities; Paris, where it is hardly a figure to say that the very walls cried out against him, as a murderer, an incendiary, and a ruffian more fit for the gibbet than the senate. To procure his return it was necessary to employ the eloquence of Chabot, Danton, and Robespierre; and the more effectual aid of pike and bludgeon men, who terrified the respectable electors, and sanctioned the proceedings of voters of their own class[h]. As soon as Marat had obtained a seat in the legislature, he redoubled his audacity and virulence; previous to their meeting he declared that if they did not settle the principles of government in eight days, no good was to be expected from them; he denounced in his placards many of the newly-elected members, as aristocrats and counter-revolutionists, the generals who commanded the armies, as traitors, and the ministers, except Danton, as enemies of

Elected member of the convention.

19th September.

---

[f] Pagès, vol. i. p. 479, 480. Peltier's late Picture, vol. ii. p. 477. Conjuration de d'Orleans, vol. iii. p. 208.
[g] Quoted by Pagès, vol. ii. p. 39. See also Garat's Memoirs, p. 26.
[h] Impartial History, vol. ii. p. 183. Moore's Journal, vol. i. p. 387—391. Appel à l'Impartiale Postérité, vol. ii. p. 69. It must be observed that Robespierre in his defence against Louvet's accusation, which is very pointed on this subject, denies having recommended Marat.—See ROBESPIERRE.

freedom,

freedom. So little was he satisfied with the state of things while the Brissotines bore sway, that the very day after the meeting of the convention, he excited the Jacobin club against them. He persevered in his incendiary placards, and even reproached the people for their forbearance in not perpetrating new massacres. "O, people of talk!" he observed, "if you did but know how to act¹!"

4th October.

Despised in the convention.

But though he was strongly supported in, and instigated to these measures by his party in the commune and in the clubs, even they had not intrepidity enough openly to countenance him in the convention. There the hideousness of his appearance, the squalor of his attire, the infamy of his character, the audacity with which he outraged truth, decency, and order, made every one ashamed to own a connexion with him. Was a charge made on his party, of murderous principles, or views of establishing a dictator, when every one shrunk from the avowal of such designs, he was ever ready to stand in the breach, deriding the assaults of eloquence, triumphantly confessing the whole charge, justifying himself, and impudently retorting crimination, scorn, and pity on his accusers ᵏ.

Enmity to the Brissotines.

It would be an extremely tedious and uninteresting labor to relate all the motions and denunciations made by and against him, from the first sitting of the convention to the end of the year. He was the avowed contemner and scourge of the Brissotines, the unceasing opponent of Roland, whom he stigmatized in his journals, placards, and speeches in the convention, as well as at the Jacobin club, as the enemy of the republic, as a tyrant, who issued arbitrary *lettres de cachet*, and as a public peculator and defaulter¹. He was undoubtedly instigated to

---

¹ Louvet's Narrative, p. 18. 22. Moore's Journal, vol. i. p. 450. 486.
ᵏ Moore's Journal, vol. ii. p. 171. 259. Debates.
¹ Louvet's Narrative, p. 24. Roland's Appeal, vol. i. p. 118. Mercure François du 20 Octobre 1792.

these

these measures by Robespierre and Danton, and the Brissotines were anxious to confound and disgrace him. But in this they proceeded, as usual, by intrigue instead of courageous assault; they formed parties to prevent his access to the tribune, and, instead of a well-digested attack, exhausted themselves in affected declamations and feeble recriminations. A description of one of these scenes will *25th September.* shew all the atrocity and insolence of his character, and display the feeble conduct of his opponents. After a discussion in which Rebecqui and Barbaroux accused Robespierre of aspiring to the dictatorship, Marat presented himself at the tribune, to answer a part of the complaint in which he himself had been implicated. Violent murmurs arose. "It would *His speech.* " appear," he said, " that I have a great many " personal enemies in this assembly."—" That we " are all," exclaimed three-fourths of the members. Marat resumed with the most unruffled serenity: " I have a great many personal enemies in this " assembly; I call them to decency. I exhort them " to moderate their furious clamours, and indecent " menaces against a man who has rendered more " services to the cause of liberty, and to themselves, " than they are aware of. Let them, for once, " learn to listen! I am grateful to the secret hand " which has thrown in the midst of you a vain " phantom, to alarm the timid, create divisions " among good citizens, and cast a stigma on the " deputies of the city of Paris. They are accused " of aspiring to a dictatorship, a triumvirate, or a " tribuneship; this absurd accusation could not " have found credit but for my being one of the " persons to whom it applies. Well then! it " becomes an act of justice in me to declare that " my colleagues, Robespierre, Danton, and the " rest, have constantly opposed the idea of a dic- " tatorship, though I have published it in my " journals, and have had several disputes with them

" on

" on the subject. I believe I am the first, or rather
" the only political writer in France who has pre-
" sented it to the public as the only mode of crush-
" ing traitors and conspirators. If this opinion be
" a crime, I alone am culpable; on my head the
" vengeance of the nation ought to fall: but before
" I am censured or punished let me be heard.

" Surrounded by eternal machinations against the
" country; seeing the repeated conspiracies of a
" perfidious king and a detestable court; seeing
" the villany of that host of traitors, who in the
" constituent as well as the legislative assembly,
" basely sold the rights of the people; will you im-
" pute it to me as a crime to have proposed the
" only measure, in my apprehension, calculated to
" stop us on the brink of that precipice into which
" they were dragging us? When the constituted
" authorities were of no other use than to destroy
" freedom, and to murder the patriots, in the name
" of the law, will you impute it to me as a crime to
" have called down on their guilty heads, the axe
" of popular vengeance? No, the people themselves
" would disavow you; for, if they have not fol-
" lowed my advice, they have, too late, felt, of
" 'themselves, that they had no resource left to
" escape the rage of their tyrants, but by taking
" into their own hands the dictatorial power, and
" ridding themselves of traitors.

" I, more than any one, have trembled at the idea
" of those terrible commotions; and that they might
" not be always in vain, that the people might not
" be forced to renew them, I was desirous that they
" should be directed by some citizen, whose pru-
" dence, justice, and firmness might, at once, have
" secured the safety and welfare of the public. If
" the necessity of this measure could have been felt
" at the epoch of the capture of the Bastille, five
" hundred rascally heads would have fallen, and
" peace and liberty would have been established from
" that

"that period for ever; inſtead of which, for want
"of diſplaying that energy, equally prudent and
"neceſſary, a hundred thouſand patriots have been
"butchered, and a hundred thouſand more are
"threatened with the ſame fate. To prove that I
"had no view of making this dictator, tribune, or
"triumvir, (for what ſignifies the name,) a tyrant,
"ſuch as folly, preſuming on the uſe of a word,
"might have repreſented him, but a devoted victim
"to the country, whoſe lot no ambitious man
"would envy, my project was, that the duration
"of his authority ſhould be limited to a few days,
"that it ſhould only extend to the condemnation of
"traitors; and even, that a cannon-ball ſhould be
"chained to his foot, that he himſelf might always
"be within the reach of the people. All vigorous
"meaſures have, at firſt ſight, appeared abſurd to
"many, particularly to the deputies of the people;
"they were ever confident of their own wiſdom,
"and they would have ruined the country if the
"people had not trampled under foot their cowardly
"ſyſtems. My ideas, however revolting they
"might appear, tended only to the public good,
"for no perſon was ever more fond than myſelf of
"order, and the reign of juſt laws. If your ideas
"are not ſufficiently elevated to enable you to un-
"derſtand me, ſo much the worſe for you.

"Such is my opinion; I have not privately in-
"ſinuated it to a confidential circle; I have printed,
"and put my name to it. Was it the opinion of a
"madman? I was to be pitied. Was it dangerous?
"It was incumbent on men more enlightened than
"myſelf, to expoſe it, inſtead of directing againſt
"my perſon the daggers of aſſaſſination, and the
"bayonets of deſpotiſm.

"My enemies have dared to impute to me views
"of ambition. If I had been willing to ſet a price
"on my ſilence, I might have been gorged with gold;
"yet I am poor. In the ſervice of my country I
"have

"have braved misery, dangers, and insults; inces-
"santly pursued by legions of assassins, I have wan-
"dered during the space of three years from one
"subterraneous habitation to another; I have preached
"the truth when a log was my pillow. If la Fayette,
"or any other enemy of liberty, had been able to
"seize my person, the most ardent defender of
"liberty would have been no more.

"Legislators! condescend to open your eyes. In-
"stead of consuming your precious time in scandal-
"ous quarrels, dread to afford a sanction to the
"manœuvres of intrigue, by giving currency to ab-
"surd reports, artfully circulated to retard the grand
"work of the constitution; and to put my enemies
"themselves to a painful trial, let me press you to
"fulfil the true object of your mission, by immedi-
"ately perfecting the declaration of rights, and lay-
"ing the foundations of a just and free govern-
"ment."

This speech made such an impression on the convention, that they were disposed to have terminated
the discussion, by passing to the order of the day,
when Vergniaud said:

"If there is a misfortune attached to the situation
"of representative of the people, by which I am
"peculiarly affected, it is that of being obliged to
"ascend this tribune after a man still obnoxious to
"decrees of arrest, which he has not discharged."

This opening shocked the friends of Marat: "Do
"you mean the decrees of the Châtelet?" inquired
Chabot. "Or those with which he was honored for
"having overthrown la Fayette?" added Tallien.
Verginaud continued:

"It is that of taking the place of a man, against
"whom a decree of accusation has been obtained,
"and who has lifted his audacious head above the
"laws; in a word, a man dripping with calumny,
"gall, and blood." After some confusion, occasioned by the disapprobation of the galleries, Vergniaud

and denounced an address, signed by the committee of inspection of Paris, which had been previously denounced to the legislative assembly. *As this address contained nothing but the expression of the most energetic sentiments of liberty, terminated by an invitation to the departments, to unite with the Parisians to repel the enemies who threatened the capital, the orator commented on it in vain; the only sensation produced, was that of astonishment at hearing it denounced* [m].

Boileau produced a number of Marat's journal, which he pretended had been published that very

[m] I have translated this sentence from Robespierre; but to enable the reader to form a judgment of this supposed *harmless* paper, I have added it at length, as translated by Dr. Moore. Journal, vol. ii. p. 40. See also Roland's Appeal, vol i. p. 109.

"Brethren and friends! a horrid plot, planned by the court, to murder all the patriots of the French empire; a plot in which a great number of the national assembly were engaged, having, on the ninth of last month, forced the *commune de Paris* to the cruel necessity of making use of the power of the people to save the nation; the commune has neglected nothing for the service of the country.

"After the approbation which the national assembly itself bestowed on the commune, could it have been imagined that new plots were projecting in silence, which broke forth at the moment when the national assembly, forgetting that she had declared that the *commune de Paris* had saved the country, hastened to dissolve that very community, as a recompence for all its faithful services.

"Proud of possessing the full confidence of the nation, which we are resolved to deserve more and more; placed in the centre of all the conspiracies, and determined to perish in defence of the public, we cannot boast of having entirely fulfilled our duty, till we shall obtain your approbation, which is the object of all our wishes, and of which we cannot be certain, till all the departments have *sanctioned our measures for the public safety*. Professing principles of the most perfect equality, wishing no other privilege, but that of presenting ourselves the first at the breach, we will put ourselves on a level with the smallest municipality in the nation, as soon as the dangers which now threaten the country are past.

"Informed that bands of barbarians are advancing, the *commune de Paris* hastens to acquaint all the departments, that part of those furious conspirators detained in the prisons of Paris have been put to death by the people; *an act of justice which seemed indispensable, to strike terror* into the breasts of those legions of traitors hid within her walls, at the time when the citizens were about to march against the enemy. And no doubt the nation, after that long succession of treasons which have brought her to the brink of ruin, *will hasten to adopt a measure so useful and necessary*; and all the inhabitants of France will say like the Parisians: Let us march against the enemy, but, let us not *leave behind us a band of villains, to murder our wives and children*,"

morning, from which he read thefe words: "Con-
"fidering the temper of the majority of the deputies,
"I defpair of the public welfare; if in the eight
"firſt fittings, the fundamental points of the confti-
"tution be not decreed, fifty years of anarchy await
"you, from which, you can only be relieved by ap-
"pointing a dictator." This extract revived in the
affembly all the violence of its former agitations,
and there was a general outcry, *To the abbaye! To
the guillotine!* In the midſt of the tumult, Boileau
moved for a decree of accufation againſt the mon-
ſter.

Marat, with much difficulty, obtained a hearing,
and with unruffled compofure faid: "I intreat
"the affembly not to give themfelves up to fuch an
"excefs of rage againſt me, I can eafily reply to the
"new accufations of my adverfaries. They have
"not blufhed to advance the decrees of accufation
"obtained againſt me by the courtly proftitutes of the
"conftituent and legiflative affemblies. I pride my-
"felf in them, as titles of glory. I muſt obferve,
"however, to thofe who know not how to appreciate
"them, that they are annulled; the people have an-
"nulled them in calling me hither to defend their
"rights, and by that judgment have indentified my
"caufe with their own.

"As for the paper which has juſt been denounced,
"and which I am challenged to difavow—Far from
"me be fuch a difavowal—Never did untruth iſſue
"from my lips; and to fear, my heart is a ſtranger.
"But I muſt inform you, that is not, as has been
"advanced, a publication of to-day; it appeared
"ten days ago. I compofed it at a time when the
"national convention was not yet formed, when I
"was an indignant witnefs of the re-election of thofe
"unfaithful deputies, whom I had denounced, efpecially
"that faction of the Gironde, by which I am this
"day perfecuted. But an inconteftible proof of
"my wifh to remain united to you, and the real
"opinion

"opinion I have formed of the firſt labors of the
"national convention, may be found in the firſt num-
"ber of a journal, intitled, *Le Journal de la Repub-
"lique*, printed this day. That will explain to you
"my real ſentiments, much better than the treache-
"rous annotations which accompanied the reading
"you have already heard."

The paper was read, it reſtored the favorable opinion of the aſſembly. Marks of an agreeable ſurpriſe and intereſt ſucceed the impetuous ſenſations by which it had been previouſly agitated. Marat again aſcended the tribune.

"Permit me now," ſaid he, "to recal you to your-
"ſelves, and to fix your attention on the dangers of
"prepoſſeſſion and anger. What then! if by the
"negligence of my printer, my journal had not ap-
"peared to-day, you would have devoted me to
"the ſword of tyranny! But no—it would not
"have been in your power to perpetrate ſuch an act
"of iniquity. I had in my own poſſeſſion the means
"of retaining my liberty; and, if you had voted a
"decree of accuſation, this weapon ſhould have
"reſcued me from the fury of my perſecutors."

Saying theſe words, he drew from his pocket a piſtol, and put it to his head. The convention paſſed to the order of the day, on all the denunciations [n].

Marat was ſtill diſtinguiſhed, by his habitual hatred of eminent characters. When Dumouriez enjoyed the moſt flattering partiality of his countrymen, Marat exhibited himſelf as his detractor, he ſtigmatized him as an ariſtocrat, reproached him with having connived at the eſcape of the Pruſſians out of France; from ſiniſter motives, took the part of thoſe who murdered the Pruſſian deſerters at Rhetal; moved an accuſation againſt him in the convention, and in the Jacobin club; purſued him with inſults and injuries into a private company, where he was partak-

<small>Hatred of Dumouriez.</small>

<small>17th and 18th Oct.</small>

---

[n] This narrative is taken from Robeſpierre à ſes Commettans, vol. i. p. 82 to 92. See alſo Moore's Journal, vol. ii. p. 35 to 44. Debates.

ing of an entertainment; and when he set out on his expedition against Flanders, declared publicly, and in print, that he went only with a view of over-running those provinces, to make himself duke of Brabant[o].

Persecution of the king.

His exertions against the general were, however, trifling in comparison to those he used against the king and queen. To increase the miseries of their situation, to inflame the public resentment against them to the highest pitch, and to accelerate a death of unmerited ignominy; to these ends he bent all his powers. In the convention, in the clubs, in the streets; his speeches, his journals, his placards were replete with the bitterest invectives; and most flagrant untruths, against those unfortunate victims of popular frenzy and delusion. Every method was used which malice could suggest, to present the degraded monarch to the people as an object of contempt and abhorence; not only his imputed crimes, but the misfortunes which the intriguers and insurgents had brought on him, were equally held forth as motives of detestation; and the injustice the nation had already committed, or connived at, in the murder of many individuals, whose only crime was loyalty, was urged as a reason for their persevering in the same cause, and imbruing their hands in the blood

3d Nov. of the sovereign[p]. His activity on this occasion excited popular resentment; his house was once surrounded by a mob who demanded his head, and at another time, the *fédérés* vowed vengeance against him, insomuch, that he pretended to be alarmed for his safety, and, was indulged by Santerre with a guard near his place of abode[q].

---

[o] Life of General Dumouriez, vol iii. p. 260. 290. Mercure François, No. du 27 Octobre 1792, p. 239. 253. 262. Moore's Journal, vol. ii. p. 163 to 170. See DUMOURIEZ.

[p] Impartial History, vol. ii. p. 215. Moore's Journal, vol. ii. p. 280.

[q] Goudemetz's Epochs. Moore's Journal, vol. ii. p. 340.

At length his malignity was gratified, by the decree that ordered the king to the bar of the convention, and still further by the result of his trial, which he promoted with unabated rancor; combating every argument tending to mercy, and overwhelming with abuse and misrepresentation all who opposed the sanguinary measure he was resolved to carry. It was observed, that, on the day of the king's appearance at the bar of the convention, his face, for the first time, wore the smile of satisfaction; and, as an equally extraordinary phænomenon, that he was dressed in a new suit of clothes. He moved, that the crime of forestalling grain and money, of as- 10th Dec. sassinations under pretence of law, and many other charges, should be added to the king's accusation. Yet it may serve to prove the inconsistency of his character, that, the next day, he moved that all charges 11th. alluding to crimes committed before his acceptance of the constitution, should be omitted in his act of accusation, which was over-ruled by his colleagues [f].

This act of justice in him was merely fortuitous; he soon resumed his wonted ferocity; on the question of punishment, he voted for death, with execution 16th Jan. of the sentence within four-and-twenty hours; and 1793. on the question of respite, he repeated the same 19th Jan. opinions, which he accompanied with the most clamorous abuse of those who opposed them [s].

While this trial was depending, he stood candidate   Candidate for the office of mayor of Paris, vacant by the re-   for the signation of Petion, but he obtained only forty-one   mayoralty. suffrages [t]. He had been denounced by Claviere, for having, as member of the committee of inspection, refused to give any account of the effects, jewels, gold, assignats, and papers, found at the house of the treasurer of the civil list. A decree was made that they should be transmitted to the na-

[f] Debates. Moore's Journal, vol. ii. p. 507. 509. et passim.
[s] Moore's Journal, vol. ii. p. 597. Debates.
[t] Mercure François, No. du 3 Novembre 1792, p. 48.

tional

tional treasury within four-and-twenty hours. Marat, accompanied by Robespierre, went to the Jacobin club, where he was received with acclamation and enthusiasm. He was honored with the title of *magnanimous*; and his profound sagacity in recommending such numerous decollations was highly applauded. Great complaints were made of the incivism and persecuting spirit of the ministers, and he resolved to seek for refuge in his *souterrain*. Here he remained but three days, though he continued for a much longer time to date his papers from thence. He did not in them assume a style of greater moderation, but still continued to advise the cutting off of heads, the partition of property, and the plunder of the wealthy [t].

In the contest between his party and the Brissotines he was signally serviceable; for though the disgust excited by his appearance in the convention was such that even his known intimates appeared ashamed to associate with him, though Danton professed to dislike, and Robespierre denied having much connection with him, yet his intrepidity in all matters where nothing was to be apprehended but shame, and his facility in inciting insurrection and intriguing with the mob, rendered him a necessary associate in their projects. The Brissotines, who had felt the effects of his malice, were anxious to procure his expulsion from the assembly, or his execution, but he had taken too firm root in the favour of the populace to fear the result of their exertions. Brissot now wrote, and Vergniaud and Louvet declaimed, in vain; they had it in their power to have crushed him during the first administration of Roland, but his libels on the court were then too serviceable; they fostered the serpent to sting the royal family, and were afterwards them-

---

[t] Mercure François, du 10 Novembre 1792, p. 96. 110, 111. Du 17 Novembre, p. 194. Moore's Journal, vol. ii. p. 397.

selves deservedly victims to his venom. Restrained by no impulse of shame or sense of truth, he returned their sarcasms with gross abuse, their accusations with recrimination, calling them royalists, aristocrats, *muscadins*, and heaping on them every charge which was likely to inflame the public mind: he also accused them, and not without truth, of being accessaries by their connivance to the acts of the 2d of September. The opposition made by that inconsistent faction to the progress of the king's trial, afforded him a still greater opportunity of representing them to the public as royalists; and the result of that transaction rendered their destruction easy. From the period of the king's execution, Marat was affectedly held forth by his partisans as a test in revolutionary opinions; those who did not think exactly as he did were reckoned counter-revolutionists. His ascendancy was so great, that the convention was often obliged to suspend all other deliberations to attend to his egotisms, whims, and impertinences. In vain were decrees made against him, he violated them the moment they were formed, secure of impunity from the influence of the mob over the enslaved and cowardly legislature ".

His rancor against Dumouriez, which had known no intermission, led him to depreciate all his successes, and constantly point him out as a traitor to the country. The famous battle of Jemappe he treated as a treacherous exertion of the general to occasion a wanton sacrifice of the Parisian recruits *. He prophesied that he would desert like la Fayette; and to exasperate the inhabitants of the capital, asserted that his *aides-de-camp* wallowed in gold and

<small>Rancor against Dumouriez.</small>

" See Roland's Appeal, vol. i. p. 5. 119. Peltier's late Picture, vol. ii. p. 295. 493. Mercure François, No. du 29 Septembre 1792. Moore's Journal, vol. i. p. 455. vol. ii. p. 234, 235. Young's Example of France, p. 28.

* Mercure François, No. du 17 Nov. 1792. Moore's Journal, vol. ii. p. 423.

silver,

silver, and made use of assignats of fifty livres (2*l*. 3*s*. 9*d*.) to light their pipes *y*. The accomplishment of this prediction, though produced in a great degree by the treachery of the Mountain, and by his own calumnies, raised him in the eyes of the Parisians, and inflamed his vanity to the highest pitch.

Contest with the Brissotines.

He took advantage of this circumstance to redouble his attacks on the opposing faction; he charged them with being accomplices of the general, and, as president of the Jacobin club, signed an address exhorting the popular societies to unite, and by reiterated petitions compel the convention to expel those unfaithful abettors of Dumouriez, who betrayed their trust, and did not vote for the death of the tyrant. Previous to this period, Salles had denounced him for publishing an inflammatory journal, inviting the people to murder and pillage; but, as Marat was supported by the galleries, this had no other effect than to throw the convention into one of those convulsions which then generally terminated their debates. They also procured an address from the popular societies at Amiens, requiring, amongst other things, a decree of accusation against him; but the convention passed to the order of the day *z*. In return, he accused the Brissotines of having abetted the pillage of the shops which took place in February, and of the conspiracy of the 10th of March *a*. But these were only preludes to a more daring attack: he ventured to denounce three hundred deputies, as conspirators devoted to Brissot and his coadjutors; but this attempt failed of success. He soon however returned to the charge, and pointedly accused the Brissotines of being accomplices with Dumouriez; but this denunciation had

26th Feb. 1793.

1st April 12th.

---

y Life of Dumouriez, vol. iii. p. 389. 404. Louvet's Narrative, p. 30.
z Debates. *a* Brissot à ses Commettans, p. 31.

no other effect than to create a confusion so violent that the president was obliged to put on his hat. The adverse party displayed an unexpected courage and unanimity; swords were drawn on each side, and these *soi-disant* Romans, this assembly of philosophers, thirsting for blood and inflamed with mutual hatred, were more like the contending gladiators of the amphitheatre than the philosophical disputants of the portico. The president succeeded in preventing mutual carnage, and thus the affair terminated for the present[b]. In the evening sitting, Gaudet, by way of revenge, moved for a decree of accusation against Marat, chiefly on the ground of his having, as president of the Jacobins, signed the address above mentioned; to which he alleged he had put his name merely as president, without knowing or considering the contents; but, with his accustomed audacity, defended and justified them. After a debate of two-and-twenty hours, a decree of accusation was passed against him by a very large majority, and he was ordered to be sent to the Abbaye. This transaction proves, that when active and united, the Girondists could still command a majority in the convention, on some occasions at least; but their weakness, treachery, jealousy, and timidity had occasioned them to lose so many advantages out of doors, all of which their more active opponents had secured, that a single exertion produced no other good than a temporary prolongation of a struggle, the event of which might easily be foreseen. Marat at first declared that the decree against him was only obtained to excite commotion, and that he would brave the fury of his enemies; but having escaped by the connivance of his jailor from confinement, he again repaired to his vault, where he remained carefully concealed, though he continued to write and publish with unabated rancour and au-

Denounced by Gaudet.

Escapes from confinement.

[b] Debates, New Annual Register for 1793, p. 175.

dacity.

dacity[c]. He had little to fear from a trial before the revolutionary tribunal, the jurors of which were all appointed by himself, an exertion of power which the timid right side had permitted him to usurp, after a jury had been ascertained by ballot[d]. His personal timidity, however, was such, that it required all the influence of Robespierre, who had defended him in the convention, to induce him to come forward, and stand his trial[e], even though Roussillon, one of the jurors, had said to his friends in the Cordeliers club; "Fear nothing for his "life. They talk of arresting him; I invite you "to stab the first man who dares lay his sacrilegious "hands on the *friend of the people*[f]."

Partiality of the jury.

23d Apr. Surrenders himself.
At length, having himself fixed a day for his trial, Marat, the day before, surrendered himself to the keeper of the Conciergerie. He was attended to the tribunal by a great concourse of his adherents, and appeared rather as a judge than a criminal.

24th. His acquittal.
On entering the hall, he thus addressed the bench: "Citizens; you do not see before you a culprit, but "the apostle and martyr of liberty; the decree of "accusation against me has been obtained by a "group of factious intriguers." This insult on the legislature was received with general applause. His interrogatory was slight, and his answers heard by the enraptured mob with all the respect and applause due to oracles. His acquittal was pronounced without hesitation, and the hall resounded with applauses. Marat, standing on a table, said, "Citizens, "judges, and jurors, the fate of traitors against the "nation is in your hands: protect the innocent, "punish the guilty, and the country will be "saved."

31st May.

[c] Crimes de Marat, p. 13.
[d] Louvet's Narrative, p. 41.
[e] Etat de la France, par Montgaillard, p. 13. 66. Crimes de Marat, p. 15.
[f] Brissot à ses Commettans, p. 45. n.

A ludi-

A ludicrous scene and grotesque procession suc- *He is car-*
ceeded. The mob, intoxicated with joy and en- *ried in*
thusiasm, rushed towards Marat, and covering his *triumph.*
brow with crowns and branches of oak which they
had already prepared, carried him to the grand staircase of the *Palais*, where an orator commanded the
audience to pay homage to the friend of the people
so unjustly accused. The air was rent with cries of
Vive Marat! vive l'ami du peuple! and the procession moved towards the hall of the convention,
forcing every one they met to pull of their hats, and
join in the cry of *Vive Marat!* The object of these
acclamations, a little, deformed, creature, meanly
dressed, sat in ridiculous state, almost hid with civic
crowns and oak boughs, affecting with burlesque
gravity a triumphant air, and repaying the popular
fanaticism with nods, smiles, and looks of protection.

Thus escorted, he entered the hall of the conven- *Address to*
tion, having first modestly taken off his civic crowns, *the con-*
which he carried in his hand. He ascended the *vention.*
tribune and said: "Legislators of the French nation:
"I present to you, at this moment, a citizen who
"has been inculpated, but is now completely jus-
"tified; he offers you an upright heart; he will
"continue to defend, with all the energy he pos-
"sesses, the rights of man, liberty, and the privi-
"leges of the people." This harangue was received
with unbounded applause by the mob. Marat was
about to quit the tribune, but the people required
him to stay till the president should have answered
his address. The president said: "It is not cus-
"tomary to answer the addresses of citizens, unless
"they present petitions, now Marat certainly does
"not appear as a petitioner." Danton, however,
proclaimed this one of the *beautiful days* of the French
revolution. Osselin moved that the judgment of the
revolutionary tribunal should be inserted in the
bulletin.

bulletin. The convention, glorying in its insignificance, applauded and consented [g].

31st May. Expulsion of the Brissotines. It now became obvious, that one party must triumph by the destruction of the other, many tumultuous debates, and even manual skirmishes took place in the interval between the time of Marat's resuming his seat and the 31st of May, a day which decided the contest, and which, by his influence in the clubs and in the central committees, he greatly forwarded; and it must be observed, that, of his own authority, he made several alterations in the list of persons proscribed, striking out some, and inserting others, without consulting the petitioners or the convention [h].

Marat's arrogance. This triumph over the Brissotines, confirmed by the subsequent arrestation of seventy members attached to the same party, rendered the ascendancy of the Mountain uncontrollable. Marat was treated with more honour and respect than any individual since the revolution, and exerted a sway in the convention and the clubs more absolute than was ever before known in bodies styled deliberative. In fact, they submitted to all his whims and caprices, and seemed to derive to themselves honor from their submission. *3d June.* The day after the arrest of the adverse deputies, he announced a resolution not to deliver any opinion in the assembly till they should have been *17th June.* brought to trial, but as that could not be immediately done, he soon retracted the determination [i]. His extravagances were more bearable from the obvious certainty that the wretch was hastening to *His ill health.* his grave, and that nothing could save him. His constitution had never been good, and at this period,

[g] Crimes de Marat, p. 17. Brissot à ses Commettans, p. 45. Louvet's Narrative, p. 43. Pagès, v. ii. p. 74.
[h] Louvet's Narrative, p. 44. Impartial History, vol. ii. p. 301. Pagès, vol. ii. p. 80.
[i] Debates.

he was eat up with a leprous complaint; which adding its ravages to his natural deformity, and habitual filthiness, rendered him an object truly disgusting to look at, and sometimes obliged him to a retirement from business, during which he used the bath, and other medical prescriptions. On the symptoms which attended his disorder a suspicion has been founded, that a slow poison had been administered to him by Robespierre: it is even averred that he was conscious of the treachery of his colleague, who thus attempted to cut him off at the height of his popularity, that he, succeeding him in the public opinion, might make use of it to further his projects of vengeance and ambition[k]. I do not, however, consider this suggestion well-founded, but rather one of those calumnies which the resentment of all parties has been willing to add to the real crimes of Robespierre.

His days were not terminated by disease or poison; the man of blood ended his life in blood. During one of the recesses from public affairs to which disease compelled him, a young woman called at his lodging on some pretended business. She was admitted just as he was coming out of the bath. After some previous conversation she introduced the subject of the proscribed deputies, and is said to have pleaded for mercy. Marat, with his accustomed ferocity, answered that all the promoters of insurrection in the departments were doomed to death. " Then you shall precede them," she exclaimed, and drawing a knife stabbed him in the breast; he staggered, fell, and expired[l].

12th July 1793. His death.

The

---

[k] Etat de la France, par Montgaillard, p. 13. 66.

[l] *Marie Anne Victoire* CHARLOTTE CORDÉ or CORDAY, the woman who performed this remarkable assassination, was a native of Saint Saturnin des Lienerets. She was the daughter of a gentleman in easy circumstances, and had inflamed her mind by study and meditation to the commission of an act, which she thought would be beneficial to her country. But her action cannot be ascribed to patriotism alone;

Consequences of his death. The death of Marat was of great service to his party, and the period at which it took place singularly fortunate; it afforded the chiefs of his faction

---

alone; it is not improbable that she was influenced by love for Barbaroux, whom she had long known, and whose life she imagined to be at Marat's disposal. While the proscribed deputies were at Caen, she frequently came, attended by a servant, to the town-hall, and inquired for Barbaroux, to whom she pretended some business, but always conversed with him in presence of her domestic. She was apprehended immediately on the perpetration of her extraordinary attempt, and sent first to the Abbaye, and afterwards to the Conciergerie. She was put on her trial the 17th, and avowed the fact and all the circumstances, alledging as a justification, that she considered Marat a criminal already convicted by the public opinion, and that she had a right to put him to death. She added, that she did not expect to have been brought before the revolutionary tribunal, but to have been delivered up to the rage of the populace, torn to pieces, and that her head fixed on a pike would have been borne before Marat on his state bed and serve as a rallying point to Frenchmen, if any still existed worthy of that name. Her answers to the various interrogatories were brief, pointed, distinguished by good sense, and sometimes by wit. Her advocate, precluded by her confession from making any defence as to the facts, delivered a speech in her favour, in which he insisted, that her unruffled calmness and supernatural self-denial must be occasioned only by that fermentation of political fanaticism, which also armed her hand with the dagger, and that it was for them to consider what weight that moral consideration should have in the scale of justice. She was found guilty, and executed the same day. When sentence was pronounced on her she thanked her counsel for the manner in which he had pleaded her cause, which she said was delicate and generous. She desired a friend to pay the debts she had contracted while in prison, and requested of the judges, that three letters which she had in her hand, two to Barbaroux, and one to her father, might be delivered. In her way to the place of execution, she displayed a firmness and tranquillity which charmed many of the spectators, and even awed into silence those persons called revolutionary women, or furies of the guillotine, who in general pursued the victim to death with execrations and reproaches. She submitted to her fate with the same composure which marked her preceding conduct. She is described by Louvet, who saw her at Caen, to have been stout, well made, with an open air, and modest behaviour; her face that of a fine, and pretty woman combined. The circumstances which attended this extraordinary action, the privacy with which it was concerted, the resolution with which it was executed, the openness of confession, the contempt of punishment, and, above all, the execrable character of the wretch who was the object of it, have taken off so much of the horror generally felt at an act of assassination, that the name of Charlotte Corday is generally pronounced with respect and a great degree of admiration. Her Letters (or rather her Letter and Continuation) to Barbaroux, are given in the Appendix, No. V.

a fresh

a fresh topic of declamation against the fugitives, to whom, with some appearance of probability, they attributed the formation of the plot; it enabled them to accelerate the trial of those who were in their hands, and to involve many innocent persons in pretended conspiracies[m]; and it delivered them from a malignant wretch, no longer useful to their designs.

Proceedings in the convention.

The day after Marat's death, the whole city of Paris was in extreme agitation. Before the convention had commenced its sittings, the door of the hall was besieged by petitioners, who came from the sections to deplore the *friend of the people*, and invoke vengeance on his assassins. One of the petitioners expressed himself in these words: "Representatives, the passage from life to death is but a moment—Marat is no more! O crime! the hand of a parricide has snatched from us the most intrepid defender of the people—Marat is no more! he constantly sacrificed himself to the public liberty, and that was his offence—Our eyes still seek him in the midst of you—O dismal sight! he is on the bed of death—Where art thou, David? Thou didst preserve for posterity the image of Lepelletier dying for his country; thou hast now another subject to employ thy pencil. And you, legislators, decree a law founded on the circumstance; the most horrible torments are insufficient to avenge the nation for so enormous a crime; annihilate for ever both villany and crimes; instruct hireling assassins in the value of life, and, instead of cutting them off in a moment, let the dread of torture disarm those parricides who threaten the lives of the people's representatives."—No decree followed this sanguinary petition. The attention of the legislature was immediately engaged by Chabot, who related

[m] See Appel à l'Impartial Postérité, vol. ii. p. 72.

the circumstances of Marat's death, and moved for a decree of accusation against Duperret and Fauchet as accomplices with Charlotte Corday; which being reinforced by the arguments of Couthon, was granted [a].

Marat lies in state.
The death of Marat was hardly announced, when his partizans studied how to make his funeral as grand and interesting as possible. His house not being large enough to gratify the immense concourse of people whom curiosity had attracted, it was resolved to embalm his body, and deposit it in the church *des Cordeliers*. The whole building was adorned with national colours. In the middle of the nave was an elevated state-bed, surrounded with cypress, and bearing this inscription: " MARAT, " *the friend of the people, assassinated by the enemies* " *of the people: foes to the country, moderate your* " *joy, he will find avengers.*" The croud who attended to contemplate his features, were however disappointed; he was intirely disfigured, and his corpse was absolutely disgusting.

His funeral.
His funeral ceremony, which was performed by torch-light, was grand and solemn. Mournful music was heard at intervals, forming an accompaniment to songs of woe, written for the occasion. All else was silence, save the speeches made at stated intervals by orators, who came to pay the last tribute of respect to the friend of the people, and the occasional murmurs of the mob, expressing regret at the loss of their friend. The convention and the constituted authorities attended in costume, and the body was escorted by a large detachment of the national guard. Numerous groups of women, young girls, and children, were placed at proper distances, to act the part of excessive grief, and nothing was omitted which could convey the appearance of woe and regret.

[a] Debates. Crimes de Marat, p. 43.

The body was deposited in the church-yard of the Cordeliers. The eve of the ceremony, a deputation of the club of Cordeliers attended at the municipality to demand leave to present a petition to the convention, in order to obtain for Marat the honours of the Pantheon: but Chaumette, *procureur de la commune*, though himself a Cordelier, opposed this proposition. He exclaimed, " Let *ci-devant* " nobles repose in those superb temples; leave to " them their sumptuous pantheons: to *sans-culottes* " the temple of Nature belongs. I move that a " stone, a rough stone, be placed on the tomb of " Marat, with this single inscription: *Here rests the* " *friend of his country, assassinated by the enemies of* " *his country.*" This plan was adopted, and the funeral ceremony concluded with a grand and affecting piece of music in honor of the deceased.

The Cordeliers, afterwards, thought proper to honour the *heart of Marat* with a separate ceremony. They sought, in the *garde meuble de la Couronne*, for the most precious and exquisitely ornamented urn, in which they deposited the heart of Marat. The day preceding this ceremony, a member of the club read an oration which he had prepared. It had for a motto, *O Cor Jesus! O Cor Marat!* and began thus—" Heart of Jesus! Heart of Marat! ye " are equally intitled to our homage." The orator proceeded to compare the life of our Blessed Saviour with that of the friend of the people. Marat's apostles were the Jacobins and Cordeliers; the Publicans, the shop-keepers; and the Pharisees, the aristocrats. " Jesus was a prophet," said the orator; " Marat is a deity." Continuing his eulogy, he compared Marat's concubine to the Virgin Mary; the one concealed the infant Jesus in Egypt, the other saved the friend of the people from the sword of la Fayette*. This discourse was received with considerable

28th July.
His heart consecrated.

---

* I confess that I feel considerable repugnance in publishing these horrible blasphemies; but the display of mental degradation, and excessive

considerable applause; but a member of the club found cause for censure. "We must hear no more of this Jesus," he said, "it is all nonsense; republicans own no God but Philosophy and Liberty." The speech was not spoken, but the ceremony took place. The urn containing the heart was hung up with great pomp in the dome of the hall of the Cordeliers. Robespierre, and the principal members of the Mountain attended, the whole audience were decorated with red caps, and every act denoted extravagance and enthusiasm [p].

25th Nov. Idolized by the public.
Forty-eight feasts were given in honor of him [q]. It was decreed that the bust of Mirabeau should be moved from the Pantheon to make room for his [r], and images of him were distributed all over France [s]. One of the sections of Paris assumed his name; which was also given to Havre de Grace, to Port Dauphin in Madagascar, and to the isle of Bouen. His name was also applied to one of the companies of the revolutionary army, to a ship of the line, and assumed by many individuals in revolutionary committees in various parts of the country [t]. David made a picture on the subject of his death, and in pronouncing his eulogium, mentioned his acquaintance with Marat as a consolation for having come into the world too late to be personally known to Cato, Aristides, Socrates, and many other illustrious ancients [u].

Robespierre suspected.
Though these testimonies of respect were sanctioned and promoted by Robespierre; though he placed

cessive absurdity, is not without its use. It serves to shew how easily the meanest of mankind can attain a degree of impiety so abandoned as to wrest the laurel from the whole race of modern free-thinkers; and it demonstrates the justice of restraining attacks on the scripture, which would else be equally degraded by the ferocity of atheism, and the folly of fanaticism.

p Crimes de Marat, p. 83. et seq.
q Etat de la France, par Montgaillard, p. 70.
r Pagès, vol. i. p. 388. Journals.
s Etat de la France, p. 70.
t Pagès, vol. ii. p. 60. Etat de la France, p. 78. Tench's Correspondence, &c. &c.
u Miss Williams's Letters in 1794, vol. ii. p. 74.

the bust of Marat on the altar of the Supreme Being [x];
yet he has not escaped the suspicion of having been the
enemy of his fame, and the improbable accusation
of having procured Charlotte Corday to accelerate
his death [y]. After the fall of Robespierre, the
Jacobins suggested that jealousy had prevented the
canonization of Marat; and there was not sense of
virtue in the convention sufficient to prevent the
disgraceful ceremony. It was the custom to intro-
duce a bust of him on the theatre to receive the
applauses of the patriotic spectators. But at length   *Marat falls*
an end was put to these absurdities; the name of   *into con-*
the section was changed, his bust was kicked out of   *tempt.*
the Pantheon, and by the decree against premature
apotheoses, forbid to be exhibited on the theatre:
the eulogium of David is only remembered with
contempt, and the subject of it is no longer contemplated but the horror due to his crimes [z].

Marat was in person very diminutive; his head   *Descrip-*
disproportionately large; his complexion livid and   *tion of his*
cadaverous, and his countenance singularly ex-   *person and manners.*
pressive of his malignant and sanguinary disposition.
Dr. Moore says, that " to a painter of massacres it
" would be inestimable." In his dress, he affected
to set the *ton* in point of dirt and shabbiness; Chabot
was his rival in this particular, and the club of Cordeliers their humble imitators. In his own house
he is described to have been seen in the following
attire: " He had on boots, without stockings, an
" old pair of leather breeches, and a white silk
" waistcoat. His dirty shirt, open at the bosom,
" exhibited his skin of yellow hue; long dirty nails
" marked his fingers' ends, and his frightful visage
" was perfectly in unison with this strange dress [a]."

When

---

[x] Suite de l'Etat de la France, p. 36.   [y] Idem, p. 71.
[z] See Miss Williams's Letters in 1794, vol. iv. p. 9.
[a] Roland's Appeal, vol. i. p. 171. The description of his person,
dress, manners, and peculiarities, is principally taken from the fragment

When he went abroad, he wore a large round hat flouched over his eyes, so as to hide a great part of his face. He was characterised, next to his ferocity and envy, by a perseverance which did not permit him to see or acknowledge any difficulties in the way which led to the execution of his favourite project; his vanity, which made him consider himself all-sufficient, strengthened this disposition; and the general exaggeration of his ideas, in all matters relating to himself or others, made him adopt modes of action which no person but himself would have devised, and to which no times but those in which he lived could have given effect. As a philosopher, he toiled incessantly in the repetition of philosophical experiments, in hopes to enjoy the pleasure of humbling the academy of sciences, and of overturning the systems of Newton, or the opinions of Helvetius. As an orator, he wanted every advantage; he expressed himself with difficulty, his ideas were confused, his voice hollow and croaking, his words and gestures abrupt and unconnected; yet he exhibited himself in every tribune, and, in spite of contempt and derision, would be heard: he affected a solemnity in his address, and used to hold his head as high as possible, to acquire an air of dignity; callous to every appearance of dislike or disgust, he never for a moment lost the confident look of self-approbation, but retorted on his dissatisfied hearers looks and expressions of menace and contempt. His temper was sudden and violent; in conversation he could not bear the least contradiction, but flew out instantaneously into the most passionate exclamation and rancorous abuse. The extravagant wildness of his ideas will appear as well from a fact related by Brissot, as from the continual confiscations and murders he afterwards recommended:

ment of Brissot before alluded to; from the Conjuration de d'Orleans, vol. ii. p. 153. Dr. Moore's Journal, vol. i. p. 155. vol. ii. p. 165. 297.; from Roland's Appeal; and from Garat's Memoirs, p. 88.

MARAT.

In order to be cured of the cholic, he was desirous to have his belly opened, but could not find a surgeon who would undertake the operation. His passion for praise, or rather for publicity, was vast and indiscriminate; provided his name filled every mouth, he was indifferent whether it was repeated with applauses or execrations; and was jealous even of his associates, if they affected to surpass him in wickedness. Marat was not brave, though he was irascible and audacious. During the old government, he was afraid of the Bastille; and in the course of the new, under continual apprehension of personal danger and imprisonment. Love of fame was the disease of his mind; avarice had no place in it. At his death he was possessed of no more than one assignat of twenty-five sols ($1s.\ 0\frac{1}{2}d.$); madame Roland however combats this fact by a statement of the elegance of his apartments, one of which she describes as furnished with blue and white damask, and decorated with silk curtains, elegantly drawn up in festoons, a splendid chandelier, superb China vases, filled with natural flowers, then scarce, and of a high price[b]. The assertion of the Brissotine writers, that he was in the pay of the combined powers[c], is unfounded. It may be regarded as a retaliation for the accusation of venality with which they were charged by his partisans; for Marat, unsolicitous about money, too vain to think that an adequate price could be set on his services, and an utter stranger to the dictates of gratitude, was not to be purchased; nor would the attempt be made by any persons whose sagacity was superior to, or whose situation was not so desperate as that of the deluded and abandoned Orleans.

[b] Roland's Appeal, vol. i. p. 171.
[c] See Louvet's Narrative, p. 25. 30. 39. 45. 53.

GABRIEL-HONORE RIQUETTI
Comte de Mirabeau.

Among the manifold characters whom the French revolution has exposed to observation, no one has excited greater interest or occasioned more speculation than Mirabeau. Distinguished from his coadjutors by the extent of his talents, the rapidity and vigour of his eloquence, and still more by that imperious energy of decision, which is the true characteristic of genius and keeps all competitors at a distance; his revolutionary career, though short, is brilliant, and his abilities have secured to him that renown which his virtues could not have claimed. Although the vices of Mirabeau, his treachery, profligacy, and venality, entitle him to the severest censure, such is the privilege of extraordinary endowments, that he is in general contemplated, not only without horror, but with a degree of complacency; and the French revolution has produced so many other public characters who, exceeding him in every evil quality, possessed none of his claims to admiration, that if he is not purified, he is at least dignified by the comparison.

Family of Mirabeau. The ancestors of Mirabeau were emigrants from Italy. In the year 1268, Gerard Arrighetti, and Azzuccio his son, were banished from Florence for their adherence to the Ghibelline party. They took refuge in France, and established themselves at Seyne in Provence, where a grandson of Gerard Arrighetti founded an hospital dedicated to the Holy Ghost. The Italian Arrighetti was in time softened

softened to the French appellative Riquetti; and a widow of the ancient and noble family of Barras having, by a second marriage, alienated the estate in Provence known by the name of Mirabeau, it was purchased by Jean de Riquety, and erected into a marquisate by letters patent in July 1685; from which period the family of Riquety, or Riquetti de Mirabeau, became ennobled [d].

Gabriel-Honoré Riquetti de Mirabeau was born at Egreville [e]. His father was a leader of the sect of Economists, and enjoyed a considerable reputation as author of a work intitled *l'Ami des Hommes*, and several other pieces. The education of the young count was carefully attended to, but he is said to have made so little progress as by no means to prepare the minds of his acquaintance for the brilliant exertions by which he was afterwards distinguished. An anecdote which is recorded of him seems however to prove, that this apparent indocility was in fact nothing but a contempt for the routine of study designated by his tutors: a more discerning master put into his hands, at the age of fourteen, Locke's Essay on the Human Understanding, which soon occupied his entire attention; on reading the first chapter of the second book, he seemed absorbed in profound meditation; at length starting from his reverie he exclaimed, "This is the book I wanted." He studied the work with much attention, and some years afterwards meeting his tutor in a public walk, affectionately accosted him, saying, "I shall never forget that you made me acquainted with Locke [f]."

9th March 1749. Birth.

[d] Dictionnaire de la Noblesse, par M. de la Chenaye Dubois, art. MIRABEAU et RIQUETY.
[e] Anecdotes du Regne de Louis XVI. vol. vi. p. 262. The author of a pamphlet, intitled "Vie Publique et Privée de Mirabeau," says he was born at Paris. As that author is misinformed in many particulars, and seems to have entertained great prejudices against Mirabeau, I have not relied implicitly on his information; and still less on his opinions in those facts where his production is cited as an authority.
[f] Anecdotes du Regne de Louis XVI. vol. vi. p. 262.

Family

Imprisonment.

Family differences, into the merits of which it is impossible at this distance of time to penetrate, occasioned Mirabeau's father to procure a *lettre de cachet* against him. It is said by one author, that his satiric vein too freely indulged produced this act of parental severity [g]: another has not scrupled to assert, that it was occasioned by a discovery that the young count had projected the murder of his parent by poison [h]. Mirabeau himself avers that the cause of his disgrace was the intriguing disposition of a female, who led the father to apprehend that his son would disgrace himself by an ill-chosen matrimonial alliance [i]. He was however closely confined in the *Isle de Rhé*. This imprisonment took place when Mirabeau was only seventeen years of age, and lasted fifteen months, at the end of which he was liberated at his own earnest intercession [k].

1768. Serves in Corsica.

On being set at liberty, he obtained a commission in the dragoons [l], and went to serve in Corsica, which the French were then employed in subjugating, and remained there thirteen months. No authentic mention is made of his conduct in this situation; it is therefore reasonable to believe his own representation, that he behaved in such a manner as to deserve the approbation of his superior officers. He adds, that he compiled a laborious work, which was much applauded by those who have seen it, but was suppressed by his father [m]. During his stay in this island, he assumed the name of Buffière, derived from an estate belonging to his family [n].

June 1772. Marries.

At the termination of the war he returned to France, and addicted himself to every species of irregularity. The prudence or parsimony of his father prevented his allowing such a stipend as would sup-

---

[g] Anecdotes, &c. ubi supra.
[h] Vie Publique & Privée de Mirabeau, p. 2.
[i] Lettres écrites du Donjon de Vincennes, vol. i. p. 189.
[k] Vie Publique, &c. p. 3. Lettres ecrites, &c. vol. i. p. 185.
[l] Dictionnaire de la Noblesse.
[m] Lettres ecrites, &c. vol. i. p. 190.
[n] Vie Publique, &c. p. 15.

port these extravagances, and Mirabeau was consequently involved in great distress. To repair his fortune, and supply the means of gratifying his favourite passions, he turned his attention to the state of matrimony, and selected for the object of his pursuit Marguerite-Emilie de Covet, daughter of the marquis de Marignane, who then resided at Aix. The lady's fortune, which was supposed to amount to a million (43,750*l.*), was a great temptation; but the enterprise was not in other respects promising, as she was already engaged to a gentleman named la Valette, and the marriage on the point of being concluded. Mirabeau, however, found means to supplant this rival, and several others of the first families in France, who made the most unexceptionable offers, and even to obtain the consent of the marquis de Marignane°. Application was made to Mirabeau's father, who, without opposing a match so advantageous and honourable, wrote such an answer as gave no encouragement to the proposal, and refused to advance any money towards his son's establishment ᵖ.

° Mirabeau's biographer asserts, that the young lady's father at first declined the alliance; but that Mirabeau obtained his consent by the following stratagem: Early one morning he made his appearance at the coffee-house frequented by the nobility, in the same dress he had worn the preceding day, with disordered hair and tumbled linen. His friends began rallying, and hoped he had passed an agreeable evening. "Charming," said he, "for I passed it with little Marignane." The story was reported to her father, who, as the only means of preserving his daughter's reputation, consented to her marriage. Vie Publique, &c. p. 6. This account is not altogether probable, as the conduct it supposes is altogether inconsistent with the sentiments of honour entertained by the French nobility. If it had been true, in all probability the father or lover of the young lady would have challenged her supposed seducer, and she would have been shut up in a convent. I have thought it proper, nevertheless, to relate the anecdote, as there is nothing in it repugnant to Mirabeau's character; and particular circumstances might induce the marquis de Marignane to adopt a line of conduct different from what the general view of the case appeared to dictate. There is, in Mirabeau's Letters in the prison of Vincennes, a narrative of the transaction, in which an expensive intrigue is mentioned, but not described. See vol. i. p. 302, et seq.

ᵖ Anecdotes du Regne de Louis XVI. vol. vi. p. 263. Dictionnaire de la Noblesse. Lettres ecrites du Donjon de Vincennes, vol. i. p. 190.

Treatment of his wife.

From an alliance formed on such principles, and at Mirabeau's age, little felicity could be expected. His father, though he would not sanction the marriage by any thing more than a mere constrained consent, presented Mirabeau at court, made him his representative in Provence and Limousin, and maintained for a considerable time an amicable epistolary correspondence, in which he styled him a darling son, an esteemed adviser, and an useful co-adjutor [q]. The bride's fortune, however, was not immediately paid; and Mirabeau, unrestrained in his libertinisms by any considerations arising from the state he had recently adopted, soon found himself three hundred thousand livres (13,125*l.*) in debt [r]. He is accused of having treated his unfortunate wife with the most savage barbarity [s]; and the account is not improbable, considering that love was not the motive of his union, that he was naturally choleric and cowardly, and that he considered women as an object of physical indulgence rather than of social esteem [t].

Banishment.

His irregularities became so excessive, that it was thought proper to obtain a *lettre-de-cachet*, by which he was compelled to fix his residence within the limits of the city of Maurique in Provence [u].

Conduct towards his parents.

He obtained a release from this confinement, but it operated no change in his morals or conduct: on the contrary, he seemed to grow desperate, and added to his profligacy a callousness to reproof, which generally indicates the most depraved state of vicious insensibility. His father was not happy in marriage, and the disputes between him and his wife were carried to such an excess, that the lady sued for a separate maintenance. Mirabeau displayed a want of filial feeling altogether unnatural. He had fomented the disputes between his parents;

---

q Lettres ecrites, &c. vol. i. p. 189.
r Anecdotes du Regne de Louis XVI. vol. vi. p. 263.
s Vie Publique, &c. p. 7.
t Lettres de Mirabeau à Mauvillon, p. 230.
u Anecdotes du Regne de Louis XVI. vol. vi. p. 263.

and

and now, availing himself of his talents, went to his father, and, for an hundred *Louis-d'or*, prepared his memorial for the court. Having done this, he repaired to his mother, and by invectives against his father induced her to pay the same price for the same service. Both memorials were actually presented, and the unnatural son enjoyed the double lucre of his perfidy and insensibility [x].

He still pursued the career of libertinism and dishonour with such shameless effrontery, that it being again judged necessary to imprison him, he was exiled to the city of Pontarlier [y]. His sister, madame de Cabris, had associated herself with him in his disgraceful pursuits; and, in revenge for some affront offered to her, he had assaulted the baron de Villeneuve, who commenced a suit and recovered six thousand livres (262*l*. 10*s*.) damages [z]. While at Pontarlier, he fell in love with, and seduced from her husband, Sophie Ruffei, marquise de Monnier. The intrigue was for some time carried on in secret; but at length the marquis, who was seventy years of age, obtaining intelligence of the fact, to revenge the indignity he had sustained, procured an order to confine Mirabeau in the citadel of Dijon. While he was in this place, his mistress suffered great severities from her own relations; and Mirabeau's father was preparing to imprison him with more strictness, but he took advantage of the indulgence allowed him by the commandant of Dijon, broke his parole, and escaped into Holland, where he was

Imprisoned.

Intrigue with Sophie Ruffei.

---

[x] Robison's Proofs of a Conspiracy, p. 372.
[y] Anecdotes du Regne de Louis XVI. vol. vi. p. 263. I do not pretend to have been accurate in the narration of Mirabeau's juvenile adventures and the imprisonments which ensued from them. He is said, besides the banishments and confinements already mentioned, to have been detained in the chateau d'If, and the chateau de Joux; in fact, he himself afterwards boasted, in the national assembly, that in the course of his life, seventeen lettres-de-cachet had been issued against him.
[z] Anecdotes du Regne de Louis XVI. vol. vi. p. 263. Preface de Manuel aux Lettres de Mirabeau, p. 8.

joined

joined by Sophia. It ought not to be omitted, that Mirabeau juftifies this efcape, by afferting that the commandant connived at and indirectly advifed it [a].

Sentence againft him. The hufband immediately inftituted a fuit againft his wife, in which fhe was condemned to a forfeiture of dower; and a profecution againft Mirabeau, who was fentenced, by default, to pay fifty livres (2 l. 3 s. 9 d.) as a fine to the king; forty thoufand livres (1750 l.) as damages to the marquis de Monnier; and to be beheaded in effigy by the common hangman [b].

Arrefted in Holland. As the execution of this part of the fentence would have difgraced the whole family, every exertion was made to obtain a reverfal of it; and as the judgment had been obtained by default, it was conceived that it might be fet afide if the defendant could be brought within the jurifdiction of the court. His family employed the following means to get him arrefted: an *exempt de police*, named Jaquet de Douei, went to Holland decorated with the military crofs of St. Louis; and pretending to have been exiled from France by minifterial perfecution, formed an intimacy with Mirabeau, who lodged at the houfe of a tailor, and took the name of St. Mathieu. The *exempt* found means to take Mirabeau into cuftody, and both he and Sophia were brought prifoners to France. The lady, who was now pregnant, was till her lying-in confined in a private houfe, and afterwards fent to the convent of Saint Clare at Gien. Mirabeau was imprifoned in the caftle of Vincennes [c].

May 1777. Imprifoned at Vincennes.

---

[a] See Lettres ecrites du Donjon de Vincennes, vol. i. p. 387.
[b] Anecdotes du Regne de Louis XVI. vol. vi. p. 263. Preface de Manuel, &c. p. 21. 23.
[c] Preface de Manuel, &c. p. 24. Anecdotes, &c. vol. vi. p. 264. It is to be obferved, that Mirabeau compofed a laborious defence of his conduct up to this period in the fhape of a memorial to his father, in which he denies, fuppreffes, vindicates, or extenuates many of the facts included in the preceding narrative. See Lettres ecrites, &c. p. 287.

In

In this prison he remained three years and seven months, nor could his frequent letters to the ministers, in which he exclaimed against the rigour of his detention, and demanded the privilege of a trial, procure his enlargement, or any satisfactory exertion in his favour. The *lieutenant de police* was so far interested in his behalf, as to connive at a correspondence which he maintained with the object of his passion; but, fettered with this condition, that after once reading, she should return the letter to the *inspecteur de police* [d]. It is well observed by Dr. Moore, that " Mirabeau's excessive love of " pleasure would have tended to render him com-" pletely dissipated, and of course left him ignorant, " had he not employed the long intervals of con-" finement and retirement that his debauches and " his want of money obliged him to, in studies " which, with better health and more riches, he " would have neglected [e]." In the state prison of Vincennes he seems to have thought seriously of becoming an author. He had before assisted his father, and compiled some literary works, which do not appear to have been published, and had, while in Holland, formed a literary engagement with Fauche the bookseller, though none of his productions were published. In this long interval of seclusion, he applied himself more attentively to this object, and began to consider literature as a pecuniary resource. At first he employed himself in compiling a French grammar for the instruction of the offspring of his illicit amour [f]; but as it was more immediately necessary

His employments.

---

[d] Preface de Manuel, &c. p. 8. The collection of letters written by Mirabeau during this imprisonment, and after his death published by Manuel, do their author no credit as a lover, a scholar, or a man. They exhibit the grossness of appetite, without the delicacy of passion; they are often querulous without eloquence, and expostulatory without dignity.

[e] Moore's View, vol. ii. p. 212.

[f] Sophie was delivered of a girl the 7th January 1778. Manuel speaks very highly of Mirabeau's Grammatical Essay, which, according

cessary to provide for the subsistence of his infant, then in the care of a wet nurse, he complied with the corrupt taste of the times, and supplied the hawkers with obscene pamphlets, under the titles of *Le Libertin de Qualité*, *Ma Converfion*, and *Erotika Biblion*, which last unites blasphemy with indecency[g]. It is, however, but charitable and reasonable to conclude, that necessity and the corruption of the public mind alone induced him thus to debase his pen, since even while thus employed he found leisure to compose his celebrated essay *Sur les Lettres de Cachet, et les Prisons d'Etat*[h]. It was afterwards said, that he received from government five thousand livres (218 *l*. 15 *s*.) for the copy of this work, and that an edition of six thousand was found in the Bastille when that fortress was destroyed[i]. It was published and well known in the world many years before that event[k].

27th Dec. 1780. Release.

At length Mirabeau obtained his liberty, and found little difficulty in invalidating a sentence which had been pronounced merely by default, and without any examination of witnesses. His mistress recovered her dower, and an annuity was settled for her maintenance[l]. Mirabeau, however, did not continue long attached to her after obtaining his liberty.

Goes to Switzerland.

His stay in France now became impossible, from the magnitude of his debts, and the total loss of his character; he went, therefore, to reside at Neuf-

---

ing to him, comprised, in twenty-five pages, all the essential rules of the French grammar, explained all difficulties, pointed out all the exceptions to general rules, facilitated the conjugation and syntax of the irregular verbs; contained all the rules of pronunciation and prosody, and particularly explained the declension of participles. Preface de Manuel, p. 35.

[g] Preface de Manuel, p. 36.
[h] Idem, p. 38.
[i] See Le Livre rouge, and the editor's Annotations.
[k] See Lettres de Mirabeau à Chamfort, p. 1.
[l] Preface de Manuel, p. 38.

chatel in Switzerland, where he publifhed his eſſay on *Lettres de Cachet* ᵐ. For ſome years after this, almoſt all traces of Mirabeau are loſt, he ſeems to have been involved in obſcurity and penury. It appears, however, that he commenced an action againſt his father, for maintenance and arrears, in which he finally ſucceeded ⁿ. It is alſo averred, that he

Suit againſt his father, and wife.

ᵐ Anecdotes du Regne de Louis XVI. vol. vi. p. 264.

ⁿ Lettres de Mirabeau à Chamfort, p. 45. I have not been very minute in my reſearches reſpecting the origin of theſe family diſputes, as the diſcuſſion would not Intereſt the reader. The character of Mirabeau, as diſplayed in the whole of his life, does not impart a favorable prepoſſeſſion of his filial conduct, and independently of any provocation; and the temper of the elder Mirabeau as it is repreſented, does not acquit him of probable miſconduct. The complaints the father and ſon had a right to make againſt each other are thus preſented in the abſtract by Mirabeau himſelf; " What have you " done!" my father will exclaim: " Your youth afforded a preſage of " the diſorders of your more mature age. I was obliged to impriſon " you at ſeventeen, and omitting your ſmaller profligacies, this is a brief " ſketch of your life. As ſoon as you could act for yourſelf, you " contracted enormous debts;—when, in order to ſave the fortune of " my grandſon, I cauſed you to be baniſhed from my eſtates, and " confined to a city, you broke through all reſtrictions to purſue freſh " extravagances; you have drawn on yourſelf a criminal proſecution; " you compelled me to get you confined in a citadel, and then abuſed " the liberty which had been allowed you by the commandant, to " ſeduce and carry off a woman of quality. Certainly, juſtice has " not been done, but the injuſtice conſiſts in ſhielding you from the " ſeverity of the laws." In anſwer to this ſuppoſed accuſation, Mirabeau depicts his father in the following colours: " The marquis " de Mirabeau, after paſſing a moſt licentious youth, ſignalized his " more mature age by the following traits. He proſecuted one of his " brothers, in France and in foreign countries, with an inveteracy " which afforded room to ſuſpect that he wiſhed to evade the payment " of his patrimony. He has ruined himſelf in creating a political " economy. He has deteriorated the property of his wife and children " by two millions (87,500*l*.) while declaiming againſt luxury and " debts. He continued obſtinately to reſide at Paris to form a new " ſect, though he had injured his own fortune, and was continually " preaching to all his fellow-citizens retirement to their own eſtates. " Three times he infected his wife with the moſt ſhameful of maladies, " while he was in the daily habit of crying up purity of manners. He " has notoriouſly made ſettlements on his miſtreſſes, while he affected " to deplore the depravity of the age. The feeling and tender friend " of man, (*l'ami des hommes*,) whoſe exalted ſoul cannot ſtoop to vul- " gar affections, diſdains his family, and loves the whole human " race. He has perſecuted his wife, and every one of his children. " He has turned out of doors, and confined in a convent, a wife who " had brought him a fortune of fifty thouſand livres (2187 *l*.) a-year, he inſtituted a ſuit againſt his wife, claiming the cuſtody of her perſon and property, or requiring, as an alternative, that ſhe ſhould retire to a convent. He pleaded on his own behalf before the parliament of Aix. The archduke Ferdinand and his conſort, together with the moſt diſtinguiſhed perſonages of the city, were preſent. Every one was charmed with the eloquence diſplayed by Mirabeau; but the allegations of matrimonial miſconduct and unmanly cruelty were ſo ſtrong againſt him, that he loſt his cauſe[o].

1783.

Writes on the order of Cincinnatus.

In order to enable himſelf to turn his literary talents to a better account, Mirabeau had contracted an intimacy with the celebrated Nicolas Chamfort, who, if he wanted the genius and audacity of Mirabeau, poſſeſſed much more extenſive information; and who, conſcious of the feebleneſs of his own character, was content to direct that ardour in another, which he could not create in himſelf. By Chamfort's aſſiſtance, Mirabeau was enabled to produce his work intitled *Conſiderations ſur l'Ordre de Cincinnatus*. In preparing this publication, Mirabeau uſed the greateſt diligence; and beſides the advantages derived from Chamfort, viſited Dr. Franklin, then at Paris, and conſulted with him during the whole progreſs of the work. His gains

---

"and eleven children. He has withheld her alimony, contravened his moſt ſolemn engagements, and haraſſed her, from year to year, with *lettres-de-cachet*. He has obtained decrees againſt his mother-in-law, and her eldeſt ſon, to gratify his own love of guardianſhips, and becauſe he fancies himſelf an excellent manager (the beſt proof would be his own rental). He compelled his eldeſt daughter to take the veil. He has perſecuted his ſons, and refuſed them the ſlighteſt pecuniary aſſiſtance. He has attempted to extend his tyranny over one daughter who is married, and whoſe huſband made no complaint. In the ſame manner he behaved to all his children, except a daughter, who found favour in his ſight by her complaiſance to his miſtreſs, and becauſe her huſband has had the art to profeſs a paſſionate admiration of *the economical mills*." Lettres ecrites du Donjon de Vincennes, vol. i. p. 185. 187.

[o] Anecdotes du Regne de Louis XVI. vol. vi. p. 267.

were

were but small, as the English booksellers were averse to speculate on the subject, and discouraged the author [p]. The work, however, met with considerable applause.

Mirabeau had now formed a connexion with a mademoiselle Nehrat, to whom he continued attached for several years. In order to publish his work, he resolved to go to London, accompanied by this lady, who, for decency's sake, was called comtesse de Mirabeau. After a stormy passage, they arrived in England, and established themselves in Hatton-Garden. Mirabeau, after publishing the book with which he came prepared, was involved in great pecuniary distress, which he sought to relieve by forming engagements with booksellers. In consequence of these, he produced some volumes of a work called *Le Conservateur*. The original intention, as described by Mirabeau, was to analyse good books of every description, and to draw from the unformed mass of periodical publications detached pieces, which, from their brevity, were liable to be forgotten [q]. He was yet unacquainted with the English language; but conceiving that English literature would succeed in France, undertook to translate, and qualified himself for the task while performing it; he procured a grammar and dictionary, and learned the English language as he proceeded in his translation [r].

Aug. 1784, Resides in London.

---

[p] Lettres de Mirabeau à Chamfort, p. 30. 43. 87.
[q] Idem, p. 67. 74. 83.
[r] Pagès, vol. i. p. 377. To a genius like Mirabeau, such an exertion might be possible, but it ought to serve rather as a warning than an encouragement to other translators. I can hardly think the work alluded to by Pagès to have been a selection of English comedies, which, in a letter to Chamfort, he expressed an inclination to attempt (p. 93). The colloquial language of comedy was not suited to that mind which could so successfully commit a plagiarism on Burke as to make professor Wilde regret that the whole works of that inestimable writer had not been translated by Mirabeau. See Address to the Friends of the People, p. 115.

Profecutes his fecretary.

During his ftay in England, Mirabeau was obliged to profecute one Hardy, who lived with him as fecretary, for ftealing fome of his property. The prifoner was acquitted, and Mirabeau's enemies have endeavoured to fix grievous inculpations on his character for this profecution; but, on a fair review of the proceeding, he feems in no manner blamable [s].

Writes.

On his return to Paris, Mirabeau, ftill an author by profeffion, turned his attention to finance, then the moft popular topic, and produced *Confiderations fur la Caiffe d'Efcompte*, and *Confiderations fur la Banque de St. Charles*, neither of which are now much remembered. In thefe works he accommodated himfelf fo much to the principles laid down by Calonne, that he was fufpected of being hired by that minifter [t]. In fact, it is not improbable that he received fome pecuniary affiftance, and, perhaps, a promife of being employed in the diplomatic line, as that appears now to have become an object of his attention, and, for a long time, to have formed his chief ambition.

1786. Goes to Berlin.

Actuated by this motive, and invefted with fecret orders, though not recognized in any public capacity, by Calonne, Mirabeau went to Berlin. The period of his arrival was remarkable and interefting. Frederic II. diftinguifhed by the name of *Great*, was in his laft illnefs; he fent for, welcomed, and was peculiarly kind to Mirabeau, who was the laft foreigner admitted to his converfation, though many noble travellers teftified their wifhes for that honour [u].

Advice to Frederic William II.

On the demife of that illuftrious monarch, Mirabeau wrote two memorials or letters

---

[s] See Vie Publique, &c. p. 18. Seffions Papers, 1714-5, Clark Mayor.
[t] Anecdotes du Regne de Louis XVI. vol. vi. p. 265.
[u] See Mirabeau's Advertifement, prefixed to the Memorial prefented to Frederic William II. printed with the Tranflation of his Secret Hiftory of the Court of Berlin, by Bladon, 1789.

to his succeffor, in which he gave advice with equal freedom and confidence, and reviewed the state of the kingdom, and the measures of the deceased monarch, in a style bold and impressive, yet exempt from every mark of rudeness and disrespect [x]. One of his principal objects was to induce the new monarch to place the Jews, hitherto grievously oppressed, on the same footing with his other subjects. To attain this end, Mirabeau spared no labour; he did not confine his efforts to a memorial, but wrote in the French and German journals, excited others to write, and used every exertion calculated to defeat prejudice and insure success [y].

Mirabeau's conduct in this affair was not disinterested: he considered himself qualified to fill a high department in the state, and expected to obtain some post of honour. The new king, however, was disgusted with his licentious and profligate manners, shocked at his open profession of atheism, and not inclined to pay regard to his pretensions. This disappointment induced Mirabeau to connect himself with a band of writers who had united to disseminate licentious principles, both in religion and government. His audacity, his knowledge of men and manners, and particularly his talent for sarcasm, were highly useful to this junto, at whose instigation he produced several pieces tending to make those in administration the objects of public ridicule and reproach. Among these were the Letters on the Constitution of the Prussian States, the *Chronique Scandaleuse*, and, afterwards, the *Histoire secrète de la Cour de Berlin* [z].

Motives.

One of the most remarkable events which distinguished Mirabeau's residence in Berlin, was his association with a daring and dangerous sect, enemies

Becomes an illuminatus;

---

[x] The translator of this work truly afferts, that the reasoning is in a great measure borrowed from Smith's Wealth of Nations. See Translation above-mentioned, vol. ii. p. 373. n.
[y] See Lettres de Mirabeau à Mauvillon, p. 6.
[z] Robison's Proofs, p. 274, 275.

of religion, government, and all social order, distinguished by the name of ILLUMINATI.

Account of that sect.

The patronage afforded by Frederic II. king of Prussia, to Voltaire, d'Alembert, and other writers, who affected to treat the Christian religion, and revelation in general, as a mere imposture, had given such extensive credence and circulation to their opinions, that proselytes and champions were to be found in every country. Their works were greedily read, and the avenues to fame entirely ingrossed by their partisans. The wit and sarcastic vein of Voltaire, together with his acknowledged pre-eminence in many walks of polite literature, rendered opposition dangerous, as the result was, in general, the contempt of the multitude of small wits, who are ever more ready to laugh than to reason, and who can cry down an author against whom their talents would, in any other way, be employed in vain. Nor were the doctrines set up by these new philosophers devoid of external claims to popular approbation. They affected universal tolerance, and declaimed against priestcraft, and superstition alone. But from the vices they turned their arms against the establishment. By putting extreme cases of supposition, by bringing forward the most striking events recorded in history, which reflect on the conduct of priests, they facilitated the deduction, that the sacerdotal character never alters; and that because numerous instances are found of priests who have been avaricious, profligate, ambitious, or cruel; avarice, profligacy, ambition, and cruelty must necessarily form an integral part of the disposition of the whole priesthood.

They could not, however, believe that all mankind would resist the conviction of experience, and, in spite of their own observation, conclude against individuals, merely because involved in general sarcasms or undistinguishing censures. To prevent the effect of these considerations, they redoubled their attacks

attacks on those books which form the basis of the Christian religion; they laboured, with incredible perseverance, to impeach their veracity, hoping, by such means, to procure currency for the opinion, that a priest, if not cruel, was a mean, dissembling hypocrite, who, in order to eat his bread in idleness, vouched for stories he did not believe, and recommended doctrines in which he had no faith. These efforts were attended with great success, and perhaps the most important first-fruit of them was the degradation of the priesthood in the eyes of mankind; many who could not hate or despise, began to pity, and instead of contemplating them as the champions of a sacred doctrine, under whose banners they must fight to obtain an immortal reward, considered them as docile supporters of a flagrant imposture, which they wanted courage to examine, or ability to detect.

Had the efforts of this anti-christian party been confined, like those of their predecessors, to mere polemical writings, their proselytes would have been few, and their attacks speedily forgotten. But they had recourse to new arms. The sprightly genius of Voltaire, united with extensive reading, and a great facility of combination, enabled him to give diversity to the forms of assault, and instead of confining himself to dry essays, or harsh critical discussions, to strew the seeds of scepticism in every department of the sciences; to make history, philosophy, and astronomy the vehicles of his satire. That even the lighter minds might not escape infection, and that the mere readers for amusement (a numerous tribe) might be inlisted in the cause, novels and tales were fabricated, in which, while the fancy was amused by all the brilliancy and luxuriance of unbounded wit, graced with all the decorative charms which a pen of more than threescore years' experience could confer, the heart was poisoned with doubts which indolence or want of vigour would not suffer the reader

to

to remove, but which, while they flattered his vanity by easy triumphs, arising from the display of borrowed wit, fettered his judgment in chains which were never to be loosened, and which the deluded wretch mistook for ornaments because he heard them jingle.

As the assailants of religion increased in number, an opportunity offered of uniting them still more firmly, of producing that interchange of sentiment which facilitates discussion, and of subjecting every species of literature, and every topic of human curiosity, to the influence of their favourite speculations: this was the projected publication of the French Encyclopedia. To obtain the exclusive direction of this work became a favourite view of the new philosophers, and, by the influence of d'Alembert, they were enabled to accomplish it. They used their advantage with vigour and address; conscious that attacks too direct and open against a prevailing system would frustrate their own end, they adopted a mode of conduct apparently very moderate, but fraught with the most artful duplicity. In treating of certain topics, such as the existence of God, the immortality of the soul, &c. they made a point to detail those reasons which were favourable to the popular belief; but, at the same time, by reference to other articles, contrived to direct the reader's attention to arguments more forcibly urged, and more speciously advanced, tending to destroy the opinions they had at first coldly inculcated.

The sect, by these and other means, became numerous and popular; the great, influenced by the king of Prussia's example, and sensible that fame or disgrace were in the gift of those who commanded the portals of literature, opened to them their purses and their palaces. The rising generation of wits, eager to secure the same advantages, adopted the same means; any respect shewn to the forms or even to the more essential doctrines of religion, was soon decried as the mark of a grovelling genius, or an uncultured understanding.

From attacking the highest objects of human veneration, the mind is led by an easy gradation to resist the immediate depositaries of temporal authority. The hatred of kings naturally followed the endeavour to obliterate the sentiments of religious belief. Voltaire and d'Alembert, favoured by nobles and caressed by kings, were, at first, ashamed to make their authority the object of a direct attack; they indicated in their writings some enmity to royalty, but were compelled, to preserve appearances, to confine themselves to general declamations, or anonymous philippics. It was reserved for another writer, equally hostile to religion with themselves, to lay the foundation of those doctrines of liberty and equality, which, however specious, have by misconstruction and exaggerations produced so many evils, such wide-spreading anarchy, so general a depravation of morals, and such extensive misery. Rousseau, a republican by birth, an author by profession, unnoticed by the great, and endowed with a rancorous heart and gloomy disposition, was desirous of extending his fame by being the author of new systems, and by defending apparent paradoxes. He began, in essays and popular romances, to broach those extravagant, though splendid notions of liberty which, in order to make individuals free, disunite society; and, to exalt man in a fanciful scale formed by vanity, degrade him to that state in which the human species would exist if arts, manners, and civilization were unknown. A disciple of this system might boast that he was

——as free as nature first made man
Ere the base servitude of laws began,
When wild in woods the noble savage ran.

The

MIRABEAU.

The doctrines of infidelity, and those so nearly allied to them, of disorganization, found their earliest promoters in France; but with success widely different. The necessity of supporting a form of government was, from its daily contact with all their functions, obvious to those whom vanity, levity, or worse motives rendered indifferent to innovations in matters of religion; and thus, while the police maintained the strictest vigilance with respect to publications on government, the principles of infidelity, even to the excess of atheism, were openly avowed by ministers, courtiers, and even by many of the clergy.

The ridicule of things sacred was not, however, sufficient to gratify those who, with the purchase they had already gained, meditated the immense and important project of turning the whole Christian world. That atheistical philosophers, and raving enthusiasts in politics, should in small detachments, or by separate exertions, try their strength in various countries, was a matter of no great importance. Another scheme, more extensive, more operative, and more consistent, became necessary; and to give shape and execution to such a plan was the task of Dr. Adam Weishaupt, professor of canon law in the university of Ingolstadt. This man, bred under the Jesuits, was, on the abolition of their order, induced to change his views; and, from being their pupil, he became their most bitter enemy.

Weishaupt was member of a lodge of free-masons established at Munich in Bavaria, called *the Lodge Theodore of good Counsel*. This lodge corresponded with, and had formed a particular system of its own by instructions from the *Loge des Chevaliers bienfaisans* at Lyons; it was thoroughly imbued with the modern principles, and in no degree resembled the masonic institutions in England, or those which were immediately derived from or informed by them

them. This lodge occupied itself with economical, statistical, and political matters; and had arranged a system of cosmopolitism, proposing, as a fundamental position in the formation of society, that every office should be held by a man of talents and virtue, and that every kind of ability should be employed in a suitable station. The engaging pictures of possible felicity in a society so constituted were very captivating to youth; and as the members of the lodge were enjoined to promulgate their doctrines by all possible means, they obtained many proselytes.

Weishaupt had long entertained a scheme for establishing an association which in time should govern the world. The system of cosmopolitism was so favourable to his views, that he took great pains to inculcate it in the minds of those numerous pupils whom his high reputation as a professor of civil law drew to his lectures. He employed his eloquence in describing the absurdity and horrors of superstition with such effect, that his youthful audience easily underwent the inviting transition to general infidelity and irreligion. With this ascendancy over the minds of several youths of good family, he became the founder of a new sect; and his emissaries had already been very successful in procuring adherents, when the audacity of the lodge Theodore occasioned alarms in the elector of Bavaria, who discovering too late that the sect of ILLUMINATI had taken deep root, and produced the most dangerous effects in his states, endeavoured to suppress them, but in vain. He banished Weishaupt, together with two Italian marquises, and one Zwack a counsellor, his devoted adherents, and imprisoned several others.

Weishaupt sullenly retired, refusing a proffered pension, to Regensburg on the confines of Switzerland. Confiding in the early success of his projects, and the numbers of his proselytes in different countries, he boldly wrote in defence of the sect of ILLUMINATI; knowing that inquiry would inftigate curiofity, and that if fome were led to abhor and dread the new fociety, many would be induced to inquire after and embrace it, while the great majority of mankind, wrapt in fecurity, would be indifferent to its progrefs.

The principles of the ILLUMINATI, as denounced to the elector of Bavaria by fome apoftates who had not attained any very exalted rank, were thefe:—
" The order was to abjure Chriftianity; and to
" refufe admiffion to the higher degrees to all who
" adhered to any of the three confeffions. Senfual
" pleafures were reftored to the rank they held in
" the Epicurean philofophy. Self-murder was juf-
" tified on ftoical principles. In the lodges, death
" was declared an eternal fleep. Patriotifm and
" loyalty were called narrow-minded prejudices,
" and incompatible with univerfal benevolence.
" Continual declamations were made on liberty
" and equality, as the unalienable rights of man.
" The baneful influence of accumulated property
" was declared an infurmountable obftacle to the
" happinefs of any nation, whofe chief laws were
" framed for its protection and increafe. Nothing
" was fo frequently difcourfed of as the propriety
" of employing for a good purpofe the means which
" the wicked employed for evil purpofes; and it
" was taught, that the preponderancy of good in
" the ultimate refult confecrated every mean em-
" ployed, and that wifdom and virtue confifted in
" properly determining this balance." Thefe principles were denied by Weifhaupt; who was undoubtedly angry that facts of fuch importance fhould be difclofed to affociates fo young, and whofe fidelity had not been fufficiently infured: but the information gained by fubfequent difclofures fully evinces that the communication was ftrictly true.

The

The young members were not immediately admitted to a knowledge of thefe principles: had they been difclofed ere the mind was properly prepared, terror and amazement would have repelled many profelytes. To induce them to wander in the mazes of depravity, it was neceffary to decorate the entrance with emblems of wifdom and virtue: for this purpofe, when any of the elder adepts had difcovered a perfon whom they judged fit for their purpofe, (perfons whom they were no lefs careful to examine than diligent to feek,) they made a point to gain his confidence by fuch declarations and fentiments as are moft captivating to a virtuous and benevolent mind, while they fecured his gratitude and attachment by extending the refources and emboldening the efforts of his genius. At his firft entrance into the fociety, the novice was encouraged to hope every thing if he rendered himfelf worthy of a more intimate confidence. By difplaying fhewy thefes, and ufing the pupil to reafon on them with fuccefs, they imparted a habit and readinefs of difputation; and the novice, accuftomed to combat received notions as prejudices, was led by imperceptible degrees to oppofe the moft confirmed doctrines in religion and government. His gradations to the higher claffes were performed with a rapidity or procraftination proportionate to the ardour he difplayed in qualifying himfelf for the more concealed arcana and more atrocious confidence. In proportion as he advanced in the path of profelytifm, he was encouraged with new gradations, new difclofures, and new employments, till at laft, not without many occult ceremonies and formal abjurations and proffeffions, he was inftated in the full dignities of the fuperior clafs.

The degrees to be paffed through were thefe:—
1ft clafs, or nurfery; preparation, novice, minerval, illuminatus minor.—2d clafs; apprentice, fellow-craft,

craft, master, illuminatus major, illuminatus dirigens.—3d class; presbyter, prince, magus, rex.

Some pupils, whose minds were not sufficiently apt, or whose principles were too firmly rooted to answer the purposes of the sect, were initiated only in the degrees of the first class, and there left with a full persuasion of the innocence and laudable views of the society. They omitted no means which ingenuity could devise, or perseverance effect, to increase their influence, and attain a respectable and permanent establishment. They acquired the direction of colleges, and even founded schools and seminaries of their own. They assumed the entire direction of the literary taste in Germany, by promoting the sale of books favourable to their views, and suppressing such as were of a contrary tendency. This they were enabled to effect by an intimate intercourse with eminent booksellers, and by obtaining an ascendancy in the most celebrated reviews and literary journals. They founded reading-rooms and book-societies, where, for a trifling subscription, their publications were put into the hands of the indigent; where curiosity was piqued by discussion and eulogium; and content banished by disputations, in which the civil and religious condition of man was exposed, in a style which could not fail of inflaming the mind, and producing clamour and disaffection.

Nor was the female sex exempt from their arts: towards them they exhibited a mode of conduct equally insidious and pernicious. Their desire of information was studiously excited, and their attention directed to works which tended to make them dissatisfied with their station in society, and taught them to aspire to a rank yet untried. In claiming their independence, they were taught to undervalue that quality which formed their most exalted notion of honour—chastity; and no effort of mental seduction

duction or personal blandishment was omitted to reduce them to a level which, under pretence of liberty, would place them in abject subjection to their tutors: at the same time, to prevent discoveries which would have produced fatal consequences, the deluded victims were taught to carry to their own lips those baleful compositions which counteract the operations of nature, and deprive of existence the semi-animate offspring.

The great source from which they drew their members, the basis on which they rested for acquittal in case of suspicion, and the grand mass into which they affected to resolve the principles of their society, were the lodges of free-masons. Free-masonry, imported into France by some British adventurers who followed the fortunes of James II. had spread over many countries of the continent, and lodges were formed corresponding with those from whom they derived their origin. According to the different genius of different countries, this benevolent social institution was disfigured by pedantry, or disgraced by vanity and foppery; till the masonry of the continent resembled only in a slight degree the profession of the British lodges. In some states they were considered harmless, in some slightly observed, but in others regarded with the most vigilant jealousy. In the papal dominions in particular, free-masons were declared, *prima facie*, excommunicated, obliged to hold their assemblies with the most cautious privacy, and even to maintain watchmen to prevent the intrusions of the civil power. Weishaupt's new sect, as its existence was derived from a corrupt masonic lodge, affected to be an integral part of masonry, or rather a superior directing class. The degrees were similar in name, though widely different in import from the masonic degrees[*]; and the *frere insinuant*, or recruiting brother,

---

[*] I have given (Appendix, N° VI.) a genuine copy of the diploma of a highly respectable English gentleman, who was admitted a member

ther, while leading his pupils through thefe different degrees, felt extreme regret if, from his perverfenefs or incapacity, he was obliged to leave him amongft the free-mafons. This artful involution, of characters afforded the ILLUMINATI the means of repelling fufpicion, by citing the teftimony of thofe whom they had left in the mere rank of mafons, and by vouching the exemplary character of many members of that body, whofe names alone formed a fufficient guaranty that no confpiracy would be conducted by a fociety of which they were members [b].

Confequences of Mirabeau's becoming an Illuminatus.

While at Berlin, Mirabeau attracted the particular notice of Weifhaupt, who, through the medium of Mauvillon, a Frenchman, lieutenant-colonel in the fervice of the duke of Brunfwick, imparted to Mirabeau the honors of a noviciate [c]; and from his ardent character, and facility of exertion, there is every reafon to fuppofe he was fpeedily admitted to a participation of the higher fecrets of the order. Mirabeau's connection with this fociety probably produced fome of the moft defperate exceffes and daring characteriftics of the French revolution, as it facilitated the union between the confpirators and freethinkers in Paris, and thofe in the provinces and in foreign countries; as it formed the bafis of a moft extenfive confederacy and correfpondence; and as it delivered the lodges in France to the influence of the duke of Orleans, who, fome time before, by dint of money and intrigue, had

---

ber of a lodge at Palermo in 1766, at leaft nine years before Weifhaupt's fect was in exiftence. The reader will obferve, that the expreffions and allufions are ftrictly confonant with the defcriptions of Robifon in the Chapter of Schifms in Free-mafonry.

[b] It is hardly neceffary to inform the reader, that the above account of the Illuminati is derived from Memoires pour fervir à l'Hiftoire du Jacobinifme, par Barruel; and Proofs of a Confpiracy againft all the Religions and Governments of Europe, by John Robifon, A. M.— works which merit frequent and attentive perufal, and claim profound contemplation.

[c] Robifon's Proofs, p. 276.

been

been conftituted grand-mafter. In Mirabeau it produced immediately a perceptible change of manners and purfuits. All the levity and frivolity of his difpofition feemed fuddenly difcarded; he became obfequioufly obfervant of Mauvillon's inftructions, and expreffed the moft laudable defire to increafe his knowledge, eftablifh his fame, and augment his utility[d]. Among other fchemes in which he embarked was one which marks the genius and views of the Illuminati in the moft forcible manner, namely, to acquire a correct ftatiftical and topographical knowledge of every country in Europe. He acquired fuch an acquaintance with Pruffia and Saxony, and frequently expreffed his wifh and refolution to extend refearch[e].

Mirabeau rendered an important fervice to his affociates by his *Effai fur la Secte des Illuminés*. The difcoveries which had been already made refpecting the fociety had infufed a fpirit of fufpicion and jealoufy extremely dangerous to their exiftence. Mirabeau had no reafon to expect that the king of Pruffia would favour their eftablifhment in his ftates, and therefore, to avert fufpicion and make difcovery ridiculous, he produced this effay. It is written in the ftyle of a man who, heated with a new difcovery, and exafperated by the detection of concealed villany, feels impatient to impart his fentiments, and eager for their making a proper impreffion. The difclofures it contains are not new, as they had been previoufly ftated in various publications; but they are involved with fo many improbable fictions and fallacious reafonings, that a perfon who fhould after that time fpeak of the fect of *Illuminati* as a fubject of terror, or an object of jurifprudential reftraint, muft be content to father all the improbabilities introduced in Mirabeau's effay. He could not ftate any fundamental truths which were not

Publifhes Effai fur la Secte.

[d] See Lettres à Mauvillon, paffim. [e] Idem, 211, &c.

there advanced, and the ingenuity of oppofition could hardly fail of afcribing his fears and his intelligence to the fame fource, and, by confequence, of decrying the reafoner as one who, being himfelf impofed on by fables, and terrified by chimeras, was folicitous to extend impofture, and perpetuate groundlefs alarm. Robifon juftly ftyles this one of the ftrangeft and moft impudent performances that ever appeared. " Mirabeau (he adds) con-
" fided in his own powers of deception, in order to
" fcreen from obfervation thofe who were known
" to be *Illuminati*, and to hinder the rulers from
" attending to their real machinations, by means of
" this *ignis fatuus* of his own brain. He gained
" his point in fome meafure, for Nicholai and
" others of the junto immediately adopted the
" whim, and called them *Obfcuranten*, and joined
" with Mirabeau in placing on the lift of *Obfcuran-*
" *ten* feveral perfons whom they wifhed to make
" ridiculous [f]."

Returns to Paris.

When the meafure of affembling the *notables* was refolved on, Mirabeau returned to Paris, hoping that his connection with the minifter would procure him the appointment of fecretary to that affembly. He was however difappointed: the functions of the office had been divided, and fome perfons appointed before his arrival, with whom, as he pretends, he could not act; but more probably he had been entirely difregarded by Calonne. This opinion is rendered more likely by the ill fuccefs of Mirabeau's application for a miffion to Holland, which the minifter refufed, giving Mirabeau to underftand that he had better have ftayed at Berlin [g].

Feb. 1797. Publication on ftock jobbing.

He was determined neverthelefs to render himfelf confpicuous; or, in his own words, to plant himfelf

[f] Proofs of a Confpiracy, p. 370.—As Mirabeau's Effay is extremely fcarce and little known in England, I have given a general abftract of the contents, together with a tranflation of the Preface and fome remarkable paffages. See Appendix, N° VII.

[g] Lettres à Mauvillon, p. 189. 198, 199.

in

in the breach, even if he got his head broke [h]. Though Calonne's refusal engendered a coldness between him and Mirabeau, yet he did not carry his regret or resentment to the extreme of quarrelling with the minister; on the contrary, in his first publication after his arrival, called *Denonciation de l'Agiotage au Roi et à l'Assemblée des Notables*, he attacked Necker with so much vigour, as to occasion suspicions that his work was a mere venal production. He acknowledged that his book was replete with faults; that it was composed with too much rapidity to be good; that it appeared surcharged with matter, for want of arrangement; and that he paid more attention to his subject than to his plan. Yet it had a prodigious and unexampled suc- *its success.* cess: The greater part of the notables, the heads of bodies corporate, the better sort of every class, congratulated and thanked him. From the offices of notaries to the dressing-rooms of belles, he was read, extolled, and quoted. He says, " You can " form no idea of the effect it has produced, and " how likely it is to occasion an earthquake, even " under the very steps of the sanctuary [i]."

Mirabeau avers that, on his arrival in Paris, Ca- *Order* lonne had caused him to be sounded on the subject *issued to arrest Mi-* of employing his pen in the service of administra- *rabeau.* tion; but that Mirabeau declined the task, and continued to solicit a diplomatic mission. His failure in obtaining this object, and some disrespectful expressions of the minister, inflamed him to a certain degree of resentment; but his still greater dislike of Necker, and perhaps the view of attaching himself with advantage to another party, prevented his joining the opposition. The freedom of his re- *20th Mar.* marks however was so injurious and offensive to government, that though, in consequence of his pam-

[h] Lettres à Mauvillon, p. 189.
[i] Idem, p. 192. 203. 206. 243.

phlet, an order was issued tending to repress stock-jobbing, it was accompanied with one to arrest the author [k].

He escapes. On receiving information of this intention, Mirabeau was persuaded to retire from Paris, and conceal himself near Liége. Convinced that the order against him was a mere cabinet intrigue, which would soon be counteracted by other intrigues, he would have submitted to an arrest which he knew could only produce a temporary inconvenience, and in the end enhance his reputation; but he was given to understand that the Bastille was not intended for his prison, and that he would be confined in a castle in a remote province, where he might wear out his life in oblivion. This deter-
7th April. Is recalled. mined him to make his escape. He judged rightly of the motives and duration of the proceedings against him. The opposition murmured; and the ministry, five in six of whom had ever been adversarious to his arrest, now feeling a greater alarm from his absence than even his presence could inspire, began to make overtures of accommodation. Calonne himself wrote him a letter, in which he imputed the inimical measure to the abbé Perigord; and Dupont assured him that he would instantly apply to the king to permit his return to Paris; and addressed him throughout in a style the most conciliating and considerate [l].

Hopes, From the circumstances attending his recal, Mirabeau, had no reason to doubt that the ministry would be induced by fear to employ him, and that they would enable him to make an honourable retreat, that duty might keep him silent. But before his return to Paris, Calonne was dismissed, and with the new ministry such motives would operate rather
and disappointment. to prevent than occasion his employ. His hopes revived when he understood that de Brienne was, in

[k] Letters à Mauvillon, p. 201.   [l] Idem, p. 204. 208. 222.

fact,

fact, to be confidered, and would foon be appointed prime minifter[m].

Mirabeau had long entertained a contemptuous opinion of Necker[n], and, perhaps, thought that appearing as his opponent at this crifis would advance him greatly in the minifter's favour. He had a fair opportunity of doing this, as a private letter written by him had been very unhandfomely publifhed, and placed Mirabeau in fuch a fituation that he could not avoid defending his own production. He wrote a pamphlet which he defcribes in thefe terms: "I have produced a pamphlet which will "pleafe you. I have exerted my whole force as a "difputant, a calculator, and even as a fophift. It "is a pretty game of chefs, which I have played "with great caution, and he will infallibly be check "mated[o]."

Writes against Necker.

May.

Either de Brienne did not make fuch advances as Mirabeau expected, or the difcernment of Mirabeau enabled him to appreciate the importance and influence of a new faction now rifing in the kingdom, called the Orleans' party. That corrupt and abandoned confpirator eafily perceived the importance of attaching to his caufe fuch a man as Mirabeau, who was eafily induced to join a party which he hoped to govern and direct. If the plans of Orleans fucceeded he might expect the moft brilliant rewards, and even if they failed he was not without his recompence, while by uniting with minifters, he could only hope for an honourable banifhment under the name of a diplomatic employ, or an obfcure appointment without importance and without confidence. As the beft means of extending the influence of his newly-adopted patron, he imparted to him the myfteries of illuminifm, the principles of

Forms a connection with Orleans.

---

[m] Letters à Mauvillon, p. 238. 242.
[n] See Lettres à Chamfort, p. 85.
[o] Lettres à Mauvillon, p. 242. I do not know the pamphlet alluded to.

which

which sect were the more easily diffused, as Orleans was grand-master of the order of free-masons in France [p].

Goes to Berlin.

Mirabeau constantly maintained a correspondence with Mauvillon, and they were between them preparing for the press the celebrated work called *Histoire de la Monarchie Prussienne*. Mirabeau, this summer, went to Berlin to visit his friend; apparently with a view to forward their joint labour, but probably the chief object was to confer on the means of extending the influence of illuminism, and forwarding the grand projects of that society. He left Mauvillon, and proceeded to Hamburgh, where he had some negotiations to arrange with the booksellers. He did not make a long stay. The news he received from France was so congenial to his wishes, that he resolved to hasten his departure. The Orleans' faction seemed to acquire a rapid ascendancy, and Mirabeau's letters breathe confidence and exultation. He says, " As to the affairs of France, " be assured my day is coming. The kingdom is " in a blaze. The parliament has not been ba- " nished, but only commanded to go and dispense " justice at Troyes. The measure is equally ab- " surd and insulting." He expresses in four letters written to Mauvillon from Hamburgh, the greatest impatience to be in France, and go *quo trahunt fata* [q].

Sept. At Hamburgh.

Oct. Returns to France.

The elements did not second the eagerness of Mirabeau, for he had a passage of more than seventeen days, perpetually tempestuous, and was afterwards much longer than he had expected in reaching Paris. He found the public mind in a state perfectly suited to his views, and the active share his connection with Orleans compelled him to take, incroached greatly

---

[p] Robison's Proofs, p. 376. See ORLEANS.
[q] Lettres à Mauvillon, p. 255—267.

on his time'. Mirabeau immediately obtained a favourable change in his fortune, though some contrarieties of interest and the uncertainty of events kept him in suspense, and prevented his adopting those extremes into which his character would naturally have led him. In one letter he says, " A propitious gale once again blows on your " friend, and the public vessel, as well as your own " skiff, will be benefitted '." In the subsequent letter he says, " My last, such as it was, will have " led you to expect a change, if not in my destiny, " in my lot. Nevertheless, far from retarding our " meeting, the change may accelerate it. *I am,* " *however, as yet, in a mist on this subject, because I* " *do not consider sound policy exactly in the same light* " *as the masters of the magic lantern, and they, as yet,* " *see nothing but indistinct images on my side'.*" He entered deeply into public affairs, and the importance attached to his agency may be gathered from his own declaration, that during the eight days anxiety which the royal sitting (that at which the duke of Orleans made himself so conspicuous,) occasioned to the parliament, he never had a minute's leisure '.

Yet with all this exertion, Mirabeau cautiously avoided committing himself; no reproaches, no calumnies could induce him, during the contest

His exertions.

Caution.

' Lettres à Mauvillon, p. 280. In the correspondence of Mirabeau with his intimate friend Mauvillon, the name of Orleans is never mentioned, or the train of public affairs at all minutely described, though many allusions are found to the political contests and transactions of the day. A proof of the extreme caution of the Illuminati in their publications, as no doubt, much curious information personal, political, and mystical, has been suppressed. For instance, Mirabeau says in one letter (p. 283), " You may expect by the next courier some curious " details, drawn from the *Garden of the Hesperides.*" Yet no information of the kind, or any explanation of the expression, appears in the correspondence. There are also frequent allusions to the contents of previous letters which are obviously suppressed.

' Idem, p. 283. The metaphor here used seems to contain an equivocal allusion; it may as well apply to the interests of the sect which Mirabeau and Mauvillon had embraced, as the country of which Mauvillon could no longer be considered a subject.

' Idem.   ' Idem, p. 290.

between

between the king and parliament, to write a line in favour of the popular cause, and he abstained with equal care from supporting the crown [x]. He employed his leisure in perfecting, and supervising the impression of *La Monarchie Prussienne* [y]. He produced besides some pamphlets on foreign politics, among which may be numbered *Aux Bataves sur le Stathouderat*, and *Doutes sur la Liberté de l'Escaut*. Of the former he speaks with the partiality of a fond parent [z]. The latter is described by the author of "An Historical Sketch of the French Revolution," as denoting a most violent and malevolent temper [a]. At length his great work, *La Monarchie Prussienne*, issued from the press in a quarto edition of four volumes, and an octavo edition on the same day. On this production he had bestowed great pains and considerable expence, he had laboured assiduously himself, and purchased the assistance of Mauvillon. From this circumstance, and from the nature of the subject, it has been inferred that Mirabeau had, in fact, little share in the work [b]. The truth is, Mauvillon supplied the materials, and it was left to the genius and eloquence of Mirabeau to arrange, to methodize, to animate the whole. The account given in the preface to Mirabeau's letters to Mauvillon, which is strongly corroborated by the whole tenor of the correspondence, is as follows: "Among the most lively "passions of the count's friend, was that of being "useful to mankind. He had already attempted "to gratify it by several publications, and particu- "larly by developing some important truths rela- "tive to political economy. But from mediocrity "of talent, want of authority, mismanagement, or "misfortune, whatever he wrote produced but

[x] Letters à Mauvillon, p. 374.
[y] Idem, p. 297. et passim.
[a] Historical Sketch, &c. p. 75.
[b] Vie Publique, &c. p. 36.
[z] Idem, p. 348.

"little

"little effect. In this situation, he is advised by a celebrated writer to republish his Essays, to add many new ones; to support his opinions by facts known, avowed, and attested in a thousand works; he undertakes to adorn them with the magic of his style, to support them with the authority of his name, and to publish them in the most universal of all the European languages. Perish, then, the man who shall reproach Mirabeau with not being the author of *La Monarchie Prussienne*[c]." Mirabeau himself thought so highly of this production, that he expected it would change the style of writing biography and history. He mentions it in these terms: "I have had time, my dear friend, to re-peruse our whole work. Between ourselves be it said, it is truly excellent in every point of view. I am so enthusiastic in my admiration of it, that, during these seventeen days[d], I have never thought of the probability of losing my life; and really, it often seemed to depend on a turn of the die, but the regret that this precious manuscript would perish with me, immediately succeeded the anguish I felt at leaving my mistress and my son in distress[e]." The work, undoubtedly, has considerable merit, but not sufficient to justify Mirabeau's vanity.

The decree for convoking the states-general inspired Mirabeau with fresh hopes and fresh confidence[f]. The recal of Necker was not so agreeable to him; he knew that Necker disliked him, with good reason, and felt that his own contemptuous opinion of the financier was not altered. He was apprehensive that the ministerial influence would be employed to prevent his obtaining a seat in the states-general, and as the ancient laws of France

Hopes on convoking the states-general.

[c] Avant propos aux Lettres de Mirabeau à Mauvillon, p. 15.
[d] The period he was at sea in his voyage from Hamburgh to Calais.
[e] Lettres à Mauvillon, p. 269.   [f] Idem, p. 372.

were

were not then abrogated or superseded, he knew that his exclusion was very possible. A short specimen of Necker, and a cursory survey of the public mind, in a great measure quieted his alarms. He wrote to Mauvillon: "Necker must espouse the royal or the national cause; he has no other alternative. If he adheres to the first he is lost. If he adopts the latter his reign will not be long. Fear, which already assails him, in spite of his efforts, aided by resentment, will soon drive him from the helm. I do not consider his talents proportioned to the exigency of the times, and the defects of his character will frustrate the exertion of his abilities [g]."

Exertions. It now became highly important to Mirabeau to insure such a portion of popularity, as would enable him to attain the object of his wishes by means of his partisans, whatever influence might be exerted against him. He redoubled his attention to the masonic societies, and exerted himself to forward the views and disseminate the publications of the lodge *des Chevaliers bienfaisans*, of which he was a member [h]. He was attached to the Society of *Amis des Noirs*, and one of their regulating committee [i]. He also contrived to effect a reconciliation with his father, though it produced no display of affection on either side [k].

Publication. The cautious conduct he had resolved to adopt was still, in a certain degree, adhered to; for though pamphlets on the subject of the approaching meeting of the states-general daily swarmed from the press, he resolved to publish nothing on the subject till secure of his election. He would not, however, suffer an occasion so favourable to political discussion to escape him, but wrote *Observations*

[g] Lettres à Mauvillon, p. 377. 380.
[h] Robison's Proofs, p. 41. 49.
[i] Memoires du Jacobinisme, par Barruel, vol. ii. p. 447.
[k] Lettres à Mauvillon, p. 425.

d'un Voyageur Anglois sur la maison de Force, appellée Bicêtre, suivie de Reflections sur les Effets de la Sévérité des Peines, et sur la Legislation Criminelle de la Grande Bretagne. He also published a work on the liberty of the press, but I do not know the title [1].

Previous to the election for deputies to the states-general, a book was published under the title of *Histoire Sécrete de la Cour de Berlin*. It consisted of letters written by Mirabeau to Calonne during his residence in Prussia, in which Frederic II. and his successor were very disrespectfully treated, as were prince Henry of Prussia, and several distinguished personages about the court. The duke of Brunswick was greatly extolled, and Calonne abjectly flattered. The book was condemned by the parliament of Paris, as the production of an unknown author, and burned by the common hangman. No doubt was entertained by the public that Mirabeau was author of all, or the greater part of the letters, but it was not clearly ascertained whether he had consented to the publication, or whether the most offensive passages were not interpolations. Mirabeau himself disavowed the publication *in toto*, by advertisements in the French and foreign newspapers. In his letters to Mauvillon he speaks of the book as one with which he is entirely unacquainted, not having even read it, but through the veil of his renunciation it is easy to perceive the vanity of an author. His secretary, in writing to the same person, says, that to attribute the work to Mirabeau, is horrible perfidy. "They "have taken out of the office for foreign affairs, his "correspondence from Berlin, and have got it "printed to excite against him the hatred of the "powerful and the rage of the great. Much has "been added to this collection to render the sup-

1789. Secret History of the Court of Berlin.

[1] Lettres à Mauvillon, p. 402. 436. 444.

"posed

"posed author additionally odious. What could the count do? Disown the publication. He has done so, and your gazettes will attest the disavowal [m]." This explanation is by no means satisfactory. Although it might be convenient for Mirabeau to disavow the publication for fear of legal consequences, and even to write letters to Mauvillon, which he might shew under pretence of confidence at Berlin, still in the state France then was, Mirabeau could not enhance his character more than by a work tending to make courts contemptible, and degrade exalted personages. If part of the publication only was genuine, it became a point of honor in him afterwards to have distinguished between the letters he had actually written, and those which had been malevolently added. Not having done this, his tranquil acquiescence justifies the judgment of those who rank this imperfect renunciation with the similar acts of Voltaire and many others, whom fear of consequences has induced to disown publications, which a sense of rectitude could not prevent their giving to the world [n].

1789.
Mirabeau's election.

Mirabeau had acquired a fief in Dauphiny, but considering Provence as his natural situation, resolved to go there for the purpose of being elected a deputy. He was aware that if it were left to the nobility to elect their own representatives, he should be excluded by that class, but he had some hopes that all the orders would vote for each order, and in that case the influence of the *tiers etat* would secure his election, as representative of the *noblesse* [o]. On his arrival at Aix, he was received by the *tiers etat* with enthusiastic acclamation. He was met and

---

[m] Lettres à Mauvillon, p. 453. 455. 457.
[n] On this subject see the translator's Preface to the Secret History of the Court of Berlin. Pagès, vol. i. p. 270. Historical Sketch, p. 75. Anecdotes du Regne de Louis XVI. vol. vi. p. 265.
[o] Lettres à Mauvillon, p. 445.

carried

carried to his hotel, amidst reiterated cries, which proclaimed him *the defender, the tutelary angel of the people* [p]. The Bourgeoisie appointed for him a guard of honor [q], which, if his own assertion may be believed, was not unnecessary, as the rage of the priesthood and aristocracy ran so high, that he entertained fears of assassination [r]. He was rejected by the *noblesse*, who alledged that he was not competent to take a seat as representative of their order, not having a fief in Provence [s]. During a recess of sittings in the states of Provence, he is said to have qualified himself to represent the *tiers etat*, by becoming a shopkeeper. He opened a shop where he sold grocery by retail, and dressed with an apron, distributed his wares, his politics, and his bon mots [t]. It is said that curiosity attracted so many purchasers to his shop, that his sale amounted to three hundred louis-d'ors a-day, and the first day produced fifteen thousand livres (656*l.* 5*s.*). He was elected president of the order of the *tiers etat*, and always in public seated under a canopy. When he went to the play, he was escorted by fifty young men in uniform, and had a box set apart for him. Fireworks, balls, serenades, and continual dances under his windows testified his popularity. The people took off his horses and drew his carriage, and he was honored with a triumph; a crown was placed on his head, and he entered Aix amidst a discharge of artillery, and shouts of " God save the king! God " save Mirabeau!" Similar marks of respect were piad to him at Marseilles, where he was elected deputy as well as at Aix, but he took his seat for the latter [u].

[p] Lettres à Mauvillon, p. 447.
[q] Pagès, vol. i. p. 82.
[r] Lettres à Mauvillon, p. 452.
[s] Anecdotes du Regne de Louis XVI. vol. vi. p. 267.
[t] Playfair's History of Jacobinism, p. 125.
[u] Anecdotes du Regne de Louis XVI. vol. vi. p. 267. Moore's View, vol. i. p. 173. Lettres à Mauvillon, p. 456.

A popular

His eloquence.

A popular assembly was the precise sphere in which Mirabeau could display himself to advantage. He was, as madame Roland justly observes, "formed to command the vulgar, to concentrate in one focus the opinions of the wise, and to present them with that force of genius which compels obedience the moment it is displayed [x]." In the national assembly, where most of the members read their speeches, he was among the few who possessed the gift of extempore eloquence, which besides its more forcible impression afforded him great advantage in replies, and in those quick turns of sarcastic raillery which constituted his forte [y]. He continued firmly attached to Orleans, and forwarded all his views, hoping, in case of his success, to attain the situation of prime minister [z]. His opposition to the court was therefore systematic, constant, and violent.

Publishes a journal.

As a means of propagating his principles, relating the debates of the assembly in his own manner, and effectually serving his party, he undertook the direction of a daily paper, which he called "*Lettres de Mirabeau à ses Commettans.*" Its appearance was, for a short time, prevented by authority, but Mirabeau easily surmounted, or resolutely braved every impediment, and began his publication soon after the sitting of the states-general. The expectation excited by this undertaking was so favourable, that in a week after the publication of the prospectus, subscriptions to the amount of more than thirty thousand livres (1312 *l.* 10 *s.*) were lodged at his bookseller's for the first three months delivery [a]. This paper, which was afterwards continued under the name of *Le Courier de Provence*, was highly serviceable to Mira-

---

[x] Appeal to Impartial Posterity, vol. i. p. 84.
[y] See Arthur Young's Travels, p. 110
[z] Historical Sketch, p. 80. Conjuration de d'Orleans, vol. ii, p. 31.
[a] Playfair's History of Jacobinism, p. 123.

beau's views, as it gave additional weight and confequence to his party, and augmented his popularity in the capital.

Mirabeau's eloquence and manner of attack were new to the French; and though the difpofition of the public mind, and the mafs of feditious pamphlets which preceded the meeting of the ftates-general might have induced an expectation of violent proceedings, both parties feem to have regarded him with aftonifhment. The privileged orders faid that his infidious and fatal eloquence inflamed and exafperated the commons; while many of the *tiers etat* declared their apprehenfions that his exceffive zeal would be fatal to the public caufe [b]. The firft topic which agitated the *tiers etat* was the verification of orders, in which Mirabeau took a diftinguifhed fhare, and, befides the inflammatory effect of his eloquence, his quicknefs of apprehenfion, and ready perception of the ftrong and weak parts of a cafe, greatly facilitated the triumph of his party. After trying in vain, feveral meffages inviting the nobility to join with the *tiers etat* in the common-hall to verify their powers, he fuggefted the expedient of conjuring the clergy, *in the name of the God of peace*, to unite with them for the benefit of the nation. Though the clergy had the addrefs to evade this propofal, yet the refult of the meffages rendered them extremely unpopular, and made it almoft impoffible for them to maintain their point [c]. After feveral weeks of affected moderation, during which the factious leaders were trying their ftrength, and endeavouring to exafperate the public, the *tiers etat* refolved to conftitute themfelves, and leave to the other two orders the choice of joining them, or becoming odious and infignificant. On this fubject a debate of confiderable length took place, and

His boldnefs.

Judgment.

27th May.

12th June.

[b] Lettres à Mauvillon, p. 464.
[c] See Debates, Moore's View, vol. i. p. 153. Hiftorical Sketch, p. 104.

occupied

occupied the assembly for four days. Mirabeau, though ill of the ague, attended constantly, even while under the operation of sudorifics, and spoke three times from the tribune while attacked by shivering fits ᵈ. His wish was that the assembly should be declared representatives of the French people (*peuple*). In this he had great obstacles to surmount, as the term *peuple*, in French, unlike people in English, was ordinarily applied to the lower class, or mere rabble. He succeeded in removing this prejudice, but failed in his grand object. The majority adopted a motion of M. le Grand, and assumed the title of *national assembly* ᵉ. In opposing a metaphysical definition proposed by Syeyes, Mirabeau displayed great judgment, sense, and knowledge; he distinguished ably between the actual state of man in society, and the abstract representation of him which may be fitted for mere verbal discussion, and illustrated his distinction by the difference of tracing countries on a painted map, and traversing the face of the globe. In the former all is level and mountainous deserts, rivers, and abysses oppose no impediments, but the traveller is obliged to consider the face of Nature as she exists, to provide against difficulties, resist obstacles, and keep constantly in mind that he is in a real, not an imaginary world ᶠ. Though Mirabeau was not successful, still his exertions were much applauded. Some pains were taken to impress on the public a belief that he had been bribed by the court; his character afforded a foundation for the conjecture, but it was in every other respect improbable ᵍ. The assumption of a title which threatened to invest all power in the *tiers etat*, and render the nobility and clergy

15th. Political sagacity.

ᵈ Lettres à Mauvillon, p. 468.
ᵉ Debates. Histories. Young's Travels, p. 110.
ᶠ Debates. Moore's View, vol. i. p. 163. Collection of Mirabeau's Speeches in the Assembly.
ᵍ Young's Travels, p. 114.

entirely

entirely subservient to them, was a measure for which Mirabeau was not prepared. As a politician he wished for many changes in the form of government; as an individual, his ambition would have been gratified by such a change of rulers as would have enabled him to hold the highest offices in the state; but this step appeared too hazardous at the present juncture, when the ascendancy of his faction was not sufficiently confirmed. He says, "sup-
"posing the most favourable event; that the king
"should afford his sanction to the new title *we have
"arrogated to ourselves*, the result will be that they
"have played the welfare of the kingdom on a *coup*
"at *rouge et noir*, where there is no advantage,
"while I would have put it on a game at chess,
"where I was the best player." He afterwards adds, "The best means to render the revolution
"abortive is to ask too much [h]."

Whatever might be Mirabeau's private opinions, he acquiesced in the measures of his party, and would not risk the favour of the people by a decided opposition. He was highly popular in Paris; and the following anecdote will shew how great homage was paid him.—The first night, after the sitting of the assembly, that Voltaire's *Brutus* was performed, Mirabeau took a place in the fourth tier of boxes. The people perceiving him, required that he should come down to a lower box, and sent a deputation to request he would indulge them. He did more: he went and placed himself in the gallery in the midst of the people, who were unwearied in testifying their satisfaction at seeing amongst them their darling representative [i].

Popularity.

Mirabeau displayed, at the period of the royal sitting, when Necker evinced so much perfidy, and the king such benevolent and patriotic intentions [k], a degree of factious intemperance which demon-

23d June. Royal sitting.

[h] Lettres à Mauvillon, p. 469.
[i] Anecdotes du Regne de Louis XVI. vol. vi. p. 268.
[k] See NECKER.

strated

Mirabeau's conduct.

strated that no consideration could restrain him in the pursuit of a favourite object. While the *tiers etat* were waiting till the superior orders were seated, he shewed great impatience, and required the president to conduct the nation immediately to the king's presence. When the king had pronounced his truly paternal and conciliatory harangue, he ordered the deputies to depart and assemble the subsequent day; and then retired, attended by the nobility and the majority of the clergy. The *tiers etat* remained, but though animated by the applause which had attended their recent exhibition in the tennis-court, they seemed at a loss, and preserved silence. The workmen began to remove the throne and the vacant benches; still the deputies did not move: at length M. de Brézé, grand-master of the ceremonies, entered, and said to the president, "You have heard, sir, the intentions of the king." Bailly, the president, timid and uncertain how to act, answered, that the assembly was not constituted to receive orders from any one. Mirabeau was dissatisfied with this evasion, and conceiving the occasion to demand all his intrepidity, rose, and addressing himself to M. de Brézé, said, "Yes, we "have heard the intentions the king has been pre- "vailed on to express. But you, who cannot be "his organ in this assembly, you, who have nei- "ther seat, nor vote, nor any right to speak here, "you are not the person to remind us of his dis- "course. However, to avoid all equivocation and "all delay, I declare, that if you are instructed to "make us leave this place, you must return and "demand instructions to employ force. Go, and "tell those who sent you, that we are assembled by "the will of the people, and nothing shall expel "us but the bayonet[1]." The effect of this speech

---

[1] Debates. Histories. Collection of Mirabeau's Speeches. A bust of Mirabeau was afterwards made for *the friends of the constitution,* on which the last sentence of this speech was engraved. White's Translation of Rabaud's History, p. 92. n.

was the triumph of the *tiers etat*. That body, before so irresolute, commenced a virulent debate, in which the royal authority was derided, and the king's person and commands treated with indignity. Mirabeau took advantage of a moment so favourable, to move for a decree declaring the persons of members inviolable, which was instantly granted ᵐ.

The result of this day greatly augmented Mirabeau's popularity, and enhanced his importance with his party. The junction of the two superior orders with the *tiers etat*, which speedily followed, extended his influence, and with it, his power of doing injury to those he was inclined to oppose. On this event he made a speech replete with florid imagery, in which he disguised, under an appearance of philanthropic congratulation, his exultation at an event to which he had so materially contributed ⁿ.

27th. Junction of orders.

The triumph of the Orleans party over the court now seemed so certain and decided, that the conspirators pursued their operations without affecting disguise, and hardly restrained by the common rules of caution. Mirabeau was guilty of a flagrant imprudence, which nothing but a certainty of success could have occasioned. Conversing in a circle of deputies, among whom were Mounier, Bergasse, Duport, and la Fayette, he praised the duke of Orleans in terms sufficiently expressive, but with some restraint. La Fayette quitting the party, he became less guarded, and said, "Gad, gentlemen, shall I tell you my mind at once?—I think we shall never have made a step towards liberty, till we shall have effected a revolution at court."— "What revolution do you mean (said one); what is the nature of the revolution you wish?"—"I will tell you without disguise (said Mirabeau); we must raise the duke of Orleans to the post of

Exertions for Orleans

ᵐ Debates. Histories. Anecdotes du Regne de Louis XVI. vol. vi. p. 306.
ⁿ Debates. Collection of Speeches. Moore's View, vol. i. p. 274.

"lieutenant-

"lieutenant-general of the kingdom." One of the company reprefented, that it was not certain that the duke of Orleans would confent to affume the poft. "Oh, (replied Mirabeau,) make yourfelves perfectly eafy on that point; I have fpoken to the duke about it, who anfwered me in a very pleafing manner." This difcourfe alarmed Mounier, who, in a fubfequent converfation, expreffed his apprehenfions arifing from the afpect of affairs. "Why, you fimple good man (*bonhomme*)," anfwered Mirabeau, "I am as much attached to royalty as you; but what fignifies whether we have Louis XVI. or Louis XVII.; or why fhould we have a child to govern us?" Mounier expreffed fo much difapprobation at thefe fentiments, that Mirabeau, after fome vague attempts to explain away his meaning, haftily broke off the converfation°.

Addrefs refpecting the troops. 8th July.

The train, in fact, was now laid, and the explofion confidently expected. The only circumftance which reftrained the confpirators was the army under the command of marfhal Broglio, which was affembled round Paris. To remove thefe troops became an object of the utmoft importance, and to this Mirabeau bent all his efforts. In a moft eloquent and inflammatory fpeech, he reprefented to the affembly the danger of thefe preparations: he drew an exaggerated picture of the mifery of the people, the numbers and movements of the troops, and the views of the court; and concluded by moving an addrefs, praying his majefty to remove the army which occafioned fo much difquietude. Though it was known that fuch an addrefs was to be moved, and feveral members had prepared to oppofe it, the effect of Mirabeau's eloquence was fuch as to convince them of the inutility of oppofition, and that their own difgrace would be the only refult. The

---

° See Conjuration de d'Orleans, vol. ii. p. 60. Moore's View, vol. i. p. 293. Hiftorical Sketch of the French Revolution, p. 153.

address was drawn by Mirabeau, read twice, adopted, and presented by a deputation of twenty-four members, among whom were Mirabeau and Robespierre. It is a model of insidious composition, where treason is plainly shewn through the thin mask of affected loyalty, and pretended praise is bestowed on the monarch, only as the means of overwhelming him with increased reproach if he should refuse compliance with the dictates of an imperious assembly. In answer to this address, the king declared that the tumultuous state of the metropolis was the reason for surrounding it with troops; disclaimed every idea of interrupting the debates of the assembly; and offered, if the troops gave any alarm, to transfer their sittings to Noyon or Soissons, and remove himself to Compeigne, to maintain the necessary communication with them. This answer was satisfactory to the majority of the assembly, who were inclined to rely on the royal promise; but Mirabeau, alarmed at the manifestation of such sentiments, expressed violent disapprobation of the king's answer. He averred that it was a direct refusal of their request; and affecting to doubt the king's sincerity, inferred still greater treachery from the situation of the place to which he had proposed to remove them. He concluded by observing, that the absence of the troops from the capital was the principal object of the address, and not that the assembly should remove to a distance from the troops. This reasoning made great impression on the assembly; and Dr. Moore extols their moderation and respect for the king, in not renewing the petition. Mirabeau did not urge the measure; but the reason was, that in the interval between the two debates, and while he had such a measure in agitation, a second conference took place between him and Mounier. This deputy remonstrated on the impropriety of a second address; and Mirabeau, who was sensible

he

he had been too open in his expressions, and apprehended a schism in his own party, did not venture to press a measure which might have led to the most disagreeable explanations [p].

14th July. Encourages massacres and outrages.

The dismission of Necker accelerated the projected commotion; and the ascendancy of the Orleans party gave a more complete success to their proceedings than could have been expected. The pusillanimity of the duke however prevented his adherents from deriving from it those advantages to which they considered themselves entitled. Mirabeau in vain endeavoured to urge him to assume a greater share of resolution. On one of these occasions, when Mirabeau had been unsuccessfully attempting to persuade him to shew himself in Paris, he exclaimed, " What, sir, you are within four leagues of the throne, and yet will not travel to it: it is written then that Mirabeau shall never be a man of consequence [q]." Mirabeau is accused of having incited the mob to acts of violence and massacre during the tumults which succeeded the capture of the Bastille. Though this charge wants direct proof, it is rendered probable by his being the constant defender of their excesses, and the opposer of measures calculated to repress them. When Lally Tollendal was describing the deaths of Berthier and Foulon with expressions of appropriate horror, Mirabeau told him that it was a time to *think* rather than to *feel*; and, in defending the conduct of the populace, he made the following savage observation; " If these scenes which have " passed at Paris had passed at Constantinople, the " most timorous characters would say, *the people* " *have done themselves justice*, the measure of ini-

[p] Debates. Histories. Moore's View, vol. i. p. 295 to 307. Historical Sketch, p. 153.
[q] Lettre d'un François sur les Moyens qui ont Opéré la Revolution, p. 11. n. 16.

" quity

"quity was full, and *the punishment of one vizier will become a lesson to another*." He also defended the further excesses of the mobs in the provinces, and apologised for their burning castles, and other cruelties towards the nobility, on a principle of justice and retaliation.

Mirabeau had not altered his opinion of Necker, or ceased to entertain the same sentiments of rancour against him; but as the tide of popularity ran strongly in his favour, and as it was considered a measure distressing and insulting to the court, he determined to move for an address requiring the dismission of the new ministry, and the recal of the popular idol. This measure was opposed by some who remonstrated on the unconstitutional indelicacy of interfering with the appointments of the executive government; but Mirabeau's exertions surmounted all opposition, and the address was carried, when the delivery of it was rendered unnecessary by the voluntary resignation of the ministers, and the king's declaration, that he had sent to recal the favourite of the assembly.

Moves for Necker's recal.

Necker, whose vanity surmounted his judgment and his duty, was weak enough to return; and Mirabeau commenced a vigorous and successful opposition to his measures, both in the assembly and in public. An opportunity of enfeebling the minister's popularity occurred immediately on his return, when by his address to the electors of Paris, at the *Hotel-de-ville*, he had prevailed on them to decree the liberation of the baron de Bezenval, and a general amnesty. Mirabeau exerted himself among the political clubs, where he represented the transactions at the *Hotel-de-ville* as a compromise with aristocracy, rendered Necker an object of suspicion, and roused the minds of his audience to measures of severity and vengeance. The resolutions of the commune of Pa-

Opposes his measures.

---

r Historical Sketch, p. 194.
s Pagès, vol. i. p. 171.   t Histories. Debates.

ris were declared illegal, and the matter was referred to the national aſſembly, where Mirabeau and his adherents ſucceeded in eſtabliſhing their point, and the amneſty was annulled ᵘ. Conſiſtently with the principle he had determined to adopt, Mirabeau reſiſted with effect Necker's propoſal for a loan, which, had it been ſuccefsful, would have relieved the embarraſſments of the court, and rendered Necker's adminiſtration permanent. Mirabeau raiſed ſo many objections, and deducted ſo much from the advantages of the loan, that it never filled ˣ.

It was probably about this time that Mirabeau offered his ſervices to the king on certain conditions, which were rejected through the influence of Necker ʸ, who perhaps felt himſelf incapable of acting in concert with a man of Mirabeau's principles ; or more probably was actuated by perſonal reſentment alone. Mirabeau ſeems to have been indignant at the baſeneſs of Orleans, diſplayed at and juſt after the period of taking the Baſtille ; and at this time ſeems in his public conduct to have ſhewn a diſpoſition to approach the court, and even to conciliate the miniſter. In the debates on the ſhare of authority to be intruſted to the crown in the ratification of laws, he ſupported the unpopular doctrine of an abſolute *veto.* Montjoye imputes this to his attachment to Orleans, and his wiſh to be the miniſter of an arbitrary monarch ; but the other motive is full as probable ᶻ. The diſtreſs of the revenue ſtill increaſing, and the loan having been found entirely unſuccefsful, Necker brought forward a propoſition, that every individual ſhould contribute a fourth part of his revenue towards the

---

ᵘ Necker on the Revolution, vol. i. p. 234. Impartial Hiſtory, vol. i. p. 172. Moore's View, vol. i. p. 380. See NECKER.
ˣ Debates. See NECKER.
ʸ Bouillé's Memoirs, p. 248. 277.
ᶻ Conjuration de d'Orleans, vol. ii. p. 127. Mrs. Wollſtonecraft's Hiſtory, p. 332. Debates in Auguſt and September. Moore's View, and the other Hiſtories.

exigencies

exigencies of the ſtate. This meaſure alarmed the aſſembly by its violence; but Mirabeau, " more " eloquent than ever he had been, great in his geſ- " ture, in his countenance, and in his voice, pre- " vailed on the aſſembly to decree with confidence " the meaſure propoſed by Necker [a]." Though this ſignal ſervice ought to have convinced the miniſter of Mirabeau's value and importance, he could not forgive his critical animadverſions, and his previous oppoſition. He felt no kindneſs to him for ſupporting his ſecond financial plan, after overthrowing the firſt; he did not acquieſce in the propriety of an abſolute *veto*; and he fruſtrated the negotiation between the king and Mirabeau.

rejected through Necker.

Irritated at this rejection, Mirabeau attached himſelf more firmly than ever to Orleans. He contrived to render the compliment he had paid to Necker unavailing, by tacking to the decree a requeſt that the king would immediately ſanction certain obnoxious reſolutions voted on the fourth of Auguſt [b]. In the debates which followed, eſpecially thoſe which related to the limitation of the crown, and the ſettlement of a regency, he ſhewed a decided predilection for the intereſts of Orleans [c]. What could not be produced by cabal in the legiſlature it was determined to effect by external violence, and the dreadful inſurrection which took place on the fifth of October was projected and organiſed.

Attaches himſelf more firmly to Orleans.

15th Sept.

No doubt can be entertained that Mirabeau took an active ſhare in contriving and conducting this celebrated inſurrection. Mrs. Wollſtonecraft, with her uſual raſhneſs, has declared his innocence, deducing it only from his diſlike to Orleans, and the

5th and 6th Oct. Conduct of Mirabeau.

---

[a] Quoted from Rabaud's Hiſtory, p. 141. See NECKER. Debates. Hiſtories.
[b] See NECKER.
[c] Debates. Conjuration de d'Orleans, vol. ii. p. 135. Hiſtorical Sketch, p. 235.

opinion

opinion subsequently delivered by the abbé Mauri[d]. Dr. Moore states it as evident that Mirabeau did not act in concert with the duke; and says it does not appear that he had any hand in exciting the insurrection, but he certainly endeavoured to turn it to his own purposes when excited[e]. The argument of Mrs. Wollstonecraft of his contempt for Orleans is not very cogent, considering how many facts appeared in evidence to shew that he was very active in urging the proceedings of the mob. The conduct of the abbé Mauri will be mentioned hereafter. The want of concert between the conspirators, adduced by Dr. Moore, is easily accounted for by adverting to the character of the duke of Orleans, with whom it was easy to *plot*, but whose cowardice and inconsistency rendered it extremely difficult to *act* in concert. A statement of Mirabeau's proceedings during and previous to the insurrection will best elucidate his motives. For some time before this event, a great many deputies, dreading the anarchy which they had reason to apprehend from the intrigues and ambition of the popular party, had meditated a junction with the members attached to the court; and their influence had so far prevailed, that in the election of presidents, the composition of committees, and the nomination of secretaries, the friends of order were generally preferred. Mirabeau was indignant at this junction, which threatened to reduce his party to a state of insignificance, and wrote a letter replete with threats to Clermont Tonnere, who was then president, which he, with more forbearance than prudence, did not denounce to the assembly[f]. A secret committee composed of the adherents of Orleans met frequently at the duke's country-seat at Mousseau; Mirabeau was a constant attendant at

[d] History of the Revolution, p. 456.
[e] View, vol. ii, p. 50.
[f] Lettre d'un François sur les Moyens qui ont Opéré la Revolution, p. 27.

these meetings [g]; he was continually travelling to Paris, and exerting his influence in the clubs and coffee-houses [h]. On the day of the explosion, the debates were conducted with peculiar acrimony. The pretended *orgies* of the *Gardes-du-corps* afforded a ground for some accusations which Petion levelled against the queen, but wanted courage to sign his denunciation. Mirabeau, who in these extremities never lost his presence of mind, relieved Petion from his embarrassment by saying, " I begin by declar-
" ing that I consider the motion supremely impo-
" litic; nevertheless, if it is persisted in, I am ready
" to produce the details, and sign them with my
" own hand: but the assembly must first decree,
" that the person of the king *alone* is inviolable;
" and that all other individuals, whatever their sta-
" tion, are equally subject to the laws." This speech produced a series of inflammatory observations, but the denunciation was not proceeded on [i]. While the debates were going on, Mirabeau rose and whispered to the president, " Mounier, there
" are forty thousand men marching against us from
" Paris; adjourn." Many people had been observed going in and out with an appearance of great agitation, these were the agents of the conspiracy, and from them Mirabeau derived his intelligence [k]. In the course of the debate Mirabeau had behaved with great petulance, and displayed the confidence of a successful conspirator. In adverting to the king's delay in sanctioning the decrees, he renounced his own principle of an absolute *veto*, and said, " It appears to me that in an address
" to the king, it would not be improper to speak
" with the same frankness and truth which a court

[g] Moore's View, vol. ii. p. 39. Playfair's History of Jacobinism, p. 244.
[h] Lettre d'un François, &c. p. 28.
[i] Debates. Histories. Conjuration de d'Orleans, vol. ii. p. 204.
[k] Pagès, vol. i. p. 235. Conjuration de d'Orleans, vol. ii. p. 205.

" fool of Philip conveyed in this trifling sentence:
" *What would you do, Philip, if all the world were to
" say no when you say yes!.*" A deputation to the
king had been decreed, when the *Poissardes* rushed
into the hall. In the confusion which ensued, Mirabeau alone retained any authority; he alone
dared, when the clamour was such as to interrupt
the debate, to move that all persons who were not
deputies should be expelled. Though the mob did
not permit such a motion to pass, they expressed no
anger against the mover [m]. As soon as the assembly
adjourned, Mirabeau went among the rabble, who
were assailing the guards, and threatening the life
of the queen. He was among the privates of the
regiment de Flandres, the complete seduction of
whom had been only that day effected; and the Parisian women, when they lost sight of him, were continually screaming, " Where is our count Mirabeau? we want to see our count Mirabeau."
Sometimes he appeared with a huge sabre under
his arm, and sometimes disguised in women's
clothes. In this dress he was seen the next morning, uttering imprecations against the queen, and
mixing with the mob to instigate fresh violences [n].
When the assembly met, Mirabeau was at his post,
disappointed at the result of the conspiracy, and
gloomily awaiting an opportunity of turning it to
some advantage. Such an occasion soon presented
itself. The king, astonished at the audacity of treason, which, not content with violating the refuge of
his palace, sought to deprive him of liberty by a
compulsory journey to the capital, sent a message to
the assembly, requiring them to come and hold their
sitting in the hall of Hercules, that he might have
the benefit of their advice. Mounier, the president,

[l] Moore's View, vol. ii. p. 3.
[m] Anecdotes du Regne de Louis XVI. vol. vi. p. 427.
[n] Conjuration de d'Orleans, vol. ii. p. 234. 245. Robison's Proofs of a Conspiracy, p. 377.

would inftantly have complied; but Mirabeau prevented it. He faid it was not confiftent with the dignity of the affembly to go to the king, and that the freedom of debate could not be preferved within the walls of a palace. As foon as the king's fubmiffion to the orders of the mob was announced, Mirabeau moved that the affembly was infeparable from the perfon of the monarch, and that a deputation of one hundred perfons fhould accompany the royal family to Paris. The fecretary, in preparing the lift, inferted the name of Mirabeau, which Mounier immediately erafed. "Why do you take out "my name, Mounier? (faid Mirabeau); I infift on "being one of the deputation, that I may appeafe "the people in cafe of any tumult." The prefident anfwered; "Sir, thofe who have fo much "influence on the people as to *appeafe* them, may "alfo be inftrumental in *making them rebel*." Mirabeau however infifted on carrying his point; and as his word was that day a law to the affembly, he fucceeded[o]. Though the grand object of the confpiracy, that of deftroying or dethroning the king, had failed, yet the transfer of the king and affembly to Paris, where the king would be kept a prifoner, and where Mirabeau, by means of the clubs, poffeffed fo great an influence, was a fubject of confiderable triumph; and the final victory of the faction appeared to be only retarded. Mirabeau expreffed his exultation on the occafion by faying, in an addrefs to the provinces, that now "the veffel of public bufinefs would proceed in its "courfe more rapidly than ever[p]."

As there was reafon to apprehend from the manner in which thefe tranfactions are mentioned, that they would become the fubject of a judicial inveftigation, Mirabeau propofed to avail himfelf of the prefent

[o] Debates. Conjuration de d'Orleans, vol. ii. p. 266. et feq.
[p] Debates. Hiftorical Sketch, p. 267.

disposition of the assembly, and obtain such decrees as would prevent any inquiry; and instead of juridical depositions, leave the facts to be recorded by tradition alone, and forgotten when the day was past. Every thing was arranged, and the time fixed; when Orleans, from cowardice, refused to appear in the assembly, and the project was abandoned. Mirabeau was transported with rage, and vented himself in angry expressions; he declared the duke did not deserve the pains which had been taken for him; that he was base as a foot-boy; and added, that he always carried a loaded pistol in his bosom, but had not sufficient spirit to pull the trigger^q. His indignation was carried to the highest pitch, when he learned the duke's resolution to go to England. " He used imprecations worthy of " Philoctetes^r;" and afterwards declared, that so far from desiring to elevate the duke to the throne, he would not choose him for a lacquey. He made an attempt to prevent the assembly from permitting his departure, and hinted at the imperious conduct of la Fayette on the occasion; but without success^s.

19th Oct. Moves thanks to la Fayette.

Though highly displeased with la Fayette, and always personally inimical to him, Mirabeau, when the assembly began to make Paris the place of their sittings, moved a vote of thanks to the commandant of the national guard, which was carried with universal applause^t. He opposed la Fayette's proposition of a martial law, though without success; but the arguments he used were highly gratifying to the people^u.

Mirabeau's popularity;

Mirabeau had calculated rightly on the effects of his popularity in Paris, he was idolized by the mob,

^q Conjuration de d'Orleans, vol. ii. p. 289. Robison's Proofs of a Conspiracy, p. 378.
^r History of the Brissotines by Camille Desmoulins, p. 8.
^s Debates. Histories. Conjuration de d'Orleans, vol. ii. p. 350.
^t Debates. Impartial History, vol. i. p. 258.
^u Debates. Conjuration de d'Orleans, vol. ii. p. 340.

who

who carried their complaifance towards him to fuch an excefs, that he was accufed of fending meffengers when he intended to fpeak to give notice to the people that they might fill the galleries. He denied the fact, but it is far from being improbable [x]. He extended his influence by a regular attendance at the Jacobin club, where he was one of the committee of correfpondence [y], and he was the founder or promoter of various other clubs. He belonged to the club of 1789, but feeing there was no popularity attached to it, foon declined attending [z]. He alfo founded, with the affiftance of fome Swifs malcontents at Paris, a club, called the Friends of Swifs liberty, which was in fome degree encouraged by the affembly, and carried on a correfpondence with the partifans of the fame caufe in Switzerland [a].

In the courfe of this year Mirabeau's father died, but as the arrangement of his affairs took up a confiderable time, Mirabeau derived no immediate pecuniary advantage from the event [b]. Mirabeau, however, was enabled, by the large fums he received from Orleans, and afterwards from the king, to live in a very fplendid ftyle. He bought a great part of his father's library, which was one of the beft in France, and almoft all the library of the celebrated Buffon. He alfo purchafed the houfe of Fleffelles, and had agents at all the fales of books and rarities at the hotel de Bouillon [c]. Mirabeau was the firft who had propofed the eftablifhment of a city militia, a project which was difregarded at the moment, but which was afterwards embraced, and became the foundation of the national guard [d].

His profufion;

---

[x] Anecdotes du Regne de Louis XVI. vol. vi, p. 211.
[y] Conjuration de d'Orleans, vol. iii. p. 7.
[z] Expofition abrégée des Principes, &c. par Arthur Dillon, p. 34. Hiftorical Sketch, p. 587.
[a] Playfair's Hiftory of Jacobinifm, p. 351.
[b] Lettres à Mauvillon, p. 473.
[c] Playfair's Hiftory of Jacobinifm, p. 294.
[d] Pagès, vol. i. p. 137.

The command of the battalion *de la Grange Batte-lière*, the section where he refided, was beftowed on him, and he gave a fête to his comrades and a part of the national guard, which coft about ten thoufand livres (437*l*. 10*s*.). When any perfons expreffed furprife at his living fo expenfively, they were taught to believe that he was enabled to do it by the profits of his journal, which had an immenfe fale [e].

His defire to be minifter.

The abfence of Orleans, and the impoffibility of raifing popular commotions, which, in fact, were no longer neceffary either to his popularity or power, feem to have allayed the ferment of Mirabeau's mind. He began to wifh for a more regular government, where the executive branch might be reftored to a due fhare of authority by means of a minifter poffeffed of a genius for finance and government, who might fupply the place of the feeble Necker, and, by his fuperior powers, reftrain the tribe of jealous expectants. His remarks are curious and interefting. " You reafon very juftly on our " *revolution*; but it arifes among us, rather from " *devolution* than *exaltation* [f]. The party which " was able to have refifted was fo degenerate, the " inevitable effect of a long monopoly, that they " felt rather the fpite of a child, or the rage of a " woman, than a defire to operate a counter-revo- " lution. The crown is more in danger from " want of energy than from any confpiracy. Un- " lefs an able pilot is found, it is probable that the " veffel will be ftranded. If, on the contrary, the " force of events compels the appointment of a " man of parts, and infpires them with courage to

[e] Anecdotes du Regne de Louis XVI. vol. vi. p. 270.
[f] I am compelled to ufe this affected phrafeology to preferve a miferable pun. In plain language, Mirabeau means that the weaknefs of the court rather than the enthufiafm of the people occafioned the revolution. In the next fentence he completely acquits the royal family of aiming at a counter-revolution, and, of courfe, figns his own condemnation as a confpirator and calumniator.

" difregard

" disregard the opinions of mankind, and the
" efforts of subaltern jealousy, you cannot imagine
" how easy it will be to set the public vessel afloat.
" The resources of this country, and the inconstancy
" of its inhabitants, which constitutes their greatest
" fault, give birth to so many expedients, and such
" a variety of means, that in France we ought
" never to presume or to despair [g]."

Mirabeau now thought seriously of establishing the government, and extending the power of France. He entertained the same projects of aggrandizement, education, and government which have been pursued by his successors, but he was not prepared to ascend to the same height of revolutionary violence which they attained at a sudden spring. He wished to make the finances of the country respectable and flourishing, by appointing funds for the regular payment of interest; they have eased themselves of such exertions by repeated bankruptcies. He intended to produce a change of manners in his countrymen, by altering the system of education, and allowed fifteen years for the perfection of his plan; they superseded the necessity of education by the decapitation and banishment of those who expressed an opinion of their own, by which means the whole country could be brought to adopt any system of religion or government in fifteen days. Mirabeau was desirous to extend the influence of France by increasing the prosperity of other countries; his successors instead of influence have acquired an enforced and sullen obedience, and instead of inspiring gratitude by an increase of prosperity have excited universal horror and latent indignation by unparalleled rapacity and want of faith. The identity of system, however the variation in practice may have disfigured Mirabeau's plan, and the fact and time of his making his confession

Political opinions.

---

[g] Lettres à Mauvillon, p. 487. See also p. 498. for his opinion of Necker.

of faith on the subject to Mauvillon, prove that there did always exist a conspiracy against all the religions and governments of Europe, and that the same views have been constantly adhered to, though differences of education and system in the demagogues of France have given a variety to its operation. The following is an extract from Mirabeau's letter in which he delineates his plan, but the whole merits a serious perusal. " Upon the whole, I am " more than ever attached to my system. *A great* " *empire can never be well-governed but as a congrega-* " *tion of small federative states, whose federal knot is* " *in a representative assembly* presided over and " watched by the monarch. Thus by force of a " good constitution alone *we might soon have the* " *Rhine for a boundary,* and, what is more, *an irre-* " *sistible influence over all the governments of Eu-* " *rope,* by the amelioration and extended prosperity " of the whole human species. But to produce " these advantages we must have a system, we must " not be obliged, in addition to our general laws, " to make special laws, which we do not and " should not understand. *A government must be a* " *professor, not a pupil; a chief, not a slave.* The " representative of the nation must not act in a " manner contradictory to her interests. In a " word, an expiring juggler [h], must not continue " his clumsy cup-and-ball tricks, when there is no " longer any need for hocus-pocus, or mounte- " bank's tables. Comus and Pinetti must not ex- " pect to receive from an academy of sciences, the " same applauses they acquire at a fair [i]."

Exertions in the assembly;

To describe all Mirabeau's labours in the constituent assembly, it would be requisite to enter into a minute detail of every debate which took place from its commencement to the last day of his life, since no debate occurred which was not directed by his

[h] Necker.
[i] Lettre à Mauvillon du 31 Janvier 1790, p. 506. du Recueil.

judgment,

judgment, guided by his genius, or illuminated by his eloquence. I shall describe the course of his exertions on a few subjects, as they enable us to form a just estimate of his politics, without narrating historically the circumstances which preceded, or the effects which followed them. From an early attachment to the doctrines of infidelity, and as an *illuminatus*, Mirabeau was inimical to the ecclesiastical establishment, and the opposition made by the clergy to the usurpation of the *tiers etat* had exasperated him to a still higher pitch. He had frequently been heard to say, " If you wish for a revo-" lution, you must banish the Catholic religion " from France [k]." He was an advocate for the abolition of tithes, a measure which he supported with all his eloquence and influence, and finally succeeded [l]. The necessity and rapacious disposition of the assembly could not be satisfied with the tithes alone, but required that the whole wealth of the clergy should be at their disposal. The lay members of the assembly, apprehensive of censure from the invidious appearance such a motion would assume if it proceeded from them, availed themselves of the profligacy of a member of the clerical body to obtain their object. Talleyrand Perigord, bishop of Autun, was prevailed on by Mirabeau to propose the measure, which was supported by all the zeal, eloquence, and intrigue of the party. The resistance was proportioned to the magnitude of the object, and the popular party, not feeling sufficiently strong to insure a majority, more than once adjourned the debate. The mob strenuously assisted the enemies of the clergy. Placards were pasted up, containing lists of those who had opposed the motion, and offering rewards of twelve hundred livres (52*l*. 10*s*.) to any patriot who would kill them. On

against the clergy;

---

[k] Barruel's History of the Clergy, part I. p. 2.
[l] See Impartial History, vol. i. p. 193. Historical Sketch, p. 111.

the

the day when the question was finally decided, a mob, armed with pikes, assembled in the avenues to the place of sitting, and threatened to put all the bishops and priests to death, if the motion was lost [m]. Several members produced letters in which they were threatened with destruction if they persevered in opposing the measure; but Mirabeau silenced them by producing letters of similar import, which, he pretended, had been written to him by the other party [n]. This measure was followed by the suppression of all monastic establishments, and the grant of nominal pensions to the clergy, while their lands were assigned to the creditors of the state, and assignats issued on them, as a new kind of paper money. Mirabeau was one of the strongest advocates of these violent proceedings in opposition to his own sentiments, expressed in his pamphlet against the emperor, called *Doutes sur la Liberté de l'Escaut*, where, among many similar passages, he says expresfly, 'Despise the monks as much as you please, but do not rob them, for it is unlawful to rob either the most determined Atheist or the most credulous Capuchin [o].' Yet, with all this violence, Mirabeau had occasion to shew his moderation at the expence of others. He said one day at the Jacobin club, while descanting on the inveteracy displayed against the priests : " For God's " sake, gentlemen, let us not torment their con- " sciences. We have got their property, and what " signifies any thing else [p] ?" Mirabeau, as a member of the club of *Amis des Noirs*, was anxious to abolish slavery, and make the coloured inhabitants of the colonies in every respect equal with the whites; a measure supremely impolitic, in which he failed [q].

for the slaves.

[m] Barruel's History of the Clergy, part I. p. 22.
[n] Historical Sketch, p. 222.   [o] Idem, p. 373.
[p] Lettre d'un François, p. 45. n.
[q] See Impartial History, vol. i. p. 319.

Thefe meafures, and the arrangement of fome articles of the conftitution, took up the attention of the affembly during the early part of the year. Mirabeau's popularity continued to increafe, and he augmented his infolence in proportion. His appearance and manners were fuch, that an author in defcribing him fays, "When filent he refembled a favage "bear, when he fpoke, a foaming lion'." He felt no fear of the perfons to whom he was oppofed, knowing them to be attached to order, morals, and the laws. "You have nothing to apprehend from "the ariftocrats," was his expreffion to his adherents, "they neither pillage, burn, or affaffin- "ate'." Towards his opponents he behaved with the utmoft ferocity, threatening them with the vengeance of the mob on every occafion'. Yet Mirabeau was cowardly to the greateft degree. His prefence of mind never forfook him in debate, but in action, or when threatened, he exhibited none of that inflammability which diftinguifhed him on other occafions; his courage bore an inverfe proportion to his infolence ˣ. He received two or three challenges, which he always declined, with frefh infolence or unmanly pleafantry. "I will write to my "conftituents," he faid, "to know if they deputed "me to ftake my life at fword and piftol; if fo, I "fhall requeft them to nominate Saint George, or "fome equally fkilful combatant, as my fuper- "numerary ʸ."

1790. His violence,

and cowardices

As Necker's influence declined, fome friends of the king renewed a negotiation with Mirabeau for

His exertions for the crown.

ʳ Apologie des Projets, &c. p. 198.
ˢ Bertrand's Memoirs, vol. i. p. 305. Anecdotes du Regne de Louis XVI. vol. vi. p. 269.
ᵗ See Hiftorical Sketch, p. 300. Conjuration de d'Orleans, vol. ii. p. 204.
ˣ Apologie des Projets, &c. p. 192.
ʸ Anecdotes du Regne de Louis XVI. vol. vi. p. 220. For inftances of Mirabeau's tamenefs in fubmitting to infults, fee the fame volume, p. 143. 193. 202.

his assistance, which finally succeeded. It was either in consequence of this negotiation, or of Mirabeau's wish that it should take place, that many motions made by him appeared to favour the royal cause. He seems to have had some prospect of being minister, when he endeavoured to get rid of the absurd self-denying decree, by moving that ministers should have a consultative voice in the assembly. This proposition was so ill received, that instead of producing the desired effect, it only caused the exclusion to be more strongly enforced [2]. In the question respecting the power of declaring war and making peace, Mirabeau shewed his disposition to favour the court still more openly, for he maintained the unpopular though rational doctrine, that these powers ought to be vested in the king. This produced an immediate effect on the mob; it was rumoured that he was sold to the court. The hawkers cried about the streets *the grand treachery of count Mirabeau*; and Marat, who had long been his enemy, printed the opinion that he ought to be broiled on a gridiron, as the greatest traitor in the assembly. Mirabeau was now obliged to retract a part of his opinion, and compromise with the more moderate of his opponents to form a decree that war should be declared on the part of the king, in the name of the nation. Even this was not sufficient to gratify the populace. Barnave and Lameth, who had opposed him, were carried in triumph on coming out of the assembly. " I too," said Mirabeau, " had it in my power but two days " ago to have been carried in triumph, but I was " not then to learn that it is but one step from the " capitol to the Tarpeian rock [3]."

Jealousy of the populace.

22d May.

---

[2] Debates. Impartial History, vol. i. p. 284.
[3] Debates, Historical Sketch, p. 277. Pages, vol. i. p. 345. Playfair's History of Jacobinism, p. 295.

Although

Although Mirabeau assumed in public the semblance of stoical indifference, he felt the insult he had received with considerable sensibility. He says, "I have attended closely to business in the assembly, and even powerfully maintained the barrier, as you will have read in the public papers. We have here a multitude of persons whose only aim is confusion. Their audacious turbulence awes the timid, alarms the prudent, hurries away the impetuous, and rallies the factious. It was necessary to form, to guide, to render victorious a truly monarchical party, which was not easy in a nation so fickle, which does nothing but by the impulse of the moment, or at the dictates of fashion. Now the fashion of this day is licentiousness and anarchy [b]." The prevalence of this disposition was such that he was led to apprehend it would terminate in a civil war. In a subsequent letter he says, "You must suppose, my dear friend, that my career becomes daily more perilous. In the first place, I never had any faith in the possibility of effecting a great revolution without bloodshed; and I no longer entertain a hope but that the internal fermentation, combined with intrigues, will occasion a civil war; I am not clear that such an event is not a necessary evil." It is probable, that at the time he wrote this his treaty with the king met with some obstacles, as in another part of the letter he says, "The ministry, equally treacherous and base, cannot, even for their own safety, forgive me for having rendered some services to the nation. The throne has neither conception, judgment, or free-will. The people, ignorant and anarchical, float at the discretion of every political juggler, and of their own illusions [c]."

4th Aug.

[b] Lettres à Mauvillon, p. 510.
[c] Idem, p. 517. 518.

Inculpated by Chatelet.

It is possible that some portion of jealousy felt by the ministry might arise from the return of Orleans, and a suspicion that the connexion between him and Mirabeau would be renewed. This might originate from their being jointly implicated in the charge of conspiracy on the fifth of October, and the presumption that they must unite in their defence.

7th Aug.

Of this, however, there is no appearance. When Boucher d'Argis made his report to the assembly, Mirabeau was in the frame of mind which induced him to write the letter mentioned above.

30th Sept.

Before the Chatelet had delivered in their accusation, Necker had retired, and as no impediment remained, it is highly probable that Mirabeau had made his bargain with the court, and was consequently under no apprehensions of the event of this proceeding.

Acquitted by the assembly;

To this must be attributed the phenomenon of Mauri's undertaking his defence, and the slight opposition made to the vote of exculpation which could not apply to Mirabeau without extending to Orleans also [d]. Mirabeau's guilt is strongly apparent in the depositions in the Chatelet as published, but that part can afford only very imperfect information, as the more important examinations were not committed to the press. It is said they are preserved, and will at some future time appear [e].

Bribed by the court.

Mirabeau had now entirely dissolved his connexion with Orleans, though he found it necessary to maintain an appearance of cordiality with him, and even to attach himself to the Lameths, and some other leaders of the Jacobins, in order to counterbalance the influence of la Fayette, of whose duplicity and ambition he was justly apprehensive [f]. Sensible of the disorganizing power which Orleans, by dint of

---

[d] Debates. Histories. Conjuration de d'Orleans, vol. iii. p. 81. et seq. Anecdotes du Regne de Louis XVI. vol. vi. p. 443. See ORLEANS.

[e] Robison's Proofs of a Conspiracy, p. 392. n.

[f] Bouillé's Memoirs, p. 254.

corruption,

corruption, had acquired in the army, Mirabeau proposed the bold but salutary measure of disbanding the whole military body, and re-establishing it on constitutional principles. This plan would not have been disagreeable to la Fayette, but when it was proposed in the assembly, most of the members were terrified at its audacity, and it was rejected by all parties [g]. The price Mirabeau received from the crown for his services was six hundred thousand livres (26,250*l.*) in prompt payment, and an allowance of fifty thousand livres (2187*l.*) a-month [h]. The king had much repugnance to overcome before he could repose an entire confidence in Mirabeau, or resolve to rely on a man of his character [i], but the marquis de Bouillé; to whom Mirabeau's junction with the court was communicated, was immediately sensible of its beneficial tendency. He was of opinion that the genius, talents, and firmness of Mirabeau were equal to the greatness of the emergency; and that if any man could save the king and monarchy it was he [k]. The following comparison between the characters of Mirabeau and la Fayette is so sagacious and just, that I give it in M. de Bouillé's own words: " It will appear astonishing,
" without doubt, that I should act with so much
" confidence towards Mirabeau, when my conduct
" towards la Fayette was marked with such distrust.
" The reason is obvious; avarice and ambition were
" the reigning passions of the former, and these
" the king could amply gratify when re-seated on
" his throne: now I very well knew that Mirabeau
" possessed too much discernment not to perceive
" that the gratitude and favours of a prince, whom
" he should have contributed to restore to his
" power and authority, were much to be preferred
" to popular favour, and the temporary situation of

Compared with la Fayette.

[g] Bouillé's Memoirs, p. 174. Moore's View, vol. ii. p. 170.
[h] Bouillé's Memoirs, p. 277. [i] Idem, p. 275.
[k] Idem, p. 277.

" leader

"leader of a party. La Fayette, on the contrary, was an enthusiast, and intoxicated with self-love; whose price could neither be known or reached; a description of men at all times dangerous, but particularly so during a revolution[1]."

Mirabeau's plan;

The plan which Mirabeau proposed to adopt for restoring the king to liberty and political importance, and the means and resources he possessed for putting it in execution, are thus faithfully displayed by the same candid and judicious author:—" The intention of Mirabeau was to procure the dissolution of the assembly and the liberty of the king, by the force and will of the nation itself; establishing this principle, that the representatives of the people at this assembly were not possessed of the powers necessary to make a change in the ancient constitution, such a measure being contrary to the instructions given by all the provinces to the deputies sent by them to the states-general, which instructions had neither been altered nor revoked; and that the king, being deprived of his personal liberty, could not invest with his authority the new laws that had been enacted. The validity of this objection being admitted, he then intended to procure addresses from the different departments, praying that the present assembly might be dissolved; a new one convoked, with the powers requisite for making such alterations in the constitution as should appear necessary; and that the king should be restored to his liberty, and the enjoyment of a reasonable authority. These addresses were to be supported by the people of Paris, whom Mirabeau seemed to think at his disposal, when he should have removed some of the leading men of the Jacobin faction, whom he had already denounced to the assembly. Mirabeau reckoned six-and-thirty de-

---
[1] Bouillé's Memoirs, p. 281.

" partments

"partments whose conduct he could direct, and I myself could depend upon six; besides, as I have already observed, there was hardly a department in the kingdom which was not well affected to the royal cause. Mirabeau was further to deliver to me the king and royal family either at Compeigne or at Fontainbleau, where I should have surrounded them with my best troops [m]." In this whole plan there was no violence meditated either against the assembly or individuals; the people were to be resorted to that they might remedy the evils which an usurping body had committed in their name. Nor could it with propriety be termed a counter-revolution, but merely a corrective measure, tending to restrain the vices and defects which had originated in rashness, violence, and ignorance. A new assembly, duly elected and authorized for the purpose, could have framed a constitution with greater probability of success than that which already existed. Obtaining their authority without a struggle, they would have proceeded to business without rancour, and instead of destroying every thing without reserve, they would have endeavoured to combine existing laws and establishments with such reforms as the disposition of the people and the necessity of the times suggested. Enlightened by the experience of their predecessors, they would have avoided their faults; while from a contemplation of the danger into which the kingdom had been plunged by precipitation, jealousy, and party-spirit, they would have learned moderation, forbearance, and mutual confidence. Thus the first national assembly would not have existed in vain, and the few principled members of it who survive the wreck of the times would not be under the necessity of lamenting that they have been unintentionally accessary to the destruction of their sove-

[m] Bouillé's Memoirs, p 278.

reign, the extirpation of religion, the enslaving of their country, and the conflagration of Europe.

His exertions. Mirabeau applied the whole force of his genius and all the energy of his indefatigable mind to give effect to this new plan, in the result of which he expected to be prime minister. He used all his efforts to disunite the prevailing factions, and make them jealous of and odious to each other. He had attached to himself the Lameths, Barnave his former rival in eloquence, and Duport [n]. There is reason to suppose that Mirabeau also made some attempts to conciliate la Fayette; this might be dictated either by hope or fear; there was reason to apprehend that the general had by some means obtained a knowledge of the project, and had, at his own desire, had a conference of three hours with Mirabeau, at the house of Emery, deputy for Metz, who was a confidant of la Fayette [o]. From the union of two such men, had it been possible, the greatest advantages might have been derived; but la Fayette, limited in his talents though unbounded in his ambition and vanity, could not have borne the near approach of a mind so much his superior, or have consented to embrace so grand a plan, from the execution of which hypocrisy, petty intrigue, and trivial manœuvre must have been banished. To strengthen his own party was among Mirabeau's greatest efforts. He was desirous of forming a connection with persons of talents, and of employing them in such a manner as to give effect and vigour to a new system and a new administration. Among others so applied to was Dumouriez, who undertook the embassy to Prussia, and seems to have entered cordially into Mirabeau's interests. Mirabeau also made due preparations to secure the approbation of foreign courts, and proper advances to ministers: even count Hertz-

---

[n] Apologie des Projets, &c. p. 191.
[o] Bouillé's Memoirs, p. 281. 297.

berg, the Prussian minister, though Mirabeau hated him, was complimented with numerous consultations [p].

During these transactions, Mirabeau was not inattentive to his duties in the assembly, where the debates generally turned on some articles of the constitution, in which he interested himself in proportion to their magnitude, but avoided a mode of conduct so decisive as to alarm the one, or injure the other party. He was elected one of the administrators of the department of Paris, which gave him a right to command the municipality, and drew up a proclamation, in which he strongly recommended obedience to the law, and submission to authority [q]. He was elevated to the president's chair, which he filled with dignity and moderation. He distinguished his presidency by the answer he gave to a deputation of quakers, who required permission to abstain from military duty, as it was repugnant to their religious tenets. Mirabeau's answer is one of those specimens of subtilty which rarely occur: it refuses the request of the petitioners, without leaving them reason to complain, or the power of renewing their supplication; and invalidates the reasoning of the petition, without throwing disgrace or blame on the petitioners [r]. The last words pronounced by Mirabeau in the tribune were these:—" I will oppose " the factious; I will combat them, of whatever " party or on whatever side they may be [s]."

in the assembly.

29th Jan. 10th Feb.

Conversing with Dumouriez on affairs of the utmost importance, the character of count Hertzberg became the subject of discussion. " This old

His sudden death.

---

[p] Life of Dumouriez, vol. ii. p. 115. Among Mirabeau's motives for disliking count Hertzberg, may be reckoned the pride of authorship. The count had produced a criticism on the Histoire de la Monarchie Prussienne which highly offended Mirabeau. See Lettres à Mauvillon, p. 450. 515.
[q] Historical Sketch, p. 323.
[r] Debates. Talma's Chronology.
[s] Anecdotes du Regne de Louis XVI. vol. vi. p. 271.

"fox (said Mirabeau) is surrounded by a chaplet
"of obstructions, and attacked at the same time by
"at least five or six maladies, all of which are mor-
"tal; and yet he is continually broaching new
"projects, as if he were to live a hundred years;
"while in fact one of the fatal sisters has her scissars
"ready to cut the thread that holds suspended over
2d April. "his head the sword of Damocles." In four days
Mirabeau himself was no more!

30th Mar. When his illness was announced, all Paris was in consternation and alarm: his door was crowded with inquirers, and the king himself sent for information of the state of his health. He suffered the acutest pains without betraying any unmanly symptoms of alarm or anguish. He conversed with his friends, and delivered to Talleyrand Perigord a speech which he had composed on the law then agitated in the assembly respecting testamentary devises. "It will be a remarkable circumstance (he said) "that the man who offers them this, his last tri- "bute, prepared it immediately after making his "own will "." He appeared to feel some regret at quitting life, just when he was about to have commenced an useful and truly glorious career; and he predicted, that with him the French monarchy would expire [x].

Supposed to be poisoned. The supposed cause of Mirabeau's death was a gathering occasioned by the stoppage of an issue: his heart was dried up, and a mortification had taken place in his intestines. Such was the *procès verbal* published by the surgeons who opened him [y]. The people of Paris suspected that the days of their favourite had been shortened by poison. All authors who have written on Mirabeau's death have mentioned this supposition with different degrees of

[t] Life of Dumouriez, vol. ii. p. 119.
[u] Anecdotes du Regne de Louis XVI. vol. vi. p. 272.
[x] Moore's Journal, vol. i. p. 470.
[y] Anecdotes du Regne de Louis XVI. vol. vi. p. 273.

acquiescence

acquiescence or disbelief. I am of opinion that the fact, so far as it can be decided by probability, appears almost certain. The critical period at which Mirabeau was carried off; the last words he uttered in the tribune, so well calculated to strike terror and infuse desperate resolutions in the party he had relinquished, naturally gave birth to suspicion: the extent of the project in which he was embarked implied a necessity for a diffuse confidence, and Orleans, who had his spies and agents every where, could not fail of obtaining information, if not of the whole circumstances, at least of the leading features of a plan which threatened entire destruction to all those schemes of ambition and revenge, in pursuit of which he had ruined his fortune, and exposed himself to every danger. No man was so likely as Orleans to effect the death of a dangerous opponent by violence of any kind, but in the present case poison was the most easy and effectual method. I am not qualified to discuss chirurgically or medically the probability of the cause which was supposed to have occasioned Mirabeau's death operating by such means as an acute excruciating agony, terminating an illness of three days by paralytical affections, and an incapacity to speak, though the power of writing remained till almost his last moment [2]. The suspicions of the people were appeased by the report of the surgeons who opened the body; but the reports of surgeons are not always true, and the circumstances on this occasion afforded just ground for continued suspicion. Sixty surgeons were chosen from the different sections of Paris to attend on the occasion; few of them, as they afterwards confessed, approached the body so as to examine it minutely; and there was a mob of above one hundred thousand persons collected, vowing vengeance if it should be discovered that Mirabeau's days had

[2] Anecdotes du Regne de Louis XVI. vol. vi. p. 272.

been abridged by treachery. Uncertain against whom the popular violence might be directed, it is not wonderful if these surgeons made a report contrary to their conviction, and suppressed symptoms which might have led to doubts, if not certainties of the fact[a]. But even supposing the surgeons to have declared faithfully the result of their experiment, it seems that dissection does not always afford decisive proof on the subject, and suspicion, strongly founded on the political crisis at which he died, is left to point out as her objects those whose consequence would be diminished, and whose schemes would be thwarted by his newly-adopted politics[b]. His death, however, was the greatest political misfortune that could have occurred to France. The assembly immediately lost its small share of respectability, the proceedings of the clubs assumed an unexampled audacity, and a multitude of crawling reptiles became conspicuous and noxious, whom the blaze of Mirabeau's genius would at pleasure have driven back to the caves of ignominy and obscurity.

Funeral and posthumous honours. When Mirabeau's death was publicly known, a general regret was testified by all ranks of people. The theatres were shut, the fleets lowered their topsails, and every thing wore the appearance of public calamity. M. Comps, his secretary, was so affected that he attempted to stab himself with a penknife, but was saved. The news occasioned in the national assembly a general exclamation of grief. It was immediately decreed, that the members should go into mourning; the members of the department, and of the municipality of Paris, followed their example; and it spread all over France. In a few hours after his death, the people changed the name of the street where he had resided, from *Rue de la*

[a] Playfair's History of Jacobinism, p. 296. n.
[b] Impartial History, vol. i. p. 400.

Chauffée

Chauſſée d'Antin, to *Rue de Mirabeau*. After much deliberation, and proposals to bury him at Saint Denis in company with the kings of France, and in the *Champ de Mars* under the national altar, it was decreed that the church of Saint Genevieve ſhould be a receptacle for the remains of illuſtrious men, and that Mirabeau ſhould firſt have the honour of being placed there. It was decreed that the whole national aſſembly ſhould attend his funeral. The retinue extended to the length of a league, though the national guard formed a front of ſixteen deep. All the civil and military bodies attended, as did the king's miniſters. His coffin, inſtead of a marquis's coronet, which his rank would have required before the abolition of nobility, was adorned with a civic crown decreed by the country. No ſound was heard, ſave muffled drums, melancholy martial muſic, and occaſional diſcharges of artillery. His funeral oration, a ſplendid compoſition, was delivered by Cerutti. The buſt of Mirabeau was placed in the halls of moſt of the municipalities and political clubs throughout the kingdom. In many provincial towns and cities, as Bourdeaux, Verſailles, Bayeux, and Bagneux, funeral ſervices were celebrated to his memory. At Bagneux the concourſe of people was ſo great, that ſeveral of the neighbouring villages were abſolutely ſtripped of their inhabitants; in the town only ſeven infirm perſons were left at home, and that (ſays my author) only becauſe they could get nobody to carry them[c]. At Leſneven, near Breſt, an image of Mirabeau was cut in wood, and placed on a pedeſtal in a public ſquare, for inauguration: there was a civic feaſt; the Marſeillois hymn was chanted, and, at a given word, the people, the municipal officers, the juſtices of peace, and the national guards, fell proſtrate,

---

[c] Anecdotes du Regne de Louis XVI. vol. vi. p. 273 to 279. Hiſtories.

and, with a new kind of idolatry, paid their homage to Mirabeau [d]. Funeral orations and poems of every defcription were publifhed in abundance; more than one collection was made of his fpeeches [e]; Manuel fraudulently publifhed his letters written while in the caftle of Vincennes; and his letters to Mauvillon and Chamfort have fince been committed to the prefs.

Dies infolvent. Mirabeau made a will, in which he left feveral confiderable bequefts, yet he died infolvent. It is probable that his effects were immediately diftributed, and his collection of books, &c. never fold. Some of his creditors endeavoured to poffefs themfelves of the letters which Manuel had printed and was about to publifh [f], but were at length obliged to apply to the legiflative affembly, which, after feveral debates, decreed that his debts fhould be paid by the public [g].

11th Aug. 1792. Pofthumous infults. A fhort period fubverted the fragil edifice of Mirabeau's popularity. As a friend to monarchy he firft encountered the fury of the mob. After the ftorming of the Tuilleries, his bufts were devoted to deftruction, together with thofe of la Fayette and Necker [h].

Sept. 1792. As the principles of republicanifm were more generally adopted, the refpect for Mirabeau decreafed, the ftreet named after him was, when general Montefquiou had over-run Savoy, new named *Rue de Mont Blanc* [i]. In the celebrated iron clofet feveral papers were found, or pretended to have been found, certifying Mirabeau's connexion with the court. They were produced at

---

[d] Barruel's Hiftory of the Clergy, Part II. p. 47.
[e] The only means an Englifh reader, unacquainted with the French language, can have of eftimating Mirabeau's eloquence, are fupplied by an admirable tranflation of his Speeches, made by James White, Efquire.
[f] See MANUEL.
See Debates 24th and 27th October, and 3d November 1791, and 12th January 1792.
[h] Impartial Hiftory, vol. ii. p. 115.
[i] Peltier's late Picture of Paris, vol. ii. p. 116.

the

the king's trial, and denied by him, and there are strong reasons, from internal evidence, to consider them forgeries, though the facts inferred happened to be true. When the rage of republicanism was at its greatest height, Chenier the poet, in the name of the committee of public instruction, presented a report to the convention, in which these letters were recited. It formed the basis of a decree that the remains of Mirabeau should be taken from the Pantheon, and those of Marat placed there in his stead [k]. The execution of this absurd decree (absurd as to the latter part at least) is not to be recorded amongst the disgraces of the age of terror, it was reserved to stigmatize the pretended age of moderation. It was not carried into effect till some months after the fall of Robespierre [l].

25th Nov. 1793.

Mirabeau's features were harsh, and his person clumsy. His head, which was uncommonly large, seemed to be wedged in between his enormous shoulders, and his body and limbs formed a thick unshaped mass. Yet when he applied his talents to seduction, he was more successful than many others, whose personal attractions seem much greater [m]. After the facts contained in the preceding narrative, it is unnecessary to descant on his character as son and husband. He is said to have been extremely choleric, and even brutal in the regulation of his family, frequently descending to the cowardly meanness of striking his own servants [n]. As an author he derived much of his success from his art in always writing on the topic which created the greatest share of momentary interest. He was not diligent in the selection of materials, frequently relying on the labours of his friends, as Mauvillon and Chamfort, and often adopting without reserve as

Person and manners.

Talents as an author;

---

[k] Debates. Pagès, vol. i. p. 384.
[l] Miss Williams's Letters in 1794, vol. iv. p. 10.
[m] Moore's View, vol. ii. p. 211. Pagès, vol. i. p. 389. Conjuration de d'Orleans, vol. i. p. 213.
[n] Conjuration de d'Orleans, vol. i. p. 214.

much

much as suited his subject, from the works of other authors, either ancient or cotemporary°. What he received and what he selected he made his own by the force of his genius, the propriety of his arrangement, the beauties of his style, and the elegance of his ornaments. He had an exalted opinion of his own abilities, relied on the favourable judgment of posterity, and disdained his cotemporaries. "No bankruptcy," he says in a letter to Mauvillon, "is the production of Messrs. Clavière and Brissot de Warville. Your German critics must be miserable tasters, to mistake the brewings of these gentry for my wine ᵖ."

As an orator;

His voice was forcible, loud, and commanding, except when he was agitated by passion, then it occasionally assumed the depth and compass of Stentor, and sometimes by a sudden transition was brought to resemble the treble string of a violin squeaking under the bow ᵠ. He had great rhetorical talents, and could employ them on sudden emergencies, and in all directions. This, in popular assemblies, rendered him almost irresistible. He never despaired of turning the debate. His victories were always splendid, his defeats never ignominious. He never appeared vanquished, and no man could assume a triumph over him. His talents for repartee, joined to his powers of reasoning, enabled him with equal facility to disconcert his opponents with sarcasm, or refute them by force of argument, while the greatness of his abilities and his sudden command of them enabled him, if any of his co-adjutors approached him, so as to be thought competitors, by a little effort to throw them back to their original and natural distance ʳ.

As a politician.

To appreciate Mirabeau as a

° See a remarkable instance in Wilde's Address to the Friends of the People, p. 115.
ᵖ Lettres à Mauvillon, p. 440.
ᵠ Conjuration de d'Orléans, vol. i. p. 213.
ʳ Wilde's Address, p. 104. 106. Moore's View, vol. ii. p. 211.

politician,

politician, it will be more proper to survey the end than the earlier part of his career. In his struggle for power, he disgraced himself by many violences and excesses, for which a prison or a scaffold would have been the deserved punishment. When he had attained the object of his ambition, when wealth, respect, and nobility* became his own, he was desirous to tread back the steps he had taken, and to establish a more splendid reputation, as well as a more permanent authority. Awake from the dream of popular frenzy and recovered from the delusions of illuminism, he might have rendered the most conspicuous and essential services to his country, and to the world. From his decease we may date the rapid declension of royalty, and the audacious display of disorganizing politics pursued by the demagogues of France.

* Mirabeau was not friendly to the decree for abolishing titles, armorial bearings, &c. He thus expresses himself: "It is the most difficult of all undertakings, to erase from the human heart the influence of recollections. True nobility is, for this reason, a property, no less indestructible than sacred. Forms may vary, but the worship will ever continue. Let every man be equal in the eye of the law, let every monopoly disappear, all else is but changing the object of human vanity." Lettres à Mauvillon, p. 519.

JAQUES NECKER.

As Necker is generally confidered one of the principal authors of the French revolution, his conduct and views have been examined and criticifed with fingular afperity. On one hand, thofe who have fuffered by the revolution, and attribute to him all the evils they complain of, are inceffant and intemperate in their reproaches; while thofe who think his reforms too much reftricted, and his views in many refpects too confined, and often perfonal, are no lefs inveterately his enemies; but, on the other hand, Necker priding himfelf in his integrity, and poffeffing a ftyle fufficiently eloquent, and much improved by habit, has defended his conduct in many works, equivalent in themfelves to the efforts of thofe partifans whom intereft or affection might have attached to him.

1732. Birth, education, and outfet in life.

Necker was born at Geneva; his father was profeffor of civil law in the college there[t]; he received an education much fuperior to that generally given to men intended for bufinefs[u]; but the narrownefs of his circumftances obliging him to feek fome means of gaining a fubfiftence more promifing than the walks of literature, he became clerk to a banker at Geneva, at a falary of fix hundred livres (26 *l.* 5 *s.*) a-year[x]. While he was in this fituation, Theluffon, the banker at Paris,

1758. Goes to Paris.

[t] Hiftoire Literaire de Geneve, par Jean Senebier, vol. iii. p. 90. 294. Anecdotes du Regne de Louis XVI. vol. v. p. 142.
[u] Moore's View, vol. i. p. 97. Anecdotes, &c.
[x] Moore's View, Bertrand's Memoirs, vol. i. p. 145.

wrote

wrote to his correspondent at Geneva to find him a clerk to keep his cash-books; and this correspondent, who happened to be Necker's employer, recommended him [y]. He was retained at a salary of one thousand two hundred livres (52 *l.* 10 *s.*) and gave such satisfaction by his assiduity and intelligence, that his emoluments were rapidly raised, and he was soon made cashier [z].

Great success.

In this situation he has been accused of speculating with the money of his employers [a], and reproached with having raised his fortune by means far less honourable [b]; but as no proof of these assertions has ever been brought forward, I rather incline to the decision of an accurate observer, who says, that " his greatest enemies have not been able to injure " his reputation for probity [c]." The embarrassment of the finances of France, under the administration of the abbé Terray, afforded him the means of advantageous speculation; and his employers, conscious of his sagacity and of the benefits they derived from his intelligence, admitted him partner [d]. He made a very large and rapid fortune by these speculations, and by his interference in the affairs of the East-India company, an interference equally satisfactory to the company and the public, and extremely profitable to himself. Yet it has been asserted, that he imposed on the company by false pretences, and sacrificed their advantage to his own cupidity [e].

---

[y] Bertrand's Memoirs. The author of Anecdotes du Regne de Louis XVI. gives a different account of Necker's introduction to Thelusson: he says, that immediately on finishing his education, Necker came to Paris, and was employed by Isaac Vernet; that he was suddenly dismissed from his house, and offered his services to Thelusson, who was the rival of Vernet's successor, Saladin, and received him with no other recommendation than his having been employed by Vernet, and a few false pretences, vol. v. p. 142.
[z] Bertrand's Memoirs. Anecdotes, &c. [a] Ibid.
[b] See Anecdotes, &c. vol. v. p. 144.
[c] Moore's View, vol. i. p. 146.
[d] Bertrand's Memoirs. Anecdotes, &c. [e] Ibid.

While

Marries.

While he was partner in the house of Thelusson, he made his addresses to a young lady living with madame Thelusson as companion, whose name was Susanna Curchod. This lady had previously excited amorous sensations in the bosom of Gibbon the historian, which the repugnance of his father to the match, and his own prudence, enabled him to conquer: he speaks of her with the warmth of a lover, and with that eloquence for which he is so much celebrated. " The personal attractions of " mademoiselle Susan Curchod were embellished by " the virtues and talents of the mind. Her fortune " was humble, but her family was respectable. Her " mother, a native of France, had preferred her " religion to her country. The profession of her " father did not extinguish the moderation and phi- " losophy of his temper, and he lived content with " a small salary and laborious duty, in the obscure " lot of minister of Crassy, in the mountains that " separate the Pays de Vaud from the county of " Burgundy. In the solitude of a sequestered vil- " lage he bestowed a liberal and even learned " education on his only daughter. She surpassed " his hopes by her proficiency in the sciences and " languages; and in her short visits to some re- " lations at Lausanne, the wit, the beauty, and " erudition of mademoiselle Curchod were the theme " of universal applause. The report of such a " prodigy awakened my curiosity; I saw and loved. " I found her learned without pedantry, witty in " conversation, pure in sentiment, and elegant in " manners; and the first sudden emotion was " fortified by the habits and knowledge of a more " familiar acquaintance. * * * * The minister of " Crassy soon afterwards died; his stipend died " with him; his daughter retired to Geneva, where, " by teaching young ladies, she earned a hard sub- " sistence for herself and her mother; but in her " lowest distress she maintained a spotless reputation
" and

" and a dignified behaviour. A rich banker of Paris,
" a citizen of Geneva, had the good fortune and
" good sense to discover and possess this inestimable
" treasure; and in the capital of taste and luxury
" she resisted the temptations of wealth, as she had
" sustained the hardships of indigence. * * * * In
" every change of prosperity and disgrace he has
" reclined on the bosom of a faithful friend; and
" mademoiselle Curchod is now the wife of M.
" Necker, the minister, and, perhaps, the legislator
" of the French monarchy [f]."

On Necker's marriage, his share in the bank was increased; and, on Thelusson's death, he established a house of his own, taking into partnership with him Mess. Girardot and Haller [g]. The rapidity of his rise, and the extent of his establishment, put it out of doubt that he must have been more indebted to the mysteries of stock-jobbing, than to the regular course of the banking business for his fortune.

1765.

His reputation for financial knowledge, aided by a favourable impression he had made in some literary productions, was such, that at the period when France was about to embark in the American contest, he was pointed out by M. de Pezay, who had great influence with the minister Maurepas, as a proper person to succeed M. de Clugny, recently deceased, as director of the finances [h]. It is said by several writers, that he owed his appointment to an intrigue amongst the bankers of Paris, who wished to avail themselves of his communications during the war, and to his own urgency and perseverance with M. de Pezay, who engaged M. de Maurepas in his interests so effectually, as at last to vanquish every obstacle [i]. Necker was the first

Made director of finances.

July 1776.

---

[f] Gibbon's Miscellaneous Works, vol. i. p. 73.
[g] Anecdotes, &c.
[h] Moore's View. Anecdotes, &c. vol. v. p. 133.
[i] Anecdotes, &c. Bertrand's Memoirs. Playfair's History of Jacobinism, p. 68.

protestant

protestant who, since the revocation of the edict of Nantz, had held any important place in the administration of France [k]; and some extraordinary circumstances must be supposed to have contributed to his elevation. He himself attributes it wholly to the deranged state of the finances, and the decline of public spirit [l]; but it is not impossible that it was favoured by the intrigues alluded to; and perhaps by a little bribery, which was known to be a sure passport to the favour of M. de Pezay [m].

<small>Comptroller general</small> But whatever might be expected from Necker's talents and exertions, he had not at first access to the king, a circumstance which impeded his designs and hurt his pride, but which he contrived to surmount by creating a financial dispute between M. Taboureau, the comptroller-general of finances, and himself, which occasioned that minister to retire <small>July 1777.</small> in disgust, and Necker obtained his situation [n]. Even when he had immediate communication with the king, he found great difficulty in effecting the reforms he desired; he had many prejudices to surmount, and many discordant interests to reconcile; so many, that even late in life he mentions the difficulties of his situation with some feeling and more vanity. " I still remember," he says [o], " that " high dark staircase to M. de Maurepas' apart- " ments, which I used to ascend with fear and de- " jection, uncertain how a new idea might succeed " with him, which occupied all my attention, and " which often tended to produce an increase of the " revenue by some just but severe operation. I still " remember that cabinet, placed under the roof of

---

[k] Impartial History, vol. i. p. 14.
[l] Sur l'Administration de M. Necker, par lui même, p. 8.
[m] Moore's View. M. de Pezay is said to have been only a *soi disant* marquis; but having fortunately obtained an introduction to M. de Maurepas, he acquired an entire ascendancy over him. Anecdotes, &c. vol. v. p. 162.
[n] Moore's View. Bertrand's Memoirs. Anecdotes, &c.
[o] Sur l'Administration de M. Necker, p. 13.

" the

"the palace of Verfailles, but above the king's apartments, and which, by its fmallnefs and fituation, really feemed the effence (and a very refined effence too) of human vanity and ambition. There was I obliged to difcourfe on reform and economy to a minifter grown old in the pomps and formalities of a court. I remember the addrefs I was obliged to ufe to fucceed, and how, after many repulfes, I fometimes obtained a little attention to the public, as a recompence for the refources I found in the midft of war. I ftill remember the kind of bafhfulnefs I felt when I introduced, in the difcourfes I ventured to addrefs to him, fome of thofe grand moral ideas with which I was animated. I then appeared as gothic to this old courtier as Sully did to the young ones, when he appeared at the court of Louis XIII."

Plans of economy.

The ftate of the finances was at this period very much deranged, though not fo much as to gain credit for the affertion of Rabaud, that a peaceable adminiftration of fifty years, without wars and without wants, would have been infufficient to effect a remedy of diforders[p]. Necker, however, notwithftanding the confidence of his boafts, difplayed no genius capable of producing any great national advantage. The principal act which diftinguifhed his adminiftration was the fuppreffion of the *intendans des finances*. It is of little import at prefent to difcufs the poffible utility of thefe officers; but their fuppreffion was certainly no great national benefit, as the price of their places was refunded to them, and the intereft of the money was nearly equivalent to their falaries, befides the inconvenience of difburfing the capital. Thefe places were filled by old and diftinguifhed members of the king's council, and the fuppreffion could only diminifh the influence of the crown, without producing any real

[p] Rabaud's Hiftory of the Revolution, p. 34.

Mode of raising supplies.

benefit to the nation [q]. The American war, so contrary in every respect to the true interests of France, had commenced at this period; and Necker undertook to carry it on without laying any new imposts. This he was enabled nominally to perform by means of his credit amongst the monied people, and perhaps by the exorbitant sacrifices he made to them, at the public expence. His system was the most absurd and puerile ever invented; he borrowed money for the exigences of one year, and the next borrowed another sum sufficient for the expences of the current year and the interest of the year or years preceding; relying, for a final liquidation, on the precarious resource of an untried, and perhaps impracticable economy. By these means he maintained a forced and artificial credit, but set the example of those improvident loans which occasioned the final stagnation of the finances [r]. In the course of his administration, he borrowed in this way five hundred and thirty millions (23,187,500*l.*), on terms extremely advantageous to the lenders; and subsequent ministers, in the space of ten years, increased the sum to upwards of fifteen hundred millions (65,625,000*l.*), for which no provision was made [s].

Aspires to a seat in the council.

The improvident character of the French, and the triumph of Necker's partisans, prevented the public from speculating too minutely on the consequences of this system. His popularity increased, and with it his vanity; he was no longer contented with the situation of comptroller-general of the finances, unless he could be admitted to a seat in the privy council, for which his religion disqualified him. He made application to M. de Maurepas on

[q] Moore's View. Bertrand's Memoirs. Anecdotes, &c.
[r] Impartial History, vol. i. p. 17. Historical Sketch of the French Revolution, p. 32. Historical Essay on the Ambition and Conquests of France, p. 109.
[s] Anecdotes, &c. Exposition, &c. par Arthur Dillon, p. 4.

the

the subject; but the old minister, wishing perhaps to get rid of him quietly, and make him the author of his own disgrace, advised him to write a letter to the king, requesting a seat, and a dispensation with the customary oath. Necker wrote accordingly; and not receiving any answer for two days, was so irritated that he waited on the queen and offered his resignation, which, to his great mortification, was instantly accepted. This event is attributed, not without some appearance of probability, to the resentment of the parliaments, arising from the establishment of provincial administrations, and the dislike conceived against him by the queen and the count d'Artois [t]. May 1781. Resigns.

Some time previous to his resignation, Necker had published his *Compte rendu*. This method of submitting the views of government and operations of finance to the judgment of the public, was not new: Turgot [u] had set the example, and other ministers before Necker had followed it. His book however was written with more art, and had a greater effect on the public mind, as it was long considered and quoted as the only work which placed the affairs of France in a clear light, and gave occasion to Necker's partisans to hold him out, long after his retreat, as the only man capable of restoring order, and re-establishing public credit. Popular opinion was, for some time after the publication, divided; but it is now generally treated as a splendid delusion [x]. Jan. 1781. Publishes his Compte rendu.

Necker's

---

[t] Bertrand's Memoirs. Moore's View. Historical Sketch, p. 33. Anecdotes, &c. The lively author of this last work relates several instances of the dislike of M. de Maurepas to Necker; particularly a sharp reply when the comptroller, relying on his importance, threatened to take post-horses and return to Geneva. " Sir," said Maurepas, " I " must inform you that foreigners who have been finance ministers in " this country, cannot have post-horses without the express command " of the king." Vol. v. p. 176.

[u] Wilde's Address to the Friends of the People, p. 315.

[x] Moore's View, vol. i. p. 101. Historical Sketch, p. 32. Bertrand's Memoirs, vol. i. p. 151. Of this work Maurepas said to the king,

Observations on Necker's administration;

Necker's first administration undoubtedly paved the way for all the evils which have befallen France since that period, by putting a new and dangerous mode of supply into the hands of ministers; and by suppressing, in a harsh and wanton manner, several offices which, though he might imagine them unnecessary, had been of great service to his predecessors, and might have averted many errors of his successors. His intentions however were perfectly honest, and he had the good of the country at heart. It is but just to give his own statement of the benefits of his administration, which, though much exaggerated, is not, I am persuaded, wilfully misrepresented.—" I was so fortunate (he says) in " the five years of my first administration, that, in " the midst of a war which gradually brought on a " want of extraordinary supplies to the amount of " one hundred and fifty millions (6,562,500*l.*) a " year, the public funds, which sunk in England " from thirty to thirty-five *per cent.*, were gradually " rising in France; and almost all the loans which " were opened were filled in eight days [r]." He also gives himself great credit for the establishment of provincial assemblies, the publicity given to the affairs of finance, and the abolition of mortmain tenures [z].

His disinterestedness.

One singularity attended his conduct in office; that he received no salary or fees of any kind. He states the amount of what he thus renounced, allowing at the rate fixed by the reformed economy of the national assembly at the time he wrote, at two hundred thousand livres (8750 *l.*), independent of his appointments as minister of state, fixed at twenty

---

king, that it was written *with as much truth as modesty*. And the critics, punning on the title, called it a *Conte bleu*. Anecdotes, &c. vol. v. p. 177.
[r] Sur l'Administration de M. Necker, p. 9.
[z] Ibid. p. 16, 17.

thousand livres (875 *l.*). Besides the income annexed to those places, he refused without exception all the indirect emoluments, fines, gifts, presents from corporations and individuals, boxes at the theatres, and all other advantages which had been enjoyed by his predecessors, and often amounted to very large sums [a]. This disinterestedness has not escaped the animadversion of his adversaries: they assert that, as he still continued a partner in the house of Girardot and Haller, he could make more by stock-jobbing in a day than he would derive from his salary in ten years; and that therefore there is more affectation than reality of virtue in the circumstance [b]. There is, however, no proof offered of the justice of these insinuations, and Necker himself meets them in the most manly and satisfactory manner.—" I defy any man (he observes) to aver " that, directly or indirectly, I have had the smallest " interest in any *business whatever*; that I have " had the most trifling share in any speculation in " the public funds; or that I have procured places " for any of my relations or dependants in any of " the offices in my own department, or in that of any " other minister." He adds to this assertion, that, in the beginning of the American war, he advanced to government two millions two hundred thousand livres (96,250 *l.*), at five *per cent.*, which he never on any change of affairs sold out or received, and which he ultimately left behind him [c].

A few years after his retreat, his daughter, who had received a most accomplished education, and was author of several ingenious works, married the baron de Stael, the Swedish ambassador in France.

1786. Marriage of his daughter.

[a] Sur l'Administration de M. Necker, p. 399. Anecdotes, &c. vol. v. p. 167.
[b] Playfair's History of Jacobinism, p. 68. Apologie des Projets & de la Conduite des Chefs de la Revolution, p. 12.
[c] Sur l'Administration de M. Necker, p. 401, 403.

He publishes De l'Administration des Finances.

1784.

During his retreat he was employed in literary pursuits, in assisting the efforts of his friends to force him again into the cabinet, and in keeping up the prepossession of the public in his favour. He published his laborious work on the Administration of Finances; and to make himself better known, and enjoy the buzz of his own celebrity, visited the southern provinces of France. His book was received with enthusiasm, and read with the greatest avidity and admiration. It certainly contains many accurate statements and ingenious deductions, but abounds with that vanity, egotism, and self-sufficiency, which are his characteristics [d]. The true character of the book may be appreciated from the mention made of it by the revolutionary historian Rabaud: he says, "It did perhaps more "good than a long and wise administration; for it "spread knowledge far and wide, and *sowed the* "*seeds of the present patriotism* [e]."

In a recent publication, Necker has asserted that, at the time of his retreat in 1781, he had left the finances in a "perfect equilibrium [f]." This assertion is, at least, doubtful, considering the acknowledged insufficiency of the means he employed to maintain a balance between the receipt and expenditure, and the embarrassments felt by his immediate successors, which rendered them incapable of proceeding without having recourse to the most extraordinary means. Calonne had written an essay to prove that the statements in the *Compte rendu* were false; that instead of a surplus there was an immense deficit in the supplies. Necker, notwith-

1787. Writes an answer to M. de Calonne.

---

[d] Anecdotes, &c. Sur l'Administration, &c. p. 20. Bertrand's Memoirs, vol. i. p. 157. and see the work itself. I suppose this to be the publication alluded to by the author of the "Impartial History," which he confounds with the *Compte rendu*, and with Necker's Answer to Calonne. See vol. i. p. 25.
[e] Rabaud's History of the French Revolution, p. 29.
[f] On the French Revolution, vol. i. p. 13.

standing

standing the king's express prohibition, published an answer, in which he refuted this assertion, and laid the whole blame of the deficit on Calonne. For this conduct he was banished to his country-seat at St. Ouen. It is probable that this offence was not the sole cause of his disgrace: he is said to have been extremely assiduous in procuring writers, painters, and engravers, to impute errors to the administration, and throw ridicule on the person of M. de Calonne. If his banishment was intended as a punishment, it was too slight to produce either respect or terror; if it was intended to weaken his party, the place was ill chosen on account of its vicinity to Paris [g].

Apr. 1787.
Is banished to St. Ouen.

It was probably during his retreat at this place that he wrote his Essay on the Importance of Religious Opinions; a book which, though it contains no great originality of thought, or strength of argument, is written in a style which claims applause for its elegance. The recollection of having produced it seems to have afforded the author some satisfaction in the moment of disgrace, and may probably afford him pleasure when others, of more apparent importance, are obliterated from his memory, or only recur to it attended with sentiments of vexation and disgust [h].

1788.
Writes De l'Importance des Opinions Religieuses.

While he was at St. Ouen, the affairs of France were drawing to a crisis. Calonne had been driven from the helm by the intrigues of the archbishop of Sens, the errors of whose administration embarrassed the court, and rendered the recal of Necker absolutely necessary. His party had not been idle in influencing the popular judgment in his favour;

Exertions of himself and friends

[g] Anecdotes, &c. vol. v. p. 200. 309. 330. Conjuration de d'Orleans, vol. i. p. 63. Rabaud's History of the Revolution, p. 41. Necker, on the French Revolution, vol. i. p. 29 acknowledges himself to have been wrong in this transaction, but pleads that he was impelled to this act of disobedience *by a lively sense of honour*.
[h] Sur l'Administration, &c. p. 22. On the Revolution, vol. i. p. 292.

his work on the administration of finances was generally read during the first assembly of the notables; and the facts contained in it opposed to the statements of that minister [l]. His wife, animated by a spirit of dislike to a court where she could never hope to shine, and feeling indignation at the banishment of her husband, whom she idolized, redoubled her efforts to acquire popularity. She had founded an hospital, and was unremitting in her attendance to the necessities of those who were reduced to make it their abode. She visited the other hospitals, the prisons, and even private houses whereever misery was to be found, stimulated by the desire of raising a conspicuous reputation, and making the name of Necker dear to the people [k]. The political club of females, of which his daughter, the baroness de Stael, was a distinguished member, and the band of political writers, whom the imprudence of the minister had exempted from all restraint, contributed to the recal of the popular favourite [l].

His recal resolved on.

Before the retreat of de Brienne, Necker had been sounded, on the part of the king, to know if he would undertake the administration of the finances, in conjunction with that minister. The seat in council, which had before occasioned his dismission, was to have been conceded: but he rejected the proposal [m]. The increasing turbulence of the people, the growing distress of the court, and a consciousness of his own incapacity and want of popularity, at length compelled de Brienne to resign; and he left his advice to the king, to recal Necker, and convene the states-general [n].

25th Aug. 1788.

---

[l] Sur l'Administration, &c. p. 21.
[k] Idem, p. 397. Playfair's History of Jacobinism, p. 68. Apologie des Projets, &c. p. 18.
[l] Conjuration de d'Orleans.
[m] Necker on the French Revolution, vol. i. p. 29.
[n] Impartial History, vol. i. p. 32. Moore's View, vol. i. p. 87. Anecdotes, &c. vol. v. p. 201.

The

The reinstatement of Necker took place imme- *His rein-*
diately on the resignation of the archbishop of Sens; *statement in office.*
and the queen and count d'Artois are said to have
been no less strenuous in recommending it than de
Brienne himself°. The whole court vied in feli- *Behaviour*
citating the return of a minister from whom the re- *of the court.*
storation of tranquillity and the salvation of the
country were expected. He is said to have had a
private audience of three quarters of an hour with
the queen; and it is asserted that she herself wrote
the letter requesting his return ᵖ: but he himself
makes no mention of these circumstances. He says
the king received him in the queen's closet, and in
her presence; that the king's great good-nature
made him feel some embarrassment on account of
the banishment of the preceding year; but he spoke
to his sovereign only of his devotion and respect;
and from that moment replaced himself on the same
footing he had formerly maintained ᑫ. Monsieur,
on his first public appearance in quality of minister,
complimented him on the occasion, avowed the prejudices he had formerly entertained against him,
and professed a hope that the experience of his mature age would correct the errors of his youth ʳ.

The circumstances which marked his return to *State of*
administration were not calculated to inspire con- *the public*
fidence or impart satisfaction. The ferocity which *mind,*
marked the public rejoicings on the expulsion of
his predecessor, the riots and military execution
which followed, did not presage a calm and stable
administration. In fact, the task he had assumed of
guiding the helm of state, at this particular juncture,
was extremely difficult. Circumstances and indivi-

° Rabaud's History, p. 55.
ᵖ Anecdotes, &c. vol. v. p. 201. Conjuration de d'Orleans, vol. i. p. 165.
ᑫ On the Revolution, vol. i. p. 29.
ʳ Anecdotes, &c. vol. v. p. 202. Conjuration de d'Orleans, vol. i. p. 166.

dual

duals had undergone an entire change since his retreat in 1781. The people, who were at that time, gay, careless, and indifferent to public affairs, now devoted their whole time to the study and discussion of politics. Books, inimical to the interests of government, which were formerly procured from Geneva and London, and circulated in a clandestine and sparing manner, were now boldly published at the *palais royal*, and distributed gratis. A prince, who in 1781 had been considered with the contempt and disregard due to profligacy and cowardice, was now at the head of a violent, numerous, and active party, conferring popularity, or taking it away at pleasure, and by means of the public opinion, making hasty strides towards obtaining the rule of all public measures. The kingdom was plunged in the greatest distress, and, besides the ferment occasioned by political discussion, was agitated with the fear of wanting the first necessary of life. These appearances, however, did not intimidate Necker: the public opinion was his idol; he flattered himself that the more it was permitted to operate without restraint, the greater would be its influence in his favour, and he relied with too much confidence on his own sagacity and resources to feel the least dismay.

His popularity. In fact, his popularity, at this period, was at an unexampled height; the people seemed to look up to him as their only hope, and even to lay themselves at his feet. His return was a complete victory of the public voice over the court, and it has been said, with great truth, that the king was exactly reduced to the state of a bankrupt, who had surrendered his effects to his creditors*.

Recals the parliament and ob- The first step of his administration was to recal the banished members of the parliament of Paris,

---

* Wilde's Address, p. 393. Playfair's History of Jacobinism, p. 85. Sur l'Administration, &c. p. 26.

and to reinstate that body in its functions, in oppo- *tains sup-*
sition to the odious measure of the *cours plenieres* [t]. *plies of money.*
His next exertion was to relieve the embarrassments
occasioned by the distress of the treasury, which, at
the time of his return to office, contained no more
than 500,000 livres (21,875*l*.) [u]. This he effected
by persuading the different public bodies to remit
to him the money they had in hand; by prevailing
on the receivers general, and other persons employed in the finances, not to retain their salaries,
which he promised to repay them in 1789, and by
obtaining loans from the body of notaries of Paris,
and the six mercantile companies [x]. Thus, to use
his own expression, " by sailing with a side wind,
" by using all possible circumspection, and employ-
" ing every exertion in a confined space, he was
" enabled to guide the feeble vessel of state, with-
" out wreck or damage till the opening of the
" states-general [y]."

But a more difficult task awaited him, in the *His exer-*
necessity of finding supplies for the capital, which *obtain a*
occasioned him the greatest uneasiness. He gives *supply of*
himself credit for having saved Paris and the king- *grain.*
dom in general from the horrors of famine [z]. He
obtained from all parts of the kingdom circumstan-
tial information of the quantity of the crops of the
current year, and what remained on hand from
preceding years. He made inquiries into the wants
of other countries, and the resources to be expected
from them, and with all speed obtained an order *7th Sept.*
from the king in council prohibiting the exportation *1788.*
of grain. He offered a bounty for the importation, *23d Nov.*
which procured considerable supplies from Great
Britain and Ireland, till the exportation was pro-

---

t Moore's View, vol. i. p. 102. Rabaud, p. 55, &c.
u Sur l'Administration, &c. p. 28.
x Anecdotes, &c. vol. v. p. 202.
y Sur l'Administration, &c. p. 29.
z Necker on the Revolution, vol. i. p. 31.

hibited,

hibted, from Italy, and the northern kingdoms, and from North America. As this scarcity continued almost during the whole course of his administration, he was obliged to rely not only on the premiums offered in the name of government, but to use his own personal credit with some merchants, Hope of Amsterdam particularly; and he wrote a very pressing letter in 1789, to Mr. Pitt, requesting him to prevail on the king or the parliament to permit the exportation of a limited quantity of grain, but notwithstanding the support given to this request by the French ambassador, it failed of success [a].

Observation on them.

Such is his own account of his exertions, and the success which attended them. The policy by which they were dictated is very doubtful. Necker has not escaped malevolent imputation of having shared with Orleans in his speculation in grain, to participate with him in the profit and popularity resulting from it. He has been accused of sharing with foreign merchants the profits of their premiums, and of buying up grain himself, exporting, and relanding it in order to obtain money and popularity [b]; and a fact related by the marquis de Bouillé, if it does not prove, at least strongly supports these accusations. The marquis says, "Having
" at Metz, and in the province under my com-
" mand, corn sufficient to subsist the troops,
" amounting to twenty thousand men for eighteen
" months, on being pressed by the people, whose
" provisions were almost totally exhausted, and still
" more by the administrative bodies, who could not
" possibly supply them, I proposed to the govern-
" ment to distribute the half of this grain among
" the towns and villages, on condition of again

[a] Sur l'Administration, &c. p. 367. 373. 377. 380.
[b] Conjuration de d'Orleans, vol. i. p. 187. Apologie des Projets, &c. p. 46.

" receiving

" receiving it the enfuing harveft; which might
" have been done without any inconvenience, yet
" was rejected: notwithftanding this refufal of the
" miniftry, I refolved, however, to execute my
" project, and for this I was afterwards thanked by
" M. Necker himfelf, though he at firft refufed his
" confent to the meafure ^{c}." If we can acquit Necker
of criminality in thefe tranfactions, his own account
convicts him of the greateft imprudence. The
publicity given to the apprehenfion of dearth by the
inquiries, and the *circumftantial informations* obtained
at home and in foreign countries, gave room to all
the operations of fpeculifts, and facilitated the fuccefs of their attempts to increafe the public diftrefs,
and inflame the public mind. The premiums,
freight, and other charges, which, according to his
own account ^{d}, amounted to upwards of feventy
millions (3,062,500*l*.), were an enormous load on
an exhaufted treafury, and tended to keep up the
price of the commodity at home, as the poffeffors
of grain could hardly be expected to fell it cheaper
than the importers. It cannot be fuppofed he was
entirely unacquainted with the fchemes of the duke
of Orleans; he has even been accufed of abetting,
but if that was not the cafe he certainly took a very
improper courfe to counteract them ^{e}. His effay on
the legiflation of grain, which he wrote previous to
his firft adminiftration, is very contemptuoufly fpoken
of; and his meafures for the fupply of France are
much decried by perfons well qualified to judge,
and of deferved credit in commercial and agricul-
tural affairs ^{f}.

All thefe efforts would have been infufficient in times fo critical to have kept alive the popular predi-

1775.

Prepares to convene the ftates-general.

^{c} Bouillé's Memoirs, p 91.
^{d} Sur l'Adminiftration, &c. p. 374.
^{e} Conjuration de d'Orleans, vol. i. p. 185. Playfair's Hiftory of Jacobinifm, p. 87.
^{f} Playfair's Hiftory of Jacobinifm, p. 69. Arthur Young's Tra-
vels, p. 105.

lection,

lection, but he was known to be engaged in forwarding the national wish for assembling the states-general. His conduct in this particular has been more forcibly arraigned, and more strenuously defended than in any other; in fact no event so important has occurred, and the turn given to it by the force of his single decision renders him responsible for all its consequences on France and on Europe. The complaints against him on this subject may be reduced to four heads. 1. His having urged the assembling of the states-general at a period so stormy and critical: 2. His procuring a double representation for the *tiers etat:* 3. His leaving undecided the important question, whether the proceedings should be taken by orders or by poll: and 4. His neglecting to influence the elections so as to secure a majority, resolved to maintain the laws and constitution, and to exert themselves only in the reform of abuses.

Examination of his conduct.

On the first of these subjects, Necker excuses himself by observing, that the irritated state of the public mind could by no means be attributed to him; that he was not the author of those financial embarrassments which occasioned it; that the reform of internal abuses could only be expected from the states-general; that the inundation of political pamphlets which overwhelmed the public, owed its origin to an *arrêt* of his predecessor, and that the king, who had pledged himself to convene the states-general, was too religious an observer of his promise, to have endured a minister who advised a breach of it [t]. Without cavilling on the precise truth of each of these assertions, it is very obvious that they were insufficient to justify the measure they were intended to defend. Necker knew, that the promise of convening the states, was made under

---

[t] See Necker on the Revolution, vol. i. p. 30. and the following. Sur l'Administration, &c. p. 33. and the following.

an idea that the finances were irretrievably embarrassed, that such an impression was in a great measure derived from his writings, and from the reports of his friends and agents. He knew that at the time it was given, a rash minister had, by an unpopular innovation, and unjustifiable and absurd proceedings, created an irreparable breach between the constituted authorities, between the king and the parliament. He knew that his popularity and ascendancy were sufficient to have restored harmony, to have given energy to the government, and content to the well-disposed part of the community. He knew, and has acknowledged, that the state of the finances was not such as to require any extraordinary intervention [h]. In fact this was a mere pretence to make himself of consequence by alarming the king with false terrors, and insinuating to the people unfounded hopes [i]. It is of little importance to whom the licentiousness of the press was to be attributed, its existence was a subject of universal astonishment [k]; its force was derived from an idea of public distress and exemptions of the privileged orders; the former Necker might have demonstrated to be a mere phantom, the latter, possessing as he did the entire confidence of the court and nobility, he might easily have acquired the credit of modifying or abrogating, without injury to the constitution. But the king's promise!— This indeed was a terrible obstacle. If the people had been convinced that their welfare was effectually secured without the intervention of an authority to the effects of which they were strangers, they would have been very little solicitous about a strict compliance with a promise from which they

---

[h] Sur l'Administration, p. 36.
[i] On the Revolution, vol. i. p. 31.
[k] Necker himself is accused, and I believe justly, of having increased and favoured this licentiousness in order to promote the success of his own views. See Bouillé's Memoirs, p. 88. 126.

could

could have derived no advantage. I am far from being inclined to question the stedfast virtue of the unfortunate Louis; but had prudent and vigorous measures been adopted, and a little delay interposed, the popular ardour would have cooled, and the states-general have met for no other purposes than thanks and congratulatory addresses. It has been observed that Calonne convoked the notables, not to discuss but to admire his plans [1]; the same may be said of Necker with respect to the states-general. He looked forward with confidence to their meeting [m], and anticipated the pleasure of placing a line of forbearance between the power of the superior, and encroachment of the inferior orders. A splendid vision, fit to inflame the fancy of a young speculist, but a shameful result of his age and experience.

Second objection examined.

The same motives which induced him to effect the convocation of the states-general, undoubtedly influenced him to promote the double representation of the *tiers etat*. His perseverance in this point is remarkable, and no propriety of intention can acquit him of the blame attached to the consequences. Conscious of this truth, Necker has defended himself with great warmth, and at much length, though without any great effect. His apology rests principally on the uncertainty of the antient precedents; on the eagerness of public expectation; the diffusion of light; and the unimportance of number, if the estates voted by order [n]. Every consideration which could be drawn from

---

[1] Impartial History, vol. i. p. 25.
[m] In [proof of this assertion, see Sur l'Administration, &c. p. 31, 32, 33, and the following pages, where this objection is discussed by himself. This work was published in 1791, and intended to be read in France. His book called "On the French Revolution" must be perused with more caution on this particular topic, as it was written five years later, when more horrible calamities had resulted from his fatal error.
[n] On the Revolution, vol. i.

these

these principles, ought to have produced a decision in the mind of the minister contrary to that he adopted. The uncertainty which prevailed in times of darkness and ignorance could not be any ground of determination, and the desire of distinction, the affectation of knowledge, and the solicitude to gratify public expectation, which were prevalent, should have made him very cautious of trusting those powers to a greater number than was absolutely necessary. A great body of the *tiers etat* in 1614, had a great body been really collected, would have been of small importance, easily overpowered by argument, easily dispersed by force; but in 1789, a very small body, supported by the public opinion, strong in intelligence, and active in research, could not have been restrained or dispersed by any power possessed by government: had they only equalled either of the other orders, they would have been respectable and indivisible, but the pride and imposing aspect of a large majority, or duplication, could not fail, as in fact it happened, to render them haughty, restless, turbulent, and overbearing; in short, to occasion the subjugation and destruction of the other two classes. Necker could not err through ignorance, as he had taken every possible means to obtain information; he certainly was not malicious enough to wish the overthrow of that prince who placed the most implicit confidence in him, and for whom he constantly professes the sincerest affection; vanity alone must have influenced his determination, the wish to do good, and the fond expectation of making himself illustrious in the eyes of a numerous and enlightened assembly, perverted his judgment, and occasioned this egregious error. Imperfectly acquainted with the laws and customs of France, he appointed certain persons to search into historical registers, for the forms of convening the states-general on preceding occasions; but as their report, in all probability, contained nothing in support of his favourite plan, he never published it. The parliament of Paris passed a decree, to the surprise of most people, that the states should be convened in the same manner as in 1614; but this step, in which they exceeded their authority, only exposed them to unpopularity and contempt, and accelerated their annihilation, without altering the resolution of the minister. He prevailed on the king to convene the same notables as had been assembled by Calonne; they were divided into six committees, the majority of all of which, except one, recommended the model of 1614; that one was the section of Monsieur, where, by the majority of a single vote, the question of a double representation was carried in the affirmative. Yet the concurrence of all these opinions could not alter the determination of Necker[o]. The only reason he gives for this invincible obstinacy is, that though it occasioned him a great deal of pain to differ in opinion from the notables, yet this difference was insurmountable, because the impulse of his conscience, and the welfare of the state, according to his ideas, (*selon mes lumières,*) imposed on him as a rigorous duty to follow the line of conduct he adopted on that memorable occasion [p].

Third objection examined. Necker says in his own defence, that the great question in 1789, and at all times, was not the respective number of the deputies of the three orders, but their manner of deliberating, by head or by bailiwick, with the orders conjoined or separate [q]. If he was really impressed with the importance of this question, and felt all the consequences which must result from its decision, it is matter of great astonishment that he should not fix

[o] Moore's View, vol. i. p. 106—113. Bertrand's Memoirs, vol. i. p. 157. Exposition abrégé, par A. Dillon, p. 8. See also the Impartial History, Rabaud, &c. &c.
[p] Sur l'Administration, &c. p. 44.
[q] On the Revolution, vol. i. p. 66.

it on some certain basis, but leave it open to the determination of the parties themselves, assembled and judging with asperity of each other's views and encroachments. The notables declared their opinion in favour of a separate consultation, and of voting by orders, which left to the *tiers etat* their due share in the deliberative administration. Necker, in affecting to leave this question open, while he decided that of double representation, betrays a share of duplicity which derogates much from his moral character; he must have previously resolved it in his own mind, for, in fact, the decision of the one question virtually determines the other. It is mere affectation to say, that if the states-general voted by orders, the numeration of the *tiers etat* was a matter of indifference. If the *tiers etat* equalled in number the other two estates collectively, it is manifest they could carry every point, without affecting the least deference to them, if they voted by poll; or if they only equalled one of the other two, their body united, availing itself of cabal, clamour, and public opinion, would assuredly have been able, on most questions, to have secured a majority. A body composed of many members is more imposing in its general appearance, and attaches to itself a greater share of consideration than would be bestowed on one of half its magnitude; and it was obvious that should the *tiers etat*, composed of a double number, by obstinate clamour, by exciting the people, or through the necessities of the state, ever succeed in obtaining a consultation, or joint operation with the other orders, their victory would then be complete, and the clergy and nobility for ever chained to a dependence on them. To leave, therefore, the determination of this question to the states-general assembled, was, in fact, as Rabaud says[r], giving the victory to the stronger, and as he had already de-

[r] History of the Revolution, p. 65.

cided, on his own authority, to which party that epithet should apply, he had resolved to be answerable for all the consequences of the determination of both these important questions [*].

Fourth objection examined. At least it might have been expected, that Necker having determined on an experiment so novel and hazardous as that of throwing so large a share of power and consequence into the hands of the *tiers etat*, would have endeavoured to prevent the abuse of it, by influencing the elections, so as to procure the return of as many of the king's friends and men of moderate views as possible. The author of the essay on the importance of religious opinions could not be ignorant that, in France, religion was falling into contempt, and that the ministers of it were regarded with jealousy and hatred. He could not be uninformed of the bias given to the public opinion by the swarm of pamphlets daily issued; or of the efforts of the duke of Orleans and other persons to give effect to this perversion of judgment by influencing the elections, and procuring the *cahiers*, or intended instructions to the deputies to be written in a style corresponding with their dangerous views. It was then his duty, as a faithful servant of the crown, to have counteracted these attempts by an exertion of his popularity, and by the interposition of his influence. This, he says, his sense of honour forbad, nor did he think it necessary, as it was of less importance that the king should have friends in the states-general than in the nation at large [†]. Weak and miserable sophistry! If every speculative egotist was permitted to share the popular suffrage, what portion could possibly be left for the monarch? And what could defend his rights and those of the privileged orders, in the present state of the popular mind, from invasion

---

[*] Moore's View, vol. i. p. 104. Pagès Histoire Secrete, vol. i. p. 80. Historical Sketch, p. 52. See also the other histories of the period. [†] On the Revolution, p. 89.

and

and destruction, but a due care to counteract those who were openly forming a party against them, and whose influence over the public opinion threatened the most alarming consequences. But though his sense of honour prevented his influencing any returns favourable to the superior orders, he did not feel the same delicacy with respect to the *tiers etat*, for whom, besides their advantage of double representation, he contrived to procure such a preponderance in the clerical body, as was alone sufficient to insure success to any attack they might choose to make on the privileged orders. This was effected by overpowering the suffrages of the beneficiaries, dignitaries, and great proprietors of church lands, by admitting the salaried curates, who, in every respect, relating to the purposes of their convocation, belonged to the *tiers etat*, to a numerical equality of vote. On the other hand, the canons and monks, who were attached to the higher order of the clergy, were deprived of their counterpoise by a regulation which restricted their sending more than one in ten of their number to the electoral assemblies. Hence the great disproportion between the *curés* and the higher clergy in the assembly of the states [u]. In like manner to overwhelm the

[u] Exposition abrégé, par Arthur Dillon, p. 12. M. de Bouillé says: "The states-general consisted of men very proper for the execution of Necker's purposes. The ecclesiastical members were principally chosen from among the inferior clergy, without livings or property, opposed to those of the higher order, who were fewer in number. Among the representatives of the nobility were many of those subtle, daring, enterprising men, who had introduced themselves with a view to corrupt and divide that order: lastly, the third estate were allowed a double representation. This assembly was open to that description of men, so numerous and dangerous in France, who lived by their talents, their literary abilities, and their industry, deriving their importance from the weakness and credulity of mankind—lawyers, principally of the lowest class, physicians, artists, writers of little or no eminence, and men without either rank or property." The author adds in a note, "Of three hundred members which represented the clergy, two hundred and eight were possessed of no ecclesiastical dignity: of six hundred members who represented the *tiers etat*, three hundred and seventy-four were professors of the law." Memoirs, p. 88.

influence of landed proprietors, he procured special decrees of council, forbidding the country electors from interfering or voting in elections for towns and cities, but permitting the inhabitants of these to vote in the country bailliages, by which means a great number of provincial lawyers and needy speculists were returned, to the exclusion of the more respectable cast of candidates [x]. He also shewed his decided preference of the *tiers etat* by suspending, by order of council, all judicial proceedings commenced in Britanny, on account of the popular insurrections [y].

In these observations I have, in some measure, anticipated events; but to resume the course of narration: soon after the dissolution of the notables, the minister made a report to the king in council, which was afterwards published, wherein he displayed a shallowness, egotism, and vanity, entitled to commiseration; he traversed, with a sophistry unworthy a minister, the decisions of the notables, and giving as a motive the *imposing minority* of the notables, and what he calls *le bruit sourd de l'Europe*, decided the most important questions which had engaged their attention, in a manner entirely different from them. He determined that the *tiers etat* should have a double representation, but *advised* them not to insist on voting by poll, but always in different orders; he flattered their vanity and elevated their insolence, by attributing to them all the knowledge and respectability which remained in the kingdom; he insulted the crown by an affectedly philosophical declamation on the advantages of an abridged jurisdiction; and to shew that the probable mischiefs of his measures were not out of his contemplation, that they might probably produce the disorganization of all authority, the influx of

Report to council. Dec. 1788.

---

[x] Bouillé's Memoirs, p. 14.
[y] Bertrand's Memoirs, vol. i. p. 159.

all

'all licentioufnefs, he *modeftly* affures the king, as a recompence for what he might fuffer, that he would ftill retain the power *of difmiffing the minifter who had influenced his deliberations* [z].

Necker's conduct in the whole of this bufinefs appears fo remote from wifdom and fo perverfe, that his motives are not eafily defined. I do not believe he was influenced by avarice; his fortune was already made; and againft the charges of gratifying religious pride by the abafement of the clergy, and of indulging his natural prejudice in favour of democracy, by the debafement of the fuperior orders, he has ably defended himfelf [a]. He avows, indeed, that one of his motives was the hope of retaining his fituation, in fpite of the will of the fovereign [b], but even that defire, and all the reft of his conduct may be referred to the impulfe of vanity, which in him prevailed as a paffion, and fubdued reafon. Flattered by the popularity conferred on him by circumftances, raifed by the corrupting influence of unvaried fuccefs to a peculiar complacency of felf-contemplation, it is not wonderful that he was fo far the dupe of his own confidence, as to believe that when once he had advanced his popularity to the higheft pitch, by gaining for the people, in oppofition to the notables and the privileged orders, what they fo ardently defired, he fhould be able to mould their reprefentatives to his will, and, by exerting his influence between them and the king, be enabled to bring

Obfervations on his conduct.

---

[z] Moore's View, vol. i. p. 113 to 120. Expofition, &c. par Arthur Dillon, p. 10. Wilde's Addrefs, p. 392.
[a] On the Revolution, vol. i. p. 313. See alfo Bertrand's Memoirs, vol. i. p. 177.
[b] " J'avois connu mieux que perfonne, combien étoit inftable & " paffager le bien que l'on pouvoit faire fous un gouvernement où les " principes d'adminiftration changent au gré des miniftres, & les mi- " niftres au gré de l'intrigue. J'avois bfervé que dans le cours paffager " de l'adminiftration des hommes publics, aucune idée générale " n'avoit le tems de s'etablir, aucun bienfait ne pouvoit fe confolider." Sur l'Adminiftration, &c. p. 36.

about such reforms, both in the government and finances, as he thought necessary.

His popularity and influence. At this period Necker's popularity was unbounded, and the court placed implicit reliance on the integrity of his motives and the efficacy of his endeavours; for though the princes of the blood, except Orleans, had united in presenting to the crown a memorial respecting the inflamed state of the public mind, and the danger of a revolution in the opinion of the people respecting the necessary form of government, Necker's opinion was adopted by the council, and, in spite of the remonstrances of some of their more anxious and clear-sighted friends, recommended by the queen, and sanctioned by the king [c].

This confidence ought to have been repaid by a most zealous attention to the happiness and welfare of the royal family, but that was not the case; for though it is notorious, that during the whole of Necker's administration, the most shameful libels on them and on the whole court were profusely circulated, and produced the most baleful effect, he did not take the slightest step towards preventing or even discouraging them; and though irritable, and even vindictive at the most trifling sarcasm against himself, he suffered those against every other person to go unpunished [d].

1788-9. Severity of the winter. His report was published at a very critical period, when the people were distressed by the rigour of an excessively cold winter, alarmed by the fear of want, and supported only by the charitable donations of the rich. Necker had exhibited considerable affectation of philanthropy on this point. I have already mentioned his exertions with respect to grain, and in addition to these he made a public experiment

---

[c] Historical Sketches, p. 81. Bertrand's Memoirs, vol. i. p. 159 and 161. Wilde's Address, p. 392.
[d] See Young's Travels, p. 104. Bertrand's Memoirs, vol. i. p. 153.

respecting

respecting butchers' meat. He sent to St. Germain for an ox, had it weighed, killed, and weighed again, deducting the skin, horns, hoofs, &c. He demonstrated that the butchers sold at a profit of fifty *per cent.* but the information was the only advantage which resulted to the public, as no attempt was made to reduce the price of provisions [e]. Yet these trifles augmented the popularity of the minister, and he was desirous of deriving every advantage from it, by procuring the assembly to be held at Paris. This he has since acknowledged to be an error, and acquiesces in the propriety of their judgment who over-ruled his, and made Versailles the place of sitting. But had the operation of circumstances, and the known intrigues of persons in the capital been duly adverted to, the place of sitting should have been still farther removed from that pestilential atmosphere [f].

At length the states-general were opened at Versailles. The day commenced with an act of religion: the deputies attended the king to the church of St. Louis, where a sermon was preached by the bishop of Nancy, on the importance of religion to the well-being of a state. From church they went to the hall appointed for the states. The king was seated on a throne, the queen on one at his side, but not so high; the princes of the blood (except Orleans) were seated around; the clergy and noblesse at opposite sides of the hall; and the *tiers etat* at the lower end. The king made a speech, in which he complimented the states on their meeting, adverted to the condition of the revenue, and pointed out many objects of public importance to their attention. He was followed by M. Barretin, keeper of the seals, who said his majesty had complied with the wishes of his subjects in granting a double

5th May 1789. Assembly of the states-general.

---

[e] Playfair's History of Jacobinism, p. 96.
[f] Impartial History, vol. i. p. 68. Rabaud, p. 67. Sur l'Administration, &c. p. 61. 63. Wilde's Address, p. 490.

representation

reprefentation to the *tiers etat;* but left to the three orders to adjuft amongft themfelves the point of voting by orders or by poll. This fpeech was little attended to; but Necker's, which lafted three hours, was complimented by the moft profound and uninterrupted attention. The oration however gave but little fatisfaction; he was not beloved by the nobility or clergy, and the *tiers etat*, influenced by faction, and bent on extenfive plans of reform, received his moderate ideas with contempt and anger, and liftened with impatience to his financial calculations. Many ftrictures on his fpeech were publifhed; and from them he might have learnt more properly to appreciate his own talents and popularity [g]. It is afferted, that he paid more attention to the ftyle and delivery than to the matter of the harangue. The following character of, and anecdote refpecting it, are fupplied by Arthur Young [h].
—" The worft thing I know of Necker is his fpeech
" to the ftates on their affembling; a great oppor-
" tunity, but loft: no great leading or mafterly
" views; no decifion on circumftances in which the
" people ought to be relieved, and new principles
" of government adopted. It is the fpeech you
" would expect from a banker's clerk of fome abi-
" lity. Concerning it there is an anecdote worth
" inferting: he knew his voice would not enable
" him to go through the whole of it in fo large a
" room, and to fo numerous an affembly; and
" therefore he had fpoken to Monf. de Brouffonet,
" of the academy of fciences, and fecretary to the
" royal fociety of agriculture, to be in readinefs to

---

[g] Impartial Hiftory, vol. i. p. 73. Rabaud's Hiftory, p. 74, 75, See Obfervations on the place of fitting and manner of debating, Young's Travels, vol. i. p. 110. Amongft the moft fevere cenfors of Necker was Mirabeau, whofe journal was fuppreffed by an order of council obtained at Necker's requeft. Young's Travels, p. 113. Moore's View, vol. i. p. 201. See alfo Playfair's Hiftory of Jacobinifm, p. 116. A. Dillon's Expofition abrégé, p. 16, 17.
[h] Travels, p. 109.

" read

"read it for him. He had been present at an annual general meeting of that society, when Monſ. Brouſſonet had made a diſcourſe with a powerful piercing voice, that was heard diſtinctly to the greateſt diſtance. This gentleman attended him ſeveral times to take his inſtructions, and be ſure of underſtanding the interlineations that were made ſoon after the ſpeech was finiſhed. M. Brouſſonet was with him in the evening before the aſſembly of the ſtates, at nine o'clock; and next day, when he came to read it in public, he found ſtill more corrections and alterations, which Necker had made after quitting him: they were chiefly in ſtyle, and ſhew how very ſolicitous he was in regard to the form and decoration of his matter. The ideas, in my opinion, wanted this attention more than the ſtyle. M. Brouſſonet himſelf told me this little anecdote."

The ſtates-general were thus compoſed [1]:

The Clergy were repreſented by

Compoſition of the three orders.

48 Biſhops and archbiſhops;
35 Abbés, canons, or beneficed clergymen; and
208 Curés, or clergymen having livings with the cure of ſouls.

———
291

———

[1] Conjuration de d'Orleans, vol. i. p. 286. "The nobility and higher order of the clergy of Britanny had refuſed to name their deputies to the ſtates-general, upon the pretence that the form of their convocation was contrary to the cuſtoms and privileges of the province. The ten deputies that the higher clergy had named, were re-placed by ten curates who belonged to the order *du tiers*, at leaſt by birth; but the twenty-one deputies which the nobleſſe of Britanny ought to have ſent, were not replaced by the other provinces; therefore the order of the nobility had, in the ſtates-general, twenty-one members leſs; and the order of the tiers had about ten members more than they ought." Bertrand's Memoirs, vol. i. p. 183.

The Nobility, by

 18 Grand baillis, fenechaux, or heads of diftricts;
224 Gentlemen, or men of family; and
 28 Magiftrates of the fuperior courts.

270

The Tiers Etat, by

  2 Ecclefiaftics, or beneficed clergymen;
 12 Gentlemen of family;
 16 Phyficians;
 18 Mayors, or heads of corporations;
162 Officers of bailliages, or inferior courts of juftice;
176 Bourgeois, merchants, land-owners, and farmers; and
212 Lawyers.

598

Impolicy of the proceedings with refpect to drefs, &c.   The latter order having fo great a majority, and being fo completely in poffeffion of the public predilection, it would have fhewn wifdom as well as moderation in the two fuperior orders, and in the court, to have acquired a fhare in the good opinion of the people, if poffible, by treating them with apparent refpect and diftinction. This however was not done. On the day of their proceffion to Verfailles, the drefs was arranged by an order from the court: that of the clergy and nobility was pompous and impofing, and the wealth and tafte of many of the wearers enabled them to render it brilliant and dazzling: that of the *tiers etat* confifted merely of a little black ftuff cloak, fuch as was worn by fome of the profeffion of lawyers, and which, joined to any other drefs than black, which many of the members did not wear, had a mean and ridiculous appearance. But the effect on the populace was entirely

entirely different from what this spectacle might have been expected to produce. At the approach of every individual of the superior orders, (except Orleans,) silence, or clamorous reproach intermingled with threats, prevailed; while the humbly-clad members of the favourite order were hailed with shouts of *Vive le tiers etat*; and many of them friends of Orleans congratulated by name. In like manner their reception in the hall of assembly inspired disgust: to the clergy and nobility, both the folding doors were thrown open; to the *tiers etat*, only one. The distinction may be maintained by precedent; but so much of established usage had been already foregone, and the people were disposed to demand a relinquishment of so much more, that sound policy would have dictated a little flexibility on the occasion; for the temper of the people, notwithstanding the new lights they had gained from philosophy, was not sufficiently philosophical to look on these trifles with unconcern, or even without considerable rancour [k].

The *tiers etat*, obedient to the injunctions of the party who procured the return of the majority, and heated by the applauses and instigations of the pamphleteers, lost no time to avail themselves of the advantage which their superiority in number gave them over the other two classes. They resisted every step which tended to establish a precedent of their sitting in different chambers, or voting by orders; they would not even proceed to a verification of their powers, unless the other two orders would meet with them in the common hall. The nobility and clergy, sensible that they were contending for their existence, opposed this measure with great obstinacy for several weeks, the majority of each refusing to take a step which had an obvious

Obstinacy of the tiers etat.

[k] Pagès, vol. i. p. 98. and Moore's View, vol. i. p. 146. et seq.

tendency

tendency to their political destruction. Public business was at a stand; the people became clamorous; the king proposed a conciliatory measure in vain; the *tiers etat* resolutely rejected every plan but an unconditional association of all the orders, and a community of debate and operation. Encouraged at length by the partiality of the people, and anxious to do something in their new character, the deputies, after sending repeated messages inviting the clergy and nobility to join them, proceeded to a verification of their powers. They were at this time joined only by three curés: these men, disgusted at their want of importance amongst the dignitaries of the church, threw themselves into the arms of the *tiers etat*, who received them with transport, looking on the event as a prelude to a complete victory on their part. They proceeded to business without loss of time; and having, after a debate of much length, and in which great affectation of verbal precision was displayed, adopted the name of THE NATIONAL ASSEMBLY, set about reforming the state, with an eagerness which promised dispatch. They declared the total illegality of all the existing taxes, permitting them, however, to be provisionally collected for the present, and till their further order, or dissolution, from what cause soever. They further declared, that they would take into consideration the national debt; but that for the present the creditors of the state were under the safeguard of the honour of the French nation. The majority of the clergy, after a long discussion in what manner they should verify their powers, resolved to join the national assembly [1].

17th July 1789.

Necker proposes a royal sitting.

Meantime the minister, whose vanity had led him to suppose that he could restrain the disorderly motions of the assembly whenever he thought proper; whose equivocal declarations at

---

[1] Impartial History. Rabaud. Conjuration de d'Orleans, &c.

their

their first meeting, and whose conduct since, had produced and inflamed much of the acrimonious spirit they betrayed; alarmed at the importance of the steps already taken, advised the king to proclaim a royal sitting without delay, and there to deliver a speech, containing a plan of government or declaration of rights, which he had composed, and which he expected would tend much to conciliate the minds of the *tiers etat*. The confidence of the king was not in the least abated, and he resolved to follow this advice without delay. Accordingly, on 20th June. the day the clergy had appointed to join the national assembly, the heralds proclaimed a royal sitting for the 22d; and that, in consequence of the preparations which must necessarily be made in the halls of the three orders, a suspension of the sittings must take place till after that day. This produced the famous oath of the tennis-court, and the subsequent resolutions and transactions [m].

During this interval, while the king was at Marli, Necker's and the plan of his declaration or speech at the royal plan of government session was under discussion in the council, he was altered in induced to make some alterations in the words or council. form of it. Necker, who had been used to see his dictates implicitly followed, seems to have resented this proceeding. Some writers have asserted that the alterations were very immaterial, a mere change of words [n]: Necker asserts that his plan was altered in many important particulars, and specifies some, but does not give the whole in its perfect state, alleging that it was burnt by a friend to whom he had lent it [o]. Bertrand, however, has pointed out many of the variations, which seem very reasonable, and nothing more than the temperate efforts of the king's relatives and counsellors to prevent the royal authority and the privileges of the

[m] See BAILLY. [n] Moore's View, vol. i. p. 232.
[o] On the Revolution, vol. i. p. 172, 173.

superior

superior orders from being unconditionally laid at the feet of the *tiers etat* [p]. I shall resume the discussion of Necker's conduct; but first relate the transactions of the day, only premising, that Necker's intended resignation was generally circulated and credited.

23d June. Royal sitting.

In the midst of jealousies, alarms, and evil impressions, the royal sitting was held. The streets of Versailles were lined with guards, the hall of the states was surrounded, and none but deputies admitted [q]. While the nobility and clergy were taking their places, the *tiers etat* were obliged to shelter themselves in an out-house from the rain, and when admitted, were not accommodated with seats. These were most injudicious measures, and tended to increase the prevailing jealousy, and add to the discontents of the day. The king arrived soon after the deputies were placed, attended by a pompous retinue, the princes of the blood, the dukes and peers: four heralds and their king at arms were placed about the throne and in the middle of the hall; before the throne was a table, at which the ministers were seated, except Necker, who did not attend. This circumstance, which seemed to indicate a disapprobation of the measures in agitation, increased the dissatisfaction of the members; and their gloom received a still deeper shade from the accident of M. Paporet, one of the king's secretaries, falling down in an apoplectic fit, and expiring in the hall.

The king's speech.

Thus surrounded by disgust, prejudice, and dissatisfaction, divested of the only person whose countenance would have restored to him, in any degree, the good opinion of the small portion among those subjects who remained untainted by the contagion of disloyalty, he opened the session by an introduc-

[p] Memoirs, vol. i. p. 162.
[q] Arthur Young's Travels, p. 118.

tory discourse, after which the plan was read. It annulled the proceedings of the national assembly; recommended the liberty of the press, subject to certain restrictions; and the abolition of *lettres-de-cachet*, if it could be done consistently with the well-being of individuals and of the public. The king was restrained from imposing any new tax without the consent of the national representatives, and all exemptions from the payment of taxes were done away: the *corvées* were abolished: the distinction of orders was to be preserved, allowing, however, the three estates to meet and debate in common, with the king's approbation. Many other reforms were proposed, and the whole plan evinced a disposition to consult the real good, and anticipate many wishes of the people, which was certainly entitled to the greatest gratitude from their representatives. It was received with a profound silence, rather indicative of discontent than approbation; and the king, having ordered the assembly to separate and meet him there the next day, retired, attended by the nobility and part of the clergy.

The assembly, notwithstanding this order, delivered by the king in person, and enforced by a message delivered by M. de Brézé, grand-master of the ceremonies, commenced an active debate, or rather a series of vituperative protests against the proceedings of the day, which Camus called by the contemptuous and unpopular name of *a bed of justice*. They entered into resolutions declaratory of their adherence to their former decrees, that the persons of the deputies of the people were inviolable, and denounced penalties of high treason against those who should molest them. They seemed to contemn the bounties offered so freely by the king, which, if they did not amount to all that sanguine and interested speculists could desire, formed however a basis on which might have been erected a permanent temple of national felicity. The demagogues of the assembly

Proceedings of the assembly.

bly seemed jealous left the purity and benevolence of the king's intentions should be impartially considered by the people, and to have seized with malignant avidity the opportunity offered by the appearance of the marquis de Brézé, to sanction an act of audacious rebellion, and openly contest the palm of public favour with the king [r].

Observations on Necker's conduct.

The whole conduct of Necker on this occasion was so extraordinary, and so remote from propriety, as to justify the reproaches with which the royalist writers have assailed him, and to give strong suspicions of his caballing with the Orleans faction to maintain his power. The ostensible pretence for his absence was his attendance on a sick sister-in-law; but whatever may be said of the feelings of humanity and consanguinity, the man who undertook, in times so replete with trouble and peril, to manage the affairs of a great kingdom, was bound to suspend for a time their dictates, in order to perform duties more important. Necker well knew that much of the clamour raised on the false report of an intended dissolution of the assembly, was the work of a party, and had been at the pains to contradict it in writing; yet he did not possess firmness of character or self-denial enough to risk the loss of any of that popularity of which he was so foolishly enamoured, by appearing to support a measure against which he had some reason to think an outcry would be raised. The *illness of a sister-in-law* was but a weak excuse for evading the duties of his station, knowing as he did that, but a few days before, the king had been *forced* to receive a deputation of the assembly, and give his attention to business, although afflicted by the recent *death of a son*. Necker has been at great pains to justify himself in his two apologetical publications. In that published

---

[r] For the narrative of this day's proceedings and remarks on it, according to their different principles, see Rabaud, Moore's View, Pagès, Bertrand, &c. &c.

in 1797, and addressed to the world at large, who had seen with astonishment the result of his measures, he uses arguments and assertions to the following purport: he says that, from the material alterations which had been made in his plan, he was determined to retire from administration, but would not give in his formal resignation before the session, which was to be held the next day. For this he gives no reason, but says, "The delay was not long; and without attaching an *indiscreet importance* to myself and my actions, I thought this a *proper forbearance*. I did not however attend at this solemn assembly: it was not right for me to do so; for, if I had, the public would have considered my resignation as a resolution decided by the want of success of a measure which I had advised. It was too much also, I confess, that *those who carried it against me should oblige me to quit the ministry, and at the same time force me to ruin myself in the public opinion, by ostensibly concurring in a step absolutely contrary to my views and counsels*[*]." This sentence is remarkable for vanity and treachery. If Necker really intended to quit the ministry, (which I do not believe to have been the fact,) to whom was this *proper forbearance* shewn?—Not to the king or the court; for to the court he does not hesitate at this distance of time to express his malevolence; not to the king, for he would not assist him even with his presence, but by his absence made his repugnance to his plan the more striking and obvious. His forbearance was selfish: he saw that a division was likely to arise between the king and his subjects; he resolved, instead of carrying the weight of popular opinion which he then possessed to the side of royalty, to contribute all in his power to the success of the opposing faction: in a word, he resolved to be the

[*] On the Revolution, vol. i. p. 202.

minister of the assembly, and not of the king. Though he had not announced his intended resignation to the king, it had been spread assiduously enough among the people, and was, by the arts of his party, universally deprecated [*]. He had been for some time in fear that the party in the cabinet adversarious to his views would gain the ascendancy; and therefore resolved, by a marked opposition to them, to ruin them in the public opinion, regardless of the consequences to the king, if his own authority was secured. In this view of the subject, it is not too much to suppose that, by a refinement of treachery, he proposed the royal sitting, a novel, and, as he himself confesses, a very bold and delicate measure [†]; and then, availing himself of the differences in council, refused to sanction the prosecution of it, but left the court to contend with the disgrace in which he had involved them. At least this is certain, that the measure, to have been efficacious, should have been suggested much sooner: it should also have been preceded by conciliatory declarations, and announced as an instance of royal benevolence. Instead of this, Necker permitted it to be whispered about with all the mysteriousness which begets distrust, to be announced with an air of authority already grown odious to the populace: he permitted the line of separation to be drawn between the sentiments of the court and those of the public; and instead of any attempt to harmonise them, aggravated the slightest shades of distinction, and eagerly attached himself to the popular side.

Thus far I have examined Necker's defence as held out in his last publication, but in his preceding apology, written in 1791, he appears not to have so well digested his spleen, or prepared his story; in that he shews more anger, and exhibits his reso-

[*] See Arthur Young's Travels, p. 108. 114 to 118.
[†] On the Revolution, vol. i. p. 185. 293. Sur l'Administration, &c. p. 110.

lution to be popular with lefs referve[a]. He there accufes the council of having perverted his plan from its original meaning, and fays, "that, by de-grees, though they appeared to retain *part of his project, they refcinded all that conftituted its effence, all that could render it agreeable to the commons.*" He obferves, with the mean infidioufnefs of a man who wifhes to return to office, in fpite of the king, who at the time he wrote was ftill king, "It was a remarkable fingularity, that the court fhould think the ftyle, rather firm and lofty, which was proper when the king enjoined the two fuperior orders to unite themfelves with the commons, *in their labours for the public good*, was equally applicable to a ftep, *the fenfe of which was abfolutely different.*" In the following page he fays, "I defended my ideas and combated the innovations with the greateft ftrength; I courageoufly refifted the opinions of the princes called in to this difcuffion, and after preferving, to the laft moment, my hope of effecting the triumph of reafon, I confidered what line of conduct I ought to adopt, as to myfelf individually, and after a deliberate examination, and many internal ftruggles, occafioned by the difficulty of the conjuncture, I thought that I could not, in honour, attend the fitting of the 23d of June, or retain my place in the miniftry; and if I did not make the king acquainted with my final determination, it was for fear of receiving a pofitive order, which it would have been impoffible for me to obey."

Much of the agitation of this memorable day is, doubtlefs, to be attributed to the faction of Orleans, as his friends and privy-counfellors were moft active in promoting it[x], but Necker, if he be ac-

23d June. Further events and conduct of Necker.

---

[a] Sur l'Adminiftration, &c. p. 109 to 112.
[x] Conjuration de d'Orleans, vol. i. p. 297, et feq. See alfo Young's Travels, p. 117. See ORLEANS.

quitted

quitted of being the accomplice, claims his full share in all the events by which it was distinguished. His popularity was so great, that the king was apprehensive of the consequences of his rumoured resignation, and in the evening sent for him to the palace, and both he and the queen pressed him to retain his situation. This was exactly what he had expected and wished, the humiliation of the court, and his own exaltation, were complete. As he went to this interview, and while he was there, an immense mob followed him, and rushed into the court of the palace, shouting, "*Vive Necker! No resignation!*" but there was no cry of *Vive le Roi* [y]! The indecency of this distinction alone ought to have induced the minister to recede from the applauses of the populace, and return by the inner passage from the palace to the comptroller-general's hotel. But this coarse incense was suited to his taste; he did a thing quite unusual to ministers, and which he himself had never done before, he returned to his own apartment on foot across the court where the populace were assembled, enjoying their acclamations, affecting to yield paternally to their solicitations that he would remain in office, and permitting himself to be hoisted on their shoulders and displayed in triumph [z]. But though he gained a temporary increase of popularity, it is probable that he lost more than proportionately the real means of popularity, for he counteracted by remaining in administration the views of the friends of Orleans, a deputation from whom had waited on him, and intreated him, almost on their knees, to resign, for the sake of embarrassing the queen's party [a].

[y] Moore's View, vol. i. p. 248. Bertrand's Memoirs, vol. i. p. 167.
[z] Moore's View. Bertrand's Memoirs, ubi supra. Young's Travels, p. 121. See also the different histories.
[a] Young's Travels, p. 120. Sur l'Administration, &c. p. 115.

The nobility, and thofe of the clergy who had not yet joined the *tiers etat*, were in the utmoſt conſternation at the aſpect of affairs. The king, diſtracted by contrary councils, and biaſſed by his declared reſolution not to permit the ſhedding of blood in his quarrel, recommended, and finally inſiſted on, the junction of the two ſuperior orders with the lower, which accordingly, in ſpite of the remonſtrances of the duke of Luxembourg, took effect, though without dignity or advantage, as near fifty of the nobility, headed by the duke of Orleans, had taken the ſame ſtep two days before. *The nobility join the tiers etat. 27th June.*

Mean time the duke of Orleans and his party, by their intrigues with the guards, by their ſeditious meetings and harangues in the *palais royal*, by their criminal ſpeculation in grain, and by the various other methods detailed in the life of that conſpirator, were accelerating the exploſion which was to place him at the ſummit of his wiſhes. Theſe events becoming known to the court and the friends of the king, induced him to call in the foreign troops, and to give the command to M. Broglio. The conduct of Necker gave riſe to much uneaſineſs, his wiſdom or his loyalty muſt be impeachable; every meaſure he had recommended to the king had increaſed his embarraſſments, while it added freſh laurels to the brow of the miniſter. Orders for money on the treaſury ſigned with his name, and afterwards diſavowed by him; orders ſent into the provinces, ſigned with his name, forbidding the holders of corn to ſend it to the capital, were brought forward, yet with a ſupineneſs hardly credible in his ſituation, he took no pains to detect and puniſh the authors. He was undoubtedly apprized of the turbulent meetings at the *palais royal*, and the ſeduction of the military, yet took no care to prevent, and cautiouſly avoided ſanctioning with his name, any of the meaſures taken to counteract them. Theſe circumſtances, joined to a deſponding report *Progreſs of events.*

report he made to the committee of provisions in the national assembly, gave occasion to some persons near the throne, who were pressing for the formation of an entire new ministry, to represent him as a monopolizer of grain, a report which the mercantile occupations of his life rendered not incredible. They added, that he was devoted to the faction which agitated the capital, and his conduct was not sufficiently unequivocal to belie the assertion [b].

11th July. Necker's dismission. Urged by these representations, the king sent him an order to quit the kingdom in four-and-twenty hours. He acknowledges himself to have been astonished at this event, and almost incredulous of its reality [c], but the manner of his obedience is highly creditable to him; he was at dinner when the order was brought, and, without the least appearance of concern, said to the count de la Luzerne, the person who brought it, "We shall meet at the council." After dinner he pretended a headach, and having quitted the company who had been dining with him, without the least intimation of what had happened, prevailed on his lady to accompany him in his carriage, as if for an airing, and then first communicating to her his dismission, drove to St. Ouen, his country seat, where he slept that night; and the next morning, notwithstanding the indisposition of madame Necker, proceeded on his journey towards the frontier with the celerity of an express [d].

Observations on it. The banishment of Necker was, under all circumstances, the most imprudent measure which the court could possibly have taken. They knew the fermentation at Paris; they knew they could not

---

[b] See the Historians of the time, particularly Pagès, vol. i. p. 222. 255. Conjuration de d'Orleans, vol. i. p. 284.
[c] Sur l'Administration, &c. p. 117. On the Revolution, vol. i, p. 214.
[d] Sur l'Administration, &c. p. 119. See also the Histories.

depend

depend on the fidelity of the troops, and they knew that thefe agitations and defections were produced by the ambition of the firft prince of the blood. If the king had retained the minifter, the explofion then meditated would have wanted at leaft one pretext, and if he had any attachment to the king, his credit with the people might poffibly have been reforted to with advantage. If, on the other hand, he was inclined to the oppofite party, his prefence would have been a very trifling fanction to their proceedings, and the view of a king, befet by traitors, ruined by duplicity, and betrayed and abandoned by the minifter in whom he confided, would have prefented to his fubjects a fpectacle fo interefting as to have caufed many to rally around his ftandard, whom contrary fenfations drove into the arms of the infurgents. Necker's conduct appears to have been founded on this principle; he thought his own popularity perfectly eftablifhed, and his confidence in himfelf led him to believe he could avert all the miferies of France, if his views were not thwarted by thofe whom ambition led to defire his place; whom intereft led to oppofe his economy; or whom the pride of unqueftioned authority led to reject his conciliatory plans, or refent the freedom with which they were propofed, and the earneftnefs with which they were recommended. He faw in oppofition to thefe a ftrong party, headed by a weak, profligate and uncertain character, and apprehended that when fuccefs fhould have enabled them to humble thofe who formed the obftacle to his views, he could by means of his popularity guide and reftrain the party whom he meant to ufe only as his tools, and when ufed throw them by. Alas! he did not fee that he was the tool, that his popularity was fictitious, and that the fame hands which placed the laurel on his brow could, in fpite of his talents or merits, fnatch it
away

away for ever[*]. His banishment, at the present moment, afforded a pretext to the faction of Orleans to accelerate their plans for subverting the government. The person who brought the news from Versailles to Paris was considered a liar or a lunatic, and was with difficulty preserved from the fury of the mob; but when the report was fully confirmed, and many falsehoods added respecting the intended dissolution of the assembly, the burning of Paris, and the murder of the inhabitants, they burst into acts of the most furious violence. They carried the bust of the minister, covered with crape, about the streets, together with that of the duke of Orleans, and made them a rallying point for the disaffected. The national assembly believed, or pretended to believe, that in the dismission of Necker their own ruin was involved; they made haste to strike terror into the new ministry, by decreeing them responsible for all the events which should take place in consequence of the public fermentation; and that Necker had carried with him the confidence of the nation.

12th July.

His recal. Shortly after the events of the 14th July, the assembly were induced, by the interference of the municipality of Paris, to address the king to remove his present ministry, and recal Necker. The effect of this indecent interference in the province of the executive power is incalculable, had it been resisted; but the ministry, of their own accord, resigned their situations the day the address was voted; and the king dispatched a message to Necker the same day, inviting his return. He had, before the receipt of this letter, gained intelligence of the revolution from the

---

[*] He became afterwards fully sensible of this truth, and acknowledges, that, but for the ardent eloquence of M. Lally, he should have sunk gently into oblivion after the 11th of July. Sur l'Administration, &c. p. 423.

duchess

duchefs de Polignac [f], who, flying from the popular fury in a lefs circuitous direction than the ex-minifter, had overtaken him at Bafil, and apprized him of the recent events. Had he poffeffed a great mind, he would have rejected the proffered return to power, obvioufly procured for him by force; and by neglecting his extorted commands, have fhewn, in the moft unequivocal manner, his compliance with the *wifhes* of the king. Had he poffeffed only a moderate portion of genuine philofophy, and felt the pure affection which a virtuous mind entertains for a high reputation, inftead of the appetite, which fools and knaves often poffefs in common with wife and honeft men, for popular acclamation, he would have followed his plan of retirement, poffeffing the regrets and good wifhes of a mighty nation, and the refpect of a very great portion of Europe [g].

Necker, however, decided otherwife. He wrote to the king and to the national affembly, accepting their invitation. To the king he ufes a very chilling phrafe; " I return to receive your orders, and " afcertain on the fpot, whether my indefatigable " zeal and entire devotednefs can yet be of any " fervice to your majefty. *I am convinced that this* " *is your wifh, fince you deign to affure me of it.*" To the affembly he fays; " Worthily to reply to " *that ennobling mark of your regard* far exceeds my " feeble powers: but at leaft, gentlemen, I may be " allowed to offer you the homage of my refpectful " gratitude [h]." When Necker had refolved to re-

23d July. Determines to return.

[f] Memoires de la Ducheffe de Polignac, par la Comteffe Diane de Polignac, p. 37. Hiftories.

[g] Subfequent events, which have thrown light on the caufes and combinations which produced thofe acts which preceded M. Necker's difmiffion, and his own conduct and writings, have contributed to weaken thofe fentiments; but if they had not been fo brilliant at that moment, they would have been more general and permanent.

[h] See the Letters and Anfwers in Necker on the French Revolution, vol. i. p. 225. That to the king is in the ftyle of a perfon fullenly conferring a favour: that to the affembly, in the ftyle of a man highly honoured and proportionately grateful.

turn,

turn, there was one essential service to be rendered to the king, which, had he been honestly desirous of it, might have tended to tranquillize the country, and give permanence to the throne. I owe the suggestion to Bertrand, and transcribe his own words: " To have rendered his zeal useful to the king and
" the state at that period, he had but one line of
" conduct to adopt, which was, to have immediately
" presented himself to the assembly, and after hav-
" ing thanked them for the concern with which
" they had honoured him, to have candidly an-
" nounced to them, that he was the author of the
" declaration of the 23d of June, as it had been
" read in the assembly, except some expressions
" which had been altered, which by no means al-
" tered the sense of it; that he solemnly persisted in
" the opinion, that the form of government esta-
" blished by that law, according to the wishes ex-
" pressed in the majority of the instructions, was
" the only one proper for France; therefore his
" conscience, his honor, and his zeal, made it his
" duty not to return into administration till the
" assembly had declared their adherence to the
" declaration of the 23d of June. The general
" confidence and vast credit which M. Necker en-
" joyed at that moment enabled him to give the
" people whatever impression he pleased, and to
" have made it impossible for the assembly to
" have rejected his propositions. It was in his
" power at this period to have had many abuses
" corrected, the monarchy wisely limited and pre-
" served, and by so important a service he would
" have secured to himself as long a ministerial ca-
" reer as his ambition could have desired [1]." A mode of conduct formed on this outline would have rendered him respectable, and procured him a numerous body of friends.

[1] Memoirs, vol. i. p. 70.

His progress through the country was, in its truest sense, a triumph. Acclamations of multitudes, an escort of troops, respect and veneration, attended him the whole way[k]. His interposition effected what the king's influence could not have done, in saving the life of the baron de Bezenval. His return was celebrated at Paris with all the demonstrations of joy which a hasty, sanguine, and capricious people could give. He was introduced in great pomp to the national assembly, where he was complimented by the president in an elegant speech, which was ordered to be printed, that all France might attest and approve the homage paid by their representatives. His reply was brief, and contained nothing remarkable. He went the next day to Paris, accompanied by his colleague, M. de St. Priest; they were met at the barrier by an immense multitude, who took the horses from the carriage, and drew it themselves to the *Hotel-de-ville*. Here he was received by the commune, and complimented by Bailly, the mayor. The mob without insisted on seeing him, and he shewed himself in the balcony, accompanied by his wife and daughter. On his return to the *commune*, he took occasion to mention the situation of Bezenval, and to advert to the scenes which had lately disgraced the capital. The liberation of the baron, and a general amnesty, were instantly decreed by acclamation; and the minister, happy in the success of his efforts, retired. Intoxicated with homage and applause, he was incapable of seeing that his popularity had reached its height, and that its decline was to be dated from that moment. The districts of Paris were excited to protest against the acts of the *commune*; and the assembly, on the motion of

His journey and arrival at Paris.

29th July.

---

[k] See the Histories, and Arthur Young's Travels, p. 143.

Mirabeau,

Mirabeau, reversed them [1]. In short, he had risen to as great an eminence in the public opinion as the faction of the *palais royal* judged it expedient to permit; and while his return was celebrated by illuminations and fire-works, his disgrace was resolved on [m].

Proposes loans.

7th Aug.

Little cabal, very small efforts of intrigue, were necessary in the present circumstances to render the decline of the minister's popularity certain. The payment of taxes was refused in many provinces, and the power of paying them was taken from many persons by the burning their houses and plundering of their estates by mobs. Necker represented to the assembly, in a long speech, the distressed state of the revenue; that the treasury contained only four hundred thousand livres (17,500*l.*), chiefly in notes of the *caisse d'escompte*, then in a state of bankruptcy:

---

[1] The BARON DE BEZENVAL was commandant of the Swiss guards at the æra of the revolution. He was said to have encouraged de Launay to defend the Bastille, and to have promised him a reinforcement; this suggestion rendering his stay in Paris unsafe after the 14th July, he solicited and obtained from the king leave to return to Switzerland, his own country. In his way thither he was arrested at Villenaux by the national militia, just as Necker was passing. He immediately wrote to the municipal officers, requesting his liberation, which they declined granting till they should receive an order to that effect from the permanent committee at the Hotel-de-ville. Necker solicited and obtained it; but the assembly decreed that the baron should be kept in safe custody near the place where he was arrested, till he could be tried; he being, in the mean time, under the protection of the law. He was conducted to Brie-Comte-Robert, and committed to the castle. It was fortunate for him the messenger dispatched with the decree of the assembly used expedition enough to prevent his return to Paris with those dispatched by the districts, as a mob of thirty thousand people were waiting for him at the Grève, with a gallows and rope, ready to have executed judgment on him in their summary way. When the court of the Chatelet was erected into a tribunal for the trial of crimes of *læsæ nation*, he was arraigned before them; and it appearing that he had, in the whole of his conduct, merely acted in obedience to the commands of his superiors, he was acquitted. The baron survived his acquittal but a short time. He died at Paris.

[m] See the various histories. Necker himself speaks with great feeling and anger of the resolution entered into to unpopularise him (*dépopulariser*). Sur l'Administration, &c. p. 132. 409.

and

and after describing the causes of the difference between the receipt and expenditure, proposed a loan of thirty millions (1,312,500 *l.*), to answer the current expences for two months, in which time he hoped the constitution might be nearly, if not entirely finished. The contractors were to have five *per cent.* and a certain *bonus :* but the restoration of public credit would have fixed the minister and the royal authority too firmly to suit the views of the faction ; they therefore diminished the advantages of the proposal, and reduced the interest to four and an half *per cent.:* the consequence was the utter failure of the scheme, as three weeks elapsed after the decree, and not a tenth part of the money was subscribed. Another loan of eighty millions (3,500,000 *l.*) was then proposed on the minister's original plan ; but the public confidence was departed, and it met with no success [n]. *27th Aug.*

In September, the public mind was agitated by the question, what share of the legislative power should be confided in the crown; and whether the king was to have a prohibitory control over the acts of the assembly ? This debate was carried on with singular acrimony and violence for a fortnight. One party maintained, that the decrees of the assembly should have the force of laws, without the royal sanction : the other, that the king should have an absolute negative on all decrees. This question produced many others; such as, those of the king's inviolability, and the descent of the crown; but the main point was still undecided. Necker presented a *memoire* proposing a middle measure, namely, that the decrees of the assembly should be presented to the king for his sanction, which if he withheld during the sittings of two assemblies, both agreeing in the expediency of them, they should become laws without his consent. This was termed *1st Sept.* Debates on the *veto.*

Necker's opinion.

[n] Debates. Histories.

a sus-

a suspensive veto. The plan contains very little wisdom; the dread of committing to the crown an uncontrolled power of refusing a sanction to laws apparently unjust and inefficacious, must have originated from malignant jealousy and resolute misapprehension; and the project of protracting the consent between the executive and legislative powers, during the continuance of two assemblies, was a monster of weakness and deformity. The assembly, under a pretended terror of ministerial influence, refused to read the *memoire* of their late idol. He published it; and at length, wearied with a contest on the other alternatives of an absolute *veto*, or none at all, wherein personal acrimony increased, without making any proselytes, the assembly adopted the plan of the minister; but without any compliment to him, direct or implied.

<small>Patriotic donations.</small> Still the derangement of the finances appeared irreparable. Patriotism, or a love of distinction, had impelled many persons to make voluntary donations of their plate, jewels, and ornaments, which were denominated patriotic gifts. The king, in commiseration of the public distress for specie, had sent his superb services of plate to the mint; but these supplies were impermanent and insufficient.

<small>24th Sept. 1st Oct.</small> Necker again attended the assembly, and after drawing an alarming and just picture of the state of the revenue, and expressing his hopes of being able by economy and the equalization of taxes, to restore public credit, proposed that a contribution should be levied on every individual, equivalent to one fourth of his annual income, to be paid in fifteen months. This violent measure, which did not require all the depth of financial knowledge the minister was supposed to possess, was, after some debate, sanctioned by the assembly, to the surprise of many; Mirabeau, Necker's inveterate opponent, supported it, and proposed placing in him an unlimited confidence. This surprise was abated by Mirabeau's

<small>Necker proposes a contribution of one fourth of the revenue of each individual.</small>

Mirabeau's subsequent conduct, for when it was objected that the assembly could not, consistently with their instructions, vote any new tax till the king should have sanctioned the articles of the constitution then under his consideration, Mirabeau tacked the decree for the new impost, to the request of the assembly that the king would no longer delay to sanction the decrees relating to the constitution, and those of the 4th of August. This finesse, which a democratic writer in England has honoured with the title of a " happy combination of the " different views on the subject [o]," is neither more nor less than what was formerly practised in the house of commons of this country, tacking to a money-bill another which might be supposed less palatable to the superior orders of the constitution, a practice which they have long since discontinued, and against the legality of which many resolutions have been entered into by the lords [p].

Conduct of Necker respecting the 5th of October.

This extraordinary coalition, combined with the events then in agitation, and which so fatally broke out a few days after, have led to a suspicion that the minister was willing to make a compromise for his personal safety, or for a remnant of popularity, by conniving at, if not abetting the projects of the conspirators. Without such connivance, or an ignorance of public affairs, and the transactions of the capital, almost as culpable, it is thought impossible that so mighty an enterprise should have been formed and conducted in such a manner that the least intimation of it did not reach the court. It is considered almost impossible that, on the morning of the 5th of October, the king should have been suffered to go to Meudon to take the diversion of hunting, without receiving the least hint of the proceedings at Paris, or should never be apprized

[o] Impartial History, vol. i. p. 223.
[p] Debates. Histories. See MIRABEAU.

of them till the hall of the assembly was filled with poissardes. Had the minister no friend, no spy in Paris, who could apprize him of the dangers with which the life of the monarch and those of his family were threatened? Such a deficiency of information is unpardonable, if credible; but if Necker knew of these events and neglected to apprize the court of them, in what light must the honest men of this day, in what light must posterity view his conduct?

<small>6th Nov. Proposes to establish a national bank.</small>

The opinion of his having connected himself actively with the Orleans' faction, is believed by some authors, but the antipathy between him and Mirabeau which prevented a treaty with the king, would have frustrated an union of the kind. Necker had not what the conspirators term *energy* enough to serve their latent purposes or retain their patronage.

<small>14th Nov.</small>

He returned to his duties as a financier, and presented to the assembly a plan for establishing a national bank, to be raised on the remains of the *caisse d'Escompte*, and supplied by the sale of crown and church lands. This project first gave rise to the emission of *assignats*, which were notes or transferable acknowledgments of the receipt of monies to be refunded by the sale of those domains. This, like other innovations, or novel expedients, was very much approved at first. The people were anxious to shew their zeal by contributing largely to the patriotic donations, which were by this new plan to be funded, to answer extraordinary emergencies. But the reputation of Necker had declined, his presence gave no pleasure, he was not looked up to as the saviour of the country, but merely as a minister of some talents, and a necessary drudge in the mysterious and laborious business of finance.

<small>Decline of his popularity.</small>

This indifference was soon converted into disgust. The committee of the assembly employed in carrying into execution his econnomical plans, required a register a register of the expenditures, pensions, and donations of the public money by the court for the last twenty years, called the *red book*. The king expressed an unwillingness to comply with this request, as it would expose the profusion of his grandfather. Some of the expences of his own reign might also excite sensations of repugnance in the present state of the public mind. Camus, however, as president of the committee, pressed for the perusal of the book, alledging that it was not to be published or its contents divulged to gratify idle curiosity, but was to be made use of merely to form the basis of a report, which the committee could not draw up without it. Necker on this, with a too ready credulity perhaps, but without any apparent ill-intention, prevailed on the king to let the book be sent to the committee. To the great surprise of all honest and feeling men, the book was immediately sent to the press and published. The minister remonstrated with Camus in such a style as brought on a quarrel between them. The public took part with the treacherous president of the committee, and the press teemed with scandalous pamphlets, against the upstart, aristocrat financier [q]. Every incident of his public life, especially since his last recal, was converted into matter of reproach, and truth and fiction were exhausted in search of scandalous anecdotes of his private life [r]. Thus was the man who had been exalted to a degree exceeding all reasonable hope for acts of equivocal virtue, or small importance, degraded in the public mind to the state of a criminal, for a mode of conduct which all good men must have respected. He accelerated the downfal of his popularity by a treatise in defence of nobility, a crime in the state of opinions then prevailing in France, utterly unpardonable [s], and the unfortunate affair of Nancy,

15th Mar. 1790.

---

[q] Moore's View, vol. ii. p. 131.
[r] Sur l'Administration, &c. p. 132. 409. 424.
[s] See Historical Sketch, p. 286.

which involved all the ministers in blame, completed his debasement.

To an ear long soothed by the acclamations of popular applause, to an eye long accustomed to see every beholder bending with veneration, or animated with hope, nothing can be more irksome and insupportable than the privation of those gratifications, and the substitution of contempt and reproach for reverence and admiration. The man whose virtuous labours are directed to the public good, and to the faithful discharge of the dictates of his conscience alone, can survey with indifference the fluctuations of public opinion, and persist in his duty, though exposed to all the storms of popular outrage, but he who fixes his affections on the unstable and injudicious applause of the multitude, and sacrifices to it, in the slightest degree, his integrity and honour, once deprived of it, feels that dreary inconsoleableness which results from disappointment in an illicit object of the tenderest solicitude, and for which no internal principles, or consciousness of irreproachable conduct is left to make amends.

Demands leave to retire.

Notwithstanding all the external symptoms of this decaying popularity and influence, Necker could hardly believe the reality. The concurrence of circumstances, and the flatteries of his wife and friends, had led him into notions so extravagant, that he supposed, if he were so inclined, he could establish a new religion in France, instead of Christianity. But he was at length undeceived and alarmed for his personal safety by an insurrection

4th Sept. 1790.

which the Jacobins raised for the purpose [t], he wrote to the assembly demanding leave to retire, assigning as a cause, his ill state of health, and proffering to leave the money due to him from government, which has been already stated to amount to 96,250 *l.* sterling, together with his hotel and

---

[t] Sur l'Administration, &c. p. 424. Bertrand's Memoirs, p. 174.

furniture

furniture as pledges for the integrity of his administration. No part of this letter was deemed important enough to claim any attention, and they paſſed to the order of the day. Some of the ſections of Paris, on the news of his intended departure, aſſembled to deliberate whether it ſhould be permitted, and whether the ſum he had propoſed to leave was ſufficient to indemnify the public for what he had robbed them of, and there is no doubt that if they had been urged to it by any of thoſe perſons who were then in the habit of directing their motions, the mob would have prevented his departure and placed him in priſon. But Necker's opponents required only his abſence, and therefore diſcouraged any violent proceedings ".

This indifference was a thunder-ſtroke to Necker, it was utterly unexpected, he felt it with the greateſt ſenſibility, and acknowledges that the aſſembly, by one ſingle expreſſion of kindneſs might have retained him[x]. The whole of his book on his own adminiſtration is replete with expreſſions of the injury which his pride and honour had ſuſtained from the unkindneſs of the aſſembly. He had ſtill, however, ſome hopes of returning kindneſs, and notwithſtanding his pretended ill-health, meanly waited eight days at Paris, in expectation that ſome change of affairs would occaſion his reſtoration to office, or, as he expreſſes himſelf, he had the weakneſs to await from ſome quarter a ſentiment of juſtice or of goodneſs[y].

The journey of this degraded miniſter through France, ſo different from his triumphant entry the year before, is narrated by himſelf in ſuch pathetic terms, that I ſhould fail in doing juſtice to the ſubject if I were to relate it in any but his own

Quits Paris;

ᵘ The facts contained in the preceding narrative are taken from Moore's View, Bertrand's Memoirs, and the various hiſtories; which reſpectively contain different, but not repugnant narratives.
ˣ Sur l'Adminiſtration, &c. p. 436.   ʸ Idem, p. 426.

words,

words, the facts are corroborated by all the hiſtorians. "At length I ſet out, and I alone, indulging a long ſeries of recollections, I alone know my ſtruggles and my heartfelt pain; I ſet out, and already was I preceded by thoſe dreadful letters, thoſe fatal correſpondences which impart to the provinces ſentiments of hatred, injuſtice, and perſecution. Rapid in their effects as the wand of Medea, they appeaſe the furies, or excite them at pleaſure. I ſpeedily experienced their malign influence; I was taking a few moments repoſe, free from miſtruſt, at the poſt-houſe in the little town of Arcis-ſur-Aube, forty leagues from Paris, when I was ſurpriſed by the appearance of a great crowd of the people, and ſeveral armed men, who entered my chamber. They began by demanding my paſſports; I had three of them, and a ſpecial letter from the king. I ſhewed them; the municipality, the directory of the diſtrict agreed that they were perfectly regular, but ſome hot-headed individuals perſuaded the national guard to think otherwiſe, and violence was triumphant. They conducted us, madame Necker and myſelf, between two ranks of fuſileers, to an inn which they appointed for us, and where at firſt they talked of keeping us apart from our ſervants; but they at length contented themſelves with giving a watchword at the inn-door, and probibiting all communication with us; they multiplied poſts of ſentinels, and to fulfil all the dictates of prudence, placed a *corps-de-garde* in the rooms below. I wiſhed to write to the national aſſembly; permiſſion was granted; but with a reſervation that none of my ſervants ſhould carry the letter; it was intruſted to two citizens of Arcis, who, when they reached Paris, entered into conſultation with thoſe members of the aſſembly who were moſt inimical to me; they fixed a day and"

Is arreſted at Arcis-ſur-Aube;

Writes to the aſſembly;

"and hour for the transmission of my letter to the
national assembly, and after a debate which produced some perfidious but impotent attacks, it
was agreed that I should at least enjoy *the rights
of man*, and they forbad all further impediment to
the continuation of my journey; but they carefully abstained from expressing any disapprobation
of the national guard at Arcis. They were,
however, afraid that the president [z], who was a
worthy man, should in his answer adopt a style
resembling that of gratitude; and as one or two
members, in a moment of extraordinary boldness,
had hinted something of thanks for my services,
the president was required to communicate his
letter before he dispatched it, and he was obliged,
contrary perhaps to his own private wishes, to
confine himself rigidly to the terms dictated to
him."

After some dolorous reflections on this injustice of the assembly, and a comparative view of the facility with which they voted thanks on some occasions, and their extreme jealousy of granting them on the present, he thus continues:—" I quitted Arcis-sur-Aube, that town which perhaps at this day regrets its conduct towards me; and rein-forced with a fourth passport, that of the national assembly, continued my route. But, on my arrival at Vesoul, I was detained by the people: they stopped my carriage, cut the traces, held the most threatening language, and I had great difficulty in escaping from their undiscerning fury. At night the servants who were following me incurred a still greater danger; they were tumultuously seized, the trunks which were in their carriage were opened, the padlocks broke, their contents were industriously examined; and from the inside of the house where these iniquities were

Proceeds on his journey;

Stopped at Vesoul.

His servants arrested and his trunks broke open.

[z] Bureau de Puzy.

" transf-

" transacting, they cried to the mob without,—
" *Stay, stay, we will give you notice when we find any
" thing.* They only wanted therefore a pretence to
" commit the greatest violences; fortunately they
" found none; the papers were a collection of the
" principal letters of thanks and kindness which I
" had received for some time past: the manuscript
" books contained the accounts of my domestic ex-
" pences: they were therefore obliged to let my
" servants depart, who for near five hours consi-
" dered themselves between life and death, and in
" their danger bound themselves by vows, which
" after their deliverance they immediately ful-
" filled [a]."

Arrives at Copet.

Thus, after a journey replete with disgrace, insult, and danger, he arrived at his estate at Copet, where he still resides [b]. The oblivion from which he was rescued by M. Lally, and which he appears so much to have dreaded, now so completely enshrouds him, that all the abuse of his adversaries, who are to be found in all parties, and three works of considerable size, besides smaller ones, which he has published since his retreat, are insufficient, amongst those who are not immediate sufferers by the revolution, to make him personally the topic of a moment's convers- ation. The popular indignation was carried to such

[a] Sur l'Administration, &c, p. 426.
[b] Gibbon thus describes his misery after his retreat: " I passed four days at the castle of Copet with Necker; and could have wished to have shewn him, as a warning to any aspiring youth possessed with the dæmon of ambition. With all the means of private happiness in his power, he is the most miserable of human beings: the past, the present, and the future, are equally odious to him. When I suggested some domestic amusements of books, building, &c. he answered with a deep tone of despair, ' *Dans l'état où je suis, je ne puis sentir que le coup de vent qui m'a abbatu.*' How different from the careless cheerfulness with which our poor friend lord North supported his fall! Madame Necker maintains more external composure, *mais le diable n'y perd rien.* It is true that Necker wished to be carried into the closet, like old Pitt, on the shoulders of the people; and that he had been ruined by that democracy which he had raised." Gibbon's Miscellaneous Works, vol. i. p. 213.

extremes

extremes at the period of the 10th of August 1792, that his busts and statues were assiduously sought out, and destroyed with all the marks of ignominy and hatred shewn to those of kings[c].

The conduct of Necker on every occasion has been so amply discussed in the preceding pages, that it is unnecessary to speak of it otherwise than in general terms. That he was a principal cause of the French revolution is admitted by writers of every description, by persons whose principles and styles are opposite as those of Bertrand and Pagès: yet it is his fate to have no defenders; the royalist writers load him with execration, as a monster, the stigma of the human race; while the republicans despise him as a shallow egotist, with views narrow and contracted, and an understanding too limited to form a grand universal scheme of government[d]. He indirectly confesses that the revolution was his work, when he says, that " the precipitation with which " the states-general were promised, and the impa- " tience with which the execution of this engage-

His character,

---

[c] Peltier relates a curious anecdote of a bust of Necker, which may shew the instability of popular favour. A sculptor of the name of Houdon, had been ordered to make a bust of this minister soon after the 14th of July. " The artist, confined in his work- " shop, had no idea that, in the short time which elapsed from his " receiving the order till his finishing the bust, the people could " possibly have expelled from their temple the idol they before wor- " shipped. Houdon therefore having exerted himself to complete it, " comes all covered with sweat and dust, bringing the precious " marble, carefully wrapt up in matting a few days after the ex- " pedition to Nancy. What an unfortunate circumstance! The " blood of the brethren and friends of Chateauvieux had been shed: " Necker was one of the king's privy council: not a member of the " common council dared to express his approbation of the bust: it " was rejected with contempt; and the artist thought himself very " lucky in being suffered to take it home, with the hope of selling it " at some future day, as an historical monument of popular ingrati- " tude." Late Picture of Paris, vol. ii. p. 110.

[d] See Bertrand's Memoirs, vol. i. p. 177. Pagès Histoire Secrete, vol. i. p. 267. 319. Playfair's History of Jacobinism, p 67. Apologie des Projets, &c. p. 185. Arthur Young's Example of France, &c. p. 47. 83. Also an admirable delineation of his character in Bouillé's Memoirs, p. 516.

" ment

"ment was hurried on, produced baneful confequences [e]." Now no perſon hurried on the performance of the king's promiſe ſo much as himſelf,
as he owns with ſome ſelf-gratulation in his publication in 1791 [f]. In defence of his general conduct
he very frequently recurs to the force of public opinion; but this is a mere cant word; the public opinion is not the law of a wiſe man or a great ſtateſ-
man, it is a powerful machine which he ought to direct, but never ſuffer himſelf to be drawn in by its
impetuoſity, or cruſhed by its weight. It is well
ſaid by Mallet du Pan, that Necker fell a victim to
public opinion, after having offered incenſe to it as
an idol, inſtead of governing it as the ſlave of experience and genius [g]. His vanity, which was in
ſome degree defenſible, conſidering how much it
was inflamed by the public and every one about
him, occaſioned moſt of his errors; but his deſire
of retaining his place led him to adopt meaſures and
form coalitions to which a virtuous and conſiſtent
man, whatever might have been his ultimate views,
would not have condeſcended. His political integrity is much applauded; I think it has ſome
ſhades; but admitting it to be unſullied, it affords
but a feeble excuſe for the evils he has occaſioned.
In private life, an honeſt motive extenuates erroneous conduct, but a miniſter is juſt as culpable for
the effects which are derived from want of ſkill,
as for thoſe which reſult from evil intentions. Necker is acknowledged even by his enemies to have
been humane, juſt, and benevolent; a good huſband,
father, and friend. His vanity made him deſirous
to monopoliſe admiration, which wiſh the partiality
of his family might conſiderably augment; and it
was accompanied with a jealouſy of others, and a

[e] On the Revolution, &c. vol. i. p. 199.
[f] Sur l'Adminiſtration, &c. p. 31.
[g] Mercure François, Hiſtorique & Politique, vol. du 25 Avril
juſqu'au 22 Juin 1791, p. 238.

vindictive

vindictiveness when attacked, which derogates much from his character as a philosopher [h].

It remains only to speak of him as an author. and writ- I cannot even give a complete list of his works. ings. Those which have fallen under my observation display marks of assiduous research and copious information, but are written in a style so laboriously polished as to incur the charge of affectation. Bertrand justly places him amongst the distinguished writers of the age. The works of Necker which I have read are the following: his *Compte rendu*, and *De l'Administration des Finances*, both of which contain striking facts, ingenious calculations, and deductions for the most part sanctioned by reason; his treatise *De l'Importance des Opinions Religieuses* is preferable to all his other writings: I have quoted many passages of his book intitled *Sur l'Administration de M. Necker par lui même*: it appears from the exordium, that he retired to Copet in a fit of dogged sullenness, and thought that his incensed pride would be best appeased by a stately silence; this however approached too much to a state of nullity, and seemed to accelerate his journey to the shades of oblivion, he therefore adopted the excess of egotism. Mallet du Pan, speaking of this book, says, it proves that he was led away by events to which he knew not how to oppose either the force of action or the *vis inertiæ* [i]. He next published an essay *Du Pouvoir Executif*, which contains many maxims of the highest importance, and which, if duly attended to, would have spared the country to which it was addressed many woes and much disgrace. The writers of the literary part of the *Mercure François*, men of different opinions from

---

[h] See his character in most of the authorities before quoted, particularly Dr. Moore and Bertrand. See also remarkable instances of his vindictiveness in Bertrand's Memoirs, vol. i. p. 153. and la Bastille devoilée 7me livraison, p. 108.

[i] Mercure François, ubi supra.

Mallet du Pan, affected to defend the constitution against his attacks[k]; and Peltier acknowledges, that the work is subject to no reproach but the name of the author[l]. His last publication, *On the French Revolution*, has been discussed in many particulars where the author defends his own conduct. The information it contains is not so extensive as might have been expected, but the facts disclosed in it are related with force and effect, and many of the observations on events posterior to his retreat, particularly on the present constitution, are worthy of peculiar attention. Those parts of the work which apply to himself are not to be implicitly relied on; the disposition to place too much confidence in them will be considerably checked by an attentive comparison of them with the corresponding parts of *L'Administration de M. Necker*. He commenced his literary career with his essay on the *Legislation of Grain*, which Playfair and Arthur Young, as has already been said, speak of with disrespect. I am not acquainted with that, or his writings concerning the *East India Company*. In 1773, he wrote the *Eulogium of Colbert*, which gained him the crown at the French Academy; and in which, with great finesse, he decried the administration of Terrai, while praising his illustrious predecessor[m]. He also wrote, while the king's trial was depending, a defence of him, under the title of *Reflections addressed to the French Nation*, &c. which Peltier calls the Funeral oration of Louis XVI.[n] It may however have afforded Necker some pleasure to know, that this production met the eye of the unfortunate sovereign in whose behalf it was composed[o]; and Gibbon mentions it with approbation[p].

[k] Mercure François Literaire, du 31 Août 1792, p. 77.
[l] Late Picture of Paris, vol. i. p. 117.
[m] Anecdotes, &c, vol. v. p. 161.
[n] Late Picture of Paris, vol. i. p. 396. 402.
[o] Journal de Clery, p. 138,
[p] Gibbon's Miscellaneous Works, vol. i.

LOUIS-PHILIPPE-JOSEPH
Duc d'ORLEANS.

THE conspiracy entered into by the duke of Orleans, so undefined in its tendency, so baleful in its effects, contributed more perhaps than any other cause to give that extraordinary violence and ferocity to the French revolution, by which it was disgraced even in its earliest stages [q].

[q] The history of this conspiracy, including the whole public and private life of the duke, has been detailed by Montjoye, in a work in three volumes octavo, intitled *Histoire de la Conjuration de Louis Philippe Joseph d'Orleans*, from which, where no other authority is cited, I have derived my information. I should not, however, ascribe events of such magnitude and importance as those which are deduced from this conspiracy to such a cause, if I did not entertain the firmest conviction of the author's *general* correctness. This conviction arises, 1st, From the obvious coincidence of historical truth with the circumstances stated by Montjoye. 2d, From the concurrent testimony of most authors who have written, and most orators who have spoken on the subject of the revolution, as well royalists as republicans, in support of most of the facts detailed by Montjoye; evidence of which I shall often avail myself to support the assertions I feel authorised to make. 3d, Besides the foregoing reasons, I am induced to give the more credit to Montjoye, from his having already received that homage from men of the greatest discernment and most established fame, as well as those who, from their attachment to republicanism, would be more anxious to suppress or disavow every narrative from the pen of a strenuous royalist. Among the former may be mentioned professor Robison, the abbé Barruel, and the author of an Historical Essay on the Conquests and Ambition of France. Among the latter, the historian and circumnavigator Pagès. In mentioning Montjoye's *general* correctness, I wish it to be understood that I am perfectly sensible that a few historical, biographical, and chronological mistakes are found in his work; but the grand outline is drawn with truth, most of the principal figures correctly designed, and the whole piece (notwithstanding occasional blemishes of no great importance) a correct though shocking picture of the times.

ORLEANS.

13th Apr. 1747. Birth. Louis-Philippe-Joseph, first prince of the blood, duke of Orleans, Chartres, Nemours, Montpensier, and Etampes, count of Beaujolois, Vermandois, and Soissons, was born at St. Cloud. The notorious impurity of his mother, Louisa-Henrietta de Bourbon-Conti, was such as to have inspired his grandfather the regent with doubts of his legitimacy, which he retained till the hour of his death, though the arguments of his confessor induced the regent on his death-bed verbally to alter his judgment.

Person. Orleans was above the middle size, strong, and robust; his appearance was dignified in a very remarkable degree, when he chose to infuse into it that elevation which his rank demanded, though it was generally debased by vulgar affectation. His face possessed in his youth a considerable share of sweetness and beauty; the delicacy of his skin, before his debaucheries had incrusted it with pimples, and the softness of his blue eyes, gave him rather an effeminate appearance; but his youth, quality, and good-nature inspired the most favourable prepossession. During the life of his father, he was

Disinclination to study. known as duc de Chartres. He was so little disposed to improve his mind by the ordinary means, that, as soon as he was emancipated from his tutor, he bade adieu to every kind of study, or if he occasionally began any, his hatred of mental fatigue occasioned a speedy dereliction. This disinclination to literature confined the resources of his mind, and by limiting his means of communication, prevented at a later period the discovery of his political intrigues, by preventing him from leaving permanent traces of his conduct. Where a man of abilities would have made an harangue, he gave a hint; and not having the faculty of speaking or writing well, indirect insinuations, messages bearing no stamp of authenticity, and bribes which the receivers would be anxious to disavow, were his only engines.

He

He passed his youth in grofs, open debauchery, *Dissipation.* which at once astonished and corrupted the city of Paris. His wealth afforded means of unbounded gratification, and his birth made his excesses the *ton*, and gave an air of superior consequence to those who frequented his society, many of whom injured their fortunes, their health, and even lost their lives, by the pernicious influence of his example. In his debauchery there was none of that courtly elegance, which, making the pursuit of pleasure the object of refined minds, produces, with the evils attendant on licentiousness, those finished manners which improve the age, and those spirited effusions which delight posterity: his was of that coarse description where gratification alone is considered; the established systems of morality, and the sprightly efforts of exuberant fancy, are equally disregarded. Amongst the victims of his example is to be enumerated the prince de Lamballe, son of the duc de Penthiévre, high admiral of France, who was carried off at a very early age[r]. This event opened a new view to the avarice and ambition of Chartres; he formed a matrimonial alliance with the only surviving sister of his deceased friend, that he might secure the greater part of the family estate to himself.

The object which most flattered his ambition was the hope of attaining the exalted and lucrative post of high admiral. It was held by his father-in-law, the duc de Penthiévre, but Chartres expected a grant of the reversion. To qualify himself for this situation according to the rules of the French navy, he went on board the fleet commanded by d'Orvilliers, and was successively promoted from the rank of midshipman to those of lieutenant, captain, *1778. Serves in the navy.*

---

[r] I state this fact after Montjoye and Peltier (Picture of Paris, vol. ii. p. 17.) in the mildest terms. Playfair says, that Chartres killed the prince de Lamballe by leading him, on purpose, where he was to contract a mortal disorder. History of Jacobinism. p. 81. n. See also Memoires pour servir à l'Histoire du Jacobinisme, vol. ii. p. 462.

commodore,

commodore, and finally vice-admiral. In all probability he would have attained the object of his wishes, but in the action with Keppel off Ushant he betrayed such ridiculous emotions of fear as drew on him the deserved contempt of the navy, and of the city of Paris. The king would not grant him the reversion he desired; but to gratify his ambition in some degree, made him colonel-general of hussars, a rank created for the express purpose. Chartres bore the sarcasms and ridicule of the Parisians with that stoicism which is supplied by an indifference to public opinion; but the censure implied in the preferment given by the court, which, instead of encouraging his pretensions to naval promotion, indirectly seemed to dismiss him from the fleet, rankled in his mind, and first produced that hatred of the royal family which so materially influenced his subsequent conduct[a]. Through life he was distinguished by an implacability of disposition; he was not morose, on the contrary, remarkably mild, accessible, and beneficent to his servants and dependants, but he could not forgive.

Continues dissipated.

After leaving the fleet his time was divided between the pursuits of sensuality, the sports of the field, and the employments of the gaming-table. He occasionally travelled in a desultory manner, without system, or apparent view of improvement. He frequently visited England, and contracted that taste for the dress, manners, and diversions, particularly horse-racing, which afterwards extended itself amongst his countrymen, and was distinguished by the name of *Anglo-manie*. He affected the appearance of an English jockey, though he was never slovenly, but rather in the contrary extreme.

Becomes a free-mason.

It was probably in England that he first became a free-mason. That society had long been established in France, though greatly corrupted and

[a] Bouillé's Memoires, p. 323.

disfigured.

disfigured. On the death of the comte de Clermont, late grand-mafter, Chartres afpired to fucceed him. As the fituation imparted a degree of authority and importance of which mere Englifh freemafons can have no comprehenfion, the attainment required an exertion of great addrefs, and a profufion of promifes and bribes. The candidate was not fparing of thefe, and finally fucceeded [t]. Having attained this object, he ufed all his efforts to render free-mafonry general in France, and fucceded fo well, that in three or four years after his election, he was at the head of two hundred and fixty-fix new lodges of mafons, diftinguifhed by various appellations, but all emanating from the fame focus [u]. As they acquired extenfion and celebrity the freemafons began to adopt new fancies, to *improve*, as they termed it, their original inftitution, and affume imaginary dignities derived from antiquity. Chartres was a zealous patron of thefe innovations. He vifited and encouraged the new lodges, heard with complacency their introductory harangues, already tinctured with atheifm, and the doctrines of liberty and equality [x]. The *loge des Chevaliers bienfaifans* was formed at Lyons, as a fuperior lodge to the reft, and the members pretended to revive in their own perfons the order of Knights Templars. Chartres, among others, had fo much complaifance for this abfurdity as to fubmit to the clerical tonfure. Several of the moft diftinguifhed characters in the French revolution, as Efpremenil, Bailly, Syeyes, Fauchet, Lequinio, Maury, Mounier, were members of this fociety, but there is no trace of any formal confpiracy at this early period, although in their difcourfes they made vigorous attacks on the principles of religion and government [y].

1781. Grand-mafter.

1784. Patronifes innovations.

[t] Robifon's Proofs of a Confpiracy, p. 381.
[u] Idem, p. 49. 101. 381.   [x] Idem, p. 41.
[y] Idem, p. 49. See alfo Memoires pour fervir à l'Hiftoire du Jacobinifme, par Barruel, vol. ii. p. 461.

VOL. II.   P   His

His character was not in the mean time improving. He made himself additionally ridiculous on the score of cowardice, by ascending in an air-balloon from St. Cloud, with two adventurers of the name of Robert. Such a frolic, in a prince of the blood, was contemptible at best, but he was so much terrified at the appearance of danger in a new form, that he lost all presence of mind, and tore the taffeta to facilitate the descent of the machine by the evasion of the gas. The step was what wisdom and courage would have dictated, but he was known to possess so little of either, that the Parisians laughed at him without reserve, and said he had exhibited his cowardice in three of the four elements.

Ascends in a balloon.

After the death of his father, he injured himself more effectually in the minds of the people by an act founded only in insatiable avarice. Anxious to increase an already overgrown fortune, and careless of the convenience or opinion of others, he entered into a speculation to surround the gardens of the *palais royal* with buildings. Those who occupied the houses already erected, who had embellished, furnished, and paid for them, according to the apparent beauty and pleasantness of the situation, found themselves on the point of being shut out from a charming prospect, and reduced to inhabit a narrow street. They remonstrated, the duke was obstinate. They commenced a lawsuit, and were cast. They again attended the duke, and pointed out to him how his conduct would excite the ill opinion of the people; "I would not give a single half-crown for their good opinion," was his answer. This act of dishonourable selfishness was succeeded by another, so unjust and meanly rapacious as to be worthy only of the basest sharper. He let some shops and houses in the *palais royal* on leases, for which he exacted premiums from the tenants, and immediately afterwards sold the premises.

1785. His avarice

and injustice.

mifes. A fale, by the rules of the civil code, then prevalent in France, annulled a leafe, or other temporary demife [z].

When M. de Calonne affembled the notables, Orleans, as prince of the blood, was appointed prefident of one committee. His reputation was fo odious, and his conduct fo mean, that his committee was diftinguifhed by the title of *Comité des Ladres*, or committee of *ſkin-flints*. This arofe from the parfimony of Orleans, who did not, like the other princes, keep a table at Verfailles, but returned every night to Paris. An anecdote, however, is recorded of his conduct in this affembly, which does him great honour. He attended his committee one day, and addreffed them in thefe words: " Gentlemen, you are about to read a memorial " on certain feignorial rights. If you fanction it, " I fhall lofe four hundred thoufand livres (17,500*l*.) " a-year. I could not fubmit to this lofs with a " good grace, and might perhaps make fome un-" guarded remarks. I think it moft prudent, and " moft delicate for me to retire, and give no opi-" nion on the fubject. I have obtained leave of " abfence for a few days, of which I fhall imme-" diately avail myfelf." The committee requefted that he would forbear delivering his opinion, if he thought proper, but that he would continue to prefide; he perfevered, however, in his refufal, from a dread of conftraining the voters [a].

1787. Conduct in the firft notables.

After the diffolution of this affembly, Orleans, as ufual, lived in a ftate of luxurious fenfuality, furrounded by a court of his own, formed of perfons whofe fimilarity of character prevented reflection or reproach. He retained a gloomy hatred againft the king and queen, on account of his not having obtained the reverfion of the place

Oppofition to the court.

[z] Playfair's Hiftory of Jacobinifm, p. 81. n.
[a] Anecdotes du Regne de Louis XVI. vol. vi. p. 77. 84.

of high-admiral. His firſt diſplay of ſyſtematic oppoſition was during the unpopular adminiſtration of the archbiſhop of Sens. The *palais royal* had long been the refuge of a herd of malecontents, who took advantage of the ſtate of finances to excite the public diſcontent, by inflammatory and ſeditious writings, and every other means in their power. A regular council, compoſed partly of theſe, partly of ſome diſaffected members of the parliament, anxious for innovation, was held nightly, at which the ſteps to be taken in the debates of the ſubſequent day, were arranged and regulated. The duke's purſe was profuſely opened to pay the writers and orators who clamoured for a convocation of the ſtates-general, and his influence on the parliament was ſuch as to produce that line of conduct which occaſioned their baniſhment to Troyes [b]. This act of ſeverity, however, exceeded the wiſhes of his highneſs, he feared that at ſuch a diſtance from the fermentation of the capital, and the vortex of his influence, they might abate the fervour of their attachment, and diſcontinue their oppoſition. Beſides, he was not deſirous to ſee them inveſted with too great a ſhare of popularity, as their eſtimation was not a primary object, but ſubordinate to the views which he now began to entertain. He therefore induced them to make that conceſſion which produced their recall, and diminiſhed their reputation with the public.

Forms connexion with Mirabeau. While affairs were in this ſtate, and the public mind extremely agitated, Mirabeau returned to Paris from Berlin, where he had been on a viſit to his friend Mauvillon. Mirabeau had been diſappointed by Calonne of the ſecretaryſhip of the notables, and the archbiſhop of Sens had not encouraged him according to his own eſtimate of his pretenſions. He ſaw that he had nothing to expect from the

[b] See DE BRIENNE.

court,

court, and was therefore rejoiced to see an opposition party rising in the kingdom. He considered Orleans a fit man to be the ostensible head of such a party, as birth, wealth, and independence were in him united. The impression made by his past conduct might be effaced by a few popular acts; and his want of talents, his ambition, and his rancour were circumstances rather favourable than detrimental to the views of Mirabeau. In the existing state of the public mind, it was greatly advantageous to Orleans that he had never received money from the treasury, and his wealth, by whatever means augmented, was contemplated with less malignity than that of any nobleman or prince who was attached to the court [c].

Mirabeau saw the great advantages and influence which might be derived from the societies of freemasons, of which Orleans was grand-master, he therefore readily acceded to the overtures made by the duke, and imparted to him the mysteries of illuminism. From this period the systematic perversion of the masonic lodges in France began [d].

Becomes an Illuminatus.

In conformity with the plans of his new coadjutors, Orleans distinguished himself by resisting de Brienne's proposal for a loan of four hundred and twenty millions (18,375,000*l*.). In this instance he displayed consummate address, and, for the only time in his life, courage and consistency. The archbishop, apprehensive that his project would meet with strenuous opposition, sounded the members of the parliament. All the friends of Orleans promised their hearty co-operation, while, in fact, they meditated the most determined opposition. The minister, deceived by these promises, prevailed on the king to hold a royal sitting, for the purpose of registering that and other decrees. The oppo-

Opposes loan.

---

[c] Historical Sketch of the French Revolution, p. 54.
[d] Robison's Proofs, p. 385.

fition refolved to hinder the regiftration, and, as the conftitution of a royal fitting permitted it, to caufe the queftion to be argued and put to the vote,

7th Nov. The fitting was opened; Lamoignon, the keeper of the feals, declared his majefty's pleafure to be, that every member of the parliament fhould deliver his fentiments without referve. A debate of nine hours took place, in which feveral agents of the duke fpoke in a ftrain neither agreeable to the king or relevant to the queftion. Tired at length of a debate fo protracted and unufual, his majefty rofe, and commanded the regiftration of the decrees. The members, not prepared for an oppofition to the king's exprefs orders, fat filent, the clerk was preparing to fulfil his office, when Orleans arofe, and cafting a glance of expreffive indignation at his faction, afked the king in an abrupt and haughty tone, if the prefent was a royal fitting or a bed of juftice? "A royal fitting," anfwered the king. "Then, Sire," replied the duke, "permit me to "lay at your feet, and to depofit in the bofom of "this court, my proteft, that I confider the re- "quired regiftration illegal, and that it will be "neceffary, for the exculpation of thofe who may "otherwife be thought to have fanctioned it, to "declare, that it is done by the exprefs command "of the king." Had the firmnefs difplayed on this occafion formed part of the general character of Orleans, he might have afpired to the moft exalted fituations in confequence of the fubfequent difturb- ances, and even have changed the fucceffion of the crown, but avarice rather than ambition in- fluenced his conduct even in this inftance. He held a million of a former loan, which would have been materially depreciated by the fanction of that which was then in agitation.

The king anfwered the duke by faying, in a laconic manner, that he had directed nothing but what was perfectly regular, and having perfifted in

his

his commands, retired with his ministers. As soon as he was in his carriage, Orleans returned to the hall, accompanied by the duke of Bourbon, his brother-in-law. His faction represented the late transaction as illegal in the most flagrant degree, and they finally prevailed on the parliament to protest against any participation which might be imputed to them in the registration of the king's edict, a step which was sure to render the proposed loan illusory.

The king retiring to his palace, complained, not of the duke's protest, which in itself was sufficiently extraordinary, but of the harsh, objurgatory tone in which it was delivered, and of the insolent conduct of several members of the parliament, and was finally prevailed on to banish Orleans to his estate at Villiers-Cotteret; and two of his faction, Sabbatier and Freteau de St. Just, to different parts of the country[c]. This measure was far from politic: advantage was taken of the notorious bad character of the parties punished; but when any individual can assume the appearance of a victim in the popular cause, compassion and admiration speedily follow; the public grants an amnesty of all past errors, and the danger of speaking against the idol of the day procures general forbearance. Not only the parliament of Paris, but those of Thouloufe and several other provinces, took up the cause of the exiled members, and in numerous addresses solicited their recall, mixing with their petitions remonstrances in the true revolutionary style; but without effect.

Orleans banished.

Petitions in his favour.

This banishment, inflaming the vindictive temper of Orleans, gave an energy to his conduct, which in him could only be derived from revenge and hatred. It gave him, for the first time, a taste of

His rage.

[c] See Impartial History, vol. i. p. 28. Rabaud's History, p. 48. Moore's View, vol. i. p. 66.

the intoxicating draught of popularity, and a knowledge of the advantages he might obtain from having a strong hold on the public mind. To secure this popularity, he bought to his interest several journalists of Paris, who joining their voice to that of the parliaments, attached an importance to his name of which it had never before been thought susceptible [f]. His desire of vengeance stimulated him to adopt every measure which could be devised to embarrass the monarch, and excite discontent. Amongst these was a monopoly of grain, by which an artificial famine might at any time be produced; and by affording or denying to the public the means of subsistence, a violent clamour produced, and tranquillity as suddenly restored [g]. To effect this, he laid his plans, and appointed his private agents, while at Villiers-Cotteret; but conscious that Paris must be the centre of action, and yet unwilling to compromise his hatred to the king by condescending to personal solicitation, he employed his duchess, whose excellent character made her as much beloved and respected at court as he was despised, to request his recall, in which she easily succeeded.

and projects.

His recall.

1788. His resentment,

On his return to the *palais royal*, Orleans prosecuted his schemes of vengeance and aggrandizement with greater earnestness than ever. In addition to

---

[f] See Pagès, vol ii. p. 71.

[g] This attempt has been doubted by many; and by some critics of Montjoye's work treated with unmerited ridicule. The argument drawn from the impossibility is extremely futile, considering the vast fortune and unlimited credit possessed by Orleans; and that the transaction should in justice be viewed as a profitable speculation, rather than a disadvantageous expenditure. I think it impossible, on a candid consideration of the events of the 5th and 6th of October 1789, and the immediate facility of supply which took place when Orleans was driven from France by la Fayette, to doubt the reality of this part of the duke's conspiracy. It may receive some additional confirmation from its being positively charged in a report made by St. Just, April 15th, 1794, when interest had totally ceased to influence the question, when the means of knowledge remained among the accomplices, but Orleans was executed and forgotten.

ORLEANS.

the journalists in his daily pay, he established a regular committee to discuss his affairs, suggest plans, and direct his operations. His partisans formed a club, called *les enragés*, which was of great importance in extending his influence, and one of the roots of the Jacobin society [h]. From these meetings and clubs most of the parties who afterwards directed the affairs, and divided the public mind in France, derived their origin. The money and patronage of Orleans drew them from poverty and obscurity, and enabled them to acquire that popularity which they afterwards turned against his interest, his life, and his fame [i]. It is not easy to define the exact views of the conspirators, or the precise tendency of the hopes of Orleans: it is probable, that though ostensibly the head, he was in fact the mere instrument of a cabal [k]. His partisans would, to gratify their own ambition, have elevated him to any dignity, or they would have conspired with equal alacrity against him. They flattered his vanity and ambition alternately with hopes of possessing the throne or regency, according to the fluctuations of public affairs [l]. Avarice might have restrained him, had ambition alone directed his pursuit, but revenge gave a stronger impulse; and that passion, his dependents, long prac-

Efforts,

and views.

---

[h] Bouillé's Memoirs, p. 80. See also Notice sur la Vie de Syeyes.
[i] The existence of an Orleans' faction from the very beginning of the revolution, can hardly now require proof. However, for the perfect satisfaction of the reader's mind, he is referred to the following works: Bertrand's Memoirs; Bouillé's Memoirs; Garat's Memoirs; Life of Dumouriez; Moore's View; Histoire Secrete, par Pagès; Historical Sketch of the French Revolution; Barruel's History of the Clergy, and History of Jacobinism, passim; Brissot à ses Commettans, p. 15.; History of the Brissotines by Camille Desmoulines, p. 8.; Louvet's Narrative, p. 9. et passim; Roland's Appeal, vol. i. p. 45. 59.; Playfair's History of Jacobinism, p. 80. et passim. I could cite many more authorities, but think it unnecessary; more especially as I frequently adduce their testimonies in support of the various facts contained in the subsequent part of the narrative.
[k] Historical Sketch, p. 235.
[l] See Robison's Proofs, p. 391. Moore's View, vol. ii. p. 375.

tifed in the arts of libelling and invective, and prepared to give effect to every defperate fuggeftion, were beft able to gratify.

Difcontent of the army.
Meantime the imprudence of the minifter opened to him another fource of feduction which could not fail to produce the moft deftructive effects. The *cours plenieres* were about to be eftablifhed; and as a ferious oppofition was expected in all parts of the country, foldiers were to be fent into all the cities and towns in France, to enforce obedience to the will of the fovereign when promulgated. This was but an ungracious talk at a time when the government of France was fo enfeebled, that an oppofition to its meafures was decidedly and triumphantly difplayed, and carried with it the good wifhes of a majority of the nation. The officers, many of whom, as well as the privates, had been admitted to the clubs of corrupted mafonry, were diffatisfied with their duty, and a few infinuations from the duke and his agents fo completed their difguft, that they commanded with reluctance, and a relaxation of difcipline and inattention to the will of the officers was introduced among the foldiery, which, reinforced by bribes and other allurements, in the end completely diforganized them, and fubverted the government.

13th July. Hurricane.
The hurricane which occurred in this year, by increafing the diftreffes of the country, and putting the fubfiftence of the poor more immediately in the power of Orleans, facilitated all his fchemes, and rendered their execution certain. Hail-ftones of prodigious fize defolated the country, and deftroyed the hopes of the farmer. The decree which permitted the exportation of grain, one of the greateft follies of De Brienne's adminiftration, gave credibility to the report induftrioufly circulated by the duke's partifans, that the court had caufed the greater part of the fcanty harveft to be exported to England, to ftarve the people of France.

At

At length the unpopular minister, tired of a situation for which he had demonstrated himself every way unfit, retired, and Necker, the only man supposed capable of effecting the salvation of France, assumed his place. Necker, to perpetuate his popularity, patronized with all his influence the convocation of the states-general. The expectation of this grand event, acting upon the sanguine temper of Frenchmen, inflamed by the numerous seditious pamphlets which daily issued from the press, produced repeated acts of riot and disorder. The parliament of Paris, sensible, from the style in which the new systems, every where profusely distributed, were written, that their importance, and even their existence, were as much endangered by the proposed convocation as by the establishment of the *cour pleniere*, exerted their declining influence to maintain order, check the riotous disposition of the mob, and punish the more atrocious of the libellers; but their exertions came too late. The inclination to tumult had got too firm possession of the populace; the numerous and well-paid band of libellers had too much at stake to desist from their practices, and the parliament only exposed itself to contempt and hatred. *Necker's administration.*

Orleans saw with pleasure the tide of public favour flowing from the parliament; he wanted engines of greater power to effect his plans, and therefore, during the convocation of the *notables* which preceded the assembling of the states-general, seldom attended their meetings, and never presided [m]. He courted the *tiers etat* by all the means of blandishment which his wealth and influence afforded; nor did he omit, while extending his own popularity, proportionately to vilify the reigning branch of the family. His libellers were indefatigable and audacious in a degree without example: writings and *Notables. Seditious meetings at the palais royal.*

[m] Impartial History, vol. i. p. 46. Moore's View, vol. i. p. 110.

speeches

speeches were industriously circulated, in which the king and queen were accused of occasioning all the miseries of the people. These events had a considerable effect in relaxing the vigilance and discipline of the police. Coffee-houses were open day and night in the precincts of the *palais royal*, where seditious persons were constantly haranguing against the government, and, mounted on tables and stools, attracted the attention of the mob in the gardens to their abuse of the royal family, from which, however, the duke of Orleans was constantly excepted, as a worthy descendant of Henry IV. Many of these coffee-house and field orators, who before had neither bread or shoes, were now well clothed and supplied with money, without the exercise of any other industry than their trade of defamation, without any other resource than the duke's coffers. Nor was his encouragement of these incendiaries confined to secret benefit or tacit approbation. It was become a practice, from the affected way in which the virtues of Henry IV. were held out to admiration, particularly from the pointed allusion constantly made to his benevolent wish that every peasant in the kingdom should have his fowl in the pot every Sunday, for large groups of the necessitous and idle to assemble every day near his statue on the *pont-neuf*, and force all who passed by to do homage to the figure. This fact was public, and could not be unknown to the duke; he took advantage of it to raise his popularity: he went in his carriage to the *pont-neuf*, and performed his obeisance to the statue, accompanying it with the most encouraging demeanour and condescending familiarity to those who exacted the ceremony.

Hard winter.

In this memorable year every thing conspired to promote the plans of Orleans. The presumption and weakness of the archbishop of Sens, the imprudent measures of his administration, and the effects of the hurricane, were sources of great embarrassment and perplexity.

perplexity. The winter was one of the most severe ever known in France; the poor were totally unable to procure subsistence; the price of bread would have been raised in a very distressing manner in consequence of the hurricane alone, but the additional scarcity produced by monopoly filled the duke's coffers with ready money, threw the poor upon the benevolence of the opulent, and enabled him to secure great popularity. The nobility in general exerted themselves to relieve the distresses of the needy; some had fires constantly in their halls, where meat was dressed, and bread distributed. Many prelates and nobles incurred debts to a very great amount by their acts of charity. Orleans too distributed his alms, but the papers being all in his pay, magnified his donations to an extent infinitely exceeding the truth, and though he never gave in proportion to his fortune, the constant recurrence of their applauses made it appear that he was almost the only benefactor of the poor[n]. He adopted a measure exceedingly ostentatious, to increase this opinion: he did not make his distributions in the manner followed by others, but hired some coach-houses in the suburbs of St. Germain, where fires were kept all day, and victuals delivered in his name. He promised in the papers large pecuniary contributions, but his performance of that promise was limited to a paltry gift of three thousand livres (131*l.* 5*s.*). These acts, however, increased the predilection of the public. The people, ever ready to assign some ostensible cause for their miseries, attributed the scarcity to the court, and contrasting that idea with the ostentatious munificence of the duke, expressed a reliance on him as their only friend and only hope.

<small>Distress of the poor.</small>

<small>Donations of Orleans.</small>

The inefficient voice of public opinion was not all he aimed to acquire, more was necessary to the

<small>1789. Efforts in forming a party.</small>

[n] Playfair's History of Jacobinism, p. 96.

execution

ORLEANS.

execution of his plans: he was desirous to obtain a band of ruffians, who should be ready at all times to rise in open insurrection and execute his schemes. Such a band would want an ostensible leader, inferior to himself in dignity, yet capable of giving weight to his commands, but not of importance enough to be dangerous at any future period. To gain such a person, he first tried Reveillon [o], and afterwards

[o] REVEILLON was a paper-manufacturer in the *fauxbourg* St. Antoine. On the 27th of April 1789, a mob was collected, who got a figure representing Reveillon, and drew it about the street in a most tumultuous manner, asserting, that he intended to reduce the wages of his journeymen; and that he had asserted that wheat bread was too good for the populace, but potatoe flour would do well enough. They proceeded to the *Grève*, where they hung this effigy, and afterwards burnt it. The military made an attempt to disperse the mob, but failed. Reveillon, who was an elector of the *tiers etat*, applied to the *lieutenant de police*, and the colonel of the *gardes Françoises*, for a military force to protect his house, which they readily granted: they sent so many soldiers as occupied all the apartments of his mansion, and filled the avenues, before which barriers were placed to prevent the mob from breaking in. The populace assembled the next day in vast numbers, consisting of men and women; they repaired to Reveillon's house, and attempted to force the passage, loading the soldiers all the while with the most opprobrious language, and pelting them with large stones and bricks. The military maintained their station a long time, but at length the mob succeeded in getting past the barriers, and into the house, which they immediately pillaged, destroyed the furniture, burnt the books, and rushing into the cellars, drank every kind of wine and spirit there. The military were at length reinforced by a considerable body of Swiss guards, with two pieces of artillery; they required the populace to disperse, which they refused; the officers then ordered the soldiers to fire over their heads, which instead of intimidating, increased their insolence. They charged the military with such arms as they had; old swords, muskets, bludgeons shod with iron, staves with knife-blades, sword-blades, or spikes at the end, and a volley of stones. The officers, finding their moderation produced no good effect, ordered the men to fire, and take possession of the house. Their passage was disputed, foot by foot, by the people within, which occasioned a very great carnage; two hundred of the mob are supposed to have been killed, and many hundreds wounded. A few soldiers were killed, and about four-score wounded. At length they succeeded in clearing the house, which was almost demolished, and in dispersing the rioters. The scene which presented itself in the cellars was shocking beyond description: many had drunk themselves dead with brandy and wines, and many were poisoned by having mistaken casks of vitriolic composition, used by Reveillon in his business, for common spirits, and drunk them with the same avidity. The faction who had excited this riot, endeavoured, according to their custom, to throw the blame on the court; and their account

ORLEANS.

afterwards Henriot [P], but they being both independent in their circumstances, resisted his advances,

---

count has been copied by many historians. They say that the court did it to be justified in drawing so great a body of troops round the capital as would overawe the proceedings of the states-general. This account is improbable for the following reasons: 1st, The popular Necker was minister at the time; and the sums known and acknowledged by the democratic writers to have been distributed to influence the mob, could not have issued from the beggared treasury without his knowledge. 2d, The court never knew the art of employing a mob on any occasion; they had a horror of a meeting of the populace, and had no notion at that time of giving any detailed reasons for the manner in which his majesty chose to employ his troops; nor could they, after the burning in effigy of the ex-minister De Brienne; the daily meetings at the *palais royal*, the known relaxation of the police, and tumultuous state of the city in general, need a specific act to justify such a measure. 3d, Three persons were taken up as ringleaders, two of whom were executed; the third, a woman, pleaded her belly; none of these applied for a pardon, or made any discovery tending to criminate any person belonging to the court. 4th, In all the subsequent distresses and disgraces of the royal family and their adherents, when the most frivolous reports were collected with the most culpable assiduity, no person was found hardy enough, though sure of easy credit and ample reward, to involve any of them in such an accusation, otherwise than had been done by venal orators, and in lying journals. An attempt was made to impute this transaction to the comte d'Artois, through an abbé le Roy, a reputed dependent of his, against whom Reveillon had a suit depending. This abbé, both before and after the transaction, was so involved in poverty and distress, that though, after the improbable report was circulated of his being the promoter of the riot, and distributer of the money, he presented himself to await the stroke of justice, his former protector declined all proceeding against him, and even waved that he had already engaged in, on account of his abject misery, which extended even to a want of the most common necessaries; a situation hardly to be fallen into so soon by a man employed to subsidize the rabble of one of the suburbs of Paris. It could not be the spontaneous movement of the populace, because the fact of money having been distributed, is incontestibly proved by the averments of writers on both the royalist and republican sides; but there is no room to doubt that it was a premeditated effort of the Orleans' party to intimidate the court, to give audacity to their faction in the states-general, and, by the ruin of Reveillon and Henriot, who had refused to combine with them, to increase the influence of their vile associate, Santerre. Reveillon was, for a short time, a voluntary prisoner in the Bastille, considering that as the only shelter from the malice and inveteracy of his pursuers.

P HENRIOT was a saltpetre-manufacturer in the *fauxbourg* St. Antoine. His house was plundered and destroyed at the same time with Reveillon's. He had the prudence not to expose himself to further vengeance by making any complaint; and his loss being inconsiderable in comparison with that of Reveillon, has been seldom mentioned in history.

and

and were inftantly devoted to deftruction. Not fo Santerre, a brewer of the *fauxbourg* St. Antoine, where the other two alfo refided. He, diftreffed in his finances, proud of notice, and anxious to diftinguifh himfelf, accepted the commiffion, and trained the rabble of the fuburbs to an implicit obedience. He was immediately received into the warm patronage and intimacy of his employer, his debts were paid, and he became a profperous and rich man [q]. A committee, amongft whom were Mirabeau, Sillery, Syeyes, Laclos, and Latouche Treville, were indefatigable in promoting the views of Orleans both by inftructions and writings. Thofe which related to the meafures to be adopted on the convocation of the ftates-general, contained many plans which have fince been executed, and were printed and diftributed with great profufion. The inftructions to the duke's *bailliages* recommended a particular and marked attention to the *tiers etat* [r]. He had befides, a difciplined and vociferous band of coffee-houfe and garden orators, amongft whom were Grammont, Camille Defmoulins, St. Huruge, and Fournier. They were conftantly and indefatigably laborious in their vocation of exalting him, and degrading the reft of the royal family. He had likewife fucceeded in feducing many principal officers of the army in the provinces, and amongft thofe reckoned moft in his interefts were generals Dumouriez, Valence, and Biron. He had been fo fuccefsful in his exertions, that feveral months before the meeting of the ftates-general, the corruption of the army might be deemed complete [s]. He had even arranged a private mode of conveying inftructions to his band of fuburb mutineers without oral or written communication, by means of the fountains at the *palais royal*. To

[q] Moore's Journal, vol. i. p. 152.
[r] See Anecdotes du Regne de Louis XVI. vol. vi. p. 108.
[s] Wilde's Addrefs, p. 491. See alfo Bouillé's Memoirs, p. 130.

augment

augment still more his popularity, he performed several acts of self-denial, and made some sacrifices at that time peculiar. He released his seignorial rights in many of his *bailliages*, and invested his tenants with the liberty of pursuing game on their own lands; he founded hospitals and schools in various parts of the country, and his friends the journalists trumpeted forth his liberality with exaggerations. Amongst others he gave at Orleans, in honour of *Jeanne d'Arc*, the patroness of the city, the sum of fifteen hundred livres (65*l*. 12*s*. 6*d*.), to be delivered annually to some young maiden by the cur*é*s, as a marriage portion, in reward of virtuous conduct and exemplary modesty [t].

These acts, many of which were really brilliant and meritorious in themselves, though performed from sinister motives, raised the popular predilection to a pitch of unexampled enthusiasm. When he appeared in the theatre, dramatic representations were suspended by the clamorous plaudits of the audience; when he visited the public walks, the throng about him was prodigious, every tongue ejaculated applauses and blessings on him, many persons incurred the danger of their lives to obtain the gratification of touching him or kissing his garments. Pity that such a display of public sensibility should have been the meed of intrigue and dissimulation; pity that it could not soften a vicious heart, or bend an inflexible disposition to a sincere assumption of those virtues by which alone it can be truly merited.

His great popularity.

The estates possessed by Orleans, scattered in so many provinces, gave him great means of influence in the return of members to the states-general, and this was much increased by the exertions of the lodges of masons [u]. He was returned by two

May. Meeting of the states-general.

[t] Miss Williams's Letters in 1790.
[u] Playfair's History of Jacobinism, p. 100.

places, but preferred fitting for Villiers Cotteret, meaning perhaps to perpetuate the memory, and excite refentment for his banifhment. His influence with the electors of Paris was irrefiftible, and procured a return of perfons entirely devoted to him in the three orders. At the meeting of the ftates-general, he obferved an oftentatious humility. He did not walk in proceffion with the princes of the blood, but with the deputies from the *bailliage* for which he was returned [x]. At the entry of the hall of affembly, one of his brother deputies, a *curé*, offered him the *pas*, which he declined, alleging that the precedence of clergy to nobility ought to be invariably maintained. The mob behaved with marked difrepect to other princes of the blood, but received him with their wonted acclamations, and the affembly itfelf hailed him with applaufe. The king expreffed furprife when he faw the duke fitting at a diftance from all the princes, and fpoke to Orleans on the fubject, who anfwered, that he could rank with his coufins any day, but on that day he thought it his duty to fit with his co-deputies, and refumed his feat.

<small>Difpleafure of the royal family.</small>

This marked feceffion from the court could not but excite indignation; the whole royal family expreffed their difapprobation of his conduct, and the count d'Artois caufed the Swifs guard which ufed to mount at the *palais royal* to be taken away. This meafure, though it did not injure him in the minds of the people, inflamed his defire of vengeance. His refentment had alfo, before the meeting of the ftates-general, received additional force from a new motive. A marriage had been in agitation between his daughter and the eldeft fon of the comte d'Artois. Had this marriage taken place, it might have prevented moft of the tragical events of the revolution. The king had but two

<small>Project of marriage.</small>

---

[x] Anecdotes du Regne de Louis XVI. vol. vi. p. 133.

fons,

sons, the eldest was dying, and the other was not considered a healthy child. The comte de Provence (now Louis XVIII.) had no children. The comte d'Artois and his sons stood next in succession, and whoever married his eldest son, was then supposed to have a fair prospect of becoming queen. It is credibly reported the queen broke off this match, with the intention of giving the princess royal to the son of the comte d'Artois, and thus ensuring a crown to her daughter by marriage, which the Salic law forbad her to claim by inheritance [y]. *Frustrated.*

In the *tiers etat*, the adherents of Orleans were the most violent in opposition to the court, and most clamorous for the union of the three orders, a measure which was known to be highly agreeable to his views. Two days after the celebrated scene in the tennis-court, Orleans dined with duke de Liancourt, he wore the smile of satisfaction while topics were under discussion which were extremely embarrassing to the court, and distinguished himself by a flippancy of conversation, and a continual titter [z]. Seeing, by the junction of the clergy with the *tiers etat*, that the nobility must finally be defeated, he made haste to acquire the earliest tribute of popularity, by presenting himself at the head of forty-seven other seceders from their own class, to join with the commons [a]. To prepare the way for this junction, a mob had been hired by the duke and his partisans, who ran about the streets of Versailles, threatening, insulting, breaking the windows, and personally assaulting those of the clergy and nobility who were strenuous for preserving the distinction of orders [b]. At length, the nobility, sensible of the impossibility of effectual resistance, and yielding to the express commands of the king, *Conduct in the assembly.* *22d June.* *25th.* *27th.*

---

[y] Historical Sketch of the French Revolution, p. 78. Bouillé's Memoirs, p. 323. n.
[z] Arthur Young's Travels, p. 117.   [a] Histories.
[b] Arthur Young's Travels, p. 122.

Q 2   reluctantly

reluctantly joined the inferior order. Orleans considered this as a real triumph. Paris was illuminated, and fire-works distributed in every street. Shops were opened where as many squibs and serpents were sold for twelve sous (sixpence), as would at other times have cost five livres (4*s.* 4½*d.*) and there was no doubt that the duke paid the difference [c]. The clergy before their junction had proposed the formation of a committee to inquire into the causes of the scarcity of corn, and suggest measures for the relief of the poor. This proposal, had it been faithfully executed, must have developed the intrigues of Orleans, but when it was renewed, he had the address to get a committee appointed, chiefly composed of individuals devoted to his interests, among whom there was not a single member of the clergy. Orleans was elected president, an office which he declined, but his having been, at so early a period, elected to it, demonstrates his great influence.

3d July.

Exertions in Paris.

Meanwhile the duke's agents in Paris were no less strenuous in their exertions than his friends in the assembly. Libels more atrocious than ever were issued against all the royal family. The orators in the gardens and coffee-houses were constantly busy, and even devoted to destruction certain persons by name as the enemies of the people. Amongst these were the count d'Artois, the prince of Condé, the prince of Conti, and several others; the list increased daily, and was known to all Paris [d]. A regular plan of insurrection was afterwards digested, the object of which was to obtain for Orleans, the appointment of lieutenant-general, or regent of the kingdom, and to secure him in that situation by the destruction of all who were supposed adver-

---

[c] Arthur Young's Travels, p. 125.
[d] Memoires de la Duchesse de Polignac, p. 29. Moore's View, vol. i. p. 283. See also Playfair's History of Jacobinism, p. 128.

sarious

farious to him. To accelerate the crisis, the scarcity of bread became daily more distressing, and the mob were exercised, from time to time, in predatory and riotous exploits.

To repel these efforts, the king was induced to order a considerable body of troops under marshal Broglio to assemble round the capital, but the precaution was adopted too late; Orleans had already been successful in seducing most of the soldiery from their allegiance. His party encouraged them in acts of insubordination, rescued them when imprisoned, and even made a party in their behalf in the national assembly[e]. The *gardes Françoises* were last seduced; they were assailed by every engine in the power of the duke and his agents. One of their officers, Validi, was base enough to teach them the duty of non-submission. In fine, money, treats, favours, the caresses of the prostitutes who lived in the *palais royal*, aided by the blandishments of women more elevated in life, and the harangues they daily heard, shook their loyalty so much, that they added to their oath, to defend the king against all his enemies, another, that they would not oppose Frenchmen[f]. This infection extended all over the provinces, and reached even to some of the *gardes du corps*. Every thing announced the immediate approach of some dreadful explosion; the plans of the conspirators were arranged, the troops under Broglio partook of the general disaffection, the coffee-house orators had made up their list of victims, and the day of their execution was fixed for the 13th of July; accident produced the explosion two days earlier with less effect, and an omission of many parts of the scheme.

Previously, however, to its arrival, to make sure of the military, a grand public dinner was given.

Efforts to seduce the army.

10th. The soldiers feasted.

[e] See Moore's View, vol. i. p. 286.
[f] See Pagès, vol. i. p. 126. 128. Lettre d'un François à un Anglois sur les Moyens qui ont Opéré la Revolution, p. 3.

The soldiers had been ordered to keep in their barracks, but to a man difobeyed the command. They were feafted till night, when ferjeants were fent to require their return. The ferjeants, unable to refift the difplay of feftivity, and the intreaties of their comrades and the courtefans, fat down with them, and encouraged the defection from difcipline. Hand-bills were thruft under the doors of the *Bourgeoifie*, inviting them to affemble and arm themfelves, and not truft their defence to mercenaries. The duke of Orleans was named in the gardens of the *palais royal*, as a proper perfon to be exalted to the regency of the kingdom, and the whole city difplayed a general and furprifing fermentation.

11th. Alarm on Necker's difmiffion.

This agitation was greatly increafed by a report induftrioufly fpread, that there would not be bread in Paris for another day's confumption, that Necker was difmiffed and banifhed, the life of Orleans in danger, the members of the affembly doomed to death, and the capital devoted to pillage and deftruction. An immenfe mob arofe, but, at firft, deftitute of a leader, contented themfelves with fome flight outrages.

12th. Outrages of the mob.

The next day an innumerable party from the *palais royal*, inftigated by Camille Defmoulins and the other orators, collecting ftrength in their paffage through the city, went with lighted torches, to fet fire to the barriers. The only oppofition they found was from the prince de Lambefc, who, at the head of a german regiment, exerted himfelf to prevent the incendiaries from accomplifhing their purpofes, and for a time fucceeded. The people, though joined by the *gardes Françoifes*, for want of a leader, attempted nothing decifive. They wandered here and there in a ftate of agitation and irrefolution. Where then was Orleans? Had he poffeffed that courage and prefence of mind, without which no man fhould prefume to act a confpicuous part in confpiracies, that day might have placed

placed the crown on his brow. His feeble mind was incapable of fuſtaining the tumult excited by his own intrigues; frightened at the exploſion of his own artillery, he remained hovering between Verſailles and Paris, terror-ſtruck, and incapable of encouraging or heading in perſon an inſurrection which promiſed him all he deſired, and which could not be effectually oppoſed; yet he could not diſcover that his want of courage muſt, in every important criſis, prevent his ſucceſs.

Tired at length of waiting in vain for a living chief, the populace were ſupplied with the ſemblance of thoſe they deſired. Two wax buſts of Orleans and Necker were procured, and carried about the ſtreets. One, Necker, being in the hands of a perſon of genteel appearance, the other of a hawker named Pepin, the mob all the while vociferating, "Hats off! Necker for ever! Orleans for ever!" In the courſe of their progreſs, a perſon handſomely dreſſed, with a ſword by his ſide, took the buſt of the duke from Pepin, and reſpectfully inſiſted on carrying it himſelf. The buſts were then covered with crape, and paraded round the *Boulevard*, the *palais royal*, to the Place de Louis XV. and to the Tuilleries. Here the proceſſion was met by a part of the regiment of the prince de Lambeſe. An inconcievable tumult enſued; the young gentleman who carried the buſt of the duke, threw it down and made his eſcape; the hawker, who was ſtill at his ſide, immediately took it up, the riot increaſed, ſtones were thrown at the ſoldiery, and the mob, confident in the aſſiſtance of the *gardes Françoiſes*, ſeemed reſolved to commence an attack. The prince de Lambeſe's troop were commanded to advance, and deſtroy the buſts, which appeared the ſtandards of inſurrection. In executing theſe orders, they wounded Pepin dangerouſly. Some ſhots were fired by both parties, and the German regiment finally obliged to retreat. The hawker was

was conveyed to the garden of the *palais royal*, where his wounds had the greatest effect in exciting and confirming seditious emotions. *To arms! to arms!* resounded in every quarter. An attempt was made to put a firelock in the hands of Pepin that he might be employed in recruiting, but being incapable of exertion, he was sent to the hospital. On this occasion a cockade was proposed for the insurgents, green was the colour first fixed on, but it was afterwards changed to the colours now called national, namely, blue, red, and white, the two former are the colours of Orleans, the latter was added after their adoption [g]. The whole of this dreadful day and night was deformed by terror and confusion. The *gardes Françoises* renounced the government of their officers, and set fire to their barracks. The coffee-houses at the *palais royal* were full of agitators during the whole time, now issuing sanguinary injunctions, now inflammatory and slanderous proclamations. The relaxation of the police permitted unbridled plunder. The banditti of the metropolis committed their depredations without restraint or respect [h].

The faction in the duke's interest passed this eventful night in extreme agitation. The fears and alarms which haunt the bosoms of conspirators, how well so ever their plans may have been arranged, permitted no repose. They discussed a thousand schemes, they revolved a thousand projects depending on the result of the insurrection. Incapable of estimating the extreme baseness of the duke's character, they sent him to Paris, that he might shew himself to the insurgents, in hopes that his appearance would produce a favourable and decisive exertion. He did shew himself indeed, but not in a

[g] See DESMOULINS. Also Playfair's History of Jacobinism, p. 145.
[h] Among other instances of depredation may be given the robbery of the charitable house of St. Lazare.

manner

ORLEANS.

manner calculated to infpire confidence or encourage zeal; he alighted in the court-yard of the *palais royal,* and then, terrified at the immenfe multitude, inftead of affuming the hero, and fhewing himfelf qualified for the part he wifhed to act, he fpoke a few incoherent words to thofe who accofted him, then flunk into a private apartment, and kept himfelf ftudioufly concealed, till his departure for Verfailles in the morning.

On the enfuing day the national guard was formed, by inrolments in the various diftricts of the city. The electors took poffeffion of the *Hotel-de-ville,* fufpended all the regular authorities, fent orders to individuals to deliver up their fire-arms and powder, ufurped the receipt of tolls and the poffeffion of public monies; and, what is ftill more extraordinary, were generally obeyed. They foon inrolled a force of fixty thoufand men, but they were without arms and without a leader. It was expected and wifhed that Orleans would offer himfelf. Such an act, putting him at once at the head of fo large a body, with the means of increafing it, would have enabled him to feize the lieutenancy of the kingdom, or even the fceptre; but the exertion was above him. After much delay, to afford time for the tardy duke to declare his refolution, the command was given to an obfcure individual, the count de la Salle d'Offemond. Arms were ftill wanting, notwithftanding the acceffion of the *gardes Fran oifes,* with all their ammunition, and fome pieces of cannon, and the quantity fupplied by ranfacking the houfes of individuals and the fhops of the armourers. At length it was fuggefted to the people, that they might be obtained at the *Hotel des invalides.* There, after fome faint refiftance, they found thirty thoufand mufkets and twenty pieces of cannon. They were equally fuccefsful at the *garde meuble de la couronne.*

13th, Formation of the national guard.

Thus

14th. Capture of the Bastille.

Thus provided with arms, and flushed with success, the insurgents proceeded to attack the Bastille, an attempt so desperate, that there is reason to believe that treachery and neglect combined to give it success. Supposing, however, the favourable issue of the enterprise to have been due to valour alone, the Parisians are disgraced by their subsequent barbarities, by the inhuman murder of de Launay the governor, together with several of his officers and privates, and of M. Flesselles the *prevôt des marchands*.

Cowardice of Orleans.

While these things were transacting at Paris, while the armed force, increased by the liberated prisoners from the *Force* and *Chatelet*, and disciplined and assisted by the *gardes Françoises*, bore down all resistance, Orleans at Versailles was acting a part worthy of his extreme pusillanimity. Mirabeau and others of his party represented to him, that now was the time to take advantage of his own popularity and the distress of the court, to press on the king the measure of appointing him lieutenant-general of the kingdom, and constituting him mediator between himself and the people. The council was about to sit, and a speech was prepared for the duke, which he had studied and went prepared to deliver. When he arrived at the palace, his native littleness of mind prevailed. The scene of confusion before him occasioned by news at which he ought to have rejoiced, the ladies of the court running distractedly about imploring succour from every one they met, the royal family in tears, the general-officers in despair, and the ministers confounded; these circumstances, which tended to promote the success of his attempt, did not inspire him with courage, but communicated contagious impressions. Instead of entering boldly with the members of the council, he loitered in the anti-chamber, hoping that he should feel less timid when the

ORLEANS.

the business of the sitting was commenced, and the members personally engaged. He strove to rally his spirits in vain, he could not assume sufficient resolution to enter the room, but waited in the antichamber till the rising of the council. At length the door opened, and the members retired. Compelled to do something, he accosted the king stammering, and said, " Sire, I come to entreat your " majesty's permission, in case the aspect of affairs " should become more perplexing, to go to England." The king surveyed him with astonishment, and quitted him without speaking a word [l].

From this period the successes of Orleans declined; he continued the part of a distinguished conspirator, but never could place his affairs in such a situation as to render the point of his ambition attainable. His party, convinced of his meanness, would in all probability have renounced him immediately, but his purse, and his influence among the lower order of people, made them continue under his banner, though they despised him [k]. The situation of commandant of the national guard having been for several days kept open by his partisans, in hopes that he would assume it, was at length taken from la Salle and given to la Fayette, who, though sufficiently imbued with revolutionary principles, was not agreeable to Orleans, and afterwards became one of his most decided opponents.

Falls into contempt.

16th.

The plan of insurrection had been so well concerted, that it took effect almost in all parts of the kingdom; the soldiers were every where in a state of insubordination. Dispatches had been sent to all the provinces on the same day, with instructions to instigate the peasants to rise, which were fatally complied with [l]. The nobility, gentry, and rich

Insurrection in the provinces.

---

[l] Moore's View, vol ii. p. 40.

[k] Mirabeau intended to have renounced him and joined the court, but was, for a time, prevented. See MIRABEAU.

[l] Young's Travels, p. 194. Pagès, vol. i. p. 170.

of

of every description were plundered and subjected to the most barbarous indignities; while, in the capital, the presses of the *palais royal* not only defended these proceedings, but encouraged them by the daily emission of atrocious libels on all persons of worth and rank in the kingdom; while the king was abused without disguise, and the most infamous falsehoods were fabricated respecting the queen.

<small>Proceedings in the assembly.</small>

Though the party of Orleans in the assembly had lost in a great measure their confidence in him, and frequently urged measures of the utmost importance without consulting him, yet, on the whole, his interests were still prevalent there, and generally attended to.

<small>4th Aug.</small>

Thus, though, from the immensity of his possessions, the decree for the abolition of privileges was injurious to him in one sense, it did little mischief, compared with that which it occasioned to the rest of the nobility. He could better afford the loss of some privileges, and had anticipated that of others by voluntary renunciations, yet the step was taken without his knowledge, and met with his hearty disapprobation. In the debates on the succession to the crown, and the regency in case of a minority, as well as on the share of power to be allowed to the king in the exercise of his *veto*, his interest was always obviously considered. To the exertions of his party are also attributed many of the severest decrees against the clergy [m].

<small>Preparations for a new insurrection.</small>

The success of the Orleans faction in exciting tumults in July, the desire of confirming and extending their ascendancy, and the hope that more favourable circumstances might result from a new insurrection, inspired them with a project, in which all the benefits would not accrue to their dastardly patron, and which no irresolution or want of energy in him could totally defeat. Orleans, on due consideration, might have been convinced that he was

[m] See Barruel's History of the Clergy, p. 17.

not calculated to assume the direction, and reap the fruits of a public commotion; but in his mind revenge was superior to ambition. He had effectual experience that, if he was not exalted, the king and queen, whom he hated with the most rancorous malignity, were degraded by his exertions, and he resolved to persevere. The emigration of the count d'Artois and his family, the ascendancy of the Orleans' faction in the assembly, the death of the king's eldest son, and frequent assurances that the surviving child and Monsieur could easily be prevented from impeding his schemes of advancement, acted as fresh stimulants, and a more desperate attempt was agreed on. Frequent private meetings of the duke's confidential agents were held at his country-seat at Mousseau, where the scheme was formed [n]; and the confidence and imprudence of the faction were so great, that they publicly announced that the duke would soon be lieutenant-general of the kingdom [o]. The duke's agents in Paris, kept in exercise by frequent acts of cruelty and violence, were prepared to execute any project which should be directed. The scarcity of bread was severe to extremity, though the harvest was just got in, and the conspirators did not scruple to assert that the calamity originated in the court alone. To give a spring, and furnish a plausible pretence for the projected insurrection, advantage was taken of the king's delay to sanction some decrees relative to the new constitution; and a report replete with calumny and falsehood was raised, respecting a treat given by the *gardes du corps* to the *regiment de Flandres*, on their arrival at Versailles. The following appears to be a correct representation of this transaction.

It was an established point of military etiquette, when a new regiment arrived where another was

1st Oct. Feast given by the gardes du corps.

[n] Moore's View, vol. ii. p. 39.
[o] Necker on the Revolution, vol. i. p. 263.

already

already stationed, for the seniors to welcome the new comers by a military dinner. The national guard of Versailles gave theirs without exciting the slightest observation. The same act of politeness was performed by the *gardes du corps* in the hall of the opera. A table in the form of a horse-shoe was spread for the company, amongst whom was the count d'Estaing, commandant of the national guard, and twenty officers of that corps. The scene represented a wood, the orchestra was filled with the regimental bands of music, who played the airs of several favourite operas. At the end of the first course, the healths of the king, queen, and dauphin were given, and drunk with the greatest unanimity. The trumpets sounded a flourish, and *vive le roi* resounded from every part. The band played the favourite air of *O Richard, ô mon roi!* from the opera of *Cœur de lion*. The soldiers, who were placed in the pit, jumped on the stage, asked for wine and glasses, drank the healths, and redoubled their applauses. Towards the end of the second course, the king, queen, dauphin, princess royal, princess Elizabeth, and several ladies of the court entered the hall, and appeared to enjoy with satisfaction the high spirits of the company. Their presence renewed their demonstrations of loyalty, the health of the royal party was drunk, and wishes for their welfare repeated with enthusiasm. The retreat of the royal spectators broke up the meeting, for every one pressed to be near them till the last moment. The musicians followed, and when they arrived in the marble court, played some lively tunes. The soldiers, with the characteristic gaiety of the nation, began dancing; no one thought of resuming his seat at table; an undistinguished mixture of troops of the line and national guards took place, and the hilarity was unbounded. The royal family again presented themselves at the windows to see the happy multitude: the soldiers, to amuse their royal spectators,

spectators, made a sort of mock attack on the palace, climbing up the colonades and scaling the balcony. This act of levity being performed, they resumed their dance, and at an early hour separated peaceably. Their rising from table so early occasioned four hundred bottles of wine to be left, which they agreed to drink out the next day but one, at a military breakfast, consisting of cold pies, hams, and cold joints served on a table in the riding-house. No one sat down, but each helped himself as he pleased. The breakfast was replete with gaiety; loyal and patriotic toasts were given; the royal family, the national assembly, and the national guards, were complimented with this notice in turn. Some of the party drank too much, and broke the bottles and glasses, but nothing like a riot took place. The same day the officers gave a dinner to twenty soldiers who could not find room at the first; and clubbed two thousand crowns, which they transmitted to the *curés* of Versailles, to distribute in bread to such of the poor as could produce proper certificates.

3d Oct.

This was the whole of that transaction which afforded a pretext for the most horrible enormities, and afterwards formed an article of accusation against the king, queen, and princess Elizabeth. It is to be observed, that it did not cost the officers so much as three half-crowns a-head; yet these moderate enjoyments were afterwards by a cant name denominated *orgies*. The most malicious calumnies were circulated, that the national assembly had been cursed, that counter-revolutionary oaths had been administered, the national cockade trampled under foot, and the black one (that of the emigrants) substituted [p]. It was every where affectedly observed,

Calumnies and misrepresentations.

---

[p] The preceding accounts of the feast are taken from Montjoye, and are confirmed by the royalist journals and news-papers. The contrary statements seem to have been fabricated principally by Lecointre

of

observed, that the profusion of the treat formed a striking contrast with the misery of the Parisians, whom the intrigues of the court deprived of bread. It was pretended, that the intention of bringing a regiment of troops of the line to Versailles, was to overawe the national assembly, and carry off the royal family to Metz.

4th Oct. Preparations for tumult.

When the plan of the conspirators was thoroughly prepared, it was announced in the *palais royal* in the evening, that there would be no bread in the capital in the morning, but that plenty would be found at St. Cloud; and it was suggested as a measure of propriety, to go to Versailles, and bring the king to Paris [q].

5th. Mob assembled.

At day-break, an immense concourse of the lowest order of women from the most infamous parts of the city and suburbs, reinforced by a great number of men in women's clothes, assembled in a tu-

---

of Versailles, afterwards deputy to the national convention. This man, however, when called as a witness on the trial of the queen, did not depose half the facts which were currently believed at the time; and there is every reason to consider his evidence as untrue. Two persons whom he alluded to by name, as having been present, were called as witnesses (Percival and d'Estaing). Percival flatly contradicted the assertions of Lecointre, who, in his explanation, equivocated and referred to hearsay; and d'Estaing was only slightly examined. No such facts as cursing the assembly, trampling the national cockade under foot, or assuming any other cockade, was advanced. (See Proces des Bourbons, vol. iii. p. 21. 64. 72. Jordan's Political State of Europe, vol. v. p. 158. 171. 174.) Rabaud de St. Etienne, though a decided revolutionist, does not, in his history, pretend that these imputed enormities were transacted in such a manner as to give a character to the entertainment; on the contrary, he allows that nothing could be apparently more innocent. He recapitulates the principal acts with which calumny branded the feast; but, in general, he ascribes them only to individuals, and does not represent them as part of a consistent general plan. (See History of the Revolution, p. 148.) One circumstance tends very much to prove that the statements made by the king's enemies were false. These pretended orgies, to which all the inhabitants of Versailles, as well as the military, were witnesses, took place on the first of October; and it was not till the fifth, when the mob were in full march from Paris, that they were denounced to the assembly by the Orleanist Petion.

q Apologie des Projets, &c. p. 91.

multuous manner. They forced every one of their own fex whom they happened to meet, and even fome whom they preffed into the fervice from fhops and other houfes, to join them, and made a hideous proceffion to the *Hotel-de-ville*, clamoroufly fcreaming for bread and arms. The *commune*, owing to the earlinefs of the hour, were not yet affembled; and the *Hotel* being but feebly guarded, was eafily forced by this band. They defeated a party of horfe fent to oppofe them, by fhowers of ftones, and took poffeffion of the hall; exclaiming that Bailly, la Fayette, and all the members of the *commune*, were fcoundrels, and fhould be hung up *à la lanterne*, a cruelty they actually attempted to practife on a baker, but he was refcued by the military. Some of them forced the armoury, and got poffeffion of two pieces of cannon, and eight hundred mufkets. Thus armed, they propofed to go to Verfailles, to afk the king for bread, and to make the affembly give an account of their conduct. A man named Maillard, one of the conquerors of the Baftille, and a known ruffian in the fervice of Orleans, inftructed on this occafion for the purpofe, offered to conduct the party to Verfailles. He took a drum to collect them, and appointed the *Champs Elyfées* for a general rendezvous, where they muftered about eight thoufand, armed with guns, piftols, broomfticks, pitchforks, pikes, fcythes, and every other weapon of annoyance which the hurry of the occafion permitted them to provide. Maillard encouraged them by an harangue, and they fet out by beat of drum, efcorted by an immenfe troop of armed men, and followed by a party of the national guards. *They depart for Verfailles.*

There is reafon to believe that this violent mob did not know exactly how they were to be employed. They had a confufed notion that they were to murder the queen, but were ready to commit any further atrocity which might be fuggefted *Sanguinary intentions.*

to them. In their way to Versailles, they abused that ill-fated princess in terms outrageous to decency, and threatened her in a manner shocking to humanity. They hardly affected secrecy in their determinations: four persons in the dress of women stopped to drink at a tavern at Seve, one was heard to say, "I cannot resolve to kill the king, it is con-
"trary to justice, but the queen, with all my
"heart:" to which another answered, "They
"must all take their chance, we shall know what
"we have to do when we get there'."

Proceedings in the assembly. The duke's partisans in the national assembly, Mirabeau in particular, apprised of the intended attack, behaved with the most indecorous contumacy. In the midst of a tumultuous debate, the avant-couriers of the insurgents arrived. Information was sent to the king, who returned immediately from hunting; and the troops, most of whom were disaffected and corrupted, were drawn up in the court-yard'.

Arrival and behaviour of the mob. These measures were scarcely taken, when the main body of the women from Paris arrived in two divisions; one by the direct road, under Maillard; the other by St. Cloud. The former went immediately to the assembly, which was just about to rise, when they required admission, and threatened to force the doors. The president consented to their introduction; Maillard was their spokesman.—
"This morning (he said) there was no bread to
"be had in Paris: I rang the tocsin, was arrested,
"and should have been hanged but for the assist-
"ance of these ladies who accompany me, and who
"saved my life. We are all good patriots, come
"to Versailles to ask for bread, and to punish those
"*gardes du corps* who have insulted the patriotic
"cockade. Those who dare to insult that cockade

' Moore's View, vol. ii. p. 52.
* See Memoirs of the KING, &c. and MIRABEAU; and for other intermediate transactions see la FAYETTE.

"shall

"shall be served thus—for it shall be worn by
every body." In concluding these words, he
tore to pieces a black cockade, and trampled it
under foot. This action exciting some murmurs,
"What (he exclaimed in the genuine cant of vulgar ignorance) are we not all brothers?"—
"Yes, (answered Mounier, the president,) all mankind are brothers; but they must not tear one
another to pieces for wearing cockades of a wrong
colour."—"The aristocrats (resumed Maillard)
are desirous to starve us; to-day a note for two
hundred livres (8*l.* 15*s.*) was sent to a miller,
with instructions to grind no more corn, and a
promise of the same sum weekly."—"By
whom?" exclaimed the royalists. Maillard, after
some hesitation, replied, "I was told it was by
the archbishop of Paris."—"Hold your tongue,
impostor, (resumed they,) the archbishop is incapable of such an action." Maillard being thus
silenced, his tumultuous attendants began with great
clamour to demand an immediate supply of bread
for the capital. The president informed them the
assembly was about to deliberate on the most speedy
means of obtaining a supply, and that they might
retire. Far from taking this hint, they seated themselves on the forms with the members, and shewed
their favour or aversion to particular speakers, in a
manner peculiar to themselves. To some they said,
"Speak to 'em, deputy:" to others, "Hold your
tongue;" in a peremptory tone, accompanied
with the grossest denominations. In fine, it was *Deput-*
agreed that the president, accompanied by six de- *ation to*
puties, should go to the king, and represent the *the king.*
state of affairs; and after requesting his unqualified
acceptance of the decrees relative to the constitution,
present the petition of the Parisian women. After
observing that they did not want laws, but bread,
the *Poissardes* insisted that six of their number should
accompany

accompany the deputies; to which the affembly was obliged to confent.

Situation of the gardes du corps.

At the gates of the palace all was confufion and uproar. The martial order of the guards at firft ftruck terror into the mob, but as they had received orders not to fire, (an order which they obeyed with a perfevering magnanimity fufficient to have excited the admiration and refpect of favages,) the populace lofing their fear refumed their petulance, and after infulting them by every means in their power, endeavoured to break their ranks. Some attempted to frighten or enrage their horfes, fome to run between them; vollies of ftones, and frequent difcharges of mufkets were employed againft this unrefifting body. In the midft of this terrible fcene Mounier arrived, attended with his female co-deputies, who were now augmented to twelve, one having hold of each reprefentative of the people by each arm. The guards at firft refufed them admittance, but when Mounier declared himfelf, they were immediately conducted to the king. The prefident made a long fpeech on the diftreffes of the poor. The king anfwered with that pathetic eloquence which is the offspring of feeling and integrity, in terms which affected his female auditors even to fainting. Separated from their abandoned companions, their fenfes no longer inflamed by hideous clamours, or inapplicable reproaches, they exerted their intellects, and animated with joy, ran out at the end of the audience, exclaiming " God " fave the king! God fave our good king! We " fhall have bread to-morrow!" This warmth was foon checked by the mob, who exclaimed that thefe women had been bribed, and faid, " If they " do not bring us an order under the king's hand, " we will have them every one hung up." One of them, in fact, was with difficulty refcued from the hands of the affaffins. They were again introduced

troduced to the king, who gave them a written paper, which satisfied those without, and the shouts of "God save the king!" were general. The guards sheathed their swords, and tranquillity seemed to be restored. This was, however, of short duration, the guards being ordered to their quarters, broke up that firm position which had kept their assailants in awe, and they were assaulted, not only by the mob, but by the national guard of Versailles. They rigidly adhered to the orders of not firing, and were alone exposed to every hostile effort, the *regiment de Flandres* having been corrupted by the agents of Orleans [†].

The assembly having, by the ill-timed perseverance of the deputation, obtained from the king an unqualified sanction of the decrees which had been presented, adjourned, but were soon recalled to their situation by the arrival of la Fayette and the national

Assembly adjourned.

[†] The difficulty of stating with exactness the cause of this attack on the *gardes du corps*, is well expressed by the author of an Historical Sketch, &c. (see p. 244). He says, "The confusion was so great that none of the historians have described it very clearly. The *gardes du corps* are accused of provoking their enemies by some rash actions, which are either denied or justified by their friends. It may be observed, once for all, that the indifference with which the patriots had treated the murders committed at Paris, had convinced the real or supposed aristocrats that they could hope for no protection from the laws, and that force alone must repel brutal force. We cannot therefore wonder if they are sometimes liable to the imputation of beginning the attack, when they once heard their lives threatened by the mob. But in this particular instance I do not find any sufficient proof that the guards had recourse to illegal violence. The *garde nationale* of Versailles was rendered averse to them, and partly from the insinuations of Lecointre, who was from the first their enemy and accuser. The regiment of Flanders had been gained by the double seduction of women and money. The king, convinced that their small number could do him no real service, sent them positive orders not to fire; and about six o'clock ordered the greatest part of them to leave the town, whilst some few still remained to guard the interior part of the palace. Whether in their retreat they fired rashly upon some of the banditti who insulted them, or whether those banditti fired purposely to throw on them the odium, seems uncertain; but the *garde nationale* of Versailles took the pretence to fire on the guards, exclaiming first that some of their men were wounded, and vengeance was denounced on the regiment from all quarters."

guard, whose sanguinary dispositions encouraged the mob and increased the danger. La Fayette having made such arrangements with the royal family as he considered necessary, advised the assembly to adjourn, which they did, and the conspirators, in various disguises, mixed with the mob and with the soldiers, whom they instigated to fresh acts of violence.

Conduct of Orleans. It is not necessary here to repeat the transactions of this dreadful night, and of the ensuing morning, in the course of which the queen's life was imminently endangered, her defenders butchered, and the king and his family, compelled to leave their blood-stained palace, were dragged by their persecutors to reside, or rather to be imprisoned, in the capital. Every circumstance tends to prove that this insurrection was organised by Orleans: the ready obedience paid to Maillard, a self-constituted leader, known to be in the pay of the duke, shews that many subordinate persons must have been employed to influence their submission, and marshal them in proper order. " The depositions at the
" Chatelet prove in the most incontestible manner,
" that during the horrors of these two days he was
" repeatedly seen, and that whenever he was re-
" cognized by the crowd, he was huzzaed with
" *Vive Orleans! Vive notre Roi Orleans!* &c. He
" then withdrew, and was seen in other places.
" While all about the unfortunate royal family
" were in the utmost concern for their fate, he was
" in gay humour, chatting on indifferent subjects.
" His last appearance on the evening of the 5th
" was about nine o'clock, conversing in a corner
" with men disguised in mean dress, and some in
" women's clothes; among whom were Mirabeau,
" Barnave, Dupont, and other deputies of the re-
" publican party, and these men were seen imme-
" diately after concealed among the lines of the
" *regiment de Flandres,* the corruption of which
" they

"they had that day completed. He was seen again
"next morning conversing with the same persons
"in women's dress. And when the insulted sove-
"reign was dragged in triumph to Paris, Orleans
"was again seen, skulking in a balcony behind his
"children, to view the procession of devils and
"furies; anxiously hoping all the while that some
"disturbance would arise in which the king might
"perish. I should have added, that he was seen
"in the morning at the top of the stairs, pointing
"the way with his hand to the mob, where they
"should go, while he went by another road to the
"king, in short he went about trembling like a
"coward, waiting for the explosion which might
"render it safe for him to shew himself[a]."

But though these transactions occasioned so much *Suspicions excited.* misery to the royal family, Orleans did not derive from them the advantages he expected. Too wicked to be a good subject, too much misguided to feel content in his exalted situation, too timid to assume a decisive part, and support and direct openly the sedition he had privately fomented, yet too devoid of sense to keep his agency an entire secret, he now not only saw the proposed end of his plan frustrated, but a general suspicion attach to himself. His party despised, and some began to desert him, others, who thought themselves sullied by appearing as senators where he was allowed a seat, gave in their resignation, and requested leave to retire. These were about an hundred, and amongst them Mounier, the president, but he did not quit his station till he had performed what he judged his duty, by requiring an investigation of the causes of the insurrection, in a manner which demonstrated that he had a well-founded suspicion, or certain intelligence of the real author. But

---

[a] Robison's Proofs, p. 377. See the KING, &c. LA FAYETTE. MIRABEAU, Histories; and particularly Mrs. Wollstonecraft's History, p. 430. 450. Bouillé's Memoirs, p. 128.

popularity was not in itself an object of desire to Orleans, his juvenile contempt of it still continued, though he used it as a means of forwarding his other views. He would not desist from the plans he had formed, nor could the ill success of his exertions, produced solely by himself, open his eyes to the weakness of his own character. His parasites, from interested motives, kept alive the delusion, and he meditated fresh projects for attaining the end of his ambition.

Orleans projects a new conspiracy.

It soon became necessary that Orleans should make a vigorous effort to raise himself by the debasement of the king, or relinquish all the projects he had so long entertained. The royal family had, since their arrival in Paris, performed an act of honourable charity, at the express request of the queen, which promised to efface every impression made to her disadvantage, and put her in possession of the full love and esteem of the nation. This was a voluntary donation from the privy purse of money sufficient to redeem from the hands of pawnbrokers all body linen, and necessary wearing apparel, pledged for any sum not exceeding a *Louis-d'or*. To counteract the favourable impressions thus excited, the usual means were resorted to. The report of the king having intended to fly to Metz, and levy war against the assembly, the *orgies* of the *gardes du corps*, and all the scandals which owed their origin to the malignant spirits of the *palais royal*, were renewed, and circulated with increased diligence. The plenty which had suddenly gladdened the capital at the king's arrival, as suddenly disappeared. New clamours were every where excited, and St. Huruge and the garden orators of the *palais royal*, were indefatigable in their efforts to excite sedition. The bakers' shops were besieged all night and every morning by a clamorous and starving multitude, and many experienced a total want of the first necessary of life. The meeting of

the

the national assembly at Paris, was with a ridiculous precipitancy fixed for the 19th, though no building was ready for their reception, and they were finally obliged to meet in the cathedral. Houses were marked with red, black, and white chalk, denoting respectively an intended murder, pillage, or burning, these were particularly applied to the dwellings of the members of the committee of subsistence, the principal officers of the national guard, and the farmers-general.

All these indications of a projected insurrection could not escape the attention of la Fayette and Bailly, whom the late dreadful catastrophe had rendered more circumspect. They exerted themselves with uncommon vigour to cause a proper supply and regular distribution of bread, and la Fayette in particular obtained full proofs of the conspiracies, and insidious manœuvres of the duke. Thus furnished, he repaired to the Tuilleries, and entered into consultation with the king, who, on this occasion, displayed his usual good sense and moderation. Had the love of vengeance possessed a place in his breast, he could now have indulged it with perfect security, but he considered the general good of his subjects, and finding by the papers laid before him by the general, that Orleans alone could open the warehouses where grain was deposited, he resolved on the more moderate and prudent measures which were afterwards adopted. Montmorin, the minister, requested Orleans to call at his house at an early hour in the morning. The duke was prepared for the subject of the conversation, by an intimation purposely given by the duchess of Coigni, and attended at six o'clock. He answered the accusations brought against him by the minister with the readiness of a man resolved to make no confession injurious to himself, and with the haughty spirit of an innocent prince unjustly accused. He continued in this strain till la Fayette burst from a closet where he was concealed, and laying

Conduct of la Fayette.

laying open all his treacheries, asked what he had to offer against the proofs deposited in the hands of the king? Orleans, conscious that he had merited peculiar severity from the general, attempted to stammer out some incoherent accounts, but succeeded so ill, that la Fayette, giving way to indignation, attempted to strike him, but missed his aim by the duke retreating, and fainting away in an arm chair. When he came to himself he was directed to wait on the king, and to obey his orders as he valued his life [x]. His majesty, after some mild though pointed observations on his conduct, voluntarily forgave him, but exacted a solemn promise that he should without delay repair to England, and from thence issue orders for an immediate supply of corn for his country [y].

16th Oct. Orleans departs for England.

When Orleans communicated these events to his associates, together with his resolution to adhere to his promise, they were thunderstruck. They attempted to shake his determination by every suggestion and every argument in their power, but in vain. His passports were expedited, and his permission to depart obtained from the assembly, although Mirabeau observed that a mission of so secret a nature resembled a *lettre de cachet*, and made pointed allusions to the imperious deportment of la

---

[x] The circumstances here related are taken from Montjoye: they are not so circumstantially detailed by any other writer, though many authors agree that la Fayette compelled him to leave France; and hint that the methods employed were the reverse of gentleness and persuasion. See Moore's View, vol ii. p. 64. Pagès, vol. i. p. 263. Bouillé's Memoirs, p. 98. Orleans himself states that he had an interview with la Fayette, in which the general told him, that his absence would be conducive to the welfare and tranquillity of France. Exposé de la Conduite de M. le duc d'Orleans, Rédigé par lui même, p. 19.

[y] This mode of proceeding is perfectly consistent with the king's character for clemency, and his rigid adherence to a given promise may contribute to account for the facility with which the exculpatory efforts of Orleans were afterwards received by the assembly, and the queen's refusal to give evidence when required by the commissioners of the Chatelet.

Fayette.

ORLEANS.

Fayette. Orleans refifted every propofal of his friends to incite a popular tumult, or to enter a proteft with the affembly, and left Paris three days before the intended explofion. It it not impoffible that the beams of virtue emanating from the king, might kindle fome congenial fentiment in the bofom of Orleans, but as la Fayette was conftantly urging his departure, it is more probable that fear alone occafioned his fidelity to his promife. His fubfequent conduct affords no light on the fubject, for though he performed the real object of his miffion with fo much exactnefs, that in lefs than a month after his departure bread was plentiful and cheap in Paris, yet, contrary to the ufual effects of compunction, he afterwards perfevered in the fame meafures as before. At Boulogne a flight attempt was made to ftop his departure by an infurrection of the people, but without effect: a deputation was fent from Boulogne, and the prefident acting extra-officially, in the name of the affembly, confirmed the permiffion given for the duke to depart. Dumouriez afferts that this miffion to England was in confequence of an intrigue of the minifter, Montmorin, who wifhed to induce Orleans to abfent himfelf from France, and to effect that purpofe, infpired him with a wifh to become duke of Brabant[z]. But the authority of Dumouriez on the fubject of Orleans is very queftionable, and the fcheme here imputed to him utterly improbable. He was never fo much in habits of intimacy with Montmorin as to be open to his efforts of intrigue; and his plans refpecting the French monarchy were too extenfive, and had involved him in a connection too complicated to admit of his forming a new engagement. If he had entertained fuch views, England was almoft the worft fpot on the face of globe he could have repaired to for countenance or affiftance,

[z] Life of Dumouriez, vol. ii. p. 100.

assistance, in a plan to excite insurrection and dismember the empire [a].

His reception affords the best refutation of such a report. He was presented at court, but hardly, according to the best authenticated reports, honoured with any notice by the august and virtuous personages who fill the throne. Their known attachment to principles and modes of conduct diametrically opposite to his, their love of virtue, and constant practice of religion and morality, occasioned that coolness which prevented his frequent visits at St. James's. His debased manners, his taste for gross licentiousness and vulgar revelry, soon took away the respect his birth and fortune inspired. He was never easy within himself; the immense projects in which he was engaged rendered him restless, and he hurried through the various rounds of pleasure, snatching at every one with a greedy hand, yet incapable of relishing what he sought with so much avidity. The turf, the gaming-table, the bottle, and the brothel, engaged him by turns; at each of these scenes, where refinement is capable of diminishing the opprobrium of pursuit, he, like a harpy, was greedy of all, and disgusted every body: Men of refinement shunned him, and losing that extensive adulation and public acclamation he had received in his own country, his time soon became irksome, and he was impatient to revisit those scenes in which his heart was so much engaged, and all his hopes concentered.

---

[a] On his own trial, Orleans gave such an account of this journey as renders it almost certain that it had no political object. He said he had letters for Mr. Pitt, which he delivered; and that as he was very intimate with the opposition-party, he was employed to preserve peace with England. Procès des Bourbons, vol. iii. p. 164. In his own "account of his conduct," Orleans states that he was intrusted with an important mission, but does not specify its nature or extent. See Exposé de la Conduite, &c. p. 26.

ORLEANS.

1790. Exertions of his party.

The duke's party in France were too much interested in his continuing the part of a conspirator, to permit him to relinquish it from despair of ultimate success. They did not abate their diligence, though their task was rendered much more difficult by his absence, and by other circumstances. The presence of a chief, however weak, vacillating, and uncertain he may be, is the soul of a conspiracy; so long as he can be resorted to, and personally give directions, there is an order, a method, a spirit in the proceedings, which in his absence they necessarily want. But, in the present case, the fears of the faction had a different source, they apprehended a reflux of the public opinion in favour of the royal family. They renewed their intrigues and calumnies, but they were not always attended with effect, for the people of Paris being relieved from the fear of famine, and not under the influence of accustomed instigation, did not so readily adopt the pernicious projects of the conspirators. La Fayette, actuated by vanity and imprudence, unintentionally assisted the Orleanists by his unnecessary cruelty to the royal prisoners, and by his jealous vigilance, and unmanly persecution of every one who seemed warmly attached to their cause.

June. His return.

At length the imprudence of la Fayette and Bailly led them to project the confederation. The scheme of assembling so many armed men from the provinces at Paris, afforded an opportunity the conspirators could not overlook of trying by means of insurrection to forward their plans. They lamented the absence of their chief, as an irreparable obstacle, and exerted all their manœuvres to accelerate his return. La Fayette, on the other hand, opposed it, but in that inconsiderate manner which marked most of his proceedings. Instead of applying directly to the king for his interference, he, by his own authority, sent an aid-de-camp who waited on the duke, requiring him to continue in London.

London. This inexpert agent had the folly to commit these orders to writing and leave it in the duke's hands. He immediately wrote to his chancellor, who was a member of the assembly, to lay these facts, together with his desire to take the civic oath, and be present at the intended ceremony before the legislative body, and move for his recall. The favourable reception of this motion was facilitated and increased by a pamphlet published at the time, and pretended to be written by himself, called "a Narrative of the Conduct of the Duke of Orleans, during the French Revolution." La Fayette, detected in his shallow politics, had no opposition to make to the motion of the count de la Touche, he affected to explain away the mission of M. Boinville, his aid-de-camp, but the duke's recall was decreed. He arrived in Paris and took the civic oath, but the shortness of the time, the press of business, and the good disposition of the *fédérés*, did not afford him an opportunity of trying the success of any schemes. The confederation day passed, contrary to his wishes, and to the fears of many, without the smallest popular commotion. He gave a public dinner the next day in the hall of the *palais royal*, at which some attempts were made in his favour, but without success.

11th July.
Arrives in Paris.

15th.

Proceedings in the Chatelet.

During the absence of Orleans, the assembly, under the influence of his faction, had referred Mounier's denunciation of the transactions of the 5th and 6th of October, to the Chatelet; hoping, by their ordinary means of bribery and terror, and by the agency of their friends, to prevent serious inquiry. To render the efforts of this court abortive, they limited their instructions to the night of the 5th of October, denying them the means of inquiring into the causes of the insurrection in the morning, or any of the events of that day, prior to the arrival of la Fayette and the national guards at Versailles. Their view appears to have been, either to involve

ORLEANS.

involve the whole transaction in impenetrable obscurity, or to throw the odium of it on the general. The committee in the assembly furnished very few proofs, and those of the most vague description; and every engine was employed to induce the court to acquit the parties implicated. The judges of the Chatelet proceeded in the execution of their duty with great steadiness, secrecy, and patience. They applied to the committee for more proofs; which being delayed, they exerted themselves to make such discoveries as should enable them to form a true report. They were about to have reported on the subject, when the duke's party, having gained intelligence of the spirit of their proceedings, wrote to him in England for instructions; and, in consequence of his answer, employed all means in their power to procure delay. They caused the municipality to present to the court seventy-five additional proofs; which protracted the inquiry till Orleans had obtained permission to return to France. The 7th Aug. court at length, in spite of menaces, intrigues, and slanders, presented at the bar of the assembly a report of the evidence they had collected, accompanied with a declaration, that it involved in a charge of guilt two members of that body. The faction had the address to get the report of the Chatelet referred to a committee, in which a person entirely devoted to them had the charge of abridging it for the use of the members; and he succeeded so well in falsifying the evidence presented, in placing in a false light the facts advanced, and in recurring to the *orgies* of the *gardes du corps*, &c. that a decree was 2d Oct. easily obtained, importing that there was no ground of accusation against the parties. A speech in favour of Orleans was pronounced in the tribune by the duc de Biron, who promised, in the name of his friend, a full explanation of his whole conduct. This promise he himself repeated the next day, professing a wish to clear himself from every suspicion; but he

performed

performed his undertaking in a very imperfect manner, by an apology in the form of a *memoire à consulter*, or cafe, to which was annexed the opinion of two obscure advocates, Hom and Rozier[b]. It was answered by Malouet, and fell into deserved disregard.

Exertions of Orleans The proceedings of the Chatelet did not so much occupy the mind of Orleans, as to prevent his trying many plans to counteract the growing popularity of the king and queen, and to further the ultimate success of his ambitious views. On his return from England, he soon found his party stronger than ever[c]; but la Fayette being commander of the national guard, and Bailly mayor of Paris, were insurmountable obstacles to the exertion of his two favourite means of success, riot and famine. He laboured therefore with great assiduity to obtain their dismission[d] to bring undeserved odium on every act of the royal prisoners, and to render their situation as irksome as possible, in order to produce some act which might make them quit the kingdom, or expose them to the violence of the populace. In the provinces several insurrections and disturbances took place; and the inflammable mob of Paris were ready on every occasion, when not restrained by fear, to rise in arms and commit violence. They were furnished with pikes at the expence of Orleans, which were, for that reason, according to the punning genius of the French nation, denominated *Feb. 1791. Philip-piques*[e]. Santerre disciplined the mob of the *fauxbourg* St. Antoine, in hopes, by their means,

[b] It is translated into English, and forms an octavo pamphlet of eighty-three pages, published by Stockdale, 1790.
[c] Bouillé's Memoirs, p. 166. [d] Idem, p. 241. 270.
[e] Historical Essay on the Ambition and Conquests of France, p. 234. Montjoye also relates, that a caricature print was published, representing the king and the duke of Orleans playing at piquet for the crown. This emblem of royalty was slipping from the king's head; and on a label which proceeded from his mouth were these words: "J'ai ecarté les cœurs; il a pour lui les piques, & j'ai perdu la partie."

to

to wreſt from la Fayette the command of the national guard, and actually ventured to oppoſe himſelf to the general in the affair at Vincennes [f].

The king's unfortunate attempt to eſcape from the cuſtody of his perſecutors gave a great aſcendancy to the duke's party. At firſt it was ſuppoſed that, on the king's leaving the realm, a regency would be appointed; and as Monſieur had quitted the kingdom, the conſtitution pointed out Orleans as regent. That he might not appear deſirous of attaining this ſituation, he addreſſed a letter to all the journaliſts, in which he ſolemnly renounced the right given him by the conſtitution to expect the regency. This letter is written with conſiderable art, for while he makes this pretended renunciation, he alludes in pompous terms to his zeal for the public, and his ſacrifices in the cauſe of liberty [g]. The moderation thus diſplayed was merely affected, for if the aſſembly had decreed that he ſhould be regent, which, from the aſcendancy of his party, there was every reaſon to ſuppoſe, he could not have reſiſted their deciſion. On the king's return to Paris, Orleans was obſerved in a circle of deputies, a gay ſpectator of the melancholy ſcene [h]. During the king's ſuſpenſion, the queſtion of abdication and trial was preſſed in the aſſembly with all the zeal and power of his party. The aſſembly, to avoid the groſs term *decheance*, forfeiture, uſed that of *deſtitution*, privation; but in the Jacobin club, then the ſenate of the Orleaniſts, the matter was treated without ceremony or circumlocution. At that period, the project of a republic was firſt openly avowed in France; but many who affected to ſupport it were clandeſtinely promoting the advancement of their patron, by familiarizing the people to the expectation of dethroning the monarch. In all

June.
Effect of the king's flight.

[f] See LA FAYETTE. Bouillé's Memoirs, p. 299.
[g] See Anecdotes du Regne de Louis XVI. vol. vi. p. 236.
[h] Moore's View, vol. ii. p. 368.

probability the views of the party would have been crowned with success thus far;—the king would have been deposed, and the duke constituted regent during the minority of the dauphin, but for the secession of some principal leaders of his faction. Barnave unexpectedly assumed the defence of the king, and, assisted by the royalists, prevailed on the assembly to decree the completion of the constitution in the form originally intended [j]. The party had made themselves so sure of a complete victory, that they had neglected their usual precautions of packed tribunes and a hired mob. Robespierre was so astonished and enraged at this unexpected event, that he ran about the streets like a madman, exclaiming to the people, " My friends, all is lost; the " king is to be restored [k]."

Disappointment of Orleans.

17th July. Meeting in the Champ de Mars.

Baffled in their expectations from the assembly, the faction endeavoured to carry their point by means of the populace. They prepared a petition that very night, to be signed on the altar of the confederation in the *Champ de Mars* the next morning. The mob assembled, and began by murdering a hairdresser and an invalid, whose heads they stuck on pikes, and carried to the *palais royal*. The members, the Cordeliers, or *société fraternelle*, inflamed the populace with declamations and hand-bills of the most atrocious description. After several messages from la Fayette and Bailly, requiring the mob to disperse, military law was proclaimed and executed [l]. The constitution was revised and accepted by the king, and the assembly dissolved.

29th Nov. Petion elected mayor.

According to the requisition of the new constitution, la Fayette resigned the command of the national guard, and Bailly the mayoralty of Paris. This revived the hopes of Orleans, that by procuring that office for a creature of his own, he should

[j] See THE KING, &c.   [k] See ROBESPIERRE.
[l] See LA FAYETTE.

again

again be able, by a monopoly of grain, to influence the city, and, through it, the whole kingdom. Petion was elected; but the duke's views with respect to a monopoly were totally frustrated by Bailly, who caused the care of the provisions of the capital to be vested in the administrators of the department.

Sitting of the legislative assembly.

The new assembly, destitute of the experience and talents which had been the portion of their predecessors, were delivered up to a faction composed of editors of newspapers, pamphleteers, and other labourers in the lower branches of literature, who had been supported by, and were still in the pay of the duke. Amongst these were the most rancorous enemies of the king, on whom they immediately commenced an attack; but the mildness of his temper, and the resolution he had formed to abide by the constitution, which was the object of his daily study, rendered their measures abortive.

Orleans made admiral.

The peace of Europe was incompatible with the views of the new demagogues, who were resolved to procure a declaration of war against the emperor. Orleans, through the influence of Thevenard, minister of marine, who hoped to conciliate the new assembly, had been promoted to the rank of admiral [m]. This promotion it was supposed would be the more acceptable, as he had before solicited a military command, without success [n]. The insubordination of the navy was such, that most of the officers promoted at the same time resigned; Orleans and d'Estaing alone retained the rank assigned to them [o].

His desire of reconciliation with the king.

At this period, Orleans seems to have been sensible of the impolicy of his conduct: he saw the spirit of republicanism beginning to rise, and would have been happy to compromise his hopes of aggrandisement, for an honourable promotion and certain safety. His conduct on this occasion is so

---

[m] Bertrand's Memoirs, vol. i. p. 229.
[n] Anecdotes du Regne de Louis XVI. vol. vi. p. 236.
[o] Bertrand's Memoirs, vol. i. p. 310.

remarkable, that I shall not in the narrative alter a word from Bertrand [p], who gives it as a party immediately concerned, and as an eye-witness.—

"The duke of Orleans was not satisfied with writing to me, that he had accepted the rank of admiral; he likewise paid me a visit, and amongst other matters, he assured me that he set the higher value upon the favour which the king had conferred on him, because it gave him the means of convincing his majesty how much his sentiments had been calumniated. This declaration was made with an air of openness and sincerity, and accompanied with the warmest protestations of loyalty. I am very unfortunate, (said he,) without deserving to be so; a thousand atrocities have been laid to my charge, of which I am completely innocent. I have been supposed guilty by many men, because I have disdained to enter into any justification of myself from crimes of which I have a real horror. You are the first minister to whom I ever said as much, because you are the only one whose character ever inspired me with confidence: you will soon have an opportunity of judging whether my conduct gives the lie to my words.—He pronounced these last words with a voice and manner which convinced me he meant them as an answer to the air of incredulity with which I listened to him. I answered him, that I was so much afraid of weakening the force of his expressions in reporting them to the king, as he desired I should, that I begged of him to deliver them himself to his majesty. He replied, that it was precisely what he wished; and that if he could flatter himself that the king would receive him, he would go to the court the next day. I gave his majesty an account, the same evening at the council, of the

[p] Bertrand's Memoirs, vol. i. p. 310.

"visit I had received from the duke of Orleans,
"and all that had passed; adding, that I could not
"help being convinced of the sincerity of his pro-
"fessions. The king resolved to receive him; and
"the following day had a conversation with him of
"more than half an hour, with which his majesty
"appeared to be well satisfied.—I am of your opi-
"nion (said he to me) that he returns to us with
"sincerity; and that he will do all that depends
"on him to repair the mischiefs which have been
"committed in his name, and in which very pos-
"sibly he has not had so great a share as we have
"suspected.—The following Sunday the duke of
"Orleans came to the king's levee, where he met
"with the most mortifying reception from the
"courtiers, who were ignorant of what had passed;
"and from the royalists, who usually came on that
"day to pay their court to the royal family. They
"pressed round him, treading designedly upon his
"toes, and pushing him towards the door. When
"he went into the queen's apartment, where the
"cloth was already laid, as soon as he appeared they
"cried out on every side—Let nobody approach
"the dishes!—insinuating that he might throw
"poison into them. The insulting murmurs which
"his presence excited forced him to retire without
"seeing any of the royal family. He was pursued
"to the top of the stairs, and as he was going
"down, some spit over the staircase upon him.
"He hastened out, filled with rage and indignation,
"and convinced that the king and queen were the
"authors of these outrages; of which they were
"not only ignorant, but extremely concerned
"when they were informed of them. From that
"moment the duke of Orleans conceived impla-
"cable hatred, and vowed vengeance against the
"king and queen. He kept his oath but too
"well. I happened to be at court that day, and
"was an eye-witness to the scene I have just re-
"lated."

" lated." Thus was the royal caufe unintentionally injured by the royalifts, whofe conduct on this occafion demonftrates, that far from having fecret cabals and confpiracies, they did not even maintain that confidential intercourfe which was effential to their intereft.

Jacobin miniftry. The Orleanifts and republicans in the affembly ftill perfevered in their attacks; they forced on the king an adminiftration compofed of Jacobins, his moft inveterate foes. They paffed feveral decrees, by virtue of which he was required, with his own hand, to inflict the fevereft wounds on fuch of his family as had left the kingdom; to force the confcience of men for whom he had the fincereft refpect; and to furround his own dwelling with a banditti of twenty thoufand murderers, at the devotion of the Jacobins. To thefe decrees he oppofed the fhield with which the conftitution had provided him, the *veto*. They endeavoured to impel him to a frefh flight, by affected kindnefs in reprefenting his danger, and by alarming reports of the popular fury; but his refolution to remain expofed to all the fury of his enemies, deftroyed the effect of their machinations.

20th June, 1792. Attack on the palace. Fruftrated in all thefe fchemes, the Orleanifts recurred to their accuftomed meafures of popular infurrection. They took advantage of the exercife of the *veto*, and the difmiffion of the minifters, to raife a furious mob, whofe defign to murder the king and his family was averted by the fenfibility of a hired populace to the virtue and courage of thofe they were paid to deftroy. Orleans on this occafion acted with that pufillanimity which was his characteriftic, and which always prevented the fuccefs of his fchemes. Fearing to have his conduct again fubmitted to the judges of a criminal court, he left Paris a few days before the intended affault of the caftle, and went into the country, to confult with the chiefs of the army in his intereft, on the

Timidity of Orleans.

means

means of securing the fruits of his success. The head of a faction, skulking about the country *incognito*, when a decisive blow is about to be struck in the capital, is one of those novelties which the life of this weak and wicked conspirator alone can afford. In the course of his excursion he visited Valenciennes. Dumouriez says, " The duke of " Orleans made his appearance at Valenciennes, " *without any one being able to discover the motive.* " Biron protected this detestable prince. Du- " mouriez had been intimate with Biron during " twenty years; and acquainted, though upon rather " cool terms, during the same period with the duke; " but *thenceforward he distinguished his two sons, who* " *were very unlike their unworthy father* q." Let it be recollected, that when this general published his memoirs, Orleans and Biron were no longer in existence to contradict him; and that there is no cause assigned why he chose that particular æra to distinguish his two sons, and a proper estimate may be formed of the candour and veracity of the general, and the extent of the duke's intrigues. His journey and return were observed, and excited conjecture and suspicion r.

The twentieth of June not having produced all the effects expected by the conspirators, a new insurrection was organised, which succeeded to the utmost extent of their hopes. Though in the result of this conspiracy the interests of Orleans were not considered, he was very instrumental in preparing and perfecting it s. It is even said that the names, additions, and places of abode of those who were active in this conspiracy, were precisely the same with those who were employed on the fifth of October 1789 t. Orleans, however, kept as usual

10th Aug. Deposition of the king.

---

q Life of Dumouriez, vol. iii. p. 13.
r Mercure François, N° du 28 Juillet 1792, p. 277.
s Pagès, vol. i. p. 476.
t Histoire de la Conspiration du 10 Août, par M. Bigot de Ste. Croix.

far distant from the scene of action ᵘ; and his pusillanimity is said to have extended to his banditti, who fled at the first volley ˣ. Though the vengeance of Orleans was abundantly gratified by the result of this day, his ambition was severely mortified. The king was reduced to the lowest political ebb, deprived of his guards, suspended, imprisoned; but the people, instead of shouting *Vive d'Orleans!* had learned to shout *Vive la liberté* ʸ!

<small>Sept. Arrests and massacres.</small>
In consequence of the king's suspension, a national convention was decreed; and the flatterers of Orleans, or those interested to prey on his folly, led him to expect that this measure would conduce to a full and speedy attainment of all his wishes. He spared neither money nor influence to procure those persons to be returned who were devoted to him, and to intimidate and destroy the friends of the monarch and of the existing constitution. La Fayette had fled, and the disorganised armies were entirely commanded by those whom Orleans supposed to be his creatures. He procured the arrestation of many persons of influence, who were presumed to possess an attachment to the king; and that he might effectually prevent their obstructing his projects, he directed, or at least sanctioned, the <small>2d Sept.</small> horrible massacres committed in the prisons ᶻ. In these transactions his avarice as well as his ambition found a gratification, by the murder of his accomplished relative the princesse de Lamballe, which <small>Orleans changes his name.</small> he is said to have expressly commanded ᵃ. He procured himself to be returned a member to the new convention by the agency of Robespierre and Danton; and to prevent all prejudice which might arise

---
ᵘ Pagès, vol. i. p. 478.   ˣ Louvet's Narrative, p. 17.
ʸ Fennel's Review, p. 473.
ᶻ See in Gibbon's Posthumous Works, vol. i. a very interesting letter, describing the fate of several victims of these massacres, and ascribing the organization of them to Orleans.
ᵃ Peltier's late Picture of Paris, vol. ii. p. 262. 382. 384. See MANUEL.

from

from his name exciting a recollection of his affinity to the royal family, he wrote to the *commune* of Paris, renouncing his family appellative, alleging the impurity of his mother's life in proof that he was not a descendant of the Bourbons, and declaring that he was the son of her coachman. He requested of the *commune* to assign him a new name, and they conferred what they termed *the beautiful name of* EGALITE [b].

But these very measures which he imagined would strengthen his interest, and infallibly give success to his projects, frustrated his views, and produced his ruin. With his usual propensity to low company, and the disgusting familiarity of the refuse of mankind, he lavished his favour on the most abandoned and worthless of his partisans. To the utter disgust of the men of letters and superior attainments in his party, he was always surrounded by such wretches as Marat, Collot d'Herbois, Clootz, and Chabot. The massacres of September having been planned and executed by this class of his followers, and they alone enriched by them, some others of his needy partisans became angry and disgusted. The eagerness with which the people now received the abolition of royalty, suggested to some the hope of establishing a federal republic, a chimera which they pursued with ardour. Thus arose a division amongst his friends, which, in the end, left him a solitary mark for the first interested usurper to shoot at. Many of his agents, in fact, as soon as by his means they had obtained independence, and even luxury, elevated their views, they saw the solicitude of the rabble for the downfal of royalty, and affected to second it, nay even in violation of known truth, pretended to have been always republicans. To the design of their adversaries of forming a federal republic, they

Defection of his adherents.

---

[b] Moore's Journal, vol. i. p. 419. Playfair's History of Jacobinism, p. 604.

opposed

oppofed that of a triumvirate or dictatorfhip, which, flattering their refpective views and ambition, divorced them ftill more effectually from the interefts of their patron. The firft ftep taken by the convention was to decree the abolition of royalty; this was done on the motion of Collot d'Herbois, without oppofition, all the members who were prefent vied in giving this proof of their being animated with the prevailing fpirit.

Infignificance in the convention. At this period the unfortunate and worthlefs Egalité percieved the inextricable dilemma into which he was drawn. The king was depofed, but royalty was abolifhed, confequently there was no probability that he could ever be regent. Amongft other popular novelties, mention was made of an agrarian law, a fyftem which he had no longer fufficient power to counteract, and to which his remaining property was a moft inviting bait [c]. He faw that the Gironde, except a few individuals, who were fecretly his friends, hated him, and that his own worthlefs confederates, the Mountain, defrauded and betrayed him. Their rapacity drove him to the moft fcandalous expedients to raife money, and inftead of a throne he faw that he was barely purchafing a precarious protection. His importance was reduced to nothing. In the convention, which, as he had bought it with his money, he expected to ufe as a property, he was the moft infignificant of all members. He generally attended for the fpace of half an hour every

---

[c] With all his profufion, Orleans was never generous; and though he appeared to make great pecuniary facrifices, he was always tremblingly alive to an attack on his property. He carried his cupidity to fuch an excefs, that he actually made a ridiculous application to the conftituent affembly for four million one hundred and fifty eight thoufand eight hundred and fifty livres (181,949 *l.* 3 *s.* 9 *d.*), together with intereft from the year 1721, as the dower promifed to Louifa-Elizabeth d'Orleans, queen of Spain, and by her affigned over to the anceftors of the duke. This demand was referred to the next legiflative body, but I do not find that it was ever renewed. See Debates, 13th June 1791.

day, looked round him, and went out unnoticed[d]. In the army he still hoped to maintain his influence by means of Dumouriez, who continued attached to him, and ardent in promoting his son: but even on this he could not depend, as he saw his best military friends disgraced or led to the scaffold. The battle of Jemappe, which raised the spirits of the populace so high, and in the account of which Dumouriez praised Egalité's eldest son, gave him a transient gleam of sunshine, and emboldened him for the first time, to speak in the convention in praise of the general; but this hope was of short duration; Marat was busy with his libels and posting-bills, destroying the reputation, and throwing suspicion on the character of this fortunate warrior; and Pache, the war minister, was crippling all his operations.

Conduct during the king's trial.

During the king's trial Orleans displayed, in a remarkable manner, the prevalence of revenge over ambition. He could not reasonably entertain hopes that he should ever be enabled to ascend the throne after the formal abolition of royalty, and the declaration of some members, that they voted against Louis more for the crime of having been a king than for any other. Perhaps the approach of Dumouriez to the capital was in consequence of a concerted plan, to gratify, under some form, the ambition of Orleans, and inspired new hopes. There is no doubt that the Mountain used every effort of terror and conciliation to keep him firm to their interests, as they were apprehensive that even a single vote might determine the question against them. By his means, during the *appel nominal*, the doors of the convention were surrounded by assassins, who frightened with clamour, and threatened with their daggers, all whom they suspected of opposing their views[e].

---

[d] Moore's Journal, vol. ii. p. 248.
[e] Journal de Clery, p. 198.

Whatever

1793.
His votes.

Whatever were the wishes and hopes of Orleans, it might be expected that he would abstain from voting on the question which decided the fate of his unfortunate cousin, but he was reserved to exhibit depravity in all its disgusting nudity, without even the veil which fear or hypocrisy supply, when better motives are wanting. The manner in which his vote on the first question, " Is Louis guilty?" was received, might have convinced him that honour, decency, and even his personal safety required that he should abstain from giving an opinion on the other two. As soon as the monosyllable *Oui* escaped his lips, the convention, by loud murmurs, testified astonishment. On the second question, " of referring the punishment to the nation in primary assemblies," he voted with the Mountain against the reference, and the same murmurs testified the same feelings. He had an interval for reflection after these hints, before the third *appel nominal* came on. The question was " What punishment had Louis incurred?" On this point he renewed the surprise and horror of the assembly, and entailed on himself the execration of every feeling mind, by the memorable sentence which he read from the tribune: " *Uniquement occupé de mon* " *devoir, convaincu que tous ceux qui ont attenté, ou* " *attenteroient par la suite, à la souveraineté du* " *peuple meritent la mort,* JE VOTE POUR LA MORT. " Influenced by no consideration but that of per" forming my duty, convinced that all who have " conspired, or who shall hereafter conspire, against " the sovereignty of the people deserve death, I " VOTE FOR DEATH." The horror excited by this trait of villany could hardly be suppressed; the assembly was in a general ferment; one member, starting from his seat, and striking his hands together, exclaimed, *Ah! le scelerat!* many repeated that expression, and *Oh! l'horreur! Oh! le monstre*†!

---

† See Moore's Journal, vol. ii. p. 577. 580. Necker on the Revolution, vol. i. p. 403.

This conduct, which excited great indignation in the people [f], produced no other effect in the king's mind than a sense of the degraded state of his worthless persecutor. "I do not know," he said, "what I have done to my cousin to make him behave to me in the manner he has; but he is to be pitied. He is still more unfortunate than I am. I certainly would not change conditions with him [h]." Orleans is said to have been a pleased spectator of the catastrophe of this horrid tragedy. Accompanied by his eldest son, he saw with a smile, from the *Pont de Louis* XVI. the decapitation of the virtuous monarch [i].

Heroic conduct of the king.

Whatever might be the hopes of Orleans at this moment, whether he had any latent expectations from the promises or principles of the Mountain, or whether his ambition confined itself to the tranquil enjoyment of the remains of his property, cannot be determined, but the day of the king's death put an end to all his comforts. He was alarmed by anonymous notes threatening him with assassination and with poison, and loading him with every reproach: he surrounded himself with a guard of *sans culottes* formidably armed, who prevented all access to him, except after the minutest scrutiny: he never slept twice together in the same room, and frequently changed his apartment in the course of the night: he wore armour under his clothes, and took every other precaution which fear and jealousy could suggest. To the dread of assassination was added that of public impeachment; he knew that a word from the Mountain constituted his death warrant; and to obtain their forbearance, he sacrificed to their cupidity every thing which would raise money; plate, furniture, pictures, gems, all were sold. His virtuous lady, who had long mourned

Terror of Orleans.

---

[f] Journal de Clery, p. 201.
[h] Bertrand's Memoirs, vol. iii. p. 265.
[i] Peltier's late Picture of Paris, vol. ii. p. 45.

the effects of his vices and ambition, struck with the prevailing horror at his late conduct, and urged by her friends, obtained a separation from him, and retired to the house of her father.

Supposed plots in his favour. For some time after the death of Louis XVI. it was supposed that the partisans of Egalité were secretly labouring to procure his appointment to the protectorate [k]. This suspicion was carried by some to a most ridiculous excess; one deputy affirmed, that Robespierre and the *commune* of Paris had conspired to raise Egalité to the throne, and that Egalité had promised to make Robespierre prime minister *for life*, and convert the *national* into a *municipal* representation, in which the representatives of Paris should be exclusively legislators for all France [l]. *10th Mar.* A conspiracy of some kind was entered into, and excited much alarm. Orleans was generally understood to be actively concerned in it, but what end was proposed, or how it failed, are still inscrutable mysteries. Brissot exhausted his ingenuity in conjectures [m], and Garat avows his inability to explain the matter [n].

Total decline of his influence. The failure of this undefined project completed the ruin of Orleans, his few remaining partisans speedily deserted him. Before the king's death, Buzot and Louvet had moved for his banishment, but they were opposed by the Mountain, who apprehended that the loss of his vote and influence would be fatal to their views [o], and particularly by Robespierre, who virulently inveighed against this new species of ostracism [p]. They procured an adjournment of the question till after the king's trial. *23d Mar.* The popular society of Amiens sent a letter requiring an

[k] Miles's Conduct of France towards Great Britain examined, p. 150.
[l] Garat's Memoirs, p. 197.
[m] Brissot to his Constituents, p. 86.
[n] Garat's Memoirs, p. 114. 126.
[o] See Debates of 16th and 19th December 1792.
[p] See Robespierre à ses Commettans, vol. i. p. 485.

irrevocable

irrevocable decree of banishment against all the Bourbons, but as they imprudently added a request that a decree of accusation might be pronounced against Marat and some other demagogues, the convention passed to the order of the day. Robespierre also moved that *all* the relations of the late king should be banished, but with the like success.

27th.

The flight of Dumouriez, and the obvious connection of that general with the Orleans family, completely subjected Egalité to his adversaries. In vain he professed in the convention his resolution to imitate the elder Brutus, in sacrificing his son to his country; his destruction was doomed, and he had neither virtue, property, or friends to defend or console him. When the news of Dumouriez's treason arrived, la Source moved that Egalité and Sillery should be taken into custody, but having implicated Danton in his censures, the debate took another turn. He was, however, that same day struck out of the books of the Jacobin club. He was next indirectly denounced by Barbaroux, but as that deputy contented himself with requiring that Valence, and all persons connected with the family of Orleans, should be arrested, Egalité seconded the motion, and thus obtained a momentary reprieve. This lenity was perhaps merely owing to the uncertainty which attended the final event of Dumouriez's exertions, for so soon as his want of power was discovered, the proceedings of the convention became more decisive. Marat moved, that as there were no proofs against Egalité, his character of deputy should be respected, but a letter having been read relating a conversation which he had held, in which he alluded to the probability of his being king, Boyer Fonfrede moved, that *all* the members of the Bourbon family should be retained as hostages for the arrested commissioners, which was decreed. Marat, a few days afterwards, said, that he could not tell whether Phillippe Egalité was a traitor, but that he

Flight of Dumouriez.

1st April.

5th.

7th. Decree against Orleans.

12th.

he knew him to be a man without morals, without capacity, and without honour [q].

7th May. He is imprisoned. When, in consequence of the decree granted on Boyer's motion, Orleans was taken into custody, he wrote to the convention to be informed whether the decree was meant to extend to him, an affirmative burst from every mouth. He protested against his detention, on the principle of his inviolability as a representative of the people; but they passed to the order of the day; and he was conveyed to the Abbaye. At the approach of the guards who came to arrest him, he fainted away, and on his being put in prison, exhibited every appearance of abjectness and terror. He was removed to Marseilles, *11th. Sent to Marseilles.* together with several others of his family, and there confined. The first violence of his grief and fear having subsided, he gave himself up to the enjoyment of every species of luxury and debauchery in his power. He underwent an interrogatory before the criminal tribunal of Marseilles, but they having no instructions, pronounced him not guilty. They were soon however informed of the disposition of the convention, and instead of enlarging him after his acquittal, confined him in a close and damp dungeon.

7th June. Writes to the convention. From this place he wrote to the convention, humbly supplicating that they would lighten his chains, if not restore him to liberty; expressing a hope that their definitive judgment would be in his favour, and that they would grant him that liberty which he had never employed but for the good of his country. This address however produced no effect, and he was for some time apparently forgotten. *15th July.* In the report made by Billaud Varennes respecting the imprisoned deputies, he was only slightly implicated on account of his connection with Petion.

[q] See Debates.

At length, after he had suffered near six months imprisonment at Marseilles, Amar made his famous report against the Brissotines, and Orleans was implicated in many of the charges. Billaud Varennes immediately said, "Let not the convention forget one man, whom every sentence of the report accuses of the most criminal intentions: I move that Philippe Égalité be comprised in the decree of accusation which delivers all the conspirators to the revolutionary tribunal of Paris." This motion being received with applause, Billaud in continuation proposed, that the votes on this subject should be taken by *appel nominal:* this displeased Robespierre, who opposed the new motion with some asperity; and at length it was decreed in the original form. When the people were informed of the event, they expressed the greatest satisfaction, and rent the air with cries of *Vive la république*! [3d Oct. Decree of accusation.]

He was soon afterwards brought to Paris, and lodged in the Conciergerie till the day of his trial. The jailor gave him a good bed in his own rooms, and he appeared perfectly indifferent to his fate; ate, drank, and slept with apparent tranquillity, never speaking of public affairs [*]. He was at length put on his trial, together with one Coustard, also a deputy; and defended by his old agent and stedfast adherent, Voidel. The interrogatory, which is one of the iniquitous forms of Gallic jurisprudence, charged him principally with a connection with the Brissotines, and with an expression to one Poultier, a deputy, conveying an idea that he was to be king. The jury, with their customary unanimity and inattention to the prisoner's defence, found him guilty of a conspiracy against the unity and indivisibility of the republic, and he was ordered for immediate execution. [Brought to Paris. 6th Nov. Tried.]

[†] Debates.   [*] Procès des Bourbons, vol. iii. p. 158.

He was drawn to the *Place de la Revolution* in a cart, with four other perſons, who diſplayed the moſt dreadful apprehenſions; but, on this awful occaſion, Orleans exhibited an elevation of mind, which, had it been his portion in more proſperous days, would have inſured him happineſs and reputation. His being intended for execution on that day was ſo little known in Paris, that very few people were preſent when firſt he aſcended the cart, but the rumour ſoon flew and attracted innumerable gazers. They reproached him in the coarſeſt terms with all the crimes of his paſt life, his debaucheries, his aſſaſſinations, his perfidy, his vote againſt the king, every thing memory could ſuggeſt. When the cart reached the *palais royal*, with a refinement in cruelty truly Pariſian, they made it ſtop ten minutes, to obſerve the effect produced by contemplating the ſcene of his grandeur and debaucheries. On this great day he diſappointed the hopes of malevolence; he maintained, during his whole progreſs, a ſerenity of countenance and dignity of deportment altogether princely. He looked at the *palais royal*, and read the inſcription on the front denoting it to be national property, without the leaſt apparent emotion. The populace, diſappointed of their expected entertainment, at length permitted him to proceed. At a ſmall diſtance from the place of execution he entered into converſation with a prieſt who was allowed to attend the priſoners, and ſo continued till he came to the foot of the ſcaffold, where, without loſing for a moment the intrepidity ſo recently acquired, he ſubmitted to the knife of the guillotine, which terminated his exiſtence in the forty-ſeventh year of his age, in leſs than ten months after the murder of the king, which he had occaſioned by ſo much expence, ſo much intrigue, and ſo many crimes. His body was thrown without diſtinction amid the crowd of carcaſes which daily

butchery

butchery consigned to the burying-ground of St. Mary Magdalen.

Thus perished this abandoned prince, whom it is now a common mode of speech to call *the monster Egalité*. He subverted a throne without courage or consistency sufficient to avail himself of the result of his own efforts; and squandered an immense fortune with so little judgment, that at his death he scarcely possessed a single friend. He was tacitly excepted, after the fall of Robespierre, from the vote of censure which the *moderés* caused to be passed on the murderers of the other deputies, as no one had integrity or courage enough to propose including him in the list. His name will remain to posterity a perpetual warning to individuals of overgrown property, against the folly of entering into popular conspiracies, and becoming the dupes of men of desperate fortune and daring ambition [t].

Observation.

I shall avoid further discussion of the character of Orleans, by presenting to the reader the following animated comparison, which a late noble and learned author has drawn with equal spirit and feeling.

" It is afflictive to have lived to find, in an age
" called not only civilized but enlightened, in this
" eighteenth century, that such horrors, such un-
" paralleled crimes have been displayed on the
" most conspicuous theatre in Europe, in Paris,
" the rival of Athens and Rome; that I am forced
" to allow, that a multiplicity of crimes, which I
" had weakly supposed were too manifold and too
" absurd to have been perpetrated even in a very
" dark age, and in a northern island, not only not
" commencing to be polished, but inured to bar-
" barous manners, and hardened by long and bar-

---

[t] Playfair, alluding to his firmness on the day of his death, with great justice and considerable humour says, " The duke of Orleans was a coward from calculation, rather than from nature. When there was any mode of escaping, or when he had an alternative, he never risked himself." History of Jacobinism, p. 604. n.

" barous

"barous civil wars among princes and nobility strictly related;—yes, I must *now* believe that any atrocity may have been attempted or practised by an ambitious prince of the blood aiming at the crown, in the fifteenth century. I *can* believe (I do not say I do) that Richard, duke of Gloucester, dipped his hand in the blood of the saint-like Henry the sixth, though so revolting and injudicious an act as to excite the indignation of mankind against him. I can now believe that he contrived the death of his own brother Clarence; and I can think it possible (inconceivable as it was) that he aspersed the chastity of his own mother, in order to bastardise the offspring of his eldest brother:—for all these extravagant excesses have been exhibited in the compass of five years, by a monster, by a royal duke, who has actually surpassed all the guilt imputed to Richard the third; and who, devoid of Richard's courage, has acted his enormities openly, and will leave it impossible to any future writer, however disposed to candour, to entertain one *historic doubt* on the abominable actions of Philip duke of Orleans.

"After long plotting the death of his sovereign, a victim as holy as, and infinitely superior in sense and many virtues to, Henry VI. Orleans has dragged that sovereign to the block, and purchased his execution in public, as in public he voted for it.

"If to the assassination of a brother (like the supposed complicity of Gloucester to that of Clarence) Orleans has not yet concurred; still, when early in the revolution he was plotting the murder of the king, being warned by an associate that he would be detected, he said, 'No; for I will have my (natural) brother, the abbé de St. Far, stabbed too, and then nobody will suspect *me* of being concerned in the murder of my own
"brother.'

ORLEANS.

"brother.' So ably can the assassins of an enlightened age refine on and surpass the atrocious deeds
of Goths and barbarians!

"Shade of Richard of Gloucester! if my weak
pen has been able to wash one bloody speck, one
incredible charge from *your* character, can I but
acknowledge that Philip of Orleans has sullied
my varnish, and at least has weakened all the arguments that I drew from the improbability of
your having waded so deeply into wickedness and
impudence that recoiled on yourself, as to calumniate your own mother with adultery. If *you* did,
it was to injure the children of your brother;
still *you* had not the senseless, shameless effrontery,
to shake your own legitimacy. Philip of Orleans
mocks your pitiful self-partiality; he, in person,
and not by proxy, has declared his own mother
a strumpet, has bastardised himself, and for ever
degraded his children as progeny descended from
a coachman!—for what glory, for what object,
far be it from me to conjecture; who would
have a mind congenial enough to such a monster,
as to be able to guess at his motives* ?"

* See Postscript to Historic Doubts written in 1793. Lord Orford's Works, vol. ii. p. 250*.

THOMAS PAIN.

NOTWITHSTANDING the curiosity excited by the conduct and writings of Pain, and by his being the only Englishman who has appeared as a legislator in France, I should have felt an invincible repugnance to the labour of following him through all the mazes of guilt and fraud, and tracing him from a dishonest obscurity to his present state of infamous notoriety, but the more disgusting and fatiguing part of the task has been already performed with so much perspicuity and ability, that what remains becomes easy and comparatively pleasant. The publication on which I have relied for the facts stated in these Memoirs, is intitled, " The Life of Thomas Pain, the Author of the seditious Writings, intitled Rights of Man, by Francis Oldys, A. M. of the University of Pennsylvania;" a work which, from unquestionable information, I can venture to cite as the production of Mr. Chalmers, the well-known writer of the Lives of De Foe and Ruddiman. This work was first published[a] when Pain, making a violent effort to emerge from the obscurity in which he had remained ever since the peace of 1783, declared himself the opponent of Burke, and the champion of the French revolution. It has been so well received as to have passed through ten editions; and as the author himself has observed,

[a] It has been since abridged by William Cobbett, the American, who writes under the name of Peter Porcupine.

" Mr.

"Mr. Pain has noticed the Life in his Second Part of the Rights of Man; yet, however urged by intereſt, or quickened by ſhame, he has not controverted one aſſertion, he has not explained one incident; he has confirmed ſome facts, without denying any: and, of conſequence, he has admitted the *whole* of the narrative to be *true*, which indeed could not be diſputed, without contradicting dates and invalidating records." Relying on their admiſſion, and on the known character of the author, I ſhall abridge his narrative and diſtinguiſh the notes for which I am indebted to his diligence and accuracy by the ſignature O.

Thomas Pain[x] was born at Thetford in the county of Norfolk. His father, Joſeph Pain, was the ſon of a ſmall, but reputable farmer; a ſtaymaker by trade, and a quaker by religion: his mother was Frances Cocke, the daughter of an attorney at Thetford. For marrying according to the forms of the church, Joſeph Pain was expelled the community of quakers, but that benevolent ſect continued to pity his diſtreſſes through life, and to relieve his wants. The father and mother both lived to know their ſon's vices, to pity his misfortunes, to hear of his fame, but to partake little of his bounty[y]. It aroſe, probably, from the tenets of the father, and the eccentricity of the mother, that Thomas Pain was never baptized, or regularly received into the boſom of any church, though he

29th Jan. 1736-7. Birth and accounts of his parents

---

[x] This man's real name is *Pain*: his fictitious name is *Paine* with a final *e*; for, his father's name was *Pain*; and his own name was *Pain*, when he married, when he correſponded with the exciſe, and when he firſt appeared in America: but, finding ſome inconvenience in his real name, or ſeeing ſome advantage in a fictitious one, he thus changed the name of his family.—O.

[y] Joſeph Pain was buried at Thetford on the 14th of November 1786, aged 78.—Frances Pain, widow, was buried on the 18th of May 1789, and recorded to be 94: but, as ſhe was born in January 1697-8, the pariſh regiſter makes her age to be greater than it was, though ſhe had far outlived the period which is aſſigned to mortals.—O.

was confirmed by the bishop of Norwich. This last circumstance was owing to the zeal of Mrs. Cocke, his aunt, a woman of such goodness, that though she lived on a small annuity, she imparted much of her little income to his mother, while he was not very solicitous about his aged parent, amidst his cares for mankind.

Education. Pain, who was educated at the free-school of Thetford, under Mr. Knowles, was deemed a sharp boy of unsettled application, but left no performances which denote juvenile vigour or uncommon attainments; his studies were confined to reading, *Learns the* writing, and arithmetic. At the age of thirteen *trade of a* he left school to learn his father's business, and *stay-maker.* continued to work with him at Thetford for five years, except a short period during which he was employed by a cousin, who was also a stay-maker at Shipdam in Norfolk [z].

1756. At the age of nineteen he went to London, *Goes to London.* where he is supposed to have remained about two years, but no trace of him is discovered, except that he worked for some with Morris, a very noted *1758.* stay-maker, in Hanover-street, Long Acre. He *To Dover.* next established himself at Dover with Grace, a stay-maker, of whom, under pretence of an attachment to his daughter, he contrived to borrow ten pounds, to set up as a master stay-maker at Sandwich, but he neither married the lady or repaid the money.

Apr. 1759. At Sandwich he lodged with Mrs. Fisher in the *Goes to Sandwich* fish-market, at whose house he collected a congre-

---

[z] He indeed tells himself (Rights, part ii. p. 91.) what surely cannot be true, "That when little more than sixteen years of age, I entered on board the Terrible privateer, Capt. Death." He was certainly born on the 29th of January 1736-7: he was, of course, sixteen on the 29th of January 1753. But the war was not declared against France till the 17th of May 1756, when he had entered into his twentieth year. The Terrible was fitted out probably in the summer of 1756, and was certainly captured in January 1757. These facts evince how little Pain is to be trusted, when he does pretend to give a passage of his own life.—O.

gation,

gation, to whom he preached as an independent, or a methodist. He also wrote a short poem which was never published, on a person in jail, who was restored to life and reason after he had attempted self-destruction. Here he married Mary Lambert, the daughter of James Lambert, who had been an exciseman, and afterwards a sheriff's officer. She was waiting-woman to the wife of Richard Solly, an eminent woollen-draper, and is still praised by her own sex as having been a pretty girl of modest behaviour ª. Whether he was disappointed of an expected fortune, or urged by natural savageness is uncertain, but ere two months had elapsed, his ill usage of his unfortunate wife was notorious. Her former mistress, dame Solly, however, relieved her with constant solicitude. Pain soon after his marriage took a house next the Board-yard on Dolphin key, without being able to furnish it. Rutter, a respectable unholsterer of Sandwich, supplied him with such furniture as he wanted, but being embarrassed with debts and goaded by duns, he was obliged to depart from Sandwich in the night, with his wife. He took with him the stays belonging to a customer, a stove and other articles of furniture from his house, the property of the upholsterer. He left at Sandwich a bad character, which has descended to the present times, and has induced the inhabitants to remark that not a single anecdote of him is remembered which is favourable to his moral character.

and becomes a methodist preacher.

Marries.

7th April 1760. Runs away.

From Sandwich he went to Margate, where he sold the furniture he had so dishonestly obtained; an act, which, had the laws been duly enforced,

Goes to Margate.

ª In the church register there is the following entry: " Thomas
" Pain, of the parish of St. Peter's, in the town of Sandwich in Kent,
" bachelor, and Mary Lambert, of the same parish, spinster, were
" married in this church, by licence, this 27th day of Sept. 1759,
" by me William Bunce, rector. In the presence of Thomas Taylor,
" Maria Solly, John Joslin. (Signed) Thomas Pain, Mary Lam-
" bert."—O.

would

would probably have precipitated his voyage to America, and given him an additional claim to patronage in France. He stayed at Margate only while he settled his affairs, and then departed for London.

Conjectures respecting his wife.

From this period it remains uncertain what fate attended his wife; by some she is said have perished on the road, of ill usage and a premature birth: the women of Sandwich are positive that she died in the British Lying-in Hospital, in Brownlow-street, Long Acre; but the register of this charity, which is kept with commendable accuracy, evinces that she had not been received into this laudable refuge of female wretchedness: and there are others who have convinced themselves by diligent inquiry, that she is still alive, though the extreme obscurity of her retreat prevents ready discovery [b].

Convinced by long experience that he was deficient in some essential requisite, either ability or industry, to succeed as a stay-maker, he fixed his hopes on obtaining a place in the excise. To qualify himself for this situation, and obtain, in the meantime, a necessary subsistence, he retired to his father's house, and after fourteen months of study and trials, obtained a gratification of his wishes, through the kindness of Mr. Cockfedge, the learned recorder of Thetford. He was immediately sent as a supernumerary to gage the brewers' casks at Grantham, and afterwards to watch the smugglers of Alford; but he did not long retain his office, being, for some reason at present unknown, dismissed in a year after his arrival at that place.

July 1761.

1st Dec. 1762. Obtains a place in the excise.

8th Aug. 1764. Dismissed. 27th Aug. 1765. Goes to London.

He was now reduced to the most abject state of indigence, in want of food, raiment, and shelter.

[b] A diligent search in the books of the London Lying-in Hospital, in the City Road, found no such person as Mrs. Pain to have died in it during the years 1760 or 1761; nor is it true, as hath been positively asserted in the newspapers, that she is now living in the workhouse of St. George's, Southwark.—O.

In this miserable condition he returned to London, where he was supported by the disinterested benevolence of some humane individuals till he was restored to the excise. *Restored. 11th July 1766.*

His restoration, however, not being attended with immediate employment, he was obliged to accept an engagement as English usher with Mr. Noble, who kept the great academy in Leman-street, Goodman's-fields, from whom he received twenty pounds a-year, and an additional five pounds for finding his own lodging. Here he continued till Christmas, disliked by the mistress, who yet remembers him, and hated by the boys, who were terrified by his harshness. During this period he lodged with one Oliver, a hair-dresser in Whitechapel, by whom he is still recollected[c]. From Mr. Noble, who relinquished him without regret, he went to Mr. Gardnor's, a reputable school at Kensington, but he remained there only three months. *Usher at an academy.*

1767.

Among other sagacious discoveries with which Mr. Pain has, of late years, benefited mankind, there is one very remarkable, that the knowledge of a clergymen is confined to a, b, ab, and hic, hæc, hoc. Yet even this contemptible modicum of science was wanting, at this period to the accomplishment of Mr. Pain's views of interest or ambition. He was desirous of taking orders, and applied to Mr. Noble for a certificate of his qualification, which that gentleman very properly refused on account his limited education. Disappointed in his wish of regular ordination, Pain felt no abatement of his desire to be a preacher, but gratified himself by holding forth to promiscuous audiences in Moorfields, and other populous places. *Desirous to take orders.*

Becomes a field-preacher.

At length he obtained a regular employ as an excise officer, being sent, after some delays, to Lewes. *Mar. 1768. Goes to Lewes.*

[c] These references to the memory of Mrs. Noble and Mr. Oliver are taken from "The Life of Pain," and, of course, apply to the time of publishing the first edition of that work, 1792.

Lewes

Lewes in Suffex. At this place, by his devotion to the bottle, he acquired the title of a *jolly fellow*, and by greater attention to field sports than his duty, the ironical nick-name of *commodore*. He lodged at the house

July 1769. of Samuel Ollive, a tobacconist, who dying in rather bad circumstances, afforded Mr. Pain an occasion to try his ingenuity in appropriating to himself part of his effects, but he failed in the attempt, and was turned out of doors by the executor, Mr. Atterfol, with marks of indignity and distrust.

1770. But the advantages which the integrity and discernment of the executor withheld, the kindness of the widow and affection of the daughter supplied.

Opens a shop as a grocer. He returned to the house from which he had been so disgracefully expelled, opened the shop in his own name as a grocer, and on his own behalf continued

Defrauds the revenue. to work the tobacco-mill of Ollive, however contrary both the shop and the mill were to the maxims of the excise. Such was his address, or his artifice, that though he had promoted the buying of smuggled tobacco, he was able for several years to cover his practices, and to retain his protector.

1771. Marries Miss Ollive. At the age of thirty-four, he married Elizabeth Ollive, the daughter of his old landlord, who was eleven years younger than himself[a], and a woman of such accomplishments as to attract men of higher rank and greater delicacy. Pain had, however, gained her affections; and she would have him, contrary to the advice of Mr. Atterfol, her father's friend, and to the remonstrances of her own relations. This marriage began inauspiciously, and

Suspected of committing perjury. ended unhappily. Before Pain could have obtained his marriage licence, he swore that he was a *bachelor*, when he knew that he was a *widower*, if indeed his

---

[a] The following entry appears on the parish register of St. Michael in Lewes: "Thomas Pain, *bachelor*, and Elizabeth Ollive, *spinster*, were married in this church, by licence, the 26th of March 1771. By me, Robert Austen, curate. Witnesses, Henry Verrall, Thomas Ollive. (Signed) Thomas Pain, Elizabeth Ollive."—O.

first

first wife were deceased[e]. He was on this occasion instrumental too, with his understanding clear and his eyes opened, in entering on the register that he was a *bachelor*, though he knew he was a *widower*. Now the marriage-act declares it to be felony without benefit of clergy, wilfully to make false entry on the register, with intent to defeat the salutary purposes of recording truth, discriminating characters, and ascertaining property.

In this year Pain made his first effort as a public writer. His production was an election song for one of the candidates at New Shoreham. It was proposed to the poets of Lewes as a prize-subject: his song was adjudged the best, and he was rewarded with a present of three guineas. A design was formed about the same time by the excisemen, to petition parliament for an increase of salary; a sum of money was raised by common contribution, and Pain was employed to write *their case*. After many months labour, " he produced an octavo pamphlet
" of twenty-one pages, which, exclusive of *the in-*
" *troduction*, is divided into two heads; *the state of*
" *the salary of the officers of excise; thoughts on the*
" *corruption arising from the poverty of excise-officers.*
" On these topics, he says all that the ablest writer
" could have said. Truth easily slides into the
" mind, without the assistance of ability, or the
" recommendation of artifice. But if Pain's maiden
" pamphlet be inspected by critical malignity, it
" will be found, like his maturer writings, to
" abound in the false grammar of illiterature, and
" the false thoughts of inexperience. Vigour of
" sentiment and energy of manner will not be de-
" nied him. His first pamphlet will be considered

Commences author.

1772. Writes the Exciseman's Case.

[e] It is a very remarkable fact, that the marriage affidavits, within the district of Lewes, during 1771, the year of Pain's marriage, should be missing; yet, that the marriage affidavits, during 1770 and 1772, should be safe. Whether this loss happened by design, or accident, we will not conjecture, though we think the coincidence rather extraordinary.—O.

" as

"as his best performance by all those who regard truth as superior to falsehood, modesty to impudence, and just complaint to factious innovation[']" Four thousand copies of *the case* were printed by Mr. William Lee of Lewes. But even those intended for the members of parliament were not all distributed; and though Pain reinforced the arguments contained in his pamphlet, by two additional publications, each on a folio sheet, and stayed in London on the business a whole winter, no application to Parliament was made on behalf of his clients. Pain spent their money without obtaining for them any redress, and even left the printer's bill unpaid. It is worthy of remark, that in a newspaper controversy in 1779, he declared, that till the epoch of his *Common Sense*, he had never published a syllable.

1773.

While he was thus employed in every thing but his proper business, his pecuniary affairs became deranged, and he was under the necessity of making an assignment of his effects to Mr. Whitfield of Lewes, his principal creditor. About the same time, his inattention and improper conduct in his office occasioned his dismission; no previous acts of conciliation could avert his disgrace[f], nor could any subsequent efforts effect his restoration. Mr. Whitfield took possession of the property by virtue of his assign-

8th April 1774.

---

[f] This is not the only occasion on which I have used the *very words* of the author to whom I am indebted for my information respecting Pain; but as I have never seen the pamphlet in question, I do not think it proper to make use of the judgment of another person without express acknowledgment.

[g] As every scrap of a great writer is interesting to the curious, we have preserved the subjoined extract of a letter from our author to a superior excise-officer, dated at Lewes, the 24th March 1774: —"Dear Sir, I have requested Mr. Scott to put ye 3d and 4th rd. books for 74 under examination, for as I was in London almost all last winter, I have no other, which have any business in them— Request the favour (if not too inconvenient) to inquire and inform me when they are ordered—and *if you can find out the examiner, desire you will drink a bottle or two of wine with him*—I should like the character to go in as fair as it can."—O.

ment,

ment, and sold it [h]. The other creditors, thinking themselves defrauded by this preference, let loose on their debtor the terriers of the law, and he was obliged to abscond from their pursuit in the cockloft of the White-horse inn, without bedding, and, but for the female servant, without food, till Sunday set him free.

His second wife had no less reason to complain of his unkindness and brutality than his first: she bore with the greatest patience the insults, violences, and repeated beatings, which his harshness and cruelty induced him to inflict, before she sought relief by complaining to her friends. On her representations, after an unhappy union of three years and an half, they executed articles of separation, which were drawn by Mr. Josias Smith, a most respectable attorney at Lewes; she engaging to pay to her husband thirty-five pounds, and he obliging himself to claim no part of whatever goods she might gain in future. *Treatment of his wife.* *24th May 1774. Their separation.*

On leaving Lewes, he fled to London for concealment; and soon after his arrival, hearing that his wife had been kindly received by her brother, and was comfortably settled with him, he disturbed her repose by contesting the validity of the articles so recently executed; but at length a new deed was prepared in such terms as to satisfy all parties. *Goes to London.* *4th June 1774.*

After many useless efforts to obtain his restoration as an officer of the excise, Pain's friend and patron, the late George Lewis Scott, recommended him to Dr. Benjamin Franklin, as a person who could, at that epoch, be useful in America. Franklin gave *Goes to America.*

---

[h] Mr. Whitfield, by publishing the following advertisement, exposed to the whole town of Lewes the desperate state of his debtor's circumstances: "To be sold by auction, on Thursday the 14th of April, and following day, all the household furniture, stock in trade, and other effects, of Thomas Pain, grocer and tobacconist, near the West Gate in Lewes: also, a horse-tobacco and snuff mill, with all the utensils for cutting of tobacco and grinding of snuff; and two unopened crates of cream-coloured stone-ware."—O.

him a recommendatory letter to Mr. Richard Beech, wine-merchant, at Philadelphia; and one of introduction to governor Franklin of the Jerseys. Thus provided he quitted England, leaving behind him acquaintance who did not esteem, and relatives who did not regret him[1].

Sept. 1774.

On his arrival in Philadelphia, he presented his letter to Mr. Beech; but that gentleman discovering that he could not spell correctly, declined recommending him as an usher; and he was engaged by Mr. Aitkin, a bookseller, as shopman, at a salary of twenty pounds a-year. The state of America at this period was such as to afford sufficient scope for the exertions of an active mind, to whatever course it was bent, and Pain did not long remain unnoticed. Quitting the obscure and unprofitable line to which his abilities at first seemed to condemn him, he employed his genius in experiments for fixing a cheap, easy, and expeditious me-

Nov. 1774. His first employment.

Nov. 1775.

---

[1] We subjoin the following letter from Pain's mother to his wife; not only for its own merit, but because it ascertains his identity, and illustrates his character:

" Dear Daughter,   Thetford, Norfolk, 27th July 1774.
" I must beg leave to trouble you with my enquiries concerning my
" unhappy son and your husband: various are the reports, the which
" I find come originally from the Excise-office. Such as his vile
" treatment to you, his secreting upwards of 30*l.* intrusted with him
" to manage the petition for advance of salary; and that since his
" discharge, he have petitioned to be restored, which was rejected with
" scorn. Since which I am told he have left England. To all
" which I beg you'll be kind enough to answer me by due course of
" post.—You'll not be a little surprised at my so strongly desiring to
" know what's become of him after I repeat to you his undutiful beha-
" viour to the tenderest of parents; he never asked of us any thing, but
" what was granted, that were in our poor abilities to do; nay, even
" distressed ourselves, whose works are given over by old age, to let
" him have 20*l.* on bond, and every other tender mark a parent could
" possibly shew a child; his ingratitude, or rather want of duty, has
" been such, that he have not wrote to me upwards of two years.—
" If the above account be true, I am heartily sorry that a woman, whose
" character and amiableness deserves the greatest respect, love, and
" esteem, as I have always on enquiry been informed your's did,
" should be tied for life to the worst of husbands.—I am, dear
" daughter, your affectionate mother   F. PAIN."
" P. S. For God's sake let me have your answer, as I am almost
" distracted."—O.

thod of making faltpetre; and propofed the plan of a faltpetre affociation, for voluntarily fupplying the public magazines with gunpowder.

But that which elevated him to a pitch of unexpected, and, for fuch an exertion, unexampled celebrity, was the publication of the pamphlet called COMMON SENSE. Notwithftanding all the faults of ignorance and rafhnefs with which it abounds; notwithftanding the ingenious expofure of its errors, written by Dr. William Smith, which appeared under the fignature of Cato; this book was fo congenial to the public tafte, that it was univerfally perufed, and loudly praifed. The firft edition was fpeedily fold; a fecond, with a fupplement of one-third more, was immediately prepared; a German tranflation was printed; yet after all thefe editions, and all this applaufe, this wonder-working pamphlet brought the writer in debt to the publifher 29*l*. 12*s*. 1*d*. if his own ftatement may be believed [k]. In fupport of this famous work, he wrote, in anfwer to the animadverfions of Cato, fome letters in the Pennfylvania Journal, under the title of *a Forrefter*, which were more fuccefsful, from the difpofition of thofe to whom they were addreffed, than the fober reflections of the fcholar, who taught only the unpalatable doctrine of obedience. Nor did a more partial reception await a pamphlet intitled *Plain Truth*, which, as it was haftily written, was inattentively read, and little heard amidft the ravings of anarchy.

In the unfuccefsful campaign of 1776, he joined the American army, and attended them in their retreat from Hudfon's river to the Delaware. While every thing around wore the moft difcouraging afpect, he did not defpair. The congrefs fled: all were difmayed: yet Pain thanked God that he did

Publifhes Common Senfe. 10th Jan. 1776.

Joins the army.

[k] See Pain's Declaration in Almon's Remembrancer, 1780, part I. p. 295.—O.

VOL. II.　　　U　　　not

not fear. "He knew well their situation, and saw his way out of it." He endeavoured, with no inconsiderable success, to make others see with his eyes, to inspire others with his confidence. It was with this design that he published in the Pennsylvania Journal, THE CRISIS, wherein he states every topic of hope, and examines every motive of apprehension. This essay he continued to publish periodically, during the continuance of hostilities, as often as the necessity of affairs required that he should conceal truth, or propagate falsehood; that he should exhilarate despondency, or repress hope [1].

19th Dec. 1776.

The European concerns of congress were at first managed by *a committee for secret correspondence*, which was afterwards converted into *a committee for foreign affairs*, to which Pain was appointed secretary. All foreign letters, after this appointment, remained in his office; and his duty required him in future to reside with congress. He soon however embarked in a contest with Silas Deane, in which he involved Robert Morris, the celebrated financier of the American states; and perfidiously, and without regard to official decorum, retailed through the newspapers what he confidentially knew from the foreign correspondence. Of this misconduct the minister of France complained to the congress. Pain was ordered to attend. Being asked by Jay, the president, *if he were the author of the publications on Mr. Deane's affairs?* and answering, *Yes*; he was directed to withdraw. On the subsequent day he applied for an explanatory hearing; which was refused; and he was obliged to give in his resignation. He did not quietly suffer this disgrace, but wrote, though without success, to excite the people of America against the congress. The French minister, Gerard, attempted to gain him

1777. Appointed secretary to the committee.

6th Jan. 1779.

8th Jan. Resigns.

Intrigues of the French minister.

[1] The Crisis, No XIII. was published at Philadelphia on the 19th of April 1783, the same day that a cessation of hostilities was proclaimed. This was the last. Alm. Rem. 1783, part II. p. 105.—O.

over,

over, hoping to extract from him some secrets of more importance than he had before wantonly disclosed; and while he complained to the congress publicly, intrigued with Pain privately. They had several meetings, the object of which was *silence* about *Deane;* Gerard made him *a genteel and profitable offer,* but Pain was pledged to prosecute Deane; and he was determined that *pension* and *Pain* should never be seen together in the same paragraph. These intrigues were renewed, and continued for some time: Pain persisted in writing against Deane, till the Americans grew tired of the contest [m].

To

---

[m] See those intrigues detailed by Pain himself, with little prudence and no forecast, in Alm. Rem. 1780, part I. p. 294. 297. The following public papers will supply what is defective in Pain's detail:

" Sir, Philadelphia, Jan. 13, 1779.
" It is with real satisfaction that I execute the order of Congress
" for transmitting to you the inclosed copy of an act of the 12th
" instant, on a subject rendered important by affecting the dignity of
" congress, the honour of their great ally, and the interest of both
" nations.

" The explicit disavowal and high disapprobation of congress re-
" lative to the publications referred to in this act, will, I flatter my-
" self, be no less satisfactory to his most christian majesty, than
" pleasing to the people of these states. Nor have I the least doubt
" but that every attempt to injure the reputation of either, or impair
" their mutual confidence, will meet with the indignation and resent-
" ment of both. I have the honour, &c.
" John Jay.

" To the Hon. the Sieur Gerard, minister plenipotentiary of France."

" In Congress, January 12, 1779.
" Congress resumed the consideration of the publications in the
" Pennsylvania packet of the 2d and 5th instant, under the title of
" ' Common Sense' to the public, on Mr. Deane's affair, of which
" Mr. Thomas Pain, secretary to the committee for foreign affairs,
" has acknowledged himself to be the author; and also the memorials
" of the minister plenipotentiary of France of the 5th and 10th instant,
" respecting the said publications; whereupon, *Resolved unanimously,*
" That in answer to the memorials of the Hon. Sieur Gerard, mini-
" ster plenipotentiary of his most christian majesty, of the 5th and
" 10th instant, the president be directed to assure the said minister,
" that congress do fully, and in the clearest and most explicit man-
" ner, disavow the publications referred to in the said memorials;
" and as they are convinced by indisputable evidence that the supplies
" shipped in the Amphitrite, Seine, and Mercury, were not a pre-
" sent,

Pain made master of arts.

1780.

March.

To compensate for the loss of political honours, Pain now received those of the academy. The university of Pennsylvania, after the tumult of the times had driven his old antagonist the president away, conferred on him the degree of *master of arts*. He was chosen a member of the American Philosophical Society, and clerk of the assembly of Pennsylvania. On the stagnation of the congress paper credit, he published *a Crisis extraordinary*; but eloquence like his, though it might be acceptable at the moment of incipient innovation, and useful in exciting the exertions of the turbulent, and the clamours of the disaffected, was of no avail against the impressions of instant calamity and approaching ruin. He cheered the Americans from time to time with another *crisis*, till his *crisis* becoming common, was no longer a *crisis*; and was therefore read without attention, and thrown away without efficacy.

"sent, and that his most christian majesty, the great and generous ally of these United States, did not preface his alliance with any supplies whatever sent to America, so they have not authorised the writer of the said publications to make any such assertions as are contained therein; but on the contrary, do highly disapprove of the same."

To which Mr. Gerard returned the following answer:

"Sir, Philadelphia, Jan. 14, 1779.

"I have received the letter with which you honoured me on the 13th instant, inclosing me the resolve of congress in answer to the representations I had the honour to make them on the 5th and 10th.

"I intreat you to receive and to express to congress, the great sensibility with which I felt their frank, noble, and categorical manner of destroying those false and dangerous insinuations which might mislead ignorant people, and put arms into the hands of the common enemy.

"To the king, my master, sir, no proofs are necessary to the foundation of a confidence in the firm and constant adherence of congress to the principles of the alliance; but his majesty will always behold with pleasure the measures which congress may take to preserve inviolate its reputation; and it is from the same consideration, I flatter myself, he will find my representations on the 7th December equally worth his consideration. I am, &c.

"GERARD.

"Published by order of congress, CHARLES THOMSON, Sec."

At length a confcioufnefs of infignificance, or a defire of change, induced Pain to accompany the younger Laurens to France. While he was at L'Orient, preparing to return to America, the Anna Terefa packet-boat for New York was carried into France by the Madame, French privateer. This event gave him an opportunity of perufing the minifter's difpatches, which Laurens carried to congrefs when they both returned to Philadelphia[n]. He pretends that at this period he projected a fecret trip to London, in order to *open the eyes of the country with refpect to the madnefs and ftupidity of its government*[o]. It is of little confequence to difcufs the merits of an unexecuted project; but in this affertion there is fuch a mixture of abfurdity and impudence, that it claims fome notice. Pain, it feems by his own account, *had formed to himfelf a defign of coming over to England in the latter end of the year* 1780. He communicated it to general Greene, who at firft vehemently approved it; but the affair of Arnold and André happening foon after, the general became alarmed for the fafety of the profound politician, and diffuaded him from executing his fcheme. In truth, if he had really formed fuch a fcheme, the general fhewed more wifdom than belonged to the mafter of arts. The fuccefs of his plan depended only on *his getting over to England without being known, and only remaining in fafety till he could get out a publication.* The man who could form fuch a project has little right to exult over the ftupidity of others! But after all, what need was there to rifk a life fo precious by

1780. Goes to France.

May 1781.

Sept. 1781. Returns to America.

---

[n] Rights, part ii. p. 95. He there gives an account of that whole adventure, but with fome circumftances which create diftruft. The fact is, that the original difpatches, which were dated the 7th of March 1781, were publifhed in the Amfterdam Gazette of the 11th of June 1781, and were afterwards republifhed in the Englifh Regifters. Yet he pretends, with his ufual felf-fufficiency, to have feen in thofe original difpatches the ftupidity of the Englifh cabinet far more than he otherwife could have done.—O.

[o] See Rights, ubi fupra.

coming

coming to England? All his publications came through the presses of London, without his personal assistance, and without contributing very much *to open the eyes of the country*. His venom would have been as effectually circulated from America or from France then, as it is now.

<small>1782. Writes a letter to Raynal.</small> Before the American revolution was really atchieved, the abbé Raynal hastened to give his history of it ᴾ. This publication was displeasing to the Americans in general, and offensive to Pain in particular, as the abbé had, on false pretences, obtained Pain's metaphysics, and sold them as his own; thus borrowing his *morals* with his *maxims*. He poured forth his indignation on this subject in seventy-six octavo pages of intemperate criticism; and violently reclaimed his property, ascertaining it by the most indubitable marks. The pamphlet has all the characteristics of its author's other productions: the same violence, the same boldness of assumption and rashness of conclusion, the same indifference to propriety, and the same contempt of all laws, those of grammar not excepted.

<small>29th Oct. 1782. Writes his Letter to the Earl of Shelburne.</small> Pain had scarcely dispatched his letter to the abbé Raynal, when he wrote an epistle to the earl of Shelburne. The noble earl had said in parliament, it seems, in a tone which still vibrates in the ears of Englishmen, *that when Great Britain shall acknowledge American independence, the sun of Britain's glory is set for ever*. Pain reasons and laughs with the parliamentary prophet, through a little pamphlet of twenty-eight pages.

<small>19th April. Publishes his last Crisis.</small> On the day a cessation of hostilities was proclaimed, Pain published his last Crisis, which was afterwards reprinted under the title of *Pain's Thoughts on the Peace*. He concluded this valedictory oration in the following words: *Now, gentlemen, you are independent—sit down and be happy,*

ᴾ It was published at London in December 1781.—O.

But

But the country was far from being happy; nor was the magic of words sufficient to compensate for physical wants and social privations. Pain, who was no longer of use, suffered all the miseries of dependent penury. He was employed for several years in soliciting the American assemblies to grant him some reward for his labours. New York conferred on him some forfeited lands at New Rochelle, which, as they were neither tenanted nor cultivated, brought him no annual income. Pennsylvania gave him five hundred pounds, which, in spite of his protestations, was a mode of uniting *pension* and *Pain* in the same paragraph q. {1783. His rewards.}

Having stayed in America long enough to see the people awaking to order and law; to find himself no longer looked upon as a safe director or wise politician, but consigned with the most contemptuous indifference to oblivion; he quitted the United States, leaving the American citizens to build up as they could the several fabrics he had so powerfully contributed to overturn; and a young woman at New York, of a reputable family, to deplore the effects of a profligacy that will probably prevent his return to his *beloved America*. He arrived in Paris, with no other introduction than his literary fame, and the model of a bridge he had projected, which he exhibited to the French academy. That body, with their usual politeness and indifference, thanked him for the sight, but did not honour him with any further notice. {1786. Leaves America.} {1787. Arrives in Paris.}

In the autumn of the same year he returned to England, and took up his residence at the White Bear, Piccadilly. He did not make a long abode in {Returns to England, 3d Sept.}

---

q In the Maryland Journal, dated the 31st of December 1784, there is the following article: "On the 6th instant, his excellency John " Dickenson, president of the State of Pennsylvania, sent a message to " the assembly respecting Mr. Thomas Pain, the author of Common " Sense and other political pieces, strongly recommending to their " notice his services and situation."—O.

U 4   London,

London, but went to Thetford to visit his mother, to whom he had previously remitted the twenty pounds advanced on his bond, as mentioned in her letter to his wife. He now promised her an allowance of nine shillings a-week, to be paid by one Whiteside, an American merchant; but owing to the confusion in that trader's affairs, or to some other cause, this allowance was soon stopt. Before the end of the year, he returned to London, and

Publishes. published his *Prospects on the Rubicon; or, an Investigation into the causes and consequences of the politics to be agitated at the meeting of parliament.* This is an octavo tract of sixty-eight pages, and discusses a great multiplicity of topics, particularly the affairs of Holland: but it is now no longer remembered.

1788. Builds his bridge. Pain now employed himself with great assiduity in building his bridge. For this end, he made a journey to Rotheram in Yorkshire, in order to superintend the casting of the iron by Mr. Walker. While thus occupied at Rotheram, his French familiarity is said not to have much pleased the English ladies; and their displeasure induced Mr. Walker to turn Pain out of his house. The bridge, however, was at length erected in a close at Leasing-Green; being an arch constructed of iron, one hundred and ten feet in the span, five feet from the spring, and twenty-two feet in breadth. It was erected chiefly at the charge of Mr. Walker; but the project had cost the projector a large sum, which was mostly furnished by Mr. Whiteside. The bridge was shewn for some time at the Yorkshire Stingo, for a shilling[r]. As this was not the first iron bridge which was known to the English, it is not easy to discover why the projector, who had a model,

[r] Pain's bridge was taken to pieces in October 1791, in order that other erections might be built in its place, and that the rent of the close in which it stood might be paid: the timber of it was sold to the neighbouring builders, and the castings of iron were sent to Yorkshire, whence they came. — O.

should

should incur so great an expence, merely to make a show.

Whiteside having become a bankrupt, and his *Is arrested.* assignees finding six hundred and twenty pounds charged against Pain, they sued out a writ against him: he was arrested at the White Bear, and car- *29th Oct.* ried to Armstrong's lock-up house in Carey- *1789.* street. Here he lay for three weeks, at the end of which he was bailed by some American merchants; and at length compromised the business, by paying four hundred and sixty pounds which had been remitted to him from America, and giving his own note for one hundred and sixty more.

At this period, the French revolution had af- *Goes to* sumed that character of horror which rendered it *France.* too interesting to Pain for him to endure a longer absence. The capture of the Bastille, the massacres of the summer, and the imprisonment of the king on the 6th of October, were evidences of a revolutionary spirit, which promised to a mind like his the fullest enjoyment. He accordingly repaired to Paris. But the revolution of France was not like that of America; his slowness of conception, and difficulty of argumentation, were ill calculated to advance his reputation among the rapid thinkers, and fluent speakers and writers who illuminated the public mind at Paris. He could only wait in gloomy patience till some active apostle of sedition in England should, by an application of French doctrines to this country, erect a standard under which he might range himself, and by some desperate exertion rescue his name from that oblivion into which it was rapidly sinking. Nor was an opportunity of this kind long wanting: Dr. Price's *Public-* extraordinary sermon had excited the detestation of *ation of* every well-disposed man in England: that such *Reflec-* doctrines should be so promulgated, if not absolutely *tions.* a novelty, was nevertheless a perversion of the character

racter of a preacher, so abominable, and so flagrant, as to demand a public and severe reprehension. It was generally known that Burke had undertaken the task, and expectation was strained to the most interesting degree of anxiety, for the publication of the sentiments of that great politician on so important a topic. Such a work as he produced would have been dishonoured by a smaller share of expectation, and an expectation so vast could only be gratified by the work which had excited it. Language less powerful than that of the master of the sublime himself, would be inadequate duly to praise the " Reflections on the Revolution ;" its merit can only be appreciated by the never-dying rancour it excited in the minds of his opponents, a rancour which age, affliction, sickness, and even death itself could not assuage.

margin: 1790.

margin: Pain resolves to answer them.

Pain was so delighted with the prospect of obtaining public notice by being known as the antagonist of Burke, that, as he himself informs us, " as soon as he saw the advertisement of the pamphlet he intended to publish, he promised some of the friends of the revolution in France, that whenever Mr. Burke's pamphlet came forth he would answer it *." The rapid dissemination of Burke's book, without any reduction of its price, without any recommendation but its own merit, without any patronage but the public curiosity, produced a numerous, though not very formidable tribe of *answerers*. Every weapon of assault was tried, from the most ponderous argumentation, to the most frivolous raillery; but in vain: these productions have passed from the shelf of the bookseller to the shop of the trunk-maker, without animadversion from the illustrious author against whose fame they were directed, while his book continues to be read, praised, and quoted by every man of true genius,

---

* Preface to the Rights of Man, part I.

every man who is capable of admiring the vaft efforts of a vigorous mind, which, by an accurate inveftigation of caufes, delineated their certain confequences wtth all the force of prophecy. To pre- *Comes to England.* pare himfelf for this important affault, Pain came to England, and in a few months his publication faw the light. It was fubmitted to the revifal of Mr. Brand Hollis, and a committee of democrats, by whom, after fome ftruggles between the defires of the author and the wifhes of his patrons, it was fitted for the prefs. It was firft printed for Johnfon in St. Paul's church-yard, but he declined felling it. This unexpected refufal caufed a month's delay. A few copies were, however, fmuggled into private hands, and many artifices were ufed to excite and keep up a fpirit of curiofity which might be beneficial to its object.

At length this mutilated brat was delivered to the public by Jordan of Fleet-ftreet [t]. To the parent this was a moment of peculiar anxiety: befides his cares for his child, he feared or pretended to fear that the audacity of his attack might endanger his perfonal fafety. He found fhelter in the houfe of his friend Mr. Hollis, and caufed it to be generally rumoured that he was returned to France. But all thefe artifices did not fucceed in raifing the pamphlet to that degree of notice which would produce all the evil confequences the author intended. There were numbers, no doubt, who praifed it, becaufe they wifhed its tenets triumphant; there are fome who rejoice to fee real learning defied by grofs illiterature; and the Conftitutional Society, as it was called, ftrenuoufly recommended this tract to the perufal of the people. But the officers of government *13th Mar. 1791. Publifhes the Rights of Man, part I.*

---

[t] The caftrating hand of Mr. Jordan appears in the title-page; he there makes Thomas Paine *a fecretary for foreign affairs* to congrefs, inftead of *the fecretary to a committee of congrefs* for foreign affairs. The clerk of the houfe of commons, and the clerk of a committee of that houfe, are quite diftinct officers.—O.

overlooked the pamphlet and its applauders with the moſt mortifying contempt.

It is not my intention to review this publication, on which the ſenſe of the thinking part of the community is decidedly pronounced. Burke left it to find its way to notice or oblivion without his recommendation or reprehenſion; he would not deſcend from the dignity of his political eminence to engage perſonally in a conteſt, which would have been as degrading to him, as it would for Achilles to have entered the liſts againſt Therſites. In numerous critical publications the faults of ſtyle and reaſoning are expoſed, but in none better than the work to which I am ſo much indebted for information. In that publication there is a copious analyſis of "The Rights of Man," under the different heads of "Bad Grammar, Barbariſm, Soleciſm, Impro-"priety, and Nonſenſe," and to that I refer my readers [u]. But the character of the man, as an individual, would be unfairly concealed by his exertions as an author, were I to omit the following inſtance of literary diſhoneſty, which I ſhall give without a comment, in the very words of the author who firſt detected it [x]. He quotes the following ſentence of Burke: "The circumſtances are "what render every civil and political ſcheme "beneficial or noxious to mankind. Abſtractedly "ſpeaking, government, as well as liberty, is good; "yet could I, in common ſenſe, ten years ago, have "felicitated France on her enjoyment of a govern-"ment, (for ſhe then had a government,) without "inquiry what the nature of that government was, "or how it was adminiſtered?" On this paſſage he has a note in theſe words:

"I will not put it in the text, but I earneſtly beg "the attention of whoever reads this pamphlet, to "what follows in this note."

[u] Life of Thomas Pain, 10th edition, p. 65 to 79.
[x] Profeſſor Wilde of Edinburgh. See his excellent Addreſs to the Society of "Friends of the People," p. 64.

On the 23d page of the First Part of "Rights of Man," Mr. Pain writes thus:

"But Mr. Burke appears to have no idea of principles when he is contemplating governments. *Ten years ago* (fays he) *I could have felicitated France on her having a government, without inquiring what the nature of that government was, or how it was adminiſtered.* Is this the language of a rational man? On this ground Mr. Burke muſt compliment every government in the world, while the victims who ſuffer under them, whether fold into ſlavery, or tortured out of exiſtence, are wholly forgotten. It is power and not principles, that Mr. Burke venerates; and under this abominable depravity, he is difqualified to judge between them.

"I have looked into ſeveral editions of Pain, and this paragraph ſtands the fame in all of them.

"I do not believe that there is any where elſe in the world to be found an inſtance of ſuch ſhameleſs falſification. Good-breeding is due to the public, and I would not wiſh to be deficient in this reſpect. Yet there are certain things which can only be called by certain names. Mr. Pain has recorded himſelf as long as his book laſts, to be a DELIBERATE LIAR.

"An uſeful leſſon, however, ariſes from this; and I ſhall take the liberty ſhortly to enforce it.

"I do not know that this forgery, impudently glaring as it is, has been hitherto detected by any perſon. By thoſe who did not much attend to Mr. Pain, this might not be much attended to either. But with Mr. Pain's difciples (who either do not read, or read without underſtanding it, Mr. Burke's book) it would obtain thorough credit, that Mr. Burke thought any form or mode of government whatever good; and this wilful falſehood commented upon by their maſter, would be of more uſe to his fyſtem
" than

"than a thousand arguments. Once believed, it took from Mr. Burke's authority every sort of possible estimation. What was it that he defended the constitution of England, who would defend any government under the sun? With utility so great and manifest, Pain would care but little (and it might not even happen) for after detection. That detection would not again rest on the undermined authority, in whose place he had now fixed his own opinions. And as to any shame, he, and those like him, had but little acquaintance with that sensation.

"It is therefore a lesson most necessary to be attended to, (and which the detection of this forgery demonstrates,) that, where falsehoods can be of use, neither their utter improbability, nor their almost certainty of being discovered, will prevent wicked and daring men from employing them. In a time accordingly, like the present, he who, uninformed himself, grounds his approbation or disapprobation of any proceedings or opinions upon the information of men of dubious characters, who are interested to mislead, who conceal their names, or who do not give (or are not ready to give) their authorities, commits a very great evil. He encourages the propagation of falsehood for the purposes of wickedness. Nor after such an exposure as I have just now made, can any person justify himself by the common faith that is due to the common run of men. At least, on the part of Pain, there can be no question that he who is deceived has himself only to blame. It is a strange thing belief, after recorded falsehood."

The reviews of criticism, however, did not prevent Pain from receiving the applause of party, since he promoted the interests of faction. Nay, philology came in the person of Horne Tooke, who found out his retreat, after some inquiry, to mingle her

her cordial congratulations with the thanks of greater powers. *You are*, he said, *like Jove coming down upon us in a shower of gold*. Pain was highly gratified by such attentions; yet he was not happy; he plainly wished for something that was studiously withheld. Like Rousseau, he longed for prosecution. While fluttering on the wing for Paris, he hovered about London a whole week, waiting to be taken, not by the catchpoles of creditors, but by the runners of Bow-street. Yet the messengers of the press would not meddle with either his person or his pamphlet. Upon what motives government acted cannot be ascertained. Whether the ministers trusted to the good sense of England, which generally gains the ascendancy, or were not willing prematurely to engage in vindictive prosecutions, is left entirely to conjecture.

At length, Pain departed for Paris. He there formed a connexion with Condorcet, Brissot, and a few others of that stamp, who, dissatisfied with the existing government, and despairing of pre-eminence even should the views of Orleans succeed, began to broach doctrines of republicanism. The flight of the king gave an opportunity of detailing this doctrine, which was not popular, or its disciples numerous. Pain and his two associates engaged in the paper called *Le Republicain*, notwithstanding his ignorance of the French language, which was remedied by the kindness of Condorcet's wife, who translated his contributions. Pain, on this occasion, hoped to elevate himself to a great degree of notice, by a challenge to the abbé Syeyes, in which he undertook to answer all that could be advanced in favour of monarchy, in any form or space, in a work of fifty pages [y]. The abbé did not accept the challenge, and *Le Republicain* was soon discontinued.

May 1791.
Goes to Paris.

Writes Le Republicain.

[y] Moore's View, vol. ii. p. 376.

His person in danger.

At Paris, Pain met with Mr. Thomas Christie, who made some figure by his eulogium on the French revolution and constitution. On the day of the king's return they met with an adventure, which, had it been their gift to learn by experience, would have imparted some doubts concerning the pre-eminence of a popular government. At the moment when all those whom curiosity had attracted to see the king brought into the capital a prisoner, were ordered to be covered, Pain had lost his cockade. This reduced him to the dilemma of disobeying the important command of the assembly, or of appearing without a cockade, either of which amounted to a crime of *leze-nation*, and subjected the delinquent to immediate punishment. Already the fatal cry was heard, *aristocrat! aristocrat! a la lanterne!* A Frenchman, who could speak English, desired him to put on his hat. He explained his embarrassment, and the sentimental mob was with some difficulty satisfied and appeased [*].

13th July. Returns to England.
14th.

Disappointed in his expectation of notice in France, Pain returned to England, just in time to partake in the celebration of the French revolution. Yet it was deemed proper that he should not appear at the dinner, and he came not to the Crown and Anchor tavern till eight o'clock, when the celebrators had been hissed away by the multitude. Soon after this Pain retired to Greenwich, to write his Second Part of the RIGHTS OF MAN.

16th Feb. 1792. Publishes Rights of Man, Part II.

This malignant libel was published by Jordan in Fleet-street. Grown bolder from impunity, and additionally ambitious of the fame which would result from prosecution, he wrote to Jordan on the day of publication, requesting him, " If any person, " under the sanction of authority, should inquire " respecting the author and publisher, to mention

---

[*] See Mr. Thomas Christie's letter, dated from Paris, June 22d, 1791, and published in the Morning Chronicle of the 29th June 1791.—O.

" him,

" him, as he would appear and anfwer for the work
" perfonally." In this, however, he was difappointed: it required a meafure more audacious and
flagrant than that of a tranquil publication, to roufe
the refentment of an infulted government.

This work is now put out of circulation by the
verdict of a jury, and for a criticifm on it I muft
again refer my reader to " the Life of Pain,"
where he will find an ample and able difcuffion[a].
There is, however, a prefumptuous arrogance in an
infinuation in the Appendix, which deferves particularly to be refuted: it is, that the miniftry had
tampered with the printer to give them a knowledge
of its contents, and to delay the publication, that the
chancellor of the exchequer might be enabled to
avail himfelf of fome of his financial ideas, at the
opening of the feffion of parliament. Chapman
was the printer of the firft part of the *Rights of
Man*: Pain had been introduced to him by Chriftie.
Chapman was again employed to print the *fecond
part*, and about Chriftmas 1791, carried Pain to
lodge at No. 10, in Dean-ftreet, Fetter-lane; Pain,
as early as September, delivered a confiderable
quantity of copy, and took this lodging to be near
his printer. Now, he thus ftates his cafe: " on
" Tuefday fortnight preceding the meeting of
" parliament (the 17th of January 1792), *all at
" once, without any previous intimation, though I had
" been with him* (Chapman) *the evening before*, he
" fent me, by one of his workmen, all the remain-
" ing copy from page 112, declining to go on with
" the work on any confideration. *To account for
" this extraordinary conduct, I was totally at a lofs.*"
The anfwer to this ftatement is taken from *Chapman's account of the tranfaction, delivered on oath*, on
the trial of Pain[b]. He there avers, that he had

Obfervations on one of his ftatements.

[a] Page 88 to 148.
[b] See Mr. Chapman's evidence on Pain's trial, Gurney's edition, 86-7, which proves the falfehood of Pain's ftory.—O.

proceeded to work off as far as the signature *H*, when the signature *I* coming under his inspection, he observed something which, in his humble apprepreהension, *appeared of a dangerous tendency*; he therefore resolved to have nothing more to do with the work, but felt some delicacy in declaring this resolution to Pain, who had always behaved towards him with kindness and civility. From this embarrassment, however, he was relieved by Pain himself, who coming to his house on the evening of the day he had made this resolution, somewhat intoxicated with his friend Johnson's wine, began the subject of religion, *a topic he was very fond of expatiating on when drunk*. Chapman and his wife were dissenters. The *woman* defended her opinions in a manner which conquered the philosophy of the champion of the *Rights of Man*. He rose, at about ten o'clock in the evening, in wrath, declaring he had never been so insulted before, and to be on par with the loquacious female, he declared that he ever thought it his duty to be on his guard against dissenters, who were a pack of hypocrites; and desired Chapman to come to a settlement, before he proceeded any further with his work. The printer gathered courage from the overflowings of his wife's spleen, and next day sent Pain the remainder of his copy, together with a letter explaining his motives. Pain returned, to apologize, but the printer was implacable, and he was obliged to procure another person to go on with the work. This, then, is a narrative of the event, for which Pain, with his usual fallacy, declares himself utterly unable to account.

25th Jan. 1792. Within a week after Mr. Chapman had returned the copy, Pain announced the cause which delayed the publication. In the Gazetteer, Pain published that the composition being now past, the copy was given, *a few weeks since*, to *two printers*, who were to print it speedily. They printed about half of it, and

and then, being *alarmed* by *some intimations*, refused to go further; but another printer had taken it; and in the course of the next month, it will appear[c]. Pain had now told *two stories* about the cause of the delay, which invalidate each other. In the one account, the copy had been delivered to *one* printer in September 1791; in the other account, the copy was delivered to *two* printers before the 25th of January 1792. In the first account, Pain was totally at a loss to account for the printer's refusing to continue the work. In the second account, Pain says that the printers were alarmed by *some intimations*, from the messengers of the press, no doubt. Which of these accounts are we to believe; or shall we, after such palpable tergiversation, believe any account which is given by Pain?

Yet let us trace him a little further through the mazes of duplicity, that we may judge of his veracity in any case. He now tells what indeed is likely to be true, that he gave his copy to the printer in September last; let us suppose the 15th of September: from the 15th of September, to the 17th of January following, there passed away *sixteen* weeks. Now, when the memorable quarrel happened between the printer and Pain, only seven sheets had *passed through the press*; so that more

[c] In the Gazetteer of Wednesday the 25th January 1792, appeared the *following notice*, the air, and sentiments, and style, of which plainly demonstrate the *real author*,

"Mr. PAIN,
"It is known, is to produce another work this season.
"The composition of this is now past, and it was given, a *few*
"*weeks* since, to *two printers*, whose presses it was to go through as
"speedily as possible. They printed about half of it, and then, being
"alarmed by *some intimations*, refused to go further. Some delay has
"thus occurred, but another printer has taken it, and, in the course of
"next month, it will appear.
"Its title is to be a repetition of the former, 'THE RIGHTS OF
"MAN,' of which the words ' *Part the Second*' will shew that it is a
"continuation."—None but PAIN could write such an *advertisement*.—O.

than two weeks were employed on every sheet [d]. And it is a known fact, that Pain kept his proofs frequently a week, often a fortnight, and sometimes longer. He was all the *sixteen weeks* casting about for matter, receiving hints and corrections, and waiting for events. He knew that the writer who gets into a chapter of *miscellanies*, may go forward or stop short when he pleases. And Pain was plainly watching for a moment of misfortune, when he might urge discontent into fury, by publishing his *second part* on some factious night. But the parliament met, without waiting for his publication: The day of triumph passed over while he loitered in the press: The nation exulted in her prosperity, while he sat calculating with arithmetical precision, the depth of her distresses, and the benefits, but not the miseries, of anarchy.

It was owing to the foregoing causes, that Pain, who had returned his proof sheets so slowly before, was now obliged to accelerate the press. He was compelled to perform a harder task; to find plausible reasons for postponing his work, till the unpropitious day of general satisfaction. The book would have been published before the meeting of parliament, he says, " had the work appeared at " the time the printer had engaged to finish it." But this assertion, as we have already shewn, cannot be true; for no printer can perform his engagement if the author return not *the proofs*; and no printer can be benefited by the standing still of his press.

[d] Before the sad evening of the fatal quarrel, being the 16th of January 1792, the sheet *H* had been printed, now, from *B* to *H*, there are seven sheets. But the sheets *I* and *K* were also set up; now, these two may be considered as another sheet; and, of consequence, it is proved that there were no more than *eight* sheets printed in the *sixteen weeks*, from the 15th of September to the 17th of January following. This must be allowed to be very *slow printing* indeed, when even *two sheets* a day may be done with ease.—O.

Of

Of this book, which was dedicated to la Fayette, five thousand copies were printed. But notwithstanding every art to raise curiosity, this did not, for some weeks, sell with the rapidity of the *first part*. Three shillings was too great a sum for persons to give who had it only in view to distribute these new found lights, they did not even at first publicly applaud the author. A month elapsed from the time of publication, when the *Manchester constitutional society* thanked Pain for his publication, and recommended his work *as of the highest importance to every nation under heaven*[*]. Other societies followed the example of Manchester, and in order to give more rapid dissemination to the favoured publication, editions were printed on a whitish-brown paper at a small price, but to those who could not or would not buy even at that rate, the book was profusely distributed, *gratis*. It was in all shapes and all sizes, with an industry incredible, either in the whole or in extracts, thrust into the hands of all persons in this country, of subjects of every description. The sweetmeats of children and the tobacco of men were wrapped up in it, in the hope they might be tempted to read what was thus gratuitously presented.

This culpable assiduity, and the multiplication of treasonable societies gave serious alarm to government. A royal proclamation was issued, warning to the loyal and prudent part of the nation against these innovators, a prosecution was commenced against Jordan the publisher, and an information put on the file against Pain himself.

Meantime Pain had not been inactive, and the aspect of affairs was such as to open to his malignant mind the hope of a long day of horrors. Anarchy was making the most rapid strides in France; its agents here were rated at *forty thousand*; and the

Success of the work.

13th Mar. 1792.

Proceedings of government.

21st May.

Pain's occupations.

---

[*] See the Morning Chronicle of March 19, 1792.—O.

murder of the king of Sweden in his own palace afforded Pain an opportunity of exclaiming with diabolical triumph, "*Aye, you see how crowns are melting away!*" and of adding with explanatory archness, "*There is a kettle boiling in this country.*"

<small>Apr. 1792. Goes into the country.</small> He was invited by his friend Mr. W. Sharp, the engraver, to pass a few months with him in the country; and lodged at the house of one Tanner at Bromley in Kent, from which he seldom sallied <small>13th Apr.</small> forth. He attended at the anniversary meeting of the constitutional society at the London Tavern, as <small>Is arrested.</small> one of the stewards. This was the last public dinner he assisted at in England, and from this he might as well have stayed away; for the assignees of Whiteside, lured by the hope of getting in their outstanding demand, and incited by the knowledge of a fact so unusual as his public appearance, at a given time and place, sued out a writ against him for the amount of his note. This business was conducted so secretly, that the society knew nothing of the transaction. He was carried, by Wild the officer, to the King's Head lock-up house in Wood-street, till he was bailed by Johnson the bookseller, and by Wilkie another bookseller, who at Johnson's <small>17th May. Returns to London.</small> request joined in the bond. Soon after the information had been filed against him, his host at Bromley, discovering the real name and character of his lodger, gave information of his discovery to Mr. Norman, the nearest magistrate. Pain being apprized of the circumstance, made a hasty retreat from the country, and again repaired to the obscure purlieus of Fetter-lane.

<small>June. Writes in the Argus.</small> Here he was not idle: he wrote several letters in a contemptible seditious newspaper called the *Argus*; which were afterwards distributed from the pamphlet-shops, under the title of *Pain's four* <small>His Address to the Addressers.</small> *Letters on Government*. He afterwards produced his ADDRESS TO THE ADDRESSERS, which was, like the *Rights of Man*, printed on a small type and

and dingy paper, and sold for a groat. In the superior edition, it was contained in seventy-eight pages; in the inferior, in forty. It is written in his usual style and manner, without any novelty to soften his coarseness, or any information to atone for the boasts of superior knowledge. This scurrilous work was afterwards an object of legal prosecution: but Pain having, previous to its publication, withdrawn himself from the reach of those laws he had insulted and defied, the punishment fell on the publisher.

His fame now acquired its highest possible varnish in the eyes of the French legislature. He had made himself obnoxious to a regular government, to the government of England. This was a merit of sufficient magnitude to induce the Brissotines to forgive his having dedicated his book to their enemy la Fayette, and to cherish him as a fit medium for propagating those calumnies by which they intended to inflame the minds of their countrymen, and prepare them to approve the hostilities already projected against England and her allies. Accordingly Guadet, the principal orator of the party, made a speech in the legislative assembly, demonstrating how proper it would be to call Pain, Priestly, and some others, to the enviable dignity of French citizens. This was afterwards decreed, on the motion of the same orator, in terms which will afford an excellent commentary on the writings of those who maintain the passiveness, and deny the premeditated aggression of the French towards this country[f]. It must also be recollected

Made a French citizen.

24th Aug.

26th.

---

[f] "The national assembly, considering that those men, *who, by their writings and their valour, have served the cause of liberty and paved the way for the enfranchisement of nations,* cannot be looked upon as foreigners by a nation rendered free by its own knowledge and valour;

"Considering, that if five years residence in France is sufficient to obtain for a foreigner the title of French citizen; that title is much more justly due to those *who, whatever be the soil they inhabit, have consecrated their arms and their vigils to the purpose of defending the cause of the* "people

PAIN.

recollected that Pain, at the moment of receiving this homage, was under prosecution for the very writings so ostentatiously commended by the government of a country, then hypocritically pretending to maintain the relations of peace and amity.

Elected member of the convention.

In consequence of this naturalization, an attempt was made by the Brissotines to obtain his election as member of the convention for Paris; but this was frustrated by the faction of Robespierre and Marat [g]. Calais however repaired the injury done him by the capital [h]; and Abbeville was also desirous of seeing the champion of anarchy amongst her representatives, but was prevented by the knowledge of his previous election for Calais [i].

Goes to France.

He was informed of this honour by citizen Audibert, who was deputed for that purpose. He had previously secured the zealous affection of the

---

"people against the despotism of kings, of banishing local prejudices; and of extending the limits of human knowledge;

"Considering, that though it may not be permitted to hope that men will, at some period, form in social regulation, as in nature, but one family, one single association, yet the friends of liberty and universal fraternity ought not to be less dear to a nation which has decreed her renunciation of all conquests, and her desire of fraternization with all the world;

"Considering, finally, that at the moment when a national convention is about to fix the fate of France, *and perhaps to prepare that of all mankind*, it belongs to a free and generous people to call in all the intelligence they can obtain, and to submit the right of concurring in this grand act of reason to men who, by their sentiments, their writings, and their valour, have shewn themselves so eminently worthy of it;

"Decrees, that the title of French citizen be conferred on *Priestly*, *Payne*, and sixteen more." See Mercure de France, vol. de Septembre 1792, p. 14. 22. Madame Roland explains with no less force, the *true* reasons of his naturalization. " Payne was declared a French citizen as one of those celebrated foreigners whom the nation ought, with eagerness, to adopt. He was known by his writings, which had been useful in the American revolution, and *might have contributed to produce one in England*." Appel, vol. ii. p. 29.

[h] Louvet's Narrative, p. 20.
[g] Printed Lists in Political State of Europe. Goudemetz's Epochs, &c.
[i] Moore's Journal, vol. i. p. 361.

societies

focieties in England, by an oftentatious donation, real or pretended, of one thoufand pounds, the produce of the Rights of Man, to the conftitutional fociety, to be difpofed of as they might think proper [k]. He now bade a laft farewel to Fetter-lane, and, accompanied by Audibert and Mr. Froft, went to Dover. Here their trunks were diligently fearched by the cuftom-houfe officers; but nothing being found to fupport an information which had been laid, they replaced every thing as they found it. Pain, who probably thought this vigilance in a revenue officer a libel on his own conduct in the fame fituation, wrote a letter of clamorous complaint to Mr. Dundas, as did citizen Achilles Audibert. This citizen alfo publifhed a letter, in which he threatened to profecute the cuftom-houfe officer; but it appears that he was better entitled to the name of *Rodomont* than *Achilles*, as he never put his boaftful threats in execution.

After a paffage of three hours, they arrived at Calais; where, between the interpretations of Achilles, and the dumb-fhew of Thomas, the electors and the reprefentatives underftood, or fancied they underftood, mutual expreffions of good-will and devotion [l]. *16th Sept. His reception.*

He took his feat in the convention; but his ignorance of the French language reduced him to a ftate of filence not very agreeable to his difpofition. *Member of the convention.* He was, however, chofen one of the committee of the conftitution [m], after the abolition of royalty; but what in particular was the refult of his labours is not afcertained. He was alfo one of madame Roland's cabinet party, though the lady does not feem to have been impreffed with notions very ad- *11th Oct.*

[k] See Pain's Letter to the Conftitutional Society, in the Morning Chronicle of the 9th July 1792.—O.
[l] See the Letters above alluded to, and one defcribing Pain's reception, in Jordan's Political State of Europe, vol. i. p. 459 to 464.
[m] Debates.

vantageous

18th Nov. vantageous to him[n]. He assisted at a dinner given at White's hotel, to celebrate the victories gained by the French. A great number of English democrats were assembled; Mr. J. H. Stone was in the chair. They mistook the inspirations of Bacchus for those of philosophy, and in their flowing cups affected to legislate and to prophesy. They toasted " the abolition of *hereditary titles* in England:"— " THOMAS PAIN, and the new mode of advertis- " ing *good books*, by proclamation, and the court of " king's bench :"—" The approaching *national con-* " *vention* of Great Britain and Ireland :" and many similar sentiments. These drunken frolics would not deserve notice, but for the ridiculous ceremony which ensued, of sending an address on the subject, which was warmly received by the national convention[o].

His conduct on the king's trial.

With the fumes of the wine still in his head, and the din of music performed at the feast by the band belonging to the German legion still in his ears, Pain proceeded to write his opinion respecting the trial of the

21st Nov. unfortunate king. In this opinion, which was read for him in the convention, he considered Louis XVI. as a confederate in an universal conspiracy, which threatened not only the liberty of France, but that of every other nation: he considered him as a culprit, whose trial might lead all people to a knowledge and a detestation of the monarchical system, and of the plots and intrigues of their own courts: he therefore voted for the trial[p]. After such a sentence as this, and after voting the king guilty on the first *appel nominal*, with how little reason do the admirers of Pain affect to extol his merciful disposition, and exonerate him from the ignominy attached to the murderers of that unhappy monarch, on ac-

[n] Appel, vol. ii. p. 29.
[o] Jordan's Political State of Europe, vol. ii. p. 777. Debates.
[p] Debates.

count

count of his subsequent exertions [q]. On the question of punishment, he voted against death, and for banishment; and when the respite of the sentence was moved for, he delivered an opinion, which was read by Bancal. It began by stating, that it would have been better if the national convention had contented themselves with passing on Louis a sentence of imprisonment till the peace: but since they had condemned him to death, he voted for a suspension of the execution. He assigned as a reason, the necessity of not giving offence to foreign powers, particularly to the Americans, who, he assured the convention, would look with an evil eye on the execution of Louis Capet. In conclusion he said,— "France has now no ally except America, and "that ally is the only one who can furnish naval "stores. Now it happens unfortunately in the "present case, that the object of our present discus- "sion is looked upon by the United States as the "person to whom they are indebted for their li- "berty. I can assure you that his execution will "spread through the states a general affliction. If "I were capable of speaking French, I myself "would descend to the bar, and in the name of my "American brethren present a petition for a re- "spite." This observation excited the murmurs of the Mountain: Marat said that Pain was biassed by the contracted notions of his original religion, that of a quaker; Thuriot affirmed that the convention was imposed on by a false translation; Garan asserted that he had seen the original, and that the translation was perfectly correct. Bancal proceeded: " Your executive counsel have recently "nominated an ambassador to the United States of "America, who is to set sail in a few days. No- "thing could afford greater pleasure to your allies "than for him, on his arrival, to address them to

19th Jan. 1793.

[q] See Impartial History, vol. ii. p. 247.

"this

"this effect: that in consideration of the share Louis Capet had borne in the American revolution, and of the grief the Americans might feel at his execution, you had granted, him a respite. Ah, citizens! do not afford to the despot of England the satisfaction of seeing that man perish on the scaffold, who assisted in releasing from their chains my dear brethren of America [r]."

His trial.

While his attention was thus occupied with the trial of a dethroned monarch in Paris, his own trial was coming on in London; so that while he sat as a judge in the one capital, he was arraigned as a criminal in the other. The information filed against him in Easter term came on to be tried, before lord Kenyon and a special jury at Guildhall, in the sittings after Michaelmas term. The attorney-general [s], in a most able speech, stated the enormity of the offence of which the defendant had been guilty; exposed the fallacies of his reasoning; detected the rancour of his heart, affecting disguise under the semblance of virtue and moderation; and, to the utter astonishment of the court and jury, produced a letter written to him by the defendant from Paris, which for impudent mendacity, scurrility, and impertinence, exceeded whatever the imagination could suggest. It insulted the nation by calling the king Mr. Guelph, and threatened the judge, the attorney-general, and the jury, with the most horrible consequences if the trial proceeded [t]. Very few witnesses were called, and they were chiefly examined to prove his hand-writing. He had every assistance in his defence which jurisprudential knowledge could give. Five counsel held briefs for him, three of them [u] justly celebrated for

18th Dec. 1792.

[r] Robespierre à ses Commettans, vol. ii. p. 232. Moore's Journal, vol. ii. p. 587. Debates.
[s] Sir Archibald Macdonald, now chief baron of the exchequer.
[t] See the letter at length in the Appendix, N° VIII.
[u] The Hon. Mr. Erskine, Mr. Piggott, and Mr. (now serjeant) Shepherd.

learning

learning and abilities. Mr. Erſkine, in his addreſs to the jury, exerted all the powers of that perſuaſive eloquence and admirable memory for which he is ſo juſtly celebrated: he endeavoured to diſtinguiſh between the author's doctrines and intentions, and to ſhew that the one might be pure, though the other were unintentionally pernicious. "I am not," he ſaid, "aſking your opinion of the doctrines
"themſelves, you have given them already pretty
"viſibly ſince I began to addreſs you; but I ſhall
"appeal not only to you, but to thoſe who, without
"our leave, will hereafter judge, without appeal,
"of all that we are doing to-day; whether, upon
"the matter which I haſten to lay before you, you
"can refuſe in juſtice to pronounce, that from his
"education, from the accidents and habits of his
"life, from the time and occaſion of the publica-
"tion, from the circumſtances attending it, and
"from every line and letter of the work itſelf, and
"all his other writings, before and even ſince, his
"conſcience and underſtanding *(no matter whether*
"*erroneouſly or not)* were deeply and ſolemnly im-
"preſſed with the matters contained in his book;
"that he addreſſed it to the reaſon of the nation at
"large, and not to the paſſions of individuals; and
"that in the iſſue of its influence, he contem-
"plated only what appeared to *(him though it may*
"*not to us)* to be the intereſt and happineſs of Eng-
"land, and of the whole human race [x]. But the powers of oratory and genius were exerted in vain; in ſuch a cauſe no efforts could induce the jury to remove the mountain of culpability which reſted on the ſhoulders of the defendant. The reſult of the trial is well ſtated in the unornamented words of the reporter, who, purſuing his account from the concluding period of Mr. Erſkine's ſpeech, ſays,—
"The attorney-general aroſe immediately to reply

---

[x] Trial of Pain, Gurney's edition, p. 121.

"to

"to Mr. Erskine, when Mr. Campbell, the foreman of the jury, said, "My lord, I am authorised by the jury here to inform the attorney-general, that a reply is not necessary for them, unless the attorney-general wishes to make it, or your lordship. Mr. attorney-general sat down; and the jury gave in their verdict, GUILTY ⁷."" The conviction of Pain as a malignant libeller was followed by effects which were unexpected by himself, and unforeseen by his patrons. He was ere long burnt with his books in almost every village of England, with circumstances which plainly denoted popular contempt for his doctrines, and popular hatred of his person. His conviction was pursued to *outlawry*; and having joined with the convention at Paris, in a declaration of *war* against Great Britain, he became thereby a *traitor*.

1793. His insignificance. But though he had thus cast off his native country, he found that to which he had betaken himself, on the faith of solemn invitations and assurances, very different from a peaceable asylum. Attached, as far as he was capable of attachment, to the Brissotine party, he had the mortification to witness their degradation, expulsion, and execution. He was one of the seventy-three who signed the protest against the proceedings of the 31st of May. He fell into insignificance as a legislator; and to amuse himself, and contribute all in his power to the emancipation of the human mind from every religious and moral obligation, he composed, or rather compiled, for there is nothing new in it, his first part of the AGE OF REASON. In this work he attacks the bulwark of faith, with feeble arguments and clumsy ribaldry, with all the perversions and misrepresentations of fraud and ignorance.

Publishes the Age of Reason, part I.

Deprived of his seat and sent to prison. He soon found that Robespierre's castle of the Luxembourg was as impenetrable a prison as the

⁷ Trial of Pain, Gurney's edition, p. 195.

king's

king's castle of Bastille, in the taking of which he had so much rejoiced. He found that when nations were freed from the restraints of law, and raised, by the artifices of false reasoning, above the dictates of conscience, no situation, no guaranty, no participation of guilt, no plea of innocence, affords a protection. He was, by a decree of the Mountain, deprived of his seat in the convention, and soon after committed to the prison of the Luxembourg. *30th Dec. 10th Jan. 1794.*

In this situation, he exerted all the efforts his fancy could supply to obtain his liberation. A deputation of Americans residing in Paris went to the bar of the convention to reclaim him as a countryman, but Vadier, the president, informed them that Pain was no countryman of theirs, but an Englishman; and it was hinted to them by one of the committee of general safety, that their interposition was irregular, as it was only the act of individuals, without any authority from the American government[z]. In fact, he was as little beloved in America as in England; his principles were so inimical to every thing like a regular government, that Mr. Adams himself had written an answer to the Rights of Man, in which he not only cautioned the people of America, but those of England, against its doctrines. Pain, disappointed in this effort, had recourse to the club of Cordeliers, hoping that the preachers of atheism would favour the publisher of the *Age of Reason*. But that body scorned him: they sent him no other answer than a copy of his speech in behalf of the unfortunate king[a]. He had now no resource but hard drinking, disputations with Clootz in favour of the few religious principles he still affected to retain[b], and the hope that he might be able, by dint of indefatigable persever- *25th Jan. Deputation of Americans. 20th Feb. Applies to the club of Cordeliers. His employments.*

[z] Jordan's Political State of Europe, vol. vi. p. 72. Pain's Letter to Washington, p. 14.
[a] See Goudemetz's Historical Epochs, p. 86.
[b] Miss Williams's Letters in 1794, vol. ii. p. 177.

ance,

ance, to intereſt the American government in his favour[c]. The firſt of theſe enjoyments was taken from him by the increaſed ſeverities which the republican government thought proper to impoſe on the priſoners; the ſecond, by the death of the Pruſſian atheiſt; and the laſt was reduced almoſt to nothing by the difficulty of conveying letters, which he could only do through the lamp-lighter, who riſked his head to oblige him; and by his receiving no anſwers[d].

Falls ill. During his confinement he fell ill of a fever, and loſt his ſenſes for upwards of a month. It is probable, if we may believe him, that he was indebted to this circumſtance for the preſervation of his life. A memorandum was found in Robeſpierre's handwriting, after his fall, in theſe words: "To move "for a decree of accuſation againſt Thomas Pain, "for the intereſt of America as well as of France[e]."

Is renounced by America. How far the government of America was intereſted in the fate of this outcaſt cannot be aſcertained; but when Robeſpierre was no more, Pain received information, in the moſt unqualified terms, that "he was not conſidered by the American govern- "ment, or by individuals, as an American ci- "tizen[f]."

Is liberated. At length the death of Robeſpierre facilitated his reſtoration to liberty and to the legiſlative body; but thoſe events did not take place ſo ſoon as might *4th Nov.* have been expected. Mr. Monroe, the American miniſter, interceded for him, and obtained his enlargement; and, in little more than a month after- *7th Dec.* wards, a decree of the convention invited him to reſume his ſeat.

[c] Pain's Letter to Waſhington, p. 15, et ſeq.
[d] Idem, p. 17.
[e] Idem, p. 16. The ſame ſtory is told in the Preface to the Age of Reaſon, part II.
[f] Idem, p. 18.

His firſt publication, when reſtored to the dignity of a legiſlator, was a DISSERTATION ON THE FIRST PRINCIPLES OF GOVERNMENT. The occaſion of this production was the formation of the new French conſtitution, which, requiring ſome qualification of property, was not ſufficiently democratic for his approbation. He diſtributed his book as a prelude to a ſpeech which he afterwards delivered in the convention, and which met with little attention, and with ſome difficulty obtained the honours of the impreſſion. The *Diſſertation* was reprinted in London by one Griffiths, but its merits were ſo ſmall that it ſoon fell into diſregard, and though the ſale of it has not been reſtrained by proſecution, it is little read. *Publiſhes a Diſſertation.* *7th July 1795.*

Soon after this, he publiſhed A SECOND PART OF THE AGE OF REASON, in which he renewed his attack on the bible with increaſed acrimony; and, as it ſuited the views of the democratic party here to looſen the ties of public faith, it was diſſeminated, like the Rights of Man, by means of cheap editions and affected recommendations. Several anſwers appeared; but, however well meant, they all faded before the ſuperior luſtre of that produced by the learned and eloquent biſhop of Llandaff. That worthy prelate, in his APOLOGY FOR THE BIBLE, follows the aſſailant of Chriſtianity through every one of his aſſertions, expoſes his ignorance, his ſhameleſs repetition of refuted calumnies, the futility of his arguments, and the fallacy of his deductions. The arm of the law was ſtretched forth againſt the diſtributor of Pain's pernicious treatiſe. An information was filed againſt the publiſher, by the activity of the ſociety for propagating religion, rather than by government. Mr. Erſkine, by his admirable ſpeech delivered in the court of king's bench, added a never-fading leaf to his laurels; and the jury, without heſitation, acquieſced in the direction of the lord chief juſtice, and brought in a verdict of GUILTY againſt the defendant. *The Age of Reaſon, part II.*

VOL. II. Y Yet

8th April 1796. Writes the Decline and Fall, &c.

Yet Pain could not be idle; he produced a pamphlet in forty-four pages, called the DECLINE AND FALL OF THE ENGLISH SYSTEM OF FINANCE. In this work, written for the purpose of encouraging France, and causing despondency in England, he affects to demonstrate that this country is in the very gulph of bankruptcy. To prove this position he has recourse to a series of tables, by which he affects to demonstrate that every new war in which England engages must cost as much and half as much as the last preceding war. This pretended principle he affects to verify by an exposure of the expences of wars for a century past. The absurdity of such an argument must be striking to every person who considers it. No reason is given why such a ratio should be established, and the verification of it as a fact depends on six instances, two of which fail [e]. But could events perfectly confonant, be related without number, they could never make, though they might help to demonstrate a principle. For example, it was said in old times,

" When the Lord falls in the lady's lap,
" Then let England fear a mishap,"

and it was proved that for a great length of time, whenever Good Friday happened on Lady-day, some great commotion occurred that year in England. The coincidence, however, was merely casual; the same event has taken place several times since, and so far from fearing or feeling a mishap, the people of England hardly knew or noticed it. If the country sustain no greater injury from Mr. Pain's politics than from his prophecies, it will long continue rich, happy, and respectable. The book was published by Eaton in Newgate-street; and as he pretends to have entered it at Stationers'-hall, it is to be supposed that it was either sold or given to him by the author.

[e] See Decline and Fall, &c. p. 11. and the note.

Pain next published his LETTER TO GENERAL WASHINGTON, which, to the surprise of every one who is not prepared for all that the most impudent inconsistency can produce from a mind so abject and malignant, contains these and many more insulting expressions: " I KNOW, that had it not been for the aid received from France in men, money, and ships, *your cold and unmilitary conduct* would, in all probability, have lost America; at least, she would not have been the independent nation she now is. *You slept away your time in the field*, till the finances of the country were completely exhausted, AND YOU HAVE BUT LITTLE SHARE IN THE GLORY OF THE FINAL EVENT. Elevated to the chair of the presidency, you assumed the merit of every thing to yourself, and *the natural ingratitude of your constitution began to appear. You commenced your presidential career by encouraging and swallowing the grossest adulation;* and you travelled America from one end to the other to put yourself in the way of receiving it. You have as many addresses in your chest as James the Second. As to what were your views, for *if you are not great enough to have ambition, you are little enough to have vanity*, they cannot be directly inferred from expressions of your own; but the partisans of your politics have divulged the secret[b]." When Pain wrote the dedication to the first part of the *Rights of Man*, it is to be supposed he *knew* these facts, as he would call them, as well as in 1796, yet what did he say then to the very same person? " Sir, I present you a small treatise in defence of those principles of freedom WHICH YOUR EXEMPLARY VIRTUE HATH SO EMINENTLY CONTRIBUTED TO ESTABLISH. *That the Rights of Man may become as universal as your benevolence can wish*, and that you may enjoy the happiness

Aug. 1796.
Letter to Washington.

[b] Letter to Washington, p. 8.

"of seeing the New World regenerate the Old, is the prayer of, Sir, your much obliged, and obedient humble servant, Thomas Paine[i]." This was the tribute of adulation which Pain thought proper to throw in as his additional mite to Washington's Exchequer of Flattery. No one of his enemies in the utmost malignity of misrepresentation could have invented a contradiction to shew more amply the baseness of his heart, and this total want of principle and truth. Either he was ready in 1791 to answer a purpose, to adorn the brow of pusillanimity and vanity with the wreath due to valour and public spirit; or in 1796, under the impression of imaginary wrong, the desire of revenge led him to use the most barefaced calumnies, and palpable untruths: he must, therefore, be considered either as an abject sycophant, or an audacious slanderer.

Since this period, he is reputed to have published some other tracts, among which are Animadversions on Mr. Erskine's Speech respecting the Age of Reason, and a Letter to the People of France, remarkable for its inconsistency with his former doctrines, its abject flattery of the present rulers, and its puerile absurdity [k].

I am now at the conclusion of Pain's literary and political life. He still remains in France, though no longer a legislator, and the reason is well expressed by an ingenious author: "America would now prove a sterile and unproductive soil for the transplantation of such a genius, while ungrateful Europe, (the French dominions excepted,) shutting every avenue against him, bids him wander, like a second Cain, without an asylum or a resting-place [l]."

[i] I give the *whole* dedication to avoid all possible imputation of having perverted the sense by the unfair production of a part.
[k] I have not seen either of these publications, and derive my opinion of the last only from the Anti-Jacobin Review, p. 21.
[l] Tench's Correspondence, p. 183.

After

After so ample a detail of his transactions from his earliest youth to the present time, it would be superfluous to descant on his character as a man. It has been clouded by all the meaner vices, fraud, hypocrisy, rapacity, cruelty, without being illumined by the rays of one solitary virtue. He has renounced parents, wife, friends, country, and religion, without acquiring respect or confidence from those in whose favour the most important of these sacrifices have been made. He is declared an outlaw by England, renounced as a citizen by America, and, except when occasionally called into use as an humble tool, contemned and derided in France. In how little estimation he was held when his fame was at the highest, may be seen by the following character of him drawn by madame Roland. "Among the persons I was in the habit of receiving, and of whom I have already described the most remarkable, Pain[m] deserves to be mentioned. Declared a French citizen, as one of those celebrated foreigners whom the nation ought with eagerness to adopt, he was known by writings which had been useful in the American revolution, and might have contributed to produce one in England. I shall not take upon me to speak decisively on his character because he understood French, without speaking it, and I was nearly in the same situation with respect to English; I was therefore less able to converse with him myself, than to listen to his discourses with those whose political talents were greater than my own. The *boldness* of his conceptions, the originality of his style, the striking truths which he *boldly* throws out in the midst of those whom they

His character,

by madame Roland.

---

[m] She spells his name Paynes; Robespierre, in " Le Defenseur de la Constitution," calls him Penne. This slight fact is mentioned merely to shew how little chance of celebrity remains for English adventures in a country where the writers who quote them pay that homage with such ungracious awkwardness as not even correctly to acquire their appellatives.

" offend,

"offend, must necessarily have produced great effects; but *I should think him better qualified to scatter*, if I may be allowed the expression, *the flames of conflagration, than to discuss primary principles, or prepare the formation of a government* [n]. Pain is more fit to illumine a revolution, than to assist in framing a constitution. He takes up, he establishes those great principles the display of which strikes every eye, ravishes a club, and excites tavern enthusiasm; but for the cool discussions of the committee, for the regular labours of legislation, I think *David Williams* a much more proper man [o]."

I shall not enter into a review of his writings, having taken notice of several at the time of relating their publication, and others being suppressed by the laudable vigilance of the government. It would be the height of injustice to deny his claim to a certain share of popular eloquence, but it is too much to praise him for originality, unless the most unlimited mendacity and temerarious presumption merit that eulogium. He has a singular art of incorporating with the most obvious truths the most fallacious assumptions, and making such complicated results as persuade rash believers, and confiding half-thinkers, and the detection of them requires so many distinctions, that the person who undertakes to answer him incurs the censure of subtilty, from those who have not candour or knowledge enough to reflect that the greatest subtilty lies in the use of general positions. *Dolus latet in universalibus.* He also gives great effect to his arguments, by the introduction of allegories and anecdotes which are easily remembered, and make great impression, the

[n] These expressions are very much softened in the translation sold by Johnson: the original is in these words: "*Mais je le croirois plus propre à semer, pour ainsi dire, ces étincelles d'embrâsement, qu'à discuter les bases ou préparer la formation d'un gouvernement.*"

[o] Appel à l'Impartiale Posterité, vol. ii. p. 29. Translation, vol. ii. p. 41.

fallacy

fallacy of which, from the levity of their compofition, efcapes the fhafts of rigid animadverfion: fuch are the bear of Berne; the Norman who wanted to be king of America; the lame man and hare, and many others, which are introduced throughout his works, and ftated with falfe and malignant applications. The familiar appellation of " TOM PAIN," by which he is generally known, contributes to a delufion that fanctions his audacity, and apologizes for many of his errors; that he is a *young man.* But let thofe whom his example may tempt to follow his fteps recollect, that *Tom Pain* is now approaching that term which experience marks out as the limit of human life; that, at the age of threefcore, he has neither wife, child, home, nor country; that all men have renounced him, as he has renounced his GOD.

JEROME PETION.

IT has often occurred in the course of the French revolution, that the frenzy of popular predilection, the zeal of private friendship, or the temerity of individual arrogance, has occasioned the application or assumption of names and epithets to which the party for whom they were destined had so little claim, that they have been successfully converted to terms of reproach by merely repeating them ironically. The histories of ancient and modern times have been ransacked for appellatives, which have been applied with the most ludicrous impropriety, and epithets which ought only to be the meed of long tried merit, have been inconsiderately lavished on men whose names justice would have stigmatized with every mark of opprobrium and disgrace. Petion affords an instance of this kind. His partisans, with a ridiculous solemnity and affected reiteration, attached *virtuous* to his name, till, for a time, it became common in France to call him *the virtuous Petion*, though, in fact, moderate talents, excessive vanity and selfishness, inveterate rancour, and consummate hypocrisy were his principal characteristics.

Birth and profession. Petion was born at Chartres, but, till the revolution, was so totally unknown, that little can with certainty be recorded of him. He was a juvenile companion of his townsman Brissot, and, like him, bred to the profession of the law [p]. He is said to

[p] Roland's Appeal, vol. i. p. 54.

have

have been a mere pettifogging advocate, who gained a livelihood by encouraging village litigation, but of so bad reputation that many feudal lords refused him permission to plead in their courts [q]. He was also the author of some speculative, political, and moral tracts, which were afterwards collected and published in three volumes, but are so little recommended by style or matter, as to fatigue the patience without informing the understanding [r]. Petion was a member of the new lodges of masonry, and particularly of that of the *Contrat Social*, where he, together with Orleans, la Fayette, Mirabeau, and several other distinguished characters, formed the political committee [s].

Publications.

Freemason.

The connexion which Petion thus formed with Orleans might probably procure his election to the constituent assembly, though it is said he owed it to the favour of the clergy, whom he afterwards repaid with insult and persecution [t]. He was considered a devoted adherent to the duke, and for a long time acted that part with so much success, as to obtain through his means, wealth, influence, and importance [u], though it is probable that he only pretended an attachment to his patron, in order to promote his own interests, and that he was, from the beginning of his political career, at heart a republican [x]. In saying that Petion was a republican, I do not wish to be understood that he was so much attached to that form of government as to have sacrificed to his predilection any opportunity of promotion which a monarchy, a regency, a dictatorship, or a triumvirate might have afforded. Had Orleans possessed courage and consistency enough to avail himself of the opportunities which the times

1789. *Member of the constituent assembly.*

[q] Apologie des Projets, &c. p. 215.
[r] See Œuvres de Petion. [s] Robison's Proofs, p. 403.
[t] Fennel's Review, p. 429.
[u] See Pagès, vol. i. p. 460. 462, History of the Brissotines by Camille Desmoulins, passim. Conjuration de d'Orleans, passim.
[x] See Robison's Proofs, p. 376.

presented

presented for his advancement, Petion would have remained content in the situation of governor to his children, which had been promised him [y], unless some opportunity had occurred of gratifying his ambition, or his love of degrading his superiors, by adopting a different party.

Conduct in the assembly.

In the national assembly, Petion was distinguished as an adherent of Orleans, though he occasionally displayed those republican sentiments which many others affected, and which, from the beginning of the revolution, were highly popular, though the people were not, at first, prepared to approve of those actions which resulted from them. He was a member of the club Breton, where the interests of Orleans were always attended to, and the motions, afterwards made in the assembly, previously discussed [z].

20th June 1789.
23d.

He was one of the members who took the oath in the tennis-court, and, on the day of the royal sitting, displayed great warmth in reprobating the conduct of the king [a]. Petion's eloquence was not calculated to make a great impression in an assembly which contained such speakers as Mirabeau, Mauri, and Barnave, nor was his knowledge so extensive as to afford copious elucidations or important disclosures, but he constantly maintained an intimate intercourse with Brissot, and borrowed from him many hints, and even many rules of political conduct [b]. Petion was one of the cabinet council, and intimate associates of Orleans [c], he assisted in preparing the popular commotions in October, and he was the first who denounced in the assembly, the pretended *orgies* of the *gardes du corps*, though his timidity would have made him

5th Oct. Active conspirator

---

[y] Pagès, vol. i. p 470.
[z] Conspiracy of Robespierre, p. 49.
[a] Debates. Impartial History, vol. i. p. 94.
[b] Roland's Appeal, vol. i. p. 54.
[c] History of the Brissotines by Camille Desmoulins, p. 10. Conjuration de d'Orleans, vol. ii. p. 134.

completely

completely ridiculous, had he not been extricated from his embarrassment by Mirabeau [d]. He was during the tumults which occurred at Versailles on that occasion, one of the most active in exciting the mob and seducing the soldiers, and was seen with other conspirators disguised in woman's attire, and instigating acts of violence [e].

When the assembly removed to Paris, Petion contionued his labours with great assiduity, though without much celebrity. He opposed la Fayette's martial law, and was desirous to divest the king of the prerogative of making war and peace. Petion was the first who proposed the resolution, which, was adopted by acclamation, importing, that the French nation renounced for ever, all idea of conquest, and confined itself entirely to defensive war [f]. This declaration was one of the first acts of political hypocrisy, by which the French legislature attempted to impose on the rest of Europe. Petion, at the time of proposing it, knew that a scheme had been concerted for annexing Avignon to the dominions of France, which was afterwards effected in spite of this decree. This acquisition may be affectedly distinguished from a conquest, but the distinction is rather in words than in fact. The pope had not sufficient power to defend his property from the French; and the inhabitants, deluded by intrigues and alarmed by massacres, were forced to throw themselves into the arms of their treacherous neighbours. Petion was a strenuous promoter of this union; he made a speech on the subject which was ordered to be printed, and which displays a mind fraught with wickedness, and framed for iniquity [g]. He was once called to the president's chair, and on

Exertions in the assembly.

5th Dec. 1790. President.

[d] See MIRABEAU. ORLEANS.
[e] Conjuration de d'Orleans, vol. ii. p. 245.
[f] Debates. Impartial History, vol. i. p. 341.
[g] Debates. Wilde's Addrefs to the Friends of the People, p. 479.

that

that occasion highly complimented by his predecessor Lameth [h].

23d June 1791. Sent to Varennes.

But though assiduous and unremitting in his exertions, Petion never obtained a conspicuous reputation [i] till the unfortunate journey of Louis XVI. to Varennes. On that occasion he displayed a malignant joy in the anticipation that it would prove the king's ruin [k]. He was gratified, on this occasion, by being appointed one of the commissioners to escort the royal family back to Paris. The members of the deputation were particularly instructed to be attentive in preserving all the respect due to the royal dignity [l].

Brutality towards the king.

This injunction was not regarded by Petion, he exulted in an opportunity of displaying the rancour of a grovelling mind, by an unmanly triumph over his degraded sovereign. He and Barnave were seated in the coach with the royal captives. He held the dauphin on his knee during the whole journey [m]; and, in conversation, took every opportunity of insulting the king [n]. He is said to have discoursed affectedly on the necessity of bringing the king to trial, and establishing a republic. The distinction shewn by the royal family to Barnave, who preserved a more dignified and respectful demeanour, increased Petion's aversion, and rendered him the implacable foe of his king [o].

Supposed republican.

At this period, from his intimacy with Brissot, and the authors of *le Republicain*, Petion was con-

---

[h] Debates. Wilde's Address to the Friends of the People, p. 479.
[i] He is thus described in a pamphlet intitled Addresse aux Provinces, "Petion de Villeneuve, in whom you have never been able to distin- "guish any thing but the confidence of folly, and who, vile instru- "ment of factious men! resembles the criers of a fair, who are "stationed at the doors of theatres to make a noise while the farce "goes on." Quoted from Christie's Letters on the Revolution, p. 132. n.
[k] Roland's Appeal, vol. i. p. 58.
[l] Debates. Histories. Moore's View, vol. ii. p. 365.
[m] Conjuration de d'Orleans, vol. iii. p. 125.
[n] Bouillé's Memoirs, p. 406.
[o] Necker on the Revolution, vol. i. p. 349.

sidered

sidered a republican; and his conduct on the king's return tended to confirm the opinion [p]. He argued with vehemence against the king's inviolability, and for the propriety of bringing him to trial. He said, "as a citizen and public function- ary, the king is subject to the law; if above the law, he is a despot. If inviolable, he must be impeccable: then he may murder with impunity: a Nero, a Caligula, may indulge his sanguinary propensities, and have them respected." Notwithstanding the disgust excited by this unjust assimilation of Louis XVI. Petion continued in the same strain, and concluded thus: "Either the king is weak, or wicked; in either case he ought to be tried; I move, therefore, that his trial be decreed; and that it take place before the assembly, or before a convention appointed *ad hoc* [q]." These violent propositions were overruled by the address and eloquence of Barnave, and the salutary check which sedition experienced from the well-timed exertion of power in the *Champ de Mars*, so alarmed Petion, that he began to assume the veil of moderation; and declared that although he disapproved of the report of the committee, he now considered it as a law, and would support it with his life [r].

15th July. Exertions against the king.

The defection of Barnave and his party had so reduced the ranks of opposition, that Petion, Robespierre, and Buzot were almost the only systematic cavillers at the proceedings of the assembly [s]. When recovered from the momentary panic with which he had been affected, Petion resumed his wonted virulence. He had always endeavoured to favour the ascendancy of the mob; he was an advocate for the unqualified right of petitioning by every individual, without distinction; and for an unrestrained

Perseverance in opposition.

[p] Historical Sketch, p. 379.   [q] Debates.
[r] Historical Sketch, p. 385.
[s] Roland's Appeal, vol. i. p. 56.

liberty

liberty of printing and publishing, without any responsibility. " Shall non-active citizens (he said) " be deprived of the right of petitioning? You " compel them to employ force. If housekeepers, " you require that they shall sign their petitions: " suppose they cannot write, are they to be deprived " of the rights of man? As to the right of pub-" lishing *placards*; to declare a printer responsible " for the ills which may arise from a posting-bill, " or to prosecute the authors and their abettors, " would be to destroy the liberty of the press: " what can be more arbitrary than to decide, that " such and such maxims have a tendency to disturb " the public tranquillity?" He persevered in similar sentiments till the dissolution of the assembly. He said, " The sovereignty of the nation is *one*, " *indivisible, inalienable*, and *imperscriptible*. The " nation, in delegating its powers, does not dele-" gate its sovereignty; it reserves the right of ex-" ercising that, when necessary, by conventions, or " insurrections." In discussing the subject of libels, on another occasion, he said, " That a prohi-" bition to calumniate ministers by libels, amounted " to a charter of impunity; for that ministers would " never, or very rarely be convicted before the tri-" bunals. What effect (he continued) can a mo-" mentary calumny produce against a life dedi-" cated to virtue? If libels proceed from levity, " we should despise; if from folly, pity; and if " from malice, forgive them'." These sentiments which, though ridiculous from their exaggeration and absurdity, were highly popular; and his exertions to degrade the king, whom he laboured to deprive of the power of pardoning, and to distinguish by the title of chief public functionary only, confirmed the opinion that Petion was a zealous republican ". He was supposed to be en-

9th May.

10th Aug.

23d Avg.

---

t See Debates on the several days mentioned in the margin.
u Historical Sketch, p. 389. 400.

gaged

gaged in plots inimical to the state, and the friends of government watched his motions with fuspicion and jealoufy [x].

Notwithftanding thefe appearances, Petion was ftill attached to Orleans. He had been one of the moft ftrenuous advocates for his acquittal on the charges relative to the fifth of October [y]; and was one of the privy council of the *palais royal* [z]. Orleans was fo well pleafed with his fervices, that he refolved to exert his influence to get Petion elected mayor of Paris [a]; and intrufted to his care the fafe convoy of his daughter, and her governefs madame de Sillery, to London. The motives of this journey are differently ftated. Camille Defmoulins infinuates, and his opinion is adopted by profeffor Robifon, that the charms of the two females, particularly the youngeft, were employed to confirm Petion's attachment to the duke's family [b]. Madame de Sillery pretends that his attendance was merely an act of politenefs, dictated by the danger and inconvenience the ladies would experience in traverfing the provinces of France, unaccompanied by a male friend, who could on occafion harangue the people and the municipalities [c]. This does not appear a fufficient reafon for Petion's deferting Paris at a period fo interefting, when the conftitution was juft completed, and the election for mayor, and the appointment of a new commander of the national guard about to take place. There was undoubtedly fome fecret motive for this journey, but its precife object is not afcertained.

Attached to Orleans.

October. Goes to London.

Petion took leave of madame de Sillery while fhe was changing horfes, and faw her no more.

His ftay.

[x] Roland's Appeal, vol. i. p. 127. Impartial Hiftory, vol. i. p. 484.
[y] Conjuration de d'Orleans, vol. iii p. 83. 89.
[z] Hiftory of the Briffotines by Camille Defmoulins, p. 10.
[a] Conjuration de d'Orleans, vol. iii. p. 108.
[b] Hiftory of the Briffotines, p. 9. Proofs of a Confpiracy, p. 252.
[c] Précis de la Conduite de Madame de Genlis depuis la Revolution, p. 26.

He

He stayed in London but eight days [d], during which time he associated with some gentlemen who had adopted Gallic principles of reform, and honoured the revolution society with his presence at dinner [e].

Recal. When Bailly resigned the mayoralty, Orleans immediately dispatched a message to Petion, requiring his presence in Paris to fill the vacancy [f]. During his journey to London, he had spoken on the subject to madame de Sillery. He told her he entertained no doubt of being unanimously elected, but that he should decline the office. The lady expressing some doubts of his resolution, he said, "Whatever entreaties may be used, if I accept the post, I am content that you should ever consider me as the most contemptible of mankind [g]." Notwithstanding this protestation, which he frequently repeated in the course of his journey, he obeyed Orleans's summons without hesitation, and *Candidate* immediately on his arrival declared himself a candidate *for the* date for the mayoralty. His principal opponent *mayoralty.* was la Fayette, but Petion succeeded in the election. It is said, and I believe truly, that la Fayette would have had a majority, if seven-eighths of the inhabitants of Paris had not declined voting [h]. The royalists most probably did not vote on the occasion; they could not esteem Petion; although the king, justly incensed against la Fayette, was so little apprized of his competitor's malignity, and so little apprehensive of his power, that he wished him *19th Nov.* elected in preference to the general [i]. As soon as *Elected.* he had gained his election, it was announced to the

[d] Précis de la Conduite de Madame Genlis depuis la Revolution, p. 27.
[e] Flower of the Jacobins, p. 15.
[f] Conjuration de d'Orleans, vol. iii. p. 251.
[g] Précis de la Conduite, &c. p. 27.
[h] Necker on the Revolution, vol. i. p. 349. Out of eighty thousand, the supposed number of active citizens in Paris, only ten thousand four hundred and thirty two voted. See Mercure François, N° du 26 Novembre 1791, p. 289.
[i] Bertrand's Memoirs, vol. i. p. 259.

assembly,

assembly, by a letter from Petion himself, in which he requested the legislature to honour with some mark of their favour the man whom the citizens of Paris had honoured with their confidence. On the motion of Couthon, afterwards so distinguished for sanguinary ferocity, the election was recorded in the *procès verbal*, as a just tribute to a man distinguished for the goodness of his principles and his zeal for the public. It was also moved that the president should answer Petion's letter, but the proposal was over-ruled by a suggestion, that if such a practice were established, the president would be under the necessity of writing forty-four thousand seven hundred and thirty-three similar letters to different municipal officers [k].

Petion soon displayed his resolution to adhere to those principles of insurrection and insubordination to which he owed his popularity. Far from attempting to discourage, he countenanced the attacks made by the mob, under the direction of the Jacobins, on the club of *Feuillans*. He apologised for their violences in a letter to the assembly, by which he declared that Paris was divided between the friends of the people and the Feuillans, and that the law was in a state of opposition to the public opinion. The assembly on reading this letter decreed, that no club should be held in the convent of the *ci-devant Feuillans* [l]. *Encourages sedition.*

27th. Dec.

In consequence of his great influence with the Jacobins, Petion was consulted on forming the Jacobin administration [m]. Robespierre asserts, and perhaps with truth, that in this instance Petion was merely the tool of Brissot, and recommended implicitly such ministers as his political preceptor pointed out [n]. He was however in high favour with *Connection with the Jacobin ministry.*

---

[k] Debates.
[l] Ibid. Impartial History, vol. i. p. 487.
[m] Life of Dumouriez, vol. ii. p. 177.
[n] See Robespierre's Letter to Jerome Petion, Appendix, N° X.

this unprincipled administration, who, together with their fautors, exerted every effort to enhance his popularity. Dumouriez, at first by a most unwarrantable breach of faith towards the king [o], and afterwards by a misappropriation of the secret-service money, furnished him with the means of libelling the royal family [p]. The sums thus received and applied by Petion are said to have amounted to a thousand livres (43*l*. 15*s*.) a-day [q]. When the republican members of the cabinet commenced their outrageous attack on the royal prerogative, Petion and his coadjutor Manuel aided their views by endeavouring to terrify the king, that he might be induced to make his escape, which would have amounted to an abdication of the throne, and spared the faction much intrigue and exertion [r]. This project being baffled by the firmness of the king, and his resolute adherence to the constitution, Petion endeavoured to inspire the people with a continual jealousy, that the king was desirous to take the step he had so repeatedly declined. Actuated by a pretended alarm on this subject, Petion wrote to the commandant of the national guard, mentioning his suspicions, and requiring him to increase the patroles about the Tuilleries, both in number and force. The king, informed of this circumstance, wrote to the municipality, complaining of this unjust suspicion, and declaring his confidence in the national guard. He said that he was informed of all the manœuvres which had been employed to agitate the public mind, and compel him to leave the capital, but that they would be tried in vain. The effect of this letter must have been highly prejudicial to the views of the faction, had the public been permitted to peruse it calmly and without perversion; but Petion, anxious to prevent this effect,

Exertions against the king.

22d May.

23d.

---

[o] See DUMOURIEZ. [p] Roland's Appeal, vol. i. p. 79.
[q] History of the Brissotines by Camille Desmoulins, p. 38.
[r] Conjuration de d'Orleans, vol. iv. p. 170. 173. 187.

published

published a long letter animadverting on that written by the king, replete with fallacious arguments and evasive subtleties. Not satisfied with this, he procured a deputation, who unexpectedly appeared at the bar of the assembly, and denounced the publication of the king's letter as a crime against the nation. Their orator declared, that " if Petion " lost the public confidence, there was no longer any " safety for the people." The speaker was frequently interrupted on account of the irregularity of his proceeding; but, favoured by the galleries, he was heard to an end, and invited to the honours of the sitting. Though the assembly passed to the order of the day on the denunciation, the deputation was of use to those who contrived it, as it served to inflame the public mind, and increase the popularity of Petion*. A few days afterwards, a riot was organized which threatened a renewal of the scenes of October 1789; the king's guard was insulted, and the cap and flag of anarchy planted over the principal gate of the castle; the whole city exhibited an appearance of alarm and agitation, the sittings of the assembly were declared permanent, and the houses illuminated; but, probably for want of a determinate project, the insurrection subsided †.

24th.

25th.

29th.

When the Jacobin administration was dismissed, the contest between that faction and the friends of the king became more inveterate and violent than ever. Petion co-operated with his old associates, and resolved to use every means which his popularity and influence afforded to reduce the royal power to a nullity, or to render the king implicitly subservient to the ministry or regent whom he favoured. An insurrection was projected and organ-

Dismission of the jacobin administration.

* Impartial History, vol. ii. p. 32. For copies of the letters on this occasion, see Mercure François, Nº du 2 Juin 1792, p. 60.—And for the proceedings in the assembly, see Debates.
† Mercure François du 2 Juin, p. 64.

ized, in which it is most probable that the ultimate intention was to sacrifice the whole royal family; though the conspirators, not daring to avow the extent of their design, had not expressly commissioned any individual or party to perpetrate the murder. For some days before the insurrection, Petion displayed the utmost activity in exciting the mob of the *fauxbourg* St. Antoine[u]; he and Manuel covered the walls of Paris with placards highly abusive of the royal family[x]. The day before the insurrection was appointed to take place, and while the minds of the people were in the greatest fermentation, a dinner was given in the *Champs Elysées*, at which were present about five hundred guests. Anacharsis Clootz, who but two days before had proposed to depose the king, sat as toast-master; Dugazon the actor sang couplets threatening destruction to the king; and in the course of the day, Gorsas declared, that on the morrow, not the *oak*, but the *aspin* of liberty, must be planted in the garden of the Tuilleries[y]. The Jacobin club had declared their fittings permanent; and the projected insurrection was formally announced by a declaration, that the inhabitants of the *fauxbourg* St. Antoine would meet in arms and present a petition to the king, requiring him to sanction the decrees against the priests, and for forming a camp round Paris[z]. The assembly took no active measures to discourage these proceedings, and Petion openly favoured them.

On the day of the insurrection, Petion, in imitation perhaps of Orleans, absented himself from Paris: he went, no one knew wherefore, to Versailles[a]. Rœderer, *procureur-general-syndique*, appeared at the bar of the assembly, and formally an-

Preparations for insurrection.

19th June.

20th. Proceedings of the mob.

---

[u] Life of Dumouriez, vol. ii. p. 391.
[x] Conjuration de d'Orleans, vol. iii. p. 175.
[y] Fennel's Review, p. 67. Conjuration de d'Orleans, vol. iii. p. 174.
[z] Impartial History, vol. ii. p. 42.
[a] Idem, vol. ii. p. 45. Playfair's History of Jacobinism, p. 408.

nounced,

nounced, that a collection of an hundred thousand men in arms was formed on the place where the Bastille stood; that they were encouraged by the tacit approbation of the assembly and the municipality, and by the presence of three members of the legislature: he said that their intention was to present a petition to the assembly, and afterwards to go in a body to the Tuilleries: he requested the legislature to support their own dignity, by adhering to the law which forbad the presenting of petitions by armed men, and by refusing admission to the petitioners. This application produced a debate, in which the propriety of following Rœderer's advice was strongly enforced. Before this subject was fully discussed, the mob, headed by Santerre and St. Huruge, presented themselves at the door of the hall. They sent in a petition to be admitted, stating that their number did not exceed eight thousand. Lafource supported the petition, and averred, as from his own knowledge, that if they were received in the hall of the legislature, they would leave their petition there, and not proceed to the palace. Swayed by this argument, and terrified by the impetuosity of the mob, the assembly at length admitted them. Their petition was read by one Huguenin, formerly an advocate in the parliament of Nancy; he was an old man, almost seventy, remarkable for his gigantic stature, bleared eyes, and ferocious aspect. The petition or memorial was contained in eight pages, and every sentence was replete with threats and invectives against the king and queen. When he had finished, a motley and squalid band of the most wretched outcasts, drawn from all the receptacles of beggary, idleness, and infamy in Paris, marched through the hall: they were armed with pikes, rusty swords, scythes, pitchforks, twy-bills, bludgeons, pickaxes, and clubs. This miserable battalion consisted of coalmen, chimney-sweepers, shoe-blacks, wharf-porters, negroes male and female, and

and women of the lowest and most abandoned class. They carried divers ensigns, with inscriptions denoting sanguinary ferocity, occasionally intermixed with coarse and vapid ribaldry: among the latter efforts may be enumerated several pairs of ragged black breeches, which were hoisted on poles, with the inscription, *libres, et sans-culottes*; some were half naked, and carried their rags on the point of a pike; some bore on their pikes pieces of bread, cheese, or other food. This disgusting troop occupied the hall of the assembly three hours, and at their departure left with the president a banner, in token of fraternity. They then divided into three companies, one under Santerre, another under St. Huruge, and a third commanded by the Amazonian prostitute, Theroigne de Mericourt. After surmounting a slight opposition, or rather their own fears of opposition, from a guard, who were either disaffected, or would not act without orders, they occupied all the apartments in the palace, and committed those horrible outrages which endangered the lives of all the royal family, and will ever stigmatise the legislature, the municipality, and the people [b].

Conduct of Petion.

When the mob had exhausted every effort of insult and brutality which their ferocious licentiousness could dictate; when they had perpetrated every violence short of absolute murder, from which by some unaccountable impulse they were restrained, Petion made his appearance. He was driven in his carriage up to the palace, with the air of a man perfectly at leisure [c]. Convinced that the day would not produce the advantages his faction expected, that the king would not be induced by terror to sanction the decrees, and that the mob had not been duly prepared to exterminate the royal family, he

[b] See THE KING, &c. Debates and Histories. Moore's Journal, vol. ii. p. 202, et seq. Fennel's Review, p. 69, et seq. Conjuration de d'Orleans, vol. iii. p. 176, et seq. and the Journals.
[c] Playfair's History of Jacobinism, p. 408.

thought

thought it would be best to assume an appearance of kindness. He said to the king, "Sire, I was only this moment informed of your situation."— "That is extraordinary, (said the king,) for I have been in this situation above three hours[d]." Petion then assured the king he had nothing to *fear*; which produced from the king that energetic reply, in which he disclaimed the influence of so degrading a sentiment[e]. He added with pointed indignation; "Go, sir, Europe will be your judge." These words inflamed Petion's rancour, and increased his animosity against the royal family[f]. For the present, however, he restrained his anger, and dispersed the mob. Mounted on a stool, he said, "Citizens, you have now made your desires known to the hereditary representative, with that energy and dignity which become a free people, who understand their rights. The king at present knows the intentions of the *sovereign*, and will undoubtedly pay a proper regard to them. You ought now to retire with calmness and decency, that your intentions may not be calumniated." A deputation from the national assembly soon afterwards arrived, and, in their usual cant, proffered to make a shield of their bodies for the king. This ill-timed offer was rendered useless by the dispersion of the mob, who, at the command of Petion and Santerre, evacuated the palace[g].

Petion's misconduct on this occasion was so flagrant, that the directory of the department of Paris thought proper to suspend him and Manuel from their functions. When this decree was known in Paris, every exertion was made to render the

His suspension.

---

[d] Moore's Journal, vol. ii. p. 217. This assertion of Petion's must have been a falsity, or at least an equivocation; for he knew all the preparations for the event, and purposely absented himself that he might not be called on to interfere.
[e] See THE KING.
[f] Peltier's late Picture, vol. i. p. 122.
[g] Histories. Moore's Journal, vol. ii. p. 217.

authors of it odious, and to procure the reinstatement of the popular officers. Petion published, in answer to the letter of the directory of the department, an apologetical pamphlet, intitled, *General Rules of my Conduct towards the People*, in which he declared it as a fundamental principle, that he would never cause the blood of the people to be shed [h]. This declaration, which confounded every distinction between the peaceable citizen and the audacious violator of public repose, rendered him, if possible, more popular than before. Numerous deputations were sent to the bar of the assembly, who mingled with their petitions and declamations on behalf of the *virtuous* mayor, the most atrocious calumnies against the king and his advisers [i]. Danton endeavoured to excite the *commune* in Petion's behalf [k], and Robespierre wrote a severe invective against the directory of the department [l]. The king wished to decline interfering, but the assembly would not permit him to display his forbearance. He was obliged to confirm the decree of the department, and when his proclamation to that effect had been read in the assembly, and Petion presented himself at the bar to reply, Bazire insolently exclaimed, "Let us *now* hear the language of virtue and "truth." His apology, which was a series of absurd fables compiled with the most barefaced disregard of consistency or probability, was received with clamorous plaudits, he was invited to the honours of the sitting, and by a decree restored to the exercise of his office [m]. This measure was followed by the resignation of the directory of the department [n], but the rancour of Petion was not

12th July. Speech in the assembly.

13th. Restoration.

[h] Playfair's History of Jacobinism, p. 410.
[i] See Debates from 25th June to 13th July.
[k] See MANUEL.
[l] Defenseur de la Constitution, p. 431.
[m] Debates. See also Fennel's Review; Peltier's late Picture; Moore's Journal, vol. ii.; and the Histories.
[n] Impartial History, vol. ii. p. 77.

to be so appeased, he commenced an active persecution of la Rochefoucault, who had been president of the directory, and finally, with the assistance of the ungrateful Condorcet, procured his murder [o].

At the confederation, Petion was ostentatiously exhibited as the popular idol. His name was inscribed on the banners, and on the hats of the mob, whose general cry was *Vive Petion! Vive le vertueux Petion! à bas la Fayette! à bas le veto! à la lanterne les aristocrates! Petion ou la mort!* &c. Several members of the legislative assembly were insulted by the pretended conquerors of the Bastille, who said that if Petion had not been restored, they would have wreaked their vengeance on the assembly [p].

_{14th.
Popularity at the confederation.}

The faction to which Petion belonged, now displayed all the exultation of subaltern triumph with the ferocity of implacable hate; they encouraged the most flagrant insults and circulated the most atrocious calumnies against the royal family. Among other reports which gained easy credit with the mob was that of a large quantity of arms being concealed in the palace. The king, with his usual candour, invited Petion to attend and search; the mayor refused, but sent a deputation of six municipal officers, and, though they were perfectly satisfied that there was no truth in the suggestion which occasioned their visit, Petion would not certify the fact so unequivocally as to remove the popular suspicion. The arts of the faction were so successful, that the mob, who terrified and governed the city, were eager to commence acts of riot and hostility, but the fear of the national guard restrained them from attacking the palace. The night was disgraced by tumultuous and incendiary meetings, and in the day, the unrestrained rabble committed every act

_{26th July.
Rancour against the king.}

---

[o] Considerations on the Nature of the French Revolution, by Mallet du Pan, p. 46. n.

[p] Mercure François, Nº du 21 Juillet 1792. The reader is referred to this publication for a judicious description of the ceremony of the day.

of violence and fury which licentiousness and political fanaticism could suggest. Among other instances may be mentioned the attack made on d'Eprémesnil, who but a few years before had been one of the popular idols. He was walking tranquilly in the garden of the Tuilleries, when, without any known provocation, a numerous party attacked, wounded, robbed, and stripped him naked; they were about to have executed him *à la lanterne*, when he was rescued by a detachment of national guards, who carried him, though supposed to be dead, to the guard-house of the treasury. Petion attended, but unwilling to check and unable to justify this mob, he politically fainted away [q].

27th. Encourages the mob.

30th. Arrival of the Marseillois.

To encourage the rabble, and counteract their dread of the Swiss and national guards, the demagogues of Paris sent for a troop of ruffians from Marseilles, men reeking with the blood shed in lawless violence at Avignon, incapable of remorse, and rendered additionally ferocious by the concurrence of climate, education, and practice. Their march to Paris was marked by acts characteristic of their principles; robbery, rape, and murder attended their footsteps; they recruited their bands with all the abandoned wretches whom want or infamy had rendered desperate, and arrived at Paris near seven hundred in number. In their progress from the *Barriere du Trone*, where they entered, to the mayor's house, which was at the other extremity of the city, they gave a sample of the conduct they intended to maintain, by insulting and defying the inhabitants; they insisted that silken cockades should not be worn, but that worsted should be substituted, and overthrew the stalls where ribband

---

[q] See Debates and Histories. Peltier's late Picture, vol. i. p. 30. D'Eprémesnil recovered, though grievously wounded; he employed his first effort of returning strength in writing to his sovereign to beg forgiveness for that conduct which had accelerated the revolution. He was guillotined during the tyranny of Robespierre.

cockades

cockades were sold. The national guard, consisting of thirty-two thousand men, and the citizens remonstrated in vain, they were terror-struck by this handful of resolute banditti, and forced to submit. Petion received the Marseillois with cordiality and exultation, he exhorted them to be unanimous, and provided them with barracks in the *fauxbourg* Montmartre, which were afterwards exchanged for the barracks of the Cordeliers, in the section *du Theatre François*. These ruffians did not take possession of the residence assigned them by the mayor till they had signalized their own ferocity, and demonstrated the pusillanimity of the Parisians, by attacking a party of the national guard who were dining in the *Champs Elysées*, some of whom they killed and wounded, and took others prisoners, with very little resistance[r].

Encouraged by this reinforcement, Petion assumed a more decisive conduct. Actuated by his faction, the sections of Paris had been for some time in the daily habit of sending petitioners to the assembly to demand the king's suspension, while the more respectable inhabitants had attended with protests or counter-petitions. The assembly, instead of, terminating these indecorous scenes, sanctioned them by indecision, and, at length, a petition was drawn up by Chenier, the poet, and Collot d'Herbois, the actor, subscribed by a numerous tribe without distinction of sections, and presented by Petion, at the head of a deputation of the *commune*. This petition was replete with every calumny which invention had framed against the king, and every suggestion with which malice had endeavoured to blacken his intentions. It concluded by requiring a decree which should ordain " not his suspension till the " country should be no longer in danger, but his " forfeiture

3d Aug. Presents petition to depose the king.

[r] Histories. Playfair's History of Jacobinism, p. 413. Peltier's late Picture of Paris, vol. i. p. 28. vol. ii. p. 485.

"forfeiture of the crown." It is remarkable that this petition deprecates the formation of a republic, and seems only calculated to procure the deposition of Louis XVI. It says, "while we have *such* a king, liberty can never be established;" and in another place, "as it is very doubtful that the nation can ever place confidence *in the present dynasty*, we pray, &c." These expressions afford strong proofs that Petion was still attached to Orleans, and laboured for his advancement, and demonstrate the justice of Robespierre's observation, that the republic glided in by stealth among the various factions. The petition was received with acclamations, ordered to be printed and sent to the departments, and referred to a special committee [*].

10th. Conduct during the insurrection.

But although the ascendancy of faction, aided by the clamour of the galleries, had procured a favourable reception to this petition, the final event could not be intrusted to the assembly, where the royalists and constitutionalists still retained a majority. The report of the special committee was deferred, and the insurrection organized which terminated in dethroning and imprisoning the king. In that part of this work where the insurrection is described, Petion's conduct is carefully pourtrayed [†]. The leading features consist in his having been in the palace till the insurrection was in full force, and then evading his duty of protecting the royal family, by procuring an order from the national assembly requiring his attendance at the bar; his being nominated one of the three members of the new *commune*, after the old *commune* had been driven out: and his giving an order to Mandat to repel force by force, and afterwards causing that officer to be murdered and the order taken out of his

---

[*] Debates. Histories. Playfair's History of Jacobinism, p. 427. Moore's Journal, vol. i. p. 15. Peltier's late Picture of Paris, vol. i. p. 34

[†] See BRISSOT.

pocket.

pocket. The two former transactions are sufficient to stigmatize his name with indelible infamy, but those who applaud the French revolution are so far from disapproving his conduct that they consider it meritorious, and generally mention it with applause. The order given to Mandat, in which Petion did his duty, is, on the contrary, adduced as an inexpiable offence, it formed part of the accusation against the Briffotines*; and madame Roland undertakes his defence in these words ˣ: " It is not
" till lately that Petion's enemies have thought of
" saying that he went to the palace to defend it;
" while, in fact, he was exposed to the greatest
" danger while he remained there himself; it is
" not till lately that they have circulated the ca-
" lumny of his having given an order to Mandat
" to fire on the people. I ask for what purpose
" Petion, detested by the court and cherished by
" the people, should have betrayed the latter and
" protected the former, when its fall was approach-
" ing; he who had fought against it in the pleni-
" tude of power, and had already acquired popu-
" larity, what reason could he have for risking his
" popularity, when the people had the best of the
" game ʸ. I put out of the question the philosopher
" and zealous citizen, I consider only the man,
" and it is demonstrative, that under the influence
" of ambition or interest, the conduct attributed
" to Petion is repugnant to common sense; and
" that if his integrity would not, his judgment
" would have prevented his adopting it. He could
" not, from the nature of his place, march at the
" head of the insurrection; it was necessary to
" confine him, and tie his hands that he might not

---

* See the Act of Accusation against them, and the Report by Billaud Varennes, made July 15, 1793.
ˣ See Observations rapides sur l'Acte d'Accusation contre les Députés. Appel à l'Impartiale Posterité, vol. ii. p. 57.
ʸ Lorsque le Peuple avait plus beau jeu. *Orig.*

" counteract

"counteract it. The blunderers of the *commune* "forgot to do so, and I remember that Lanthemas "went twice from the mayor's hotel to the *hotel-de-* "*ville* to order a strong guard for Petion's resi- "dence." In this statement madame Roland does not relate truly, or argue correctly. It is not true that the facts relating to Mandat had, at the time she wrote, been but recently circulated, they formed part of several narratives collected at the period when they occurred, and published speedily afterwards [z]; nor was his conduct so devoid of policy as she would make it appear. Though the insurrection was strongly combined, there were many reasons to doubt its success, and Petion's hypocritical conduct was calculated, not to offend the people, but, as on the twentieth of June, to secure his immunity without prejudice to his popularity. It is also to be recollected, that at the time he gave this order (8th August), the assembly had, by the acquittal of la Fayette, shewn that they were not implicitly governed by the disorganizing faction, and the council-general of the *commune* contained many members inimical to his views, and who had shewn the greatest indifference to his cause during his suspension; it was necessary for the mayor to temporize with them till he was secure of their destruction; and accordingly, the first act of the new *commune* was to murder Mandat, and suppress Petion's order. The whole of his conduct, even according to madame Roland's statement, was a compound of stubborn malignity, treacherous hypocrisy, and pitiful cowardice [a].

[z] See Moore's Journal, vol. i. p. 149. Peltier's late Picture, vol. i. p. 144. It is however easy to suppose that the fact alluded to might be true, though not publicly recorded, as all the journals which were not devoted to the usurping ministry were suppressed.

[a] See BRISSOT. Also Impartial History, vol. ii. p. 89. Pagès, vol. i. p. 472. 478. 486. Moore's Journal, vol. i. p. 53. 144. 148. 151. Playfair's History of Jacobinism, p. 434. Account of the Revolt and Massacre, p. 19. Historical and Political Account by a National Guard, p. 13. 33. Fennel's Review, p. 355. 358, 359. Conjuration de d'Orleans, vol. iii. p. 197.

The friendly exertions of Petion's party were attended with so much success, that he was for a short time confined to his house under a guard, but when the king's suspension had been pronounced, he appeared at the bar, and thanked the assembly for their conduct[b]. As some fears were still expressed for his personal safety, he was constantly attended by two armed men as a body guard. It was even asserted that two men had attempted to assassinate him, and they were arrested and imprisoned[c]. He was deputed to attend the royal family to their prison, and in the way, and on their arrival, behaved with the most brutal insolence. He desired the queen to survey the people with more mildness, as the supercilioufness of her looks gave offence; and pointed out the place where the king was to sleep with peremptory ferociousness[d]. During their whole confinement, Petion treated the royal family with the same malignant insolence[e]. The plunder of the palace had reduced the king to such a state of penury, that he was obliged to relieve his immediate exigencies by borrowing a small sum, two thousand five hundred and twenty-six livres (110*l*. 10*s*. 3*d*.) from the Jacobin mayor; he gave a receipt for the money, which was published in the *Chronique de Paris* with an insulting comment. This act of base perfidiousness was accompanied with conduct no less mean and obdurate; when the king was reduced to the necessity of applying for money for his daily expences, his letters to Petion were received with rude indifference, and left for several days unanswered[f].

11th. Treatment of the royal family.

13th.

[b] Debates. Journals.
[c] Ibid. Moore's Journal, vol. i. p. 103.
[d] Moore's Journal, vol. i. p. 101. Fennel's Review, p. 413. See THE KING, &c.
[e] This brutality was carried to such an excess, that as Playfair justly observes, Charles I. never experienced any thing harsh or hard in comparison to what Louis XVI. suffered. History of Jacobinism, p. 609. n.
[f] Moore's Journal, vol. ii. p. 370.

Petion's

Petion's arduous situation.

Petion's popularity and ascendancy were confirmed and increased by the events of the tenth of August, he was hailed as the magistrate of the people, and his name inscribed on a flag hoisted within the precincts of the Tuilleries to commemorate that eventful day[g]. He soon found, however, that his attachment to Brissot and the ministry was incompatible with his situation in the new self-formed council of the *commune*. That body, as Petion afterwards said, instead of putting an end to the revolutionary efforts, which had already been crowned with success, thought it more dignified to enter into a state of rivalship with the legislative assembly, whose decrees they obeyed or resisted only as they were favourable or repugnant to their views[h]. But however Petion might disapprove the usurpations of the *commune*, he had not courage or integrity sufficient to oppose or resist them, he contented himself with a cold distant demeanor, and sanctioned all their measures in such a manner as to shew his internal sentiments of disgust. This conduct was sufficient to expose him to the rancour of the Jacobins, who overwhelmed him with defamation. He was not possessed of the energy requisite to stem this torrent, but threw himself helpless into the hands of his new adversaries. He wrote a canting letter to the *section des Halles* in vindication of his own conduct towards the *commune*, in which he meanly flattered them, and excused himself by general professions of zeal for the public good[i]. To conciliate still more the wavering populace, he attended the next day at the bar of the assembly, at the head of a deputation of the *commune*, and sanctioned by his presence those proceedings which demonstrated that the disorganizing

30th.

31st.

---

[g] Peltier's late Picture, vol. ii. p. 297.
[h] Petion's intended Speech on Louvet's charge against Robespierre. See Mercure François, N° du 17 Novembre 1792, p. 190.
[i] Peltier's late Picture, vol. ii. p. 291, 292.

faction in the *commune*, not content with destroying royalty, were determined to reign paramount to every other existing authority, and to brave and awe the legislature itself[k].

Thus trembling for his popularity, and ready to embrace every excess rather than risk a diminution of it, it is reasonably presumed that Petion took an active share in promoting the fatal massacres which occurred so soon after this disgraceful scene in the assembly; and the presumption receives additional confirmation from his known attachment to Orleans, and his intimacy with Manuel. He is feebly defended by Garat and madame Roland. Garat merely says that Petion was kind and humane, and had a due aversion and horror for the shedding of human blood[l]. This negative acquittal is not of great importance in itself, for even if the general assertion were true as to the rest of Petion's life, his conduct on this day might exhibit him in a new light, and alter the impression made by his former actions. The defence however is in itself of no force, for however a French revolutionary journalist and minister of state may reason, it is not possible for the thinking part of any other community to concede, that the defender of the massacres at Avignon, the employer of the Marseillois in Paris, the insurgent of the twentieth of June, and the conspirator of the tenth of August, had any horror of bloodshed. Madame Roland, speaking of Amar's act of accusation against the Brissotines, says, " The reporter
" has not, in the slightest manner, adverted to the
" massacres on the second of September; he has
" avoided a dilemma by not adopting any conclu-
" sion, for the Mountaineers have made statements
" diametrically repugnant. When Roland de-
" nounced these massacres, the Jacobins asserted
" that they were the work of the people, inflamed

2d Sept. Observations on his conduct during the massacres.

[k] See BRISSOT.   [l] Garat's Memoirs, p. 27.

"to vengeance; they considered it a crime to refrain from applauding them; and when Petion and his colleagues obtained a decree to prosecute the authors of these scenes, they called Petion and the right side enemies of the people and of liberty. Now, since this decree is fallen into neglect; now, that the Jacobins triumph, and the twenty-two are proscribed, the Jacobins themselves, and Hebert among the foremost, impudently assert that the massacres were the work of the base Petion [m]." Admitting this to be a good party argument, it is far from establishing Petion's innocence, it only shews that the Mountain were, as well as their opponents, frequently guilty of inconsistencies in argument and conduct. The facts are not, however, exactly agreeable to madame Roland's statement, Marat, even while he attributed these acts to the people, admitted and strongly asserted that Petion was a principal promoter and accomplice. He says: "As to the massacres of the second and third of September, it is an atrocity to represent them as the work of a gang of brigands: if so, the assembly, the minister of the interior, and the mayor of Paris were the malefactors; and nothing can wash them clean from the crime of not having prevented assassinations that lasted three days. But they will doubtless say, it was impossible, being equally the act of the national guards, the federates, and the people. Petion rested tranquilly at table with Brissot and his friends, and disdained to quit the party even for receiving the commissioners sent by the assembly to charge him to stop these excesses [n]." The flimsy reasonings of Petion's advocates have not been able to prevent discerning men of all nations, and of

[m] Observations rapides, &c. Appel à l'Impartiale Postérité, vol. ii. p. 58.

[n] Journal de Marat, No. 105. Quoted in Arthur Young's Example of France, a Warning to Britain, p. 28.

both

both parties, royalist and republican, from considering and accusing him as the chief contriver and promoter of these horrible transactions. Arthur Young makes an exception favourable to Marat, in stating the comparative guilt of that incendiary and Petion°. Montjoye and Peltier expressly aver, that he was the principal promoter of the massacres ᵖ; and the republican Pagès repeats the same accusation in various parts of his history, and with all the violence of unqualified reprobation ᑫ.

Leaving, however, these ill-managed efforts of exculpation, and general censures, it plainly results from all apparent circumstances, that Petion knew and consented to, if he did not command, the scenes which disgraced his mayoralty. After the suspension of the municipality, he had been invested with power to order out all the armed force in Paris, and could at pleasure have terminated a carnage which was begun and conducted only by a small band of hireling ruffians ʳ. From his window he could see the carriages full of priests designed for slaughter go over the *pont neuf* ˢ; and from rooms in his hotel he could not avoid hearing the screams of the dying, and the shouts of the murderers, in two different prisons ᵗ. The insurrection was twice announced in form, as having begun, and going to begin, yet Petion took no notice of it ᵘ. A deputation of twelve commissioners was sent to Petion by the assembly, to confer on the state of public affairs: if we may believe Marat, he sat at table with Brissot, and shewed no inclination to receive them ˣ; and when at length they were admitted, kept them till

° Example of France, &c. ubi supra.
ᵖ See Conspiracy of Robespierre, p. 74. Peltier's late Picture, vol. ii. p. 230. n.
ᑫ See Histoire Secrete, vol. i. p. 479. vol. ii. p. 40. 319.
ʳ Playfair's History of Jacobinism, p. 499.
ˢ Peltier's late Picture, vol. ii. p. 306.
ᵗ Playfair, ubi supra. ᵘ Garat's Memoirs, p. 28.
ˣ See quotation from Marat, above.

two o'clock in the morning conversing on indifferent topics, and never mentioned the massacres in the prisons. He was afterwards reproached with this fact in the convention, and feebly defended himself by saying there was no need for him to mention an event notorious to all Paris, or to descant on an evil which was then irreparable [y]. He even told a person who advised him to go to the prisons, that he did not choose to risk his popularity [z]. Towards the conclusion of the massacres, Petion made his appearance at the Bicêtre, where the mob was employed in pumping, in order to drown a few prisoners, the melancholy remains of this savage carnage, who had concealed themselves in cellars and holes under ground. He addressed the mob in the language of mildness and pretended philosophy, but when they persisted in their proceedings, calmly left them, saying, "Well, children, make an end of it [a]!"

5th Sept. 7th, 8th, 15th, 17th, 18th.

As soon as decency would permit, Petion appeared at the bar of the assembly, with a statement that Paris was then perfectly tranquil; and afterwards wrote several letters, stating the disposition of the people to return to order, and requiring that energy might be given to the law [b].

State of Paris.

At this period, Paris was in a state of unparalleled disorder; the allied armies were supposed to be within a short distance, and certain of reaching the capital; the elections for members to the convention were proceeding, but all appearance of freedom or regularity was destroyed by a mob of pike and bludgeon men, who constantly beset the electors; the populace addicted themselves to plunder to a degree so audacious, that watches, jewels, and trinkets, were snatched from

[y] See Debates, 21st January 1793.
[z] See St. Just's Report, 8th July 1793. Peltier's late Picture of Paris, vol. ii. p. 539.
[a] Peltier's late Picture, vol. ii. p. 365. Playfair's History of Jacobinism, p. 498.
[b] Debates.

the persons of their possessors in open day, and Petion stated it to the assembly as an instance of the people's sense of propriety, that some of these robbers had been murdered on the spot; the *garde-meuble de la couronne* was broke open, and plundered of jewels of immense value; all was rapacity, riot, insubordination, and terror [c]. The ministers, alarmed at the hurricane they had excited, were desirous to leave Paris, to carry the king with them, and transfer the seat of government to a more tranquil city; Danton, however, strenuously opposed the measure, and Petion rejected it with indignation [d]. It has been asserted that Petion, accompanied by Manuel and Kersaint, induced Louis XVI. to require the retreat of the combined armies; but this account, so far as it connects him with Manuel in the transaction, is disproved by Clery [e].

Notwithstanding Petion's official situation, and the strong alliance between him and the ministry, he had not sufficient influence to be elected deputy to the convention for Paris [f]. He was however returned for Eure et Loire, or Chartres, which place he had represented in the constituent assembly. His popularity was now rapidly declining; and the ill grace with which he, the instigator of commotion, now recommended subordination and obedience to the laws, contributed as much as any other circumstance to divest him of the public favour [g]. Though he was not chosen deputy for Paris, he was re-elected mayor of that city; but this was probably a manœuvre of the Mountain, to make him resign his seat for Eure et Loire; if so, he frustrated it by declining the mayoralty in the

Elected deputy to the convention.

[c] Debates. Histories. Moore's Journal, vol. i. p. 412, et seq.
[d] History of the Brissotines by Camille Desmoulines, p. 20.
[e] Pagès, vol. ii. p. 44. Journal de Clery, p. 105.
[f] Louvet's Narrative, p 20.
[g] See Impartial History, vol. ii. p. 130. Moore's Journal, vol. ii. p. 459. Pagès, vol. ii. p. 40.

most positive manner, by a short letter to the electors [h].

21st Sept. President. At the first meeting of the convention, when royalty was abolished without deliberation by three hundred and seventy-one members out of seven hundred and forty-five, Petion sat as president. He was also one of the committee appointed to revise the constitution [i], His politics at this time are extremely doubtful; he was in the confidence, and acted with the Brissotine faction; but it is said that he continued attached to Orleans, and laboured to promote his views, though the ascendancy of Marat and other worthless characters prevented his public co-operation [k]. To this uncertainty of conduct may be attributed his apparent inconsistency when Louvet made his denunciation against Robespierre. He coincided in the views of the Brissotines so far as related to the punishment and disgrace of the intended dictator, but was anxious to prevent such a discussion as would endanger Orleans; he therefore avoided supporting Louvet in the debate, and was friendly to the motion for the order of the day, but he afterwards published the speech he intended to have delivered [l].

Contest with Robespierre. The contest between Petion and Robespierre now grew to a great excess of personal rancour; in addition to his intended speech, Petion published, and posted on the walls of Paris, a letter to the Jacobin club against his rival [m]. Robespierre answered these attacks in a letter replete with humorous satire and polished ridicule, and succeeded in making his antagonist additionally contemptible [n].

[h] Mercure François, N° du 27 Octobre 1792.
[i] See Debates.
[k] See Conjuration de d'Orleans, vol. iii. p. 219. 223. Also Pagès, vol. ii. p. 12.
[l] Louvet's Narrative, p. 23, 24. See also Mercure François N° du 17 Novembre 1792.
[m] A summary of this speech and a translation of the letter to the Jacobins, are given in the Appendix, N° IX.
[n] Moore's View, vol. ii. p. 395. See ROBESPIERRE.

Petion's

Petion's exertions in the convention were neither strenuous or important; his chief efforts were employed on the king's trial, in which he acted with such timid duplicity as completely to annihilate his small remaining portion of popularity, without serving the king, or seeming attached to his cause. He appears principally to have aimed at obtaining delay, as he proposed the discussion of the king's inviolability, and remonstrated against the convention sitting as judges; but when the *appel nominal* was to decide the fate of Louis, Petion voted him guilty, reserving only a discussion on the propriety of delay º. His conduct in this particular excited great indignation among the populace, it was considered as a high crime at the Jacobin club, and Petion narrowly escaped, or rather obtained a short respite from expulsion ᵖ. *Conduct on the king's trial. 3d Dec. 5th Jan. 1793.*

In the course of these debates, Petion had some personal altercation with Lepelletier, and when that deputy was assassinated, the Mountain took advantage of the circumstance to accuse Petion as an accomplice with the murderer. A long and tumultuous debate ensued, in which Petion's conduct in many respects was virulently arraigned, and his defence was by no means proportioned to the vigour and extent of the attack ᑫ. In the contest which ensued between the Mountain and the Gironde, Petion was not active, though frequently attacked. His known connexion with Orleans restrained his efforts, and perhaps he yet retained a wish that the views of that conspirator should be crowned with success, as he could never be induced to act strenuously against him. He awaited the turn of events with childish indifference, or hypocritical levity. The following anecdote, related by Louvet ʳ, re- *21st Jan. Defeat of Petion's party.*

º Debates.
ᵖ Moore's Journal, vol. ii. p. 570. 572. See also p. 614.
ᑫ Debates. See Robespierre à ses Commettans, vol. ii. p. 241.
ʳ Louvet's Narrative, p. 35.

specting the conspiracy of the 10th of March, will shew that Petion was incredibly stupid, or so great an hypocrite that even his own faction could not depend on him. Louvet says, "That I might be
"near the convention, I had taken a lodging in
"Honoré-street, very little above the Jacobins.
"About nine in the evening, my Lodoiska, who
"had gotten home, and was expecting me, heard a
"frightful tumult and horrible cries. Ever anxious
"for me, who, with most of my friends, had lived
"for three months surrounded with dangers, con-
"stantly pursued, threatened, insulted, obliged to
"carry arms for my defence, and forced to keep
"every night from home; my dear wife came
"down, and went on till she came into the gal-
"leries of the society, from which the noise
"issued. She heard a thousand slanders, a thou-
"sand horrid speeches uttered. She saw the lights
"extinguished, and sabres drawn. She came out
"with an enraged multitude, who went to the
"Cordeliers for auxiliaries, thence to return forth-
"with, and attack the convention, Lodoiska just
"came back when I returned. Immediately I flew
"to Petion's, where some of my friends were as-
"sembled. They were conversing calmly on cer-
"tain decrees that were to be passed in the course
"of a few weeks. God knows how difficult I
"found it to rouse them from their security. At
"last I prevailed on them to refrain from appearing
"at the meeting already begun, and to assemble,
"with all the principal persons proscribed, in an
"hour's time, in a house where the conspirators
"would not expect to find us. I then repaired
"with speed to the meeting, where I found Kervé-
"l'gan, deputy from Finisterre. This brave man
"hastened to the farther part of the suburb St.
"Marceau, to alarm a battalion from Brest, which
"very fortunately arrived at Paris a few days be-
"fore, and had been detained. This battalion re-
"mained

"mained all night under arms, ready to march to our assistance at the first request, or the sound of the alarm-bell. In the mean time I went from house to house, to acquaint Valazé, Buzot, Barbaroux, Salle, and several others. Brissot went to inform the ministers of what was passing; and the minister at war, the brave and unfortunate Beurnonville, having scaled the wall of his garden, had already joined some of his friends, with whom he formed a patrole. After a ramble of two hours, in a dark night, and in the midst as it were of my assassins, I arrived at the place of rendezvous. Petion was wanting. He was in much danger, however, if he remained at his own house. I returned to seek him, and a single incident that passed will depict his character. As I was pressing him to come with me, he went to the window, and opened it; then, having looked at the weather, he said, *It rains, there will be nothing done.* Notwithstanding all I could say, he persisted in staying at home."

On the triumph of the Mountain and total defeat of the Brissotine faction, Petion made his escape from Paris, and followed the fortune of those who were of opinion that nothing but the insurrection of the departments could save France [*]. He traversed a large part of France with a party which never mustered more than nineteen in number [†]. They endeavoured to excite an insurrection in the departments, but met with very little success; their enemies were numerous, vigilant, and active; their friends few, cold, and inert. The people with great propriety distinguished between the cause of the fugitives and their own; and many who would have braved every danger to establish a good government, remained perfectly neuter in a contest, the event of which could only decide whether their

31st May. His flight.

[*] Louvet's Narrative, p. 49. [†] Idem, p. 82.

lives and properties should be at the disposal of Petion or Robespierre ᵘ. At Caen they met with a small share of protection and temporary encouragement, and had they declared in favour of royalty, would in all probability have been more confidentially treated; but finding them solicitous only for the advancement of their own faction, general Wimpfen, after trifling with them so as to prevent their success in any other quarter, finally frustrated an intended attack on the city of Vernon, abandoned their cause, and left them to their own resources ˣ. After leaving Caen, Petion and his associates wandered about for some time, exposed to every hardship, and eagerly pursued by their inveterate and active foes. Petion was peculiarly liable to be known, from the publicity of his late situation in Paris, and from the remarkable circumstance of his having grey hair at a very early age. In passing through a village named Moncontoir, he was recognised, though not apprehended ʸ. In general he bore his sufferings with fortitude, but sometimes exhibited symptoms of despair ᶻ. At length, the increasing vigilance of their enemies rendering it unsafe for them to travel in so numerous a party, the

and death. fugitives dispersed and took different routes. From this period the fate of Petion remains uncertain: by some he was said to have been found stabbed in a field in the Gironde; by others, starved to death in a cave in Languedoc. For some time after the fall of Robespierre, hopes were entertained by his adherents, that he, like Louvet and Isnard, would emerge from concealment, and again appear in the convention ᵃ: these hopes however were not verified, and doubt, mystery, and conjecture must ever attend the final moments of a man who, in the day

---

ᵘ Residence in France, edited by John Gifford, vol. i. p. 283.
ˣ Louvet's Narrative, p. 56, et seq.
ʸ Idem, p. 85.   ᶻ Idem, p. 103. 149.
ᵃ Miss Williams's Letters in 1794, vol. i. p. 168.

of pride and upstart insolence, availing himself of unmerited popularity, rivalled, endangered, and insulted his sovereign.

During Petion's flight, his wife and mother-in-law were arrested and confined in the prison of St. Pelagie [b]. They were in such pecuniary distress, that they were supported only by borrowing [c]. The mother-in-law was guillotined; of the wife's fate I am uncertain.

Fate of his wife and mother-in-law.

Dr. Moore describes Petion as a fair, well-looking man, of genteel address, and cheerful countenance, with an habitual smile [d]. Madame Roland says; "The serenity of a good conscience, and mildness "of an easy temper, with frankness and cheerful-"ness, distinguish his countenance [e]." The partiality of this description of Petion's physiognomy may be corrected by Bertrand, who says: "His "countenance, which at first sight appeared open "and agreeable, upon a nearer examination was "insipid and devoid of expression [f]." His talents were far from brilliant or extensive, even madame Roland avows, that "as an orator he was cold, as "a writer his style was loose [g]." Dr. Moore states him to have been "a man of considerable learning, "though not so much as he wished the world to "believe; of some eloquence, but by no means so "much as he believed himself; of some judgment, "though a much smaller portion than he imagined; "whereas he really possessed a very comfortable "share of vanity, of which it appears he was per-"suaded he had none at all [h]." I incline however to consider even this account too favourable to Petion's knowledge and intellects, and think he is more correctly appreciated by Bertrand. He says,

His person.

Talents.

[b] Roland's Appeal, vol. i. p. 176.
[c] Appel à l'Impartiale Postérité, vol. ii. p. 74.
[d] Moore's Journal, vol. i. p. 130.
[e] Appeal, vol. i. p. 126. [f] Memoirs, vol. i. p. 259.
[g] Appeal, vol. i. p. 127. [h] Moore's View, vol. ii. p. 402.

" Petion's

"Petion's want of information, his heavy elocution, meanly trivial or abſurdly bombaſt, made me conſider him as a man by no means dangerous. I even imagined that by flattering his vanity or ambition, he might be made uſeful to the king. His conduct has proved how much I was deceived; and I cannot, even at this diſtance of time, reflect without pain on my having been deceived by ſo ſilly a knave [i]." Petion's virtue and diſintereſtedneſs are highly extolled by madame Roland; ſhe ſays; "Petion is a truly good and honeſt man, equally incapable of doing the leaſt thing repugnant to juſtice, and inflicting the ſlighteſt injury or occaſioning the leaſt uneaſineſs to any one. For himſelf he can neglect many things, yet he knows not how to refuſe a favour to any perſon in the world [k]." The diſintereſtedneſs implied in the latter part of this panegyric is ſubject to much doubt, as Petion, in common with the reſt of his faction, was ſuſpected of having greatly enriched himſelf by the moſt palpable peculation [l]. It is no anſwer to the accuſation to ſtate, that his wife was, after his flight, left in diſtreſſed circumſtances, and when in priſon, expoſed to want: Petion, though poſſeſſed of no property, lived in a ſplendid ſtyle, and his flight was ſo unpremeditated, as not to afford him the means of ſecuring his property, which, like the confiſcated wealth of others, was embezzled, and its amount never aſcertained. The firſt part of the lady's eulogium is refuted by every act of Petion's life; which fully juſtifies the obſervation of Dumouriez, who alſo had ſufficient means of appreciating his character, that he concealed, under a mild and prudent appearance, a heart coldly wicked [m].

Moral character.

[i] Bertrand's Memoirs, vol. i. p. 259.
[k] Appeal, vol. i. p. 126.
[l] Impartial Hiſtory, vol. ii. p. 339.
[m] Life of Dumouriez, vol. ii. p. 187.

MAXIMILIEN ROBESPIERRE.

MAXIMILIEN Robespierre was born in the city of Arras[n], and an orphan from his earliest infancy. His father was a counsellor, in considerable practice, and of good reputation, but so little endowed with prudence, that he left three children in the utmost want. It has been asserted that the subject of these Memoirs was the nephew of d'Amiens, who was broke on the wheel for an attempt to assassinate Louis XV.[o], but this story is absolutely untrue. It may have been the invention of some indignant royalist, or perhaps of some friend of Robespierre himself. The good character of his father, and the distress of his children, operated so much in their favour with some of their relations that they used every exertion to procure them some effectual protection; one of them took the charge of the daughter, and the two sons were recommended to the bishop of Arras, who brought them

1759.

Robespierre's birth and education.

---

[n] The principal transactions of this blood-thirsty tyrant's life are abridged from the work of Montjoye, intitled, "*Histoire de la Conjuration de Maximilien Robespierre.*" To M. Montjoye I am indebted for all the particulars of Robespierre's early history, and for the arrangement and distribution of the whole work. I have differed with him, and with most writers who have preceded me on the subject of Robespierre's talents; and I have suppressed some parts of his narrative for brevity's sake, and others from a conviction that they sprang from misinformation or haste. All those parts of the ensuing narrative for which no authority is given, are derived entirely from him.

[o] See Peltier's late Picture of Paris, vol. ii. p. 141. 220. Apologie des Projets des Chefs de la Revolution, p. 216. Perhaps too the political romance called Couteau's Confessions may have contributed to give currency to the report.

up with a care and humanity worthy a Christian pastor. Maximilian, discovering the greatest share of genius, and no traits of those vices which afterwards marked his character, was the favourite of the worthy bishop[p], who, after leading him by the hand with infinite satisfaction through the primary avenues of science, obtained for him, by his interest, an exhibition, or annual purse, at the college of *Louis-le-grand* at Paris. While he continued in this situation, the hopes of his patron were abundantly realized; his progress was rapid and honourable, he was generally at the head of his class, and obtained several prizes. He exhibited no symptom at this period of a bad heart or depraved disposition, but every one thought he would be distinguished by his prudence, and pass through the world with some *eclat*.

The fame of his scholastic triumphs excited ardent hopes in the bosoms of his provincial friends; they recommended to him to study the law, and to make Paris the scene of his exertions, little doubting that the same success and eminence which had awaited him in the university, would be his portion in the greater scene his profession would open to him. To obviate the disadvantages likely to result from his unprovided state, recourse was had to the humanity of a gentleman of great eminence at the bar, of the name of *Ferrières*, who gratuitously received him as a pupil, and undertook to provide him with every thing he wanted, while he was prosecuting his studies. But in this situation Robespierre's deficiencies first became apparent. The acquirements of the college, as it was then regulated, were confined to a knowledge of the lives, actions, and a few of the more glaring opinions of the ancient

[p] It has been said that he repaid the kindness of this worthy pastor with ingratitude; but the fact is so slightly alleged, that I am little inclined to give it credit. See Christie's Letters on the Revolution, p. 132. n.

Romans.

Romans. A young Frenchman was brought up without any reference to the world he was about to inhabit, as if he had nothing to learn, no model to confult, but the heroes of antiquity. This learning, requiring only a good memory, and affording little fcope to the exercife of genius or imagination, opened an eafy road to puerile celebrity, Robefpierre purfued and attained it; it was flattering to the vanity, becaufe without much effort, it gave an *air recherché* to the converfation of its poffeffor. To the prevalence of this tafte it is to be attributed, that during the French revolution, the Lives of Plutarch, the Annals of Tacitus, and other memorials of the vices and virtues of the Greeks and Romans have been as conftantly quoted, and as hypocritically defcanted on, as the Holy Bible was during the civil commotions under Charles I. and the ufurpation of Cromwell. Robefpierre, who had been accuftomed to conquer fame without an effort, in this eafy level field, was difgufted at the neceffity impofed by his newly-embraced profeffion of acquiring new information; of inveftigating antiquity, of taking nothing for granted, but weighing in the balance of extreme fcrupulofity, the difference between truth and fpecioufnefs, falfehood and paradox; of examining with attention, every different complexion of men and things, of manners and motives. Ufed to the facilities of collegiate declamation, where it is only required to illuftrate a given fubject, he had not patience fufficient to go through the neceffary labour of attaining an eloquence which fhould, by its perfpicuoufnefs, ftrength, and fluency, at once convey information, obviate doubt, penetrate into the dark receffes of latent guilt, and difplay in their ftrongeft light, the interefting features of calumniated virtue. Incapable of this exertion, he fhrunk from the tafk, and from that period commenced an averfion to literature and literary characters, which he retained during the remainder of his life. At the expiration of his term of study, his friends, who now expected the accomplishment of all their hopes, and that this boasted genius would speedily attain the highest honours, sent one of his relations to partake the triumph of his first impression. On his arrival in the capital this gentleman was effectually undeceived, he found his young friend far below mediocrity in his professional line, his knowledge extremely limited, and his eloquence deficient both in dignity and correctness. He was easily persuaded by Ferrières to take him back to Arras, where dilligence might procure him a subsistence, without exposing him to comparison or competition, which must inevitably produce disgrace.

Practises at Arras. Notwithstanding the horrible celebrity which has since distinguished the name of Robespierre, no trace can be found of his professional employment, except in one solitary instance. The invention of electrical conductors, to discharge the lightning from impending clouds, made a great progress in France; it spread with singular speed from the capital to the provinces; it was patronized by the learned and polite, and opposed by the vulgar, the prejudiced, the timid, and the superstitious. Some of these machines were placed on buildings in the neighbourhood of Arras, and produced a law-suit. Robespierre, whom the fame of scholastic attainment pointed out as a proper person, was fixed on to conduct this cause on behalf of those who had adopted the conductors, but he is said to have drawn up a memorial, or case, on the subject, which was published, in which his ignorance was so manifest, his style so base, and his argumentation so perplexed, that he lost his clients, and acquired the never-ending contempt of his fellow-citizens. The cause never came into court, an amicable accommodation took place.

1789. Member of the consti- tuent af- sembly. The convocation of the states-general first afforded him an opportunity of emerging from obscurity. The opinion of the inhabitants of Arras had not

. 8 been

been able to eradicate from his mind those seeds of vanity which had been implanted there by his juvenile successes. He imagined that a large theatre alone was wanting to enable him to make a conspicuous figure. Full of this idea, he intrigued amongst the lower class of inhabitants in the district where he resided, and by incessant solicitation, by promises adapted to the imagined wants and wishes of the people to whom he looked up for support, he finally succeeded, not only in being returned to the states-general as representative of the *tiers etat*, but in being permitted to compose, in the name of his constituents, the cahiers, or instructions for himself and his co-deputies.

The talents displayed by Robespierre in the constituent assembly have been too much under-rated in consequence of the violent efforts made by Brissotine as well as royalist writers to expose him to contempt[q]. Even impartial writers, contemplating the figure he made in the convention, the gigantic power he acquired, and the dreadful means he employed in its maintenance, and comparing them with his unimportance in the assembly, have rashly pronounced that he was deficient in eloquence and ability. Robespierre came from Arras to Paris not much improved in knowledge or oratory, and he came into an assembly where, on both sides, there were seated men famous for both. He possessed neither birth or wealth to give him partisans, and his defects in speaking occasionally

His talents.

---

[q] He is thus spoken of by M. de Montgaillard, whose description will spare the necessity of numerous quotations. " ' My only wish,' " said he in 1784, ' is to be attorney-general for the parliament of Paris. " Ah! how I would make people talk of me!' In the possession of " that office he saw the means of satisfying that consuming thirst of " publicity, by which he often afterwards acknowledged himself to be " influenced. This also informs us of his motives for getting returned " to the states-general. Yet he only appeared there a stupid enthusiast. " At its dissolution, he retired, leaving no other impression than a " rooted contempt for his talents, and a total forgetfulness of his " person." Etat de la France, p. 9.

excited the laughter of the audience; but his education furnished him with modes of knowledge sufficient to give him a reputation in an assemblage so mixed and compounded, and his persevering assiduity in polishing his language, and extending his information, together with the death and secession of some of the more distinguished members, afforded him the means, before the dissolution of that assembly, of acquiring an extended and rather brilliant reputation. Garat, who is certainly a competent judge, speaks of his talents in these terms[r]: "In Robespierre, notwithstanding the nonsense and absurdity of those extemporary harangues which he daily uttered in the assembly; notwithstanding his endless tattle about the rights of man, the sovereignty of the people, principles of which he was continually talking, without ever communicating a single idea about them that was, in any degree, new or exact; In him, I fancied that I could discern, especially when he printed his compositions, the first efforts of rising genius, which was susceptible of improvement (which did actually improve) and of which the energies might one day fully expand so as to do much good or much mischief. In his style I saw a care to study and to imitate those forms of expression which possess elegance, dignity, and splendour. By those which he imitated and produced the oftenest, I could perceive that the writings of Rousseau were his great school and model."

Copies Mirabeau. In his oratory he affected to copy Mirabeau, and if he could not reach all the heights of his eloquence, he could at least obtain enough to impose on the people, and even to secure him some respect in the assembly. He resolved to attract notice by bustle and detraction, and to acquire popularity by in-

[r] Memoirs of the Revolution, p. 65.

gratiating himself with the lowest people, by flattering their caprices, extolling their virtues, reprobating all men and measures which were disliked by them, and generally by adapting his harangues entirely to their taste and comprehension.

He was a member of the society formed by Brissot and others, under the title of *Amis des Noirs*, the object of which was to procure the unconditional emancipation of all the slaves in the West Indies. In pursuit of this project he displayed that violence and inconsiderate impetuosity which characterize men who substitute passion for judgment, and pursue a favourite speculation, in contempt of every opposing motive, and declared his willingness to destroy the colonies, rather than sacrifice one iota of principle [s]. Very early in the sittings of the assembly he was so far noticed as to be included in the deputation of twenty-four, sent up, on the motion of Mirabeau, to request the king to remove the troops from the capital [t]. *[marginal: Ami des Noirs. 10th July 1789. Goes with message to the king.]*

Yet, though Robespierre was not of sufficient consequence to be claimed as a coadjutor by any party, he never failed to present himself at the tribune on almost every discussion; sometimes with prepared orations, sometimes to utter extempore remarks. He felt no timidity in pressing his principles nor any fear of contempt from the frequency of his repetitions. By degrees he polished his style, and in time gained some portion of attention. He assisted in undermining the popularity of Necker by making a speech against the amnesty obtained by him from the commune of Paris [u]. He was always extremely solicitous for the removal of the sittings of the national assembly from Versailles to Paris [x], *[marginal: Exerts himself in the assembly. 30th July.]*

---

[s] Bryan Edwards's History of St. Domingo, p. 41. 61. Historical Sketch, p. 415.
[t] Moore's View, vol. i. p. 303. Debates.
[u] Impartial History, vol. i. p. 172. Moore's View, vol. i. p. 382.
[x] Moore's View, vol. i. p. 427.

but the events of the day which produced that change were not contrived by him, nor had he the least notion of their being in agitation. He was not yet trusted, though in the debate which took place on the subject of the king's animadversion on the articles of the constitution, he rendered a service to the Orleans' faction by observing, that his majesty's message, instead of an acceptance, was a censure[y].

5th Oct.

Becomes an Orleanist and Jacobin.

He was now considered as actively attached to the Orleans' party. There was more business to do in the assembly, in the city, and in the clubs, than his superior associates could conduct without assistance. Robespierre had so far succeeded in imitating Mirabeau, that he began to be noticed by it, though not much to his advantage; the one was said to be the flambeau of Provence, the other the taper of Arras. The desire Orleans and all his party entertained to humble la Fayette and Bailly, caused Robespierre to frequent the company of Danton and Marat, who were actively engaged in the task, and through them he was often employed to convey to the people of the suburbs of St. Antoine and St. Marceau, those intimations which it was thought would be received with more readiness if sanctioned by a deputy. His eloquence and his manners were exactly suited to this class of people, and he soon became their idol, a circumstance which afterwards gave him unlimited rule in France, but the principal engine of his elevation was the Jacobin club. He was not thought worthy of a seat in the club Breton; that club, while the assembly remained at Versailles, was small and select, founded at first by the deputies from Bretagne, but when the legislative body removed to Paris, they threw open their doors to all the members of the *left side,* and to many other persons; they hired the convent belonging

---

[y] Mrs. Wolstonecroft's History, vol. i. p. 436. The other Histories and Debates.

to the Dominican, or as they were called in France, *Jacobin* friars, in the *rue St. Honoré*, and extended their influence all over the kingdom, by means of affiliated focieties, and committees of correfpondence. This club, by their pernicious agency, produced infubordination in the army and navy, and confirmed the licentioufnefs, fury, and infidelity of the populace; they deftroyed the church, diffolved the tie of laws, and brought the king to an ignominious death. The iniquity of their means was proportioned to the flagitioufnefs of their ends: they laid wealthy individuals under contribution; they fhared the plunder of thofe whofe deftruction they had occafioned; and to defray the immenfe expences they were fubject to, before their own creatures came into adminiftration, they abetted the forgery of affignats, which they were thus enabled to diftribute with incredible profufion [z]. At this club Robefpierre was indefatigable, he made motions and fpeeches of the moft incendiary defcription, and in all refpects accommodated himfelf fo well to the tafte of the people, that he was foon elevated to the prefidency, and during the remainder of his life, retained an influence the moft unlimited. Here he firft began to court the galleries and the populace of Paris in his fpeeches, by conftantly ufing a flattering cant which was fuited to their intellects, by conftantly infifting on their virtues, and calling them emphatically *the good people of Paris* [a].

This

---

[z] Bertrand's Private Memoirs, vol. ii. p. 276. See Pagès, vol. ii. p. 28.

[a] This ftyle he never afterwards difcontinued. The following are fpecimens of it from a periodical work he publifhed in 1792, called *Robefpierre à fes Commettans*. " Taken collectively, you are the moft ge-
" nerous, the moft moral of all people; and, but for your levity, the
" moft deferving of liberty." Vol. i. p. 6. " The people are naturally
" juft and peaceable; they are always guided by the moft pure inten-
" tions: the evil-minded cannot ftir them up, without prefenting to
" their view a powerful and proper motive." Vol. i. p. 405. " The
" motives

Manages the galleries.

This sort of eloquence he carried with him into the national assembly, where he already began to exercise his address, by training the galleries to particular expressions of applause and disapprobation; a manœuvre which afterwards subjected the deliberative body entirely to the dominion of the audience, or more properly to that of a party of screaming *poissardes* and vociferous *sans-culottes*, whom the leaders of the day took care to assemble. In the constituent assembly this evil was first felt: the tribunes were used to hum applause, or grumble dislike, at the use of certain phrases uttered in a certain sense. This secret was soon discovered by the *right side*, they learned, at every interval of disapprobation displayed against them, to correct the ferment by the introduction of popular phraseology, no matter however *mal à propos*. This facility of counteraction was not agreeable to the *left side*; they prepared another manœuvre; they hired companies of people to fill the tribunes, who were under the command of certain leaders; these again were directed to keep their eye on particular members of the assembly; and at a preconcerted signal, of the display of part of the pocket-handkerchief, the elevation or depression of that part of the hat in which the national cockade was placed, or other equally simple and apparently unimportant movements, they were to communicate the token of applause or censure to their band, who were thus instructed to cry up or hoot down some particular persons. The *right side* soon discovered this plan, and availed

---

" motives of the people are always pure; they cannot do otherwise
" than love the public good, since the public good is but another
" word for the interest of the people: but certain intriguers, who are
" as cunning as the people are ingenuous, as perverse as the people
" are just, seek sometimes to make an ill use even of their virtues and
" their just indignation." Vol. ii. p. 285. " The errors of the people
" are rare and impermanent; they are always the fault of fatal circum-
" stances or perverse individuals." Vol. ii. p. 291.

themselves of the discovery, by hiring their groups to oppose the friends of the *left side:* this introduced a great confusion; applause and censure were frequently bestowed at the same time by the opposite parties, and this discordance produced animosities and contentions which it was the disgrace of the assembly to suffer. At other times, the same set of men would be hired by both parties, and when contrary signals were given, remain in a confused state of suspense, undecided whether they ought to applaud or murmur; an embarrassment which has frequently occasioned the different journalists, in reporting the same speech, to attribute to the audience *violent murmurs,* and *loud and frequent applauses* [b]. This contest continued during the sitting of the constituent assembly: in the legislative assembly the *left side* managed better; and in the convention, the Mountain generally took care to have the tribunes filled with friends of their own, for which purpose the parties frequently came and took their places by break of day, and often stayed all night. Robespierre's known intrigues in this business caused a royalist writer to style him the general of the *sansculottes,* a title with which he was not displeased.

During the whole sitting of the constituent assembly, he was remarked for his exertions on every question in which the king's influence or authority was concerned. He distinguished himself by the same personal rancour which he afterwards displayed in the convention with such baleful effect. It is unnecessary to particularise instances, they occurred almost daily. He voted and spoke in favour of almost every proposition tending to narrow the king's authority, and throw contempt on his person and government. He greatly increased his popularity by the style of his speech in opposition to la Fayette's proposal of a martial law. He said, " He enter-

Adversarious to the king.

Oct. 1789. Opposes martial law.

[b] See Moore's View, vol. i. p. 422. Pagès, vol. ii. p. 29.

" tained

"tained a cordial affection for the good people of
"Paris; that their dispositions were excellent; they
"were seldom in the wrong, always meant well, and
"could not in justice be punished for mistakes they
"might commit when pinched with hunger." This,
and a great deal more of the same contemptible
cant, not only procured him the entire good-will
of the mob, but effectually deceived many who
thought themselves profound politicians; they said,
"He might be a very well-meaning patriot, but was
"far *too tender-hearted* for a statesman [c]."

Apr. 1791. Independently of his exertions against the king,
Two of his speeches he distinguished himself in the national assembly by
printed. his speeches on the re-union of Avignon, and on
the organization of the national guard, both which
were ordered to be printed [d]. He strenuously supported the right of petitioning, over which he maintained that the legislature had no jurisdiction; and
that it resided in every individual of whatever class
15th May. or country. He was no less persevering in his
efforts in favour of the people of colour, and in the
24th Sept. end obtained that fatal decree which spread desolation over the face of the French colony of St. Domingo, though it was afterwards repealed by the
16th May. same assembly [e]. He moved that the members of
one legislature should not be eligible to sit in the
next, and maintained the proposition with such jealousy, that it was finally decreed. Two points in
his conduct deserve particular notice; he was a violent defender of the right of universal suffrage, and
an affected declaimer *against the punishment of death*
30th May. *in any case*. On this subject he affected to prove,
that "the punishment of death was essentially un-
"just; that it was not the most impressive in its
"execution, but, on the contrary, that it tended to

[c] Moore's View, vol. ii. p. 72.
[d] Wilde's Address, p. 479. Mercure François Litteraire du 14 Mai 1791.
[e] Edwards's History of St. Domingo, p. 89.

"multiply

"multiply crimes instead of preventing them. A
"man can only kill an enemy when that effort is
"absolutely necessary for the saving of his own life;
"now society at large can have nothing to fear from
"a criminal whom it punishes; the criminal is to-
"tally unable to do any further mischief, and is
"tried in all the security of peace. A conqueror
"who kills his prisoners is called a barbarian; a
"grown man who kills a perverse child, whom it
"is in his power to disarm and punish, is deemed a
"monster." These and many other arguments in
the same spirit were unsuccessful with the assembly,
though warmly applauded by the galleries and populace [f].

At this period he frequented the house of Roland, then neither minister or deputy, but the confidant of Brissot, with whom, and Petion, and a few more, Robespierre met four evenings in every week, to ar-range plans for the business in the assembly on the ensuing days. He acquired the esteem of madame Roland, who thought him an honest man and firm patriot, but rather *too bashful*. He used at these meetings to say little; he advanced a few principles, without maintaining them by arguments, but care-fully treasured up the ideas which fell from the more informed men of the party, and retailed them as his own in the assembly and the Jacobin club; still eluding the reproaches this conduct drew on him, by an affectation of pleasantry and good-humoured frivolity [g]. *Frequents madame Roland's house.*

The king's departure from the capital alarmed Robespierre beyond measure; he thought Louis would not have taken that step, unless he was sure of a party in the capital who would murder all the patriots and dissolve the assembly. This panic was dispelled by the arrest and return of the king. It was in this interval that, at Petion's house, *Alarm at the king's escape.*

---
[f] For all these particulars, see Debates.
[g] Roland's Appeal, vol. i. p. 56.

Brissot

Briffot and fome others firſt ſtarted the idea of a republic, and propoſed to publiſh a paper under the title of *le Republicain*. Robeſpierre was preſent at the conſultation, and probably foreſaw in this new ſyſtem a ſchiſm amongſt the partiſans of Orleans, which would be beneficial to his intereſts: he wiſhed to act in a ſphere where he ſhould not be thwarted by their ſuperior talents, and would not therefore bind himſelf to profecute their plan, but contented himſelf with inquiring, with a ſneer, after they had been long difcuffing the ſubject, "And "pray what is a republic[h]?"

Conduct on his arreſt. 23d June.
His violence againſt the king on his arreſt was proportioned to the terror experienced previous to that event. He moved, that thoſe who ſtopped the coach ſhould receive a civic crown; oppoſed the meaſures fuggeſted for ſecuring the king's perſon, by an obſervation, that the plan introduced to the aſſembly for that purpoſe ſeemed to prejudge a great queſtion, which he wiſhed to hear ſolemnly difcuſſed.

26th June.
He alſo moved, that the king and queen ſhould be interrogated by the juſtices of peace of the circle of the Tuilleries; that as they were now to be conſidered fimply as citizens, they ought to be treated without any diſtinguiſhing forms of reſpect. On

14th July.
the ſame occaſion, he ſtrenuouſly combated the inviolability of the king, and declared he ſhould ſpeak of Louis XVI. with the ſame indifference as the emperor of China[i].

Petition of the Champ de Mars.
The event of the aſſembly's decifion on the queſtion of the king's abdication of the throne, was ſo contrary to his hopes as to deprive him of all prudence; he ran from the hall through the ſtreets, exclaiming to the groups of politicians who were aſſembled, "*My friends, all is loſt; the king is to* "*be reſtored[k]!*" He was ſo convinced that the

[h] Roland's Appeal, vol. i. p. 58.   [i] Debates.
[k] Moore's View, vol. ii. p. 406. Conjuration de d'Orleans, vol. iii. p. 142.

queſtion

question would be carried conformably to the wishes of his party, that he had omitted the precaution of securing the tribunes. After the dispersal of the tumultuous petitioners by the military, since called the massacre of the *Champ de Mars*, his panic returned with aggravated force; he was afraid of being impeached and put on his trial, and alarmed at a supposed plot of the *Feuillans*, and a dreaded defection of the Jacobins from his interest. Roland and his wife, affected at his situation, went to his lodgings in the Marsh to offer him an asylum, but he had already quitted them. He consulted Petion on the propriety of escaping to London[l]. His fears, however, were groundless; the court knew not how to punish; the constitution was completed, and the assembly dissolved[m].

Robespierre did not quit the first legislature with contempt, as M. de Montgaillard has erroneously asserted: it is true that he never was considered a great leader of a party; he was never president, and but once secretary: during the latter part of the sittings, he, Buzot, and Petion, were left almost alone on the left side[n]. His name was on the favourable side of the pillar at St. Genon[o], he was constantly a great favourite of the audience in the galleries, and the populace of Paris, who had intended, on the day of the *Champ de Mars*, to have carried his bust, crowned with laurel, in procession through the city[p]. This predilection he greatly augmented the day before the dissolution of the assembly, by his defence of the clubs. When the members quitted the hall, he and Petion were hailed with the acclamations of the populace, a civic crown was placed on their brows, and the people would have taken off their horses and drawn them home, but they declined that proof of their attachment[q].

Dissolution of the assembly.

29th Sept.
30th.

[l] Brissot à tous les Republicains, p. 192.
[m] Roland's Appeal, vol. i. p. 62.   [n] Ibid. p. 56.
[o] See BAILLY. Anecdotes du Regne de Louis XVI. vol. vi. p. 339.
[p] Historical Sketch, p. 383.
[q] Mercure François, N° du 8 Octobre 1791, p. 125.

Public accuser.

Robespierre now occupied the place of public accuser, which he soon resigned, without having ever exercised its functions; a circumstance which has excited some astonishment, and threw for the time some disgrace on his civism [r]. It is to be supposed that the attention necessary to the duties of this office was too great a drawback on the time he wished to bestow on his other avocations. He continued unremittingly his attendance at the Jacobins, where he was a principal speaker, and where his party carried every point; they commanded the applause of the tribunes, and silenced all speakers whose sentiments were opposite to theirs, by clamour and vociferation. The most popular journalists were members of this club, and spread the renown of Robespierre and the other chiefs all over the country. They despised la Fayette's impotent and ill-concerted efforts to disperse them: in fact they governed the country; they gave officers to the police, generals to the armies, and ministers to the crown. On the resignation of Bailly, Robespierre was candidate for the mayoralty; but the place being already disposed of to Petion, he obtained only a hundred votes [s].

Quarrels with Brissot.

25th April 1792.

He was soon involved in disputes with the Girondist faction, and although on good terms with Petion, was denounced by Brissot and Gaudet at the Jacobin club. It is to be presumed that the desire entertained by the Brissotine party to involve the country in war was the cause of their disagreement; for it is well known that all the members of that cabal were resolute for war, while Robespierre was a strenuous opposer of it, and for a long time afterwards retained a wish to avoid giving unnecessary offence to foreign powers [t]. The attack made on him was however attended with little success; he

---

[r] Bertrand's Memoirs, vol. ii. p. 116. Etat de la France, p. 9.
[s] Mercure François, N° du 26 Novembre 1791, p. 289.
[t] Pagès, vol. i. p. 456. Mercure François, N° du 7 Avril 1792, p. 67. See also Robespierre à ses Commettans, vol. ii. p. 326.

answered

answered it the next day but one, and his speech was printed and distributed at the expence of the society [w].

About this time he commenced a weekly publication, called *le Defenseur de la Constitution*, in which he discussed, as occasion required, all public measures and events, occasionally attacking his adversaries, and explaining his own conduct. When the constitution was no longer thought worth defending, and he was elected deputy to the national convention, he changed its appellation, and called it *Lettres de Maximilien Robespierre à ses Commettans*, under which title he continued it for some time after the king's death. From an attentive perusal of these publications, I have formed my judgment of Robespierre's style, which I think very far above mediocrity. His oratory, subjected to the disadvantages of a bad voice, and an unconquerable provincial accent [x], might fail of producing a graceful effect in discourse, but his expressions were not ill chosen, nor did they betray poverty of language or barrenness of imagination; his logic is frequently faulty in its conclusions, and he is extremely negligent of truth in his narratives; his forte is humorous reasoning, where gravity seems hardly maintainable from the ludicrousness of the subject; his sarcasms are forcible and apposite, and his irony spritely and effectual [y].

Writes a periodical work.

During the reign of the legislative assembly, the contest was changed from its former ground. In

10th Aug. His conduct.

[w] Defenseur de la Constitution, p. 37.
[x] Roland's Appeal, vol. i. p. 57.
[y] One of his best efforts in this style, his letter to Jerome Petion, is given in the Appendix (No X.). Camille Desmoulins does not scruple to say that, for its attic wit, it is equal to the best Provincials [*]; and it has been already, in part, introduced to the acquaintance of the English reader, by the extract from it in Moore's View, vol. ii. p. 396. That, and his speech in answer to Louvet's accusation abridged, will form a sufficient specimen of his powers in either species of composition.

[*] The Provincials are celebrated Letters by Father Pascal against the Jesuits. See Camille Desmoulins' History of the Brissotines, p. 66.

the

the constituent assembly, the *Constitutionels* waged war against the royalists, in the present these were attacked in their turn by the republicans. The writers and orators of that party had contrived to render their doctrine so palatable, that Orleans and Robespierre were obliged to accede to the general opinion, and affect to be zealous republicans. Republicanism became the order of the day at the Jacobins, and every thing yielded to the impulse. To reduce the royal power so much as to prevent all opposition to their scheme, the republicans planned and executed the insurrection of the 10th of August. It was much to the disadvantage of the Brissotines to be obliged to call in the aid of Danton, who was so intimately connected with Robespierre their declared enemy, but their weakness and his energy rendered it unavoidable. Though the cowardice of Robespierre kept him from being an actor in that scene; though, as Louvet afterwards told him [z], he concealed himself, like Sosia in the play, till the battle was over, yet he was named one of the council-general of the *commune*, as without the aid of his popularity their measures would have been but imperfect [a]. He was also appointed one of the judges of a tribunal erected to try criminals involved in the imputed guilt of the court on that day [b]. His exultation in the event of the contest may be learned by the account of the 14th Aug. transaction which he gave to the public [c]; and by the proposition he made in the assembly, for the erection of a column to the memory of those who

[a] See his speech against Robespierre.
[a] It seems agreed, on all hands, that Robespierre was not personally engaged in attack on the Tuilleries, or deliberating with the new council-general, on the 9th of August. See Pagès, vol. i. p. 478. 486. Peltier's late Picture of Paris, vol. ii. p. 477. Moore's Journal, vol. i. p. 497. Etat de la France, p. 10.
[b] Conjuration de d'Orleans, vol. iii. p. 208. Peltier's late Picture, vol. ii. p. 220, &c.
[c] Defenseur de la Constitution, p. 567.

fell

fell in the assault, on the place where the statue of Louis XIV. had formerly stood [d].

The events of the 10th of August placed the ministerial junto so firmly in possession of the public esteem, and appeared to invest them with so great a command over the populace by means of their Marseillois, that it became a point of the highest importance to Robespierre to counteract their influence. It has already been mentioned that he declared open war against Brissot; the quarrel involved Condorcet and all their party [e]. To snatch from the hands of this faction as much of the power of influencing the populace as they could, and to place as much as possible in the reach of persons devoted to them, was the principal aim of those who perpetrated the massacres of September. Robespierre was undoubtedly a principal contriver of these sanguinary executions. Previous to the fatal day, he had been very active in making domiciliary visits [f]; and the day preceding the massacre, he had denounced Brissot at the Jacobin club for having sold the country to the duke of Brunswick [g]. But though Robespierre had so great a share in arranging the horrible plan of the day [h]; yet on that occasion, like the former, his pusillanimity kept him from the scene of action, and he did not make his appearance till the carnage was ended. The event, however, confirmed his

2d Sept.
His executions.

1st Sept.

[d] Debates.
[e] Defenseur de la Constitution, p. 96. 99. Mercure François, N⁰ du 19 Mai 1792, p. 208.
[f] Peltier's late Picture, vol. ii. p. 479.
[g] Brissot à tous les Republicains, p. 183. Peltier's late Picture, vol. ii. p. 294. See also Louvet's Narrative, p. 17.
[h] Necker on the Revolution, vol. i. p. 433. Brissot à tous les Republicains, p. 184. Etat de la France, p. 10. It occasioned some surprise when I saw in the New Annual Register for 1794, p. 382. the following expression: "He certainly had no part in the events of "the 10th of August; and the count de Montgaillard acquits him "even of any principal share in the massacres of September." Montgaillard speaks of him in these terms: "Robespierre disparût pendant "cette crise décisive (le 10 Août). On lui a reprôché souvent la "prudence avec laquelle il se derobait aux dangers; il paroit aussi avoir "eu beaucoup de part aux massacres du 2 Septembre."

power,

power, and enabled the *commune* to domineer over the assembly with astonishing insolence [1].

Elected member of the convention.

In the interval between the 10th August and the 2d September, the assembly had decreed its own dissolution, and the calling of a national convention. In this new assembly, Robespierre's popularity, aided by the purse of Orleans, procured the return of a powerful party. The sinks of infamy and vice were raked, the retreats of obscure dabblers in literature explored, and even the refuse of foreign countries resorted to for legislators, for men whose first business it was to decide whether France should be a monarchy or not. Robespierre was returned for Paris, during the height of the carnage in the pri-

21st Sept. 1792.

sons [k]. The convention decreed, immediately on their meeting, that France was a republic. Since the 2d of September, the schism forseen by Robespierre had taken place amongst the friends of Orleans: the contrivers of the 10th of August, jealous of the overweening influence of the men of the 2d of September, formed themselves into a party under the banners of Brissot and Roland, from whom they were called Brissotines or Rolandists. These men, depending on their influence in some of the departments, were accused of a project to form what they called a federal republic; or a republic, where the different provinces, having each separate interests and rights, should be represented in one general assembly. Robespierre, on the other hand, inflated with his extensive popularity, and little attached to Orleans, whom he despised, now aspired to the dictatorship. His party, from their occupying the highest seats in the hall, were called the Mountain. The habits of intimacy which had subsisted between his colleagues and the Brissotines laid open to him all their plans, and the indiscreet efforts

---

[1] Necker on the Revolution, vol. i. p. 365. Peltier's late Picture, vol. ii. p. 141. Histories and Journals.

[k] Conjuration de d'Orleans, vol. iii. p. 214.

of Robespierre's partisans in founding different members of the convention, occasioned a disclosure of his views to the other party.

They met in the convention prepared for hostility and mutual crimination. The Brissotines had the advantage of superior talents, ministerial influence, and the *fédérés* from Marseilles. The Mountain opposed to these advantages, clamour, activity, the Jacobin club, the armed *sans-culottes*, and the journalists. But, perhaps, what principally turned the scale in favour of the latter was, that the Brissotines, seeing no farther advantage to be derived to them from riot and popular insurrection, were become the advocates of obedience to the laws, and preachers of regularity and subordination; while the Mountain, the majority of whom rather wished to perpetuate anarchy and plunder, than for any particular form of government, resisted all these efforts, and constantly secured the good-will of a clamorous populace. The Mountain gained the first prize of popularity, as the proposition for the abolition of monarchy came from them. A few days after the meeting of the convention, a regular attack was made on Robespierre, Danton, and Marat: this hostility was persevered in for a long time, and conducted with so much acrimony as to form an interesting crisis in the life of Maximilian.

Animosity against the Brissotines.

It was commenced by Kersaint, who, after stating in a speech of considerable eloquence, that assassinations were encouraged in all the departments, and blood profusely shed at the call of private animosity and revenge, continued to observe, that such crimes were not to be charged on anarchy or the want of social regulation, but that tyrants of a new description were causing citizens to butcher their fellows; brothers to murder each other: that the walls of Paris were constantly covered with posting-bills, instigating massacre and pillage; and that fresh lists of proscriptions were published every day.— " I know

24th Sept. Kersaint's motion.

"I know (he concluded) that there is some temerity in rising up against these assassins; but, should I perish by their daggers, I will shew myself worthy the confidence of my fellow-citizens." He then moved, that a committee should be appointed to frame a law against assassination; and that a guard for the convention should be furnished by the eighty-three departments, to prevent the tyranny of the council-general of the *commune* of Paris. This motion, though violently opposed by the Mountain, was at length carried, and commissioners appointed to frame the proposed law.

25th Sept. Accused by la Source.

This attack on the murderous principles of the party, was only a prelude to others on their ambition, tyranny, and fraud. The next day, Merlin of Thionville stated to the assembly, that la Source had informed him that there was a faction in the convention who had it in view to establish a dictator. La Source, though a Brissotine, evaded a personal explanation, but Rebecqui and Barbaroux, both of Marseilles, brought the matter home to Robespierre, and accused Marat and Panis of having founded them on the subject. Danton, alarmed for his party, endeavoured to avert the discussion, by moving that death should be the punishment of those who attempted to make of France a federal republic. This observation, meant to intimidate the Brissotines, was parried by Buzot, and Robespierre was obliged to ascend the tribune to defend himself: instead, however, of speaking to the point, he entered into an eulogium of his own conduct while he sat in the constituent assembly. Tired of his egotisms, a member at length exclaimed, "Do, pray, Robespierre, finish this tedious bead-roll, and give us in a few words your opinions on the point in question, not a history of your whole life." This brought him a little nearer to the point; he touched on the acts of the second and third of September; but still prevaricated as to the dictatorship: he

alleged

alleged generally the improbability of his confpiring againſt liberty; and after reflecting on thoſe who wiſhed to federalize the country, finiſhed by ſeconding the motion of Danton. The inconcluſiveneſs of this reaſoning called up Danton again; but he merely defended himſelf againſt the charge of encouraging the incendiary *placards* which were ſtuck on the walls, and left the dictatorſhip entirely unnoticed. The avowal of this intention ſurpaſſed the effrontery of both theſe men; they durſt not ſtate ſuch a wiſh in the face of the convention, and yet would not appear contemptible in the eyes of the other conſpirators by totally difavowing it. But what effort of impudence was too great for Marat? He aſcended the tribune, and acknowledged that the idea of a dictator had originated with him, and that he ſtill maintained the neceſſity of having one to counterpoiſe the intrigues of the court, and the exertions of certain corrupt deputies. This avowal turned the courſe of the debate; it became a perſonal difcuſſion relative to Marat, and Robeſpierre was forgotten [1].

But a third attack, better concerted and combined, and executed with much more ability, was made on him and his party. Roland, the miniſter of the interior, laid before the convention a memorial on the ſtate of Paris, in which he enumerated the crimes of the commune ſince the tenth of Auguſt, and plainly intimated that they had embezzled the money and other valuables ſeized at Senlis, Chantilly, l'Hotel de Coigny and other hotels, of which he had frequently demanded an account without ſucceſs. He accuſed them of having violated public and private property; of having inſtigated the murders of September; and of meditating further projects of blood and deſtruction, to gratify their ambition and rapacity. In ſupport of theſe

29th Oct. Accuſed by Louvet.

[1] See MARAT.

allegations

allegations he produced a letter addressed to the minister of justice, in which information was given, that it had been insinuated by certain persons, that the business begun in September was yet incomplete; that the whole faction of Roland and Brissot should be cut off; that Vergniaud, Gaudet, Buzot, la Source, and others, were obnoxious to the real patriots; and that Robespierre was the properest person to direct the helm of government. The reading of these papers occasioned a violent uproar, and a motion that the memorial should be printed. Robespierre ascended the tribune, but remained a long time before he could obtain a hearing, which at last was only granted him on the ground of the manifest injustice of decreeing any measure without permitting the parties interested to be heard against it. His discourse, instead of a defence, was an eulogium on himself; instead of opposing the printing of the memorial, he hardly noticed it; the admonitions of the president, and the boisterous impatience of the assembly, were equally ineffectual to restrain this propensity to self-commendation: he persevered till, animated by his own applauses, he lost all fear, and from the stores of his newly-acquired confidence drew a boastful challenge, which involved him in serious danger.—" A system of ca-
" lumny is established, (he said,) and against whom
" is it directed?—A zealous patriot.—Yet who
" is there amongst you who dares rise and accuse
" me to my face?"—" I," exclaimed some one at the end of the hall. A profound silence ensued. The speaker stalked solemnly along the hall, stopped opposite the tribune, and presented to the eyes of the confused and astonished challenger, the person of Louvet. " Yes, Robespierre, (said he,) it is I
" who accuse you." Pronouncing these words, he ascended the tribune; while Maximilian, pale and terror-struck, shrunk from sight. In vain Danton endeavoured by words of encouragement to rally

his

his spirits; in vain he appeared in the tribune, and endeavoured, by expressing a dislike of Marat, to divert the attention of the assembly; their curiosity was thoroughly aroused; and Louvet, determined to proceed, drew from his pocket a long, written oration, which he read to the assembly [m].

In his exordium he craved an uninterrupted hearing. "I am about to denounce (he said) a plot " which will astonish you; to trace scenes of woe " which will make your humanity groan; and to " unveil the guilt of men, against whom I must beg " you to suspend for a time your indignation. I " shall spare nobody, but speak the direct truth: " I shall touch the sore without hesitation, and un- " doubtedly those who are hurt will be apt to " scream."—" Put your finger in the wound, (said " Danton,) never mind those who are sore."— " I intend to probe it to the quick (replied Louvet); " but why do you, Danton, scream beforehand." In the progress of his speech he related, that a conspiracy was formed to perpetuate anarchy, to vilify the representatives of the people, to subvert liberty, and to found on its ruins the authority of a dictator: that the means used to secure applause at the Jacobin club, by a clamorous gallery, had first led to a suspicion that Robespierre, the vain-glorious Robespierre, was the head of a party, and his subsequent conduct had fully demonstrated it, and proved that he had formed a system of disorganization, by which he hoped to attain sovereign power. " The " memorable revolution of the 10th of August " (continued Louvet) belongs to the people of " Paris; Robespierre and his party have attempted " to arrogate to themseves the honour of that day, " to say that it belonged only to them:—to you!— " treacherous conspirators! the 2d of September " only belongs to you; it is stamped with your

[m] Robespierre à ses Commettans, vol. i. p 282.

"characteristics. The people of Paris know how to fight, but they do not know the vile trade of assassination. All Paris was at the Tuilleries on the 10th of August; but who were witnesses of the murders in September?—Some two or three hundred persons drawn together before the prisons by an incomprehensible curiosity. It may be asked, why then did not the citizens of Paris prevent them?—Why! because they were struck with terror, the alarm-guns had been fired, the tocsin had been sounded, their ears were imposed upon by false reports, their eyes astonished by the sight of officers in their municipal scarfs presiding at the executions; because Roland exclaimed in vain; because Danton, the minister of justice, was silent; and Santerre, the commander of the national guard, remained inactive. Soon after these lamentable scenes, the legislative assembly was frequently calumniated, insulted, and even threatened, by this insolent demagogue."

At this period, Robespierre's friends, who had before endeavoured to interrupt the speaker, could contain themselves no longer: a scene of clamour and disorder ensued, during which Lacroix and several other members attested the truth of Louvet's assertions. Robespierre attempted to obtain possession of the tribune; but was told that he ought to apply to be heard at the bar; and that, at all events, the accuser should first be permitted to conclude.

Louvet proceeded to remark, that this insolent demagogue, with proscriptions eternally in his mouth, accused some of the most deserving representatives of the people, of having sold the nation to Brunswick; and made that accusation the very day before the assassinations began. In all his bloody proscriptions the new ministers were always included, *except one*, and that one always the same. "Will
"it

"it be in thy power, Danton, (he added, darting his
"eyes on the late minister of justice,) to justify thy
"character to posterity for such an exception? Do
"not think, Robespierre, to blind us by disavowing
"Marat, that *enfant perdu de l'assassinat;* it was through
"your influence, by your harangues at the electoral
"assemblies, where you blackened Priestley, and
"white-washed Marat, that he is now a member of
"the convention." Louvet then, after relating the
opposition he made to Marat's nomination, and the
danger he incurred by it from the pike and bludgeon-men who formed the body-guard of the dictator, continued; "I accuse you, Robespierre, of
"having calumniated the best patriots, at a time
"when your calumnies amounted to proscriptions.
"I accuse you of having, as much as in you lay,
"degraded the national representation. I accuse
"you of having held yourself out as an object of
"popular idolatry; of having given out, and
"caused it to be repeated, that you were the only
"virtuous man in the republic. I accuse you of
"having tyrannised over the electoral assemblies.
"I accuse you of having aimed at sovereign authority by all means in your power." In conclusion, he implicated Marat in the charges he had
advanced; required that a committee should be
appointed to examine into the conduct of Robespierre; that a decree should be pronounced against
those monsters who excited murders and assassinations, against a faction which, from motives of
personal ambition, was tearing the republic to pieces;
and that the executive power should be invested
with authority, in all cases of civil commotion, to
call in the aid of the military force in the department
of Paris, to be employed as they should judge
expedient.

Though Robespierre, by his silly vanity, had
drawn this attack on himself, he was so unprepared
for a defence, that he was confused, destitute of

presence of mind, or words to express himself. The convention was agitated with the most violent indignation, and the galleries, not having received any instructions, remained neuter. When Louvet had finished, Robespierre appeared in the tribune; some members said he ought not to be heard but at the bar; some wished to adjourn till the morrow; Louvet voted that he should be heard immediately; but Robespierre said he only appeared there to request that he might be permitted to make his defence on the fifth of November, which was granted. Louvet avers that in this space, the coward, thinking his last hour was come, waited on him to solicit mercy, and complains that Petion, Brissot, and some others did not second his efforts with sufficient ardour [n]. He was not apprized that their connexions with Orleans were such as not to permit them to commit themselves too far in the prosecution of any of his partisans, and that, though they now ranked as virtuous republicans, they were, in fact, worthless intriguers. Barbaroux, however, seconded Louvet's efforts by a fresh denunciation against Robespierre, which he made in the interval preceding the fifth of November, but it had no other effect than attacks made out of time and place generally have, that of exciting useless indignation on one part, and producing a vigorous defence on the other.

5th Nov. Robespierre's precautions.

At length the day so important to the welfare, and even to the life of Robespierre arrived. He omitted no precaution to insure success; the galleries were filled with women properly instructed how to act; the public walks and gardens were crowded with orators, who harangued in his praise, and some fellows carried tripe on a pole, which they swore they would compel those to eat who should vote against so distinguished a patriot [o]. There is little reason to doubt that gold and terror

[n] Louvet's Narrative, p. 23.
[o] Moore's Journal, vol. ii. p. 234.

had

had also been employed to sway the decision of the members. It was, in fact, not the particular cause of Robespierre that was depending, but the cause of all his party; the coffers of Orleans, and the plunder of the murdered prisoners were devoted to the necessary expences of bribery within the assembly, and agitation without.

Robespierre took his place in the tribune, with restored spirits and confidence, and with a prepared speech, in which he proposed to vindicate his conduct from all aspersion.

His defence.

After a short exordium, in which he demanded from the convention the same patience and attention they had bestowed on the voluminous charge of his adversary; he said:

"Of what am I accused? Of conspiring to be a
"dictator, a triumvir, or a tribune; my adversaries
"seem to have no decided opinion which of these
"I aim at, but these Roman words, which are in
"themselves mutually repugnant, may be translated
"supreme power, a phrase which my accuser has
"used on another occasion. Now it must be al-
"lowed, that if such a project were criminal, it
"was still more audacious; for, to give it effect,
"it would be necessary not only to subvert the
"throne, but to annihilate the legislature, and,
"above all, to have prevented its being replaced
"by a national convention; but in that case, how
"happens it that I was the first who, in speeches
"and in writing, invoked a national convention
"as the only remedy for the ills which assailed the
"country? This proposition was denounced by my
"present adversaries as incendiary, but the revolu-
"tion of the tenth of August more than sanctioned,
"it realized the project. Need I observe, that in
"order to obtain the dictatorship, it was not enough
"for me to make myself master of Paris, I must
"also subjugate the remaining eighty-two depart-
"ments? Where were my treasures; where my
"armies?

"armies? Where the fortified places which I must have secured? All power was lodged in the hands of my enemies. The most moderate deduction I can make from these premises is, that before this accusation can acquire a character of probability, it must be demonstrated that I am absolutely mad: nor do I see that my enemies would be great gainers by this fact; for then it would remain for them to account how so many wise men should have given themselves the trouble to write so many fine discourses, so many elegant posting-bills; in short to use so many exertions in order to expose me to the national convention, and to all France as the most formidable of conspirators."

Robespierre then spoke of his connection with Marat; "This, I shall not deny, is one of the most dreadful reproaches against me; I shall give my profession of faith respecting Marat, but without saying any thing against him or in his favour, more than I actually believe, for I am incapable of betraying my own conscience to captivate the public opinion." He then proceeded to relate the circumstances of their acquaintance, which he pretended began only in January 1792, and that Marat was so dissatisfied with his opinions, that he spoke of him with contempt, as possessing neither the views or the audacity of a statesman, and, on one occasion, denounced him as a Feuillant, for not having said in a periodical paper (*le Defenseur de la Constitution*) that it was necessary to subvert the constitution.

"From the period of Marat's visit in January, (Robespierre continued,) I never saw him again till we met in the electoral assembly, and here too I meet with M. Louvet, who accuses me of having pointed out Marat for a deputy, and calumniated Priestley, in short, of having tyrannized over the electoral body by means of in-
"trigue

"trigue and terror." In answer to this accusation he says, that so far from proposing Marat as a deputy, he proposed no one, but following the example of some of his colleagues, he considered himself as performing an useful task in submitting some general observations on the rules which ought to guide the electors in the exercise of their functions. " I did not speak ill of Priestley; I could
" not speak ill of a man known to me only by his
" literary reputation, and by an insult which ren-
" dered him interesting to every friend of the
" French revolution[P]. Do you wish to know the
" real cause which united the voters in favour of
" Marat? In that critical moment, when the heat
" of patriotism was inflamed to the highest degree,
" when Paris was threatened by the approach of
" the armies of tyrants, men were less affected by
" certain exaggerated or extravagant opinions with
" which he was reproached, than by the attempts
" of those treacherous enemies whom he had de-
" nounced, and the presence of those woes, which
" he had foretold."

The orator then adverted to Louvet's charges respecting his conduct in the Jacobin club, and in the council-general of the *commune*. " I exercised,
" if my accuser is to be believed, a despotism of
" opinion at the Jacobin club, which could only be
" contemplated as the forerunner of a dictatorship.
" In the first place, I do not know what is meant
" by a despotism of opinion, particularly in a society
" of free men, unless it be the natural domination
" of principles. Now this domination is not peculiar
" to a man who happens to utter those principles,
" but belongs to universal Reason, and to all those
" who listen to her voice. You say, that since last
" January the club has been entirely governed by

[P] Alluding to the burning of Dr. Priestley's house, and to his being hanged in effigy by the populace of Birmingham.

" a faction,

"a faction, small in number, but loaded with
"crimes and immoralities, of whom I was the head,
"while all prudent and virtuous men, *like yourself,*
"sighed in silence at their oppressed condition.
"But if, since this month of January, the Jacobin
"club has not forfeited the esteem and confidence
"of the nation, and has never suspended its exer-
"tions in the cause of liberty; if, since that period
"it has displayed an increase of courage against the
"court and la Fayette; if, since that period, it has
"incurred the hatred of Austria and Prussia; if,
"since that period, it has received into its bosom
"the federates assembled to combat tyranny, and
"with them prepared the holy insurrection of the
"10th of August, what is the obvious conclusion
"to be drawn from your assertions, but that this
"handful of scoundrels have overthrown despotism,
"and that you and your party were too prudent,
"and too much friends of good order to engage in
"such conspiracies. Supposing it then to be true,
"though I am far from admitting it, that I had, in
"fact, obtained that influence among the Jacobins,
"which you so liberally impute to me, what de-
"duction could you make against me from that
"circumstance? You have adopted a very effec-
"tual and commodious method of securing your
"own triumph; you lavish the names of scoundrels
"and monsters on your adversaries, and display
"your own adherents as models of patriotism;
"thus you crush us at once with the weight of our
"own vices, and of your virtues. But by what
"right do you affect to make use of the national
"convention itself to revenge the injuries offered to
"your self-love, or to your systems? I will not
"require you to emulate the sentiments of repub-
"lican souls, but, at least, be as generous as a
"king, imitate Louis XII. and let the *legislator*
"forget the injuries sustained by *Monsieur Louvet.*"

In

In treating of his conduct in the council-general of the *commune*, Robefpierre took a rapid, but partial furvey of the operations of that body, which he defended by ingenious hypothefes, and fallacious deductions. He faid: " Intrigues vanifh " with the pitiful paffions to which they owe their " exiftence. Great actions and great characters " alone remain. We know not the names of the " factious wretches who pelted Cato in the tribune; " the eyes of pofterity are fixed only on the god- " like image of that great man. I will not con- " defcend to obferve, that I was never charged " with any kind of commiffion, that I never, in any " manner, meddled with any peculiar operation, " that I never, for an inftant, was prefident of the " *commune*, and never had the flighteft connection " with the committee of infpection, fo foully ca- " lumniated; I do not infift on thefe circumftances, " for taking the whole feries of facts collectively, I " would cheerfully confent to take upon myfelf all " the good as well as the evil deeds attributed to " that body, who have been fo often attacked, for " the fake of involving me in the inculpation.

" They are reproached with arrefts which are " ftyled arbitrary, though not one was made with- " out a previous interrogatory. When the conful " of Rome had fuppreffed Catilina's confpiracy, " Clodius accufed him of having violated the laws. " When the conful gave an account of his ad- " miniftration to the people, he fwore that he had " faved the republic, and the people applauded. " I have feen at this bar certain citizens, who are " not Clodiufes, but who, fome time before the " revolution of the 10th of Auguft, prudently " fought refuge at Rouen, emphatically denouncing " the conduct of the council of the *commune* " of Paris. Illegal arrefts! Is it then with the " criminal code in hand, that we are to appreciate " the falutary precautions which the public weal
" requires

"requires in those critical emergencies which arise
"from the impotency of the laws? Why do you
"not reproach us with having *illegally* destroyed
"the pens of those mercenaries whose trade it was
"to propagate imposture, and blaspheme against
"liberty? Why do you not institute a commission
"to collect the complaints of aristocratic and
"royalist writers? Why do you not reproach us
"for having confined all the conspirators within
"the gates of this great city? Why do you not
"reproach us for disarming suspected citizens;
"for banishing from the councils, where we deli-
"berated for the public good, the avowed enemies
"of the revolution? Why do you not, at once,
"criminate the municipality, the electoral assem-
"blies, the sections of Paris, and the primary as-
"semblies, even in the provinces? In short, why
"not criminate all public bodies who have imitated
"us? for their conduct has been in every respect
"*illegal*, as much *illegal* as the revolution, the over-
"throw of the throne, and of the Bastille; in a
"word, *illegal* as liberty itself. But what do I say?
"What I depicted as an absurd hypothesis, is a too
"certain reality. We are, in effect, accused of all
"these things, and many more. Are we not ac-
"cused of having, in concert with the executive
"power, sent commissaries into various depart-
"ments, to propagate our principles, and determine
"the people to unite with the Parisians against the
"common enemy?

"What an idea must these men have formed of
"the last revolution? Did the fall of the throne
"appear so easy before it was accomplished? Was
"nothing necessary but a *coup-de-main* at the Tuil-
"leries? Was it not also requisite to annihilate,
"throughout France, the partisans of tyranny,
"and, in course, to communicate to all the de-
"partments the salutary commotion with which
"Paris had been recently electrified? But who,
            "after

"after having sanctioned insurrection, can mark
"the precise point where the waves of popular
"tumult shall begin to subside? At this rate, what
"people could ever shake off the yoke of de-
"spotism? For if it be true that a great nation
"cannot rise by a simultaneous movement, and
"that tyranny can only be struck by the portion of
"citizens nearest to it, how shall these dare com-
"mence an attack, if, after the victory, the dele-
"gates, coming from the remote corners of the
"state, are authorized to make them responsible
"for the duration or violence of the political hurri-
"cane which saved the country. The world, and
"posterity will only survey in these events their just
"cause and sublime effect; you ought to survey
"them in the same manner. You should judge
"them, not as judges of a petty tribunal, but as
"statesmen, and *legislators of the universe*. But do
"not imagine that I invoke these eternal principles,
"for want of a veil to cover certain reprehensible
"actions; no, we have no such need; I swear it,
"by the subverted throne and rising republic."

Robespierre next treated of the massacres in September, in respect of which he observed, that Louvet's charges were vague and general. Speaking of Roland, he said, "As to the man who
"(depending on the success of defamation, the
"whole system of which he had previously ar-
"ranged) thought he might, with impunity, assert
"in print that I directed these events, I could be
"content to leave him to his own remorse, but re-
"morse implies the possession of a soul. For the
"sake of those whom his impostures may have
"misled, I will state that, before the period when
"these transactions took place, I had left off fre-
"quenting the council-general of the *commune*; the
"electoral assembly, of which I was a member,
"had commenced its sittings; and I only learned
"what was passing in the prisons by public report,
"and

" and much later than most other citizens. To
" form a correct idea of these events, the truth
" must be sought, not in those calumnious writings
" and speeches which have totally misrepresented
" them, but in the history of the last revolution."
He then proceeded to account for, and recapitulate
the events of the second of September in a fallacious
and partial manner, borrowing according to Dr.
Moore, his principal statements from a book written
by Tallien, one of the most distinguished assassins on
that day, intitled, *La Vérité sur les Evénemens du
2 Septembre* [q].

Availing himself of the inconsistency of his accusers, he said: " The most ardent zeal for the
" execution of the laws cannot justify exaggeration
" or calumny; besides, on this occasion, I can
" cite against the declamations of M. Louvet, a most
" unquestionable witness, the minister of the in-
" terior himself, who, while blaming popular exe-
" cutions in general, was not afraid to speak of the
" spirit of prudence and justice which the people
" (I use his own words) had shewn in these illegal
" transactions. What do I say? I can cite in fa-
" vour of the council-general of the *commune*, M.
" Louvet himself, who began one of his numbers
" of the *Centinel* in these words, ' Honour to the
" council-general of the *commune*, they caused the
" *tocsin* to be rung and saved the country!' This
" was in the time of the elections."

" I am assured," said Robespierre, with the most
audacious hypocrisy, " that *one* innocent person
" perished, people have chosen to augment the
" number; weep, citizens, for this cruel mistake, I
" have long wept for it: a good citizen! he was
" then my friend! Weep, even for the guilty
" victims reserved for the sword of the law, who
" fell beneath the blade of popular justice; but let

[q] Moore's Journal, vol. ii. p. 333.

" your

" your grief, like every other earthly thing, have
" an end. That fenfibility which deplores, almoſt
" exclufively, the enemies of liberty, appears fuf-
" picious. Ceafe to wave the bloody robe of the
" tyrant before my eyes, or I fhall think you are
" defirous to put Rome again in chains. In hear-
" ing thefe pathetic lamentations over the Lam-
" balles and Montmorins, fuch touching defcrip-
" tions of the confternation of worthlefs citizens,
" and fuch furious declamations againſt men,
" known by a mode of conduct the exact reverfe,
" did you not think you heard a manifeſto of
" Brunfwick or of Condé?

" To thefe alarming pictures my accufer has
" annexed the project which he imputes to me of
" *vilifying* the legiflative body, *which*, he fays, *was*
" *perpetually tormented, difgraced, and infulted by an*
" *infolent demagogue, who came to the bar to dictate*
" *its decrees.* This is a kind of rhetorical figure by
" which M. Louvet has difguifed two petitions,
" which I was inſtructed to prefent to the legiflative
" affembly, in the name of the council-general of
" the *commune,* relative to the formation of the new
" department of Paris. *Vilify* the legiflative body!
" What grovelling idea had you formed of its
" dignity? Learn that an affembly in which the
" majefty of the French people refides, can never
" be *vilified,* not even by its own acts. When it
" rifes to the elevation of its fublime miffion, how
" do you conceive that it can be *vilified* by the in-
" fenfate difcourfes of an infolent demagogue? It
" can no more be *vilified,* than the Divinity can be
" degraded by the blafphemies of atheifm; no
" more than the luftre of that planet which ani-
" mates all nature, can be dimmed by the clamours
" of the favage hordes of Afia."

Robefpierre then proceeded to narrate the circumftances which attended the prefenting of the
two petitions, in which he infifted ftrongly on the

correctness of his own proceedings, and ridiculed the timid conduct and vain-glorious language of his adversaries. He said, " Citizens, if ever, after the " example of the Lacedemonians, we erect a tem- " ple to fear, I am of opinion that the ministers of " his worship should be chosen among those who " are for ever boasting of their courage and the " dangers to which they have been exposed."

After animadverting on some other less important points of accusation, and exposing the misconduct of his opponents, he concluded thus: " Inde- " pendent of the decree respecting an armed force, " which you have used so many efforts to extort ; " independent of that tyrannical law against the " liberty of individuals and the liberty of the press, " which you have disguised under specious pre- " tences of repressing excitements to murder, you " demand for the ministry a kind of military dic- " tatorship, you demand a law of proscription " against those citizens who displease you, under " the name of an ostracism. Thus you no longer " blush openly to avow the shameful motives of so " many impostures and intrigues ; thus you speak " of a dictatorship only to exercise it yourselves " without restraint ; thus you declaim against " proscription and tyranny, that you, yourselves, " may proscribe and tyrannize; thus you have " imagined, that in order to make the national " convention blind instruments of your guilty de- " signs, it would be sufficient to pronounce a crafty, " romantic declamation, and move that they should, " without adjournment, decree the destruction of " liberty and their own disgrace! What need is " there for me to accuse men who accuse them- " selves? Let us, if possible, bury these contempti- " ble manœuvres in everlasting oblivion. May we " conceal from the eyes of posterity these inglorious " days of our history, when the representatives of " the people, deluded by base intrigues, have
" seemed

"seemed to forget the exalted destiny to which they were called. As for me, I shall make no conclusion relating personally to myself. I have renounced the easy advantage of replying to the calumnies of my adversaries by more formidable denunciations. I renounce the just vengeance which I had a right to claim against my accusers. I ask no revenge but the return of peace and the triumph of liberty. Citizens, press forward with a firm and rapid step in your glorious career; and may I, at the expence of my life, and even of my reputation, contribute with you, to the glory and welfare of our country."

This defence was heard with profound attention; it gained the applause of the galleries, and of a party in the convention. Robespierre's adversaries were by no means intimidated: after the printing of his speech had been decreed, several of them presented themselves in the tribune and at the bar, to be heard in support of the accusation; but his party were strenuous in calling for the order of the day. Some who appeared on the other side were apprehensive lest a discussion might produce a disclosure of truths injurious to their cause; some dreaded the length of debate which was like to ensue from the number of intended speakers, and the known tediousness of some of them. Louvet professed himself ready to answer every averment, and to combat all the arguments advanced by Robespierre; but both Girondists and Mountain rose to prevent his speaking. Barrere took advantage of this circumstance: he said, these petty undertakers of great revolutions ought to be more justly appreciated, and the convention no longer troubled with their manœuvres; the littleness of their abilities formed the best guaranty that they would never become Syllas or Cromwells; and concluded by the old observation, that their attention ought to be reserved for the great questions which interested the republic. The order of

Its effect.

of the day was voted. Thus terminated this great business: the Mountain obviously gained an important advantage in silencing the accusation: the printing of Robespierre's speech, which contained so many points *ad captandum vulgus*, and which was profusely distributed, confirmed his popularity, and extended the influence of his faction in the departments. The Brissotines, whom fear had induced to accede to the measure, affected to consider it a triumph; and Condorcet, in his paper, rather blamed Louvet for bringing the business forward. Louvet, however, though not informed as to particular facts relating to his own party, saw the matter in a just light. " Brissot, Vergniaud, Condorcet, and Gensonné (he says) thought that passing to the order of the day, if it saved Robespierre, would disgrace him so completely, as to to deprive him of all influence for the future: as if disgrace had any weight with that sanguinary faction, and as if physical impunity could have any other effect than to harden him in guilt. This astonishing step of the republican party grieved me to the heart. From that moment I foresaw that sooner or later the poignard-men would prevail over the men of principle: that moment I announced to my dear Lodoïska, that we must prepare for banishment or the scaffold [r]." The event, instead of tending to the disgrace of Robespierre, produced an immediate accession of popularity and respect. The manner in which Barrere treated the possibility of his ever becoming a dictator, by removing fear and suspicion, gained him a large portion of public confidence [s]. A report of the proceedings in the convention was made the same night at the Jacobin club, the members of which were rendered furious with indigna-

---

[r] Louvet's Narrative, p. 23.
[s] For a very ample and spirited account of these attacks on Robespierre, see Moore's Journal, vol. ii. p. 30 to 344. See also Debates and Histories.

tion againſt the Girondiſts, and the names of Louvet, Roland, Barbaroux, Lanthenas, Rebecqui, and Girey-Dupré, were ordered to be inſtantly ſtruck off from the liſts of the ſociety; while the dwellings of Robeſpierre and Danton were conſtantly guarded by a numerous patrole, under pretence that the *fédérés* of Marſeilles, inſtigated by the deputies, intended to murder them [t]. Louvet ſoon publiſhed the reply he had been prevented from delivering in the tribune, under the title, "*A Maximilien Robeſpierre et ſes Royaliſtes.*" Roland, ſenſible of the miſtake his partiſans had committed, repaired it as far as lay in his power, by a profuſe diſtribution of this pamphlet [u]. Briſſot, too late aware of his error in ſanctioning the motion for the order of the day, expreſſed himſelf violently againſt the meaſure, contemptuouſly of Robeſpierre's defence, and favourably of Louvet's publication [x]. Petion publiſhed a letter on the ſubject, addreſſed to the Jacobin club [y], which occaſioned Robeſpierre's celebrated anſwer. Petion had reſigned the mayoralty of Paris, and Robeſpierre was again candidate for the office, but gained only one hundred and thirty-nine votes [z].

The popularity of the Mountain, and the diſgrace of the other party, were much increaſed by the propoſed trial of the king, to which the former were urging the convention with unexampled diligence and rancour, while the others oppoſed and delayed it by all means in their power. The populace, excited by the Jacobins, were clamorous and impatient for the event: Robeſpierre was indefatigable in proſecution of the buſineſs: he ſurmounted difficulties, and repelled objections: he made motions, decrees, and ſpeeches. One of his orations on this occaſion has been much celebrated; Garat ſays that

His exertions on the king's trial.

3d Dec. 1792.

---

[t] Louvet's Narrative, p. 27. [u] Idem, p. 26.
[x] Briſſot à ſes Commettans, p. 15.
[y] See Appendix, N° IX.
[z] Mercure François, N° du 3 Novembre 1792, p. 48.

"it

"it rapidly brought the scale of condemnation to preponderate in the balance of national justice." He adds, relating a conversation between himself and Robespierre, and describing himself as the speaker: "Of all the speeches delivered on that occasion, yours made incomparably the most powerful impression on my mind. Your fundamental idea is new and unexpected, and absolutely confounds with astonishment the judgment of the hearer or reader: the style is bold and elegant; it abounds in passages glowing with passion, and in skilful transitions; it is an effort of genius; but, I confess, the logic of it appears to me very extraordinary, and entirely false.— You prove successfully enough, that it would have been lawful to put Capet to death on the 10th of August, either at the *Castle*, or in the box of the *Logographe*, in the national assembly, in which he took refuge. It would have been but the exercise of the right of war. But the right which war gives of putting an enemy to death, is confined in its operation to the time of battle. When the battle is over, the right of slaughter ceases. None but Tartars think themselves at liberty to butcher their prisoners in cold blood: none but the savages of the American forests think they have a right to devour their captives taken in war. Your speech may be a model of eloquence, but it is, nevertheless, a specimen of inconclusive logic: to your leading principles there must be other principles added, in order to prove that the law condemning Capet to the block was a grand act of national justice on the part of France; and to the whole world a great and conspicuous example, more lawful, more necessary, more useful, than the example of the trial and execution of Charles I. of England [a]."

[a] Garat's Memoirs, p. 71.

This

This criticism, which, it must be remembered, comes from the pen of a republican, is very candid and correct. Montjoye's judgment, though a staunch royalist, is far more favourable to Robespierre. He speaks of the oration in these words: "The speech which Robespierre made at this memorable epoch is perhaps the least faulty of his productions: it is far superior to all those which he had produced hitherto: the style of it is correct; the ideas are not gigantic; it is not infected with that affectation which is a certain proof of the depravation of taste, and which alone gave reputation to Mirabeau [b]."

Robespierre exerted himself incessantly during the whole course of the trial, and used all his influence to make the people partake in his ideas of precipitation and violence. The whole ferocity of his character seems to have displayed itself. He complained of the intrigues to avert the proposed end of the trial. "Louis ought to be tried (he says) as a tyrant condemned by the insurrection of the people: a process is instituted against him, as in the case of an accused citizen whose criminality is doubtful. The revolution ought to have been cemented by his death: the revolution itself is put in litigation. He ought to have been tried by the principles of the rights of man: his trial is founded on forms not applicable either to natural right or ancient law; but an equivocal and monstrous jumble of both. He is tried, not according to the spirit of republicanism, but according to the prejudices of monarchy [c]." He opposed every proposition advanced in the convention, tending to secure to the king the advantage of a fair hearing, or of a trial according to the forms of the constitution. He at

---

[b] Conspiracy of Robespierre, p. 98. See the speech at length. Robespierre à ses Commettans, vol. i. p. 193.

[c] Robespierre à ses Commettans, vol. i. p. 423.

firſt propoſed, that after the king had ſubmitted to an interrogatory, the convention ſhould decide on his fate in twenty-four hours, without ſeparating[d]. When the convention decreed that the king ſhould have counſel, a deputation from the commune preſented the plan of a decree which would have deprived him of every benefit of their aſſiſtance; the convention felt indignant at the brutality of the propoſal, but Robeſpierre, in ſpite of the prevailing clamours, defended it, and even maintained that it was too mild for the occaſion[e]. He argued and voted for the immediate death of the king; oppoſed the hearing of his counſel on the ſubject of an appeal to the people; and, after they had been heard, oppoſed the purport of their obſervations. But what enabled the convention to perpetrate this atrocious act, was a decree obtained by Robeſpierre, altering the exiſting law that two thirds of the voices ſhould be neceſſary to the condemnation of an accuſed perſon, and enabling a ſingle caſting vote to decide it[f]. That Robeſpierre's ambition urged him to many of theſe meaſures, is not to be doubted; but fear had moſt probably its ſhare in influencing him, ſince he declared at the Jacobin ſociety, that if the king were acquitted, the members of the legiſlative aſſembly, and the convention, muſt of courſe be conſidered and puniſhed as rebels[g].

16th Jan. 1793.

10th Mar. Suppoſed plot.

The popularity and influence of Robeſpierre increaſed very much after the death of the king, yet it is not aſcertained that his views led to the eſtabliſhment of a dictatorſhip; on the contrary, though it is much againſt probability, he is accuſed of ſtill entertaining intentions of placing Orleans on the throne. It is aſſerted, that a project was formed for that purpoſe, in which he was to have been aſſiſted by Dumouriez, and by a general inſurrec-

[d] Moore's Journal, vol. ii. p. 495. Debates.   [e] Idem, p. 523.
[f] Debates.   [g] Moore's Journal, vol. ii. p. 612.

tion

tion and massacre in Paris. What renders this very improbable is, that Orleans at the time was loaded with general execration, as much disliked by the republicans as the royalists, menaced, detested, and miserably impoverished. Robespierre had too much cunning, and too little generosity, to continue his attachment to a man in his circumstances; and as to Dumouriez, his army was in want of every thing, and the persevering libelists of Paris, the Marats, the Chaumettes, &c. had rendered his character suspicious to all, and abhorred by many. The conspiracy of the 10th of March is one of the inexplicable mysteries of the French revolution. To what precise end it was directed, or how frustrated, are points equally unknown. A great alarm prevailed respecting it; the Brissotines assert that the aim of the conspirators was, to murder all their opponents, to strengthen their own power and the domineering influence of the city of Paris over the rest of the republic [h]. Whatever the scheme was, it failed, some assert by reason of the cowardice of the duke of Orleans; others, by means of the vigilance and resolution of the Girondists. But the project was not without effect, it gave the party of anarchists an opportunity of obtaining a decree for organizing the *revolutionary tribunal*, that infernal engine of tyranny and horrors; of renewing the terrible outrage of *domiciliary visits*, to discover, as it was pretended, concealed traitors; and of destroying the liberty of the press.

The contest between the rival parties was now drawing to a crisis: the Jacobins had resolved the destruction of the Brissotines, and though frustrated in several of their plans, their determination was too strongly taken for disappointment to deter them from exerting every means for its final execution.

31st May. Decree of accusation against the Brissotines.

[h] Brissot à ses Commettans, p. 41. Louvet's Narrative, p. 19. 32 to 38. See also Conjuration de d'Orleans, vol. iii. p. 246. Conspiracy of Robespierre, p. 102.

The

The eloquence, the knowledge of public affairs, the interest these men had in the departments, and the majority they generally retained in the convention, rendered them dangerous to their rivals, and made it extremely probable that calamity or popular versatility would restore to them the superiority they had once attained over the public mind. Roland, in retiring from office immediately after the death of the king, had left a very forcible memorial on the state of affairs during and at the close of his administration; this, if taken into consideration by the convention, would in all probability have been published, a thing the Mountain had no reason to wish; and therefore, in spite of the ex-minister's repeated letters, refused to permit it to be reported. Marat, as president of the Jacobin club, published an address inviting all the popular societies to exert themselves in procuring the expulsion of those unfaithful deputies, who betrayed their trust in not voting for the death of the tyrant. This produced a decree for his commitment to the Abbaye prison: he was tried and acquitted, and resumed his seat in triumph [1]. It is asserted by an author of the Brissotine faction, that there was a bargain between the crowned heads in alliance against the republic, and the chiefs of the Mountain, that twenty-two of the Brissotines should be massacred: and he adds, that this plot was to be carried into execution the 20th of May: they were then to have been arrested, conveyed to a house in the suburb of Montmartre, and murdered. A forged correspondence between them and Cobourg was prepared, which after their death was to have been brought forward, and a story circulated of their having emigrated. He says they had abundant proofs of this conspiracy; but as none of these appear, as the story itself is extremely improbable, and no account given of the

---

[1] See MARAT.

means by which the plan was difclofed and fruftrated, it is not entitled to credit [k]. There is no doubt Louvet believed fome fuch plot to be in agitation, and the miferably haraffed ftate of the party during this conteft is expreffively defcribed by his obfervation that, from the 10th of March to the 30th of May, they flept from home perhaps fifty times, that is, every other night [l]. A committee of twelve had been appointed to examine into the caufes of the projected infurrection of the 10th of March; their report was ready, Rabaud de St. Etienne was to prefent it to the convention, and Hebert, one of the municipality, had been arrefted by their orders. The Mountain were fenfible that it was their intereft to oppofe thefe proceedings, and made arrangements, in private committees held at Charenton, to infure a victory. Revolutionary committees had been formed, who, under pretence of fearching for foreigners and traitors, committed the moft barefaced and impudent robberies; great numbers were fent to prifon, and it was freely intimated to them, that the fcenes of September were to be renewed. This induced many to facrifice part of their fortune to obtain their freedom, and the plunder increafed the power of the Jacobins. A central committee, compofed of Marat and feveral other furious ruffians, many of them foreigners, exerted a control over the revolutionary committees, from which they were felected, and finally ufurped the whole powers of government. This committee refolved to effect the imprifonment and death of the Briffotines; and, as a preliminary ftep, demanded of the convention a fuppreffion of the committee of twelve; which was decreed, but its report was firft to be made on the 31ft of May. On that day the central committee gave the command of the national guard to Henriot, a creature of theirs; who, at the head of fixty

---

[k] Louvet. See his Narrative, p. 53.
[l] Louvet's Narrative, p. 46.

thoufand

thousand men, with cannon, and furnaces for heating balls, surrounded the convention. The tocsin had been rung, the *generale* beat, and the whole city put into a state of consternation and insurrection. The prisoners, who thought they were to be immediately massacred, filled the air with dreadful cries. The Girondists were in the greatest confusion and alarm; some repaired to their posts in the convention; some sought safety in concealment and flight. Rabaud stood with his report in his hand, but not being able to obtain a hearing, left the hall. A deputation appeared from the *commune*, who presented a petition, demanding the heads of twenty-two members of the convention, besides the committee of twelve. The convention referred this to the committee of public safety, requiring them to

1st June. make a report in three days. Though the Mountain were not entirely succefsful in this attempt, they would not give up the point. The central committee, the next day, of their own authority arrested the ex-ministers, le Brun and Roland, and the wife of the latter. At three in the afternoon, they marched at the head of the armed force again to invest the hall of the convention, and renewed the petition of the day before. The convention had still firmness sufficient to pafs to the order of the day, and required the petitioners to support their denunciation by proofs. But this kind of proceeding was not satisfactory to the insurgents, they gave Henriot more decided instructions, and resolved on the morrow to bring the affair to a termi-

2d June. nation. Accordingly the tocsin was again sounded, the whole city under arms, and Henriot, with a considerable reinforcement, surrounded the hall. The galleries were filled with revolutionary women, armed with daggers, with which they threatened the obnoxious deputies; and all the avenues to the hall were filled with armed people, who prevented the members from retiring. It is probable that many

of

of the orders given by the revolutionary committee were extremely vague and uncertain, or perhaps kept secret from some of the apparent heads of the Mountain, for in many instances they displayed a want of unanimity which would have ruined them, had the other party been at their posts, and ready to have taken advantage of circumstances. The central committee renewed their demand: the convention again passed to the order of the day. Immediately the insurrection assumed a most formidable appearance: the cannon were pointed towards the avenues, and the members forbid to leave the place. Several battalions seized the inner posts of the hall, and prevented all communication between the deputies within and the people without. The president ordered Henriot to draw off his troops, but he returned for answer, that as soon as he had fulfilled the orders of the people, he would attend to those of the convention; but that if they refused to deliver up the traitors, he would order the cannon to be fired upon them. Danton, unacquainted with all the secrets of his party, burst into a rage at this insolence, and demanded the death of the ruffian Henriot. The convention ordered the officers next to the entrance of the hall to be called to the bar: they appeared, but gave no information towards unravelling the conspiracy. Barrere, seeing the Gironde like to be overcome, made an insidious proposal to the proscribed deputies, for the sake of peace and the good of the country, to submit, and suspend themselves from their functions. Some of them were weak enough to fall into so gross a snare; but Barbaroux and Lanjuinais resisted it, and exposed the tyranny exercised over them with so much force, that it is extremely probable, if all the rest of the deputies had been in their places, if the eloquence and credit of Brissot, Rabaud, and the others had been exercised, they would have obtained the victory,

victory, by disuniting the Mountain. The combustible soul of Danton had already caught fire; and Lacroix, another Mountaineer, had protested with vehemence against the tyranny of making the members prisoners in their own hall. The feebleness of the Brissotines afforded the president, Herault de Sechelles, a Jacobin, an opportunity to prevent the disunion of his party, by a childish trick: he insisted that the whole assembly should demonstrate how much they were at liberty, by leaving the hall. They did so; and he marched with them in the garden, till Henriot, at the head of some troops, and with his hat on, informed him he should not pass, and ordered the cannoneers to their guns. They returned to their hall, where Herault told them, that after so striking a proof, the convention could no longer have reason to complain of their want of freedom. Immediately on their return they did the very act they had so long refused, they decreed the arrest of the proscribed deputies, and the insurrection was at an end [m].

Increasing power of Robespierre.

This victory and the subsequent imprisonment of the deputies attached to the Girondists, gave Robespierre a decided ascendancy in the convention. The departments, excited by the deputies who had taken refuge there, were, some of them, in a state of formidable insurrection, but the activity, the tremendous means, and the prevailing influence of the Mountain, increased by some timely acts of apparent patriotism, at length succeeded in stifling the commotion; the deputies were hunted from place to place, some fell into the hands of their enemies, and suffered on the scaffold, some appear to have perished by famine, some were driven to the desperate

[m] For an account of these transactions, see the Histories; New Annual Register for 1793, p. 176.; Miss Williams's Letters, vol. i. p. 73.; Louvet's Narrative, p. 41 to 50.; Peltier's late Picture, vol. ii. p. 530.; Garat's Memoirs, p. 171.

resource

resource of suicide, and a few escaped, after encountering difficulties of every kind almost incredible.

The unlimited ascendancy of Robespierre arose not so much from his majority, or rather from his having destroyed all parties in the convention but his own, as from his having contrived to annihilate all remains of authority in that body. This he effected by means of the committee of public safety, which, at first, was renewable at the end of every month, but he having been appointed one of its members, and having a majority entirely devoted to him, obtained a decree from the convention to render the committee permanent, and thus perpetuate the reign of twelve tyrants, whom, as he swayed in the most absolute manner, he, in fact, was the sole ruler of the country. This atrocious body, secure of support from Robespierre, usurped many of the powers of legislation, they promulgated decrees, sent agents or viceroys into the departments, invested with unlimited authority, and several times refused to give an account of their motives to the convention. The duties of that body soon became limited to the hearing of reports from the ministers who formed the committee, which, from their fallacy, and the affectation of their style, were called *Carmagnols à la Barrere* [n], to the registration of decrees without considering of their probable effect on the country, to a patient acquiescence in, or submissive reverberation of the applauses bestowed on the committee, and on Robespierre. Their number, by reason of proscriptions, committees, missions to the departments and armies, and secessions, seldom exceeded two hundred [o]. To the original powers of the committee of public safety, Robespierre added others by means

His tyranny.

[n] Miss Williams's Letters in 1794, vol. iii. p. 61.
[o] See Etat de la France, p. 2, et passim.

of decrees gained from the complaifant convention, which feemed to promife a perpetual flavery to France. He obtained a decree, that the country fhould be in a ftate of revolution till a general peace. He obtained the appointment of a revolutionary army, with a guillotine for part of its equipage, which being compofed of ruffians of his own felection, and for whom he procured a pay of forty fous a-day, was entirely at his devotion. He obtained a decree, the moft extraordinary, perhaps, ever made by a legiflative body, authorizing the apprehenfion of fufpected perfons, and making the fufpicion of his enemies a crime in the individual, for which he fuftained imprifonment and death. Priefts, nobles, and foreigners were perfecuted without mercy or remorfe; tranfported, put to death without trial, buried in dungeons in daily fear of affaffination, or murder under colour of the law; many thoufands of thefe unfortunate claffes invoked the vengeance of Heaven on their inhuman perfecutor. The people imbibed, or were taught to affume an air of ferocity. One of the fections of Paris prefented an addrefs to the convention, in which it requefted them to facrifice *nine hundred thoufand heads*, and the revolution would be perfectly eftablifhed. The Jacobins, ftill the obedient and ready tools of Robefpierre, required of the convention that terror fhould be declared the order of the day, and that the law that members fhould be heard before the paffing of an accufation againft them fhould be repealed. Will it be believed by pofterity?—The ftupid and enflaved convention actually paffed this felf-murdering decree. They eftablifhed as principles, that pity was a fign of treafon; that the exiftence of a republic could not be maintained without the power of deftroying every thing which oppofed it. This extended alike to perfons and opinions, to fentiments avowed and acted upon, and to thofe only imputed by finifter jealoufy, jealousy, or interested surmise. It was decreed, that death should be the punishment of those who should conspire to change the republican form of government; of those who should resist the revolutionary government, of those who should harbour persons accused of conspiracies after their denunciation; of those who should correspond verbally or by writing with prisoners, and of the jailors who assisted or permitted such correspondence. All ex-nobles were banished from Paris, and obliged to submit to such strict forms of registration, as left them every hour at the mercy of the committee of public safety. It was decreed that transportation to the coast of Africa should be the punishment of those who complained of the revolution, which was extended to mean of any of the acts done by the ruling party [p].

These extraordinary powers were not granted all at once, but were never withheld when an application was made to the convention. The revolutionary tribunal, entirely devoted to the party from whom it derived its existence and authority, made with the most savage indifference, and even pleasantry, all the sacrifices required of them. The forms of inculpation, defence, and evidence were totally disregarded, and the persons whose lives were required, were merely insulted by the pretence of a trial by jury. It is, in fact, a cruel mockery to give the name of jury to a number of men permanently established in their situation; not elected by the prisoner, or subject to be challenged; deliberating in public, and pronouncing separately their opinions aloud [q]. Their deliberation was a mere farce, for one of the judges daily attended Robespierre with a list, from which he marked out a certain number with a cross, and they were devoted to certain de-

The revolutionary tribunal.

[p] On these subjects, see Debates and Proceedings of the Convention; Necker on the Revolution, vol. i. p. 438.; Pages, vol. i. p. 186. 190.; Etat de la France & Suite de l'Etat de la France, passim.
[q] See Brissot à ses Commettans, p. 37.

VOL. II.   E E   struction.

struction[r]. The powers of this tribunal were so extensive, and the decrees on which they were founded of such extraordinary latitude, that it was almost impossible for innocence to escape. The only punishment they pronounced was death, and that was applied to such indefinite crimes as *favouring the impunity of aristocracy; calumniating patriotism; seeking to vilify the revolutionary tribunal; to corrupt the public mind and conscience;* and *stopping the progress of revolutionary principles.* The necessary proofs consisted of every description of document, whether material, verbal, or written, which carries in itself a self-evidence, and when there were material or moral proofs, no witnesses were to be heard. *The rule of the sentence was the conscience of the jurors*; and the process the means which good sense should indicate to establish the solidity of the facts[s]. No person denouncing another was obliged to assign his motives, to discover his name or place of abode. The party denounced, was arrested without proof, interrogated without attention to form, insulted by the court, and condemned without mercy or hope of pardon[t].

Punishment of several members of the convention.

Invested, by the concurrence of circumstances rather than any effort of premeditation or contrivance on his part, with powers so unlimited, it was perfectly natural for Robespierre to seek his own security, in the destruction of those who could make any resistance to his authority. The Brissotine deputies were early victims to this principle. The unfortunate queen, and the worthless Egalité, the persecuted and the persecutor, fell under the same punishment, and so entirely was Robespierre master of the public opinion, that equal applauses attended these two acts, so apprently contradictory. But it

[r] Necker on the Revolution, vol. i. p. 433.
[s] See Necker on the Revolution, vol. i. p. 447. Jordan's Political State of Europe, vol. vii. p. 23.
[t] Suite de l'État de la France, p. 29.

was

was not sufficient to rid himself of those who had constantly been his opponents, some of his associates were too *volcanic* to be trusted long. Bazire, who, unconscious that he was digging his own grave, had applauded and supported the decree which deprived deputies of the privilege of being heard, was one of the earliest objects of its oppression. He, together with Chabot, Thuriot, and several others, was sent to jail, and from thence to the scaffold. But a more important operation demanded a greater exertion; Hebert, jealous of Robespierre's power, and anxious to extend his own, master of the club of Cordeliers, as Robespierre was of the Jacobins, meditated his impeachment. Maximilien, informed of the fact, resolved Hebert's destruction; yet he proceeded with caution: he first employed Camille Desmoulins to write him down, which he did with considerable wit and humour. Hebert, seeing by this that something was in agitation against him, took advantage of an illness with which his rival was attacked ", to excite the Cordeliers to insurrection. He made a speech against Robespierre, in which he declared that tyranny existed; he caused a veil to be thrown over the table of the Rights of Man, and actually succeeded in causing one of the sections of Paris to declare itself in a state of insurrection, but his triumph was short, he, with eighteen of his accomplices, was apprehended, delivered over to the revolutionary tribunal, and from them, in natural course, to the guillotine. The club was dissolved ˣ.

18th Nov. 1793.

16th Mar. 1794.

15th Mar. 1794.

Of Hebert.

The atrocities committed and excited by these people, made their destruction an act of great popularity. All who retained any respect for religion; all who wished for the re-union of their countrymen in the accustomed bonds of social intercourse; all who felt solicitous for the termination of those scenes of murder and horror which daily insulted hu-

Hopes of the people.

" Playfair's History of Jacobinism, p. 615.
ˣ See Histories. Miss Williams's Letters in 1794, vol. iii. p. 64.

manity, hailed this epoch as the dawn of that day which was to produce the accomplishment of their hopes, and gave way to the transports excited by such an expectation. The event proved the fallacy, religion was no farther re-established than by a verbal acknowledgment of the existence of a God, and a festival in honour of him, more like burlesque than religion; social intercourse became more dangerous than ever, from the increased reserve required by sanguinary edicts and frequent accusations; the torrents of blood which every day flowed from the scaffolds demonstrated too forcibly that the reign of Robespierre and that of anarchy and terror were to be coëval.

Excessive cruelty of Robespierre. Who shall describe all the horrors which at this period stained the soil of France? What mode of narration can convey to the mind of the reader an adequate idea? A general enumeration of victims would convey no distinct notion of that dreadful system which involved guilt and innocence, which respected neither old age, adolescence, sex, sickness, pregnancy, courage, or past services; while a separate recapitulation of the cases of the various sufferers would fill volumes with records of cruelty unparalleled in the annals of tyranny, without affording a clear picture of the horror, distraction, and desolation which pervaded the country. Who shall in future times obtain belief when he relates the cruelties and assassinations practised at Lyons, Marseilles, Nantz, and in la Vendée; the horrible joy with which the national convention applauded and repeated the revolutionary jokes of the assassins and encouraged their bloody progress; and the indifference with which that body suffered their own members to be snatched from them, and the citizens of Paris saw their relations and friends daily consigned to the executioner by wretches, who outraged justice by an utter contempt of all forms of jurisprudential proceeding, and humanity by the savage indifference, and even affected pleasantry with which they committed their murders[y]? Will it be believed, that the wives and children of innocent prisoners, when they went to the houses of deputies, to solicit in their behalf, were turned to indecent ridicule, and compelled to drink and dance[z]? Will it be believed, that in one of the departments, all the unmarried young women, and even all the children of a town, down to seven years old, were compelled to march in procession to the Temple of Reason, and take an oath never to marry any but true republicans[a]? "The complete portrait of "Robespierre's political life (says Freron) is re- "served for history, but we may now briefly touch "upon the oppression which he extended over us, "and over all the republic. How, in a society of "brothers and friends, a word, a gesture of his "was sufficient to procure any man's expulsion "from the Jacobin club, and how the man who was "struck out from the list of that society, was soon "struck out from the list of the living. How, "under the pretence of a revolutionary govern- "ment, he artfully contrived to set the convention "above principles, the two committees above the "convention, the committee of public safety above "the committee of general safety; and himself above "the committee of public safety. How, in this "hall, to deliver an opinion contrary to that of "Robespierre, was to obtain a passport to the "guillotine; how he filled all the prisons with "excellent republicans; how he corrupted the re- "volutionary tribunal, where judgments of death "were pronounced in terms of jocularity[b]."

To what did all this tend, or what were the spe- *Examin-*
cific objects of his views? becomes a natural question. *ation of his views.*

[y] See Pagès, vol. ii. p. 191.
[z] Brissot à ses Commettans, p. 84.
[a] Tench's Correspondence, p. 128.
[b] Speech on the Liberty of the Press. See Debates, Aug. 1794.

He has been accused by some of a conspiracy with the combined powers to dismember France; by others of royalism, or a view to restore some branch of the royal family; but either of these imputations becomes incredible when the success of the measures in war which he sanctioned, and the unabating aversion he constantly kept alive against royalty are considered. It is averred that he meant to assume the royal dignity himself, either as king, or under some other name; and that he had privately visited the princess royal in prison, with an intention to set her at liberty, and marry her [c]; but this and many other reports I consider as mere inventions of the triumphant party, and not entitled to credit. His ambition was abundantly gratified by the exalted situation to which he was raised, and in which he might have secured himself by relaxing, after the destruction of his opponents, the system of terror; but this was so far from the case, that to his last hour his thirst for blood seems to have grown more and more insatiable. Avarice had no share in his composition, for though he permitted the most iniquitous peculation in his inferior agents, his hands were clean, and he died without having amassed any property [d]. Luxury had few charms for him; he was refined rather than otherwise in his tastes, but so moderate in his enjoyments as to acquire the name of the French Cato [e]. What then had he in view? Nothing; absolutely nothing determinate. Pushed on by accident, not contrivance, raised by the fortuitous occurrences of the times, and by explosions prepared by other men, to an unexpected eminence, power had the usual effect on

[c] Pagès, vol. ii. p. 407.
[d] He is said to have encouraged the peculation of his inferior agents, that he might be enabled, at any time, to effect their destruction. Suite de l'Etat de la France, p. 34.
[e] He is said to have been addicted to liquor. See Tench's Correspondence, p. 196.

him in drawing forth the latent propensities of the heart. He was ungrateful, jealous, envious, and timid; and to these qualities, whetted by the sense of the perilous state in which he stood, must be attributed all the terrible scenes which marked his reign [f]. Blood was become his element, and he caused the effusion as necessary to his existence. Talents, virtue, birth, wealth, excited in him envy or fear, and marked out their possessors to his fury. Surrounded with men devoted to crimes, and whose ruin must have produced his own, he sought in the continuance of anarchy and proscription, the perpetuation of his own power and safety. Crimes were become familiar to him; and the depraved propensities of his heart being aroused, he no longer knew any bounds to his desire of blood. The whole period of his exaltation afforded no one instance, except in the field, which was honourable to the nation. The requisition, and rising in a mass, an idea of the most extensive sublimity, was converted into an engine of oppression; the *maximum*, that abominable offspring of tyranny and folly, was a source of endless rapacity, plunder, proscription, deterioration of provision, and famine. Religion, that corrector of the human heart, that consoling panacea for every mental wound, was proscribed; the torpid doctrine that "Death is an eternal sleep," publicly avowed, extended its influence, and blighted every affection and every principle. There never was known, in the annals of man, a period where the want of virtue was encouraged as a public boast; where Hypocrisy dressed herself in the character of Vice instead of its opposite; yet this phænomenon dis-

---

[f] Necker says of him, "No one hitherto has disclosed the reserved secrets of this unparalleled tyrant, no one has unveiled the dark combinations of his mind: thus the system of his ambition, the limit of his hopes, have remained to be guessed at; and perhaps it is of consequence to the honour of human nature to consider him as a preternatural being, with whom, even from study and observation, the mind can enter into no affinity."

tinguished

tinguished the reign of Robespierre. Every one who valued his own safety was forced to applaud and repeat sentiments which made his blood run cold; and many who had incurred suspicion were obliged to boast of actions they had never committed, and at which their hearts recoiled. How could it be otherwise when informing, treachery, calumny, and assassination were erected into virtues; when the sentiments of nature were carefully extinguished, and fury, perfidy, and inhumanity lighted up in their stead. The servant denounced his master, the friend betrayed his friend, brothers accused their brothers, fathers their sons, and children their parents; they were applauded, and received the homages of their corrupted country. Men of genius and talents in every class excited the rage of the tyrant, they were classed as a new aristocracy; it could not, in every instance, be fear which occasioned this sentiment; men of letters might have unfolded and held him up to detestation, but what had he to fear from artists, chymists, and the actors of the *theatre François?* It was envy, the base offspring of a cold, contracted heart, acted upon by the recollection of disappointment in one of the roads to celebrity. The nobles were, in the most wanton manner, confined and moved from prison to prison; every avenue to the city presented the disgusting spectacle of one or more cart-loads of these unfortunate personages of both sexes and of every age, from infancy to extreme old age, exempt from a charge of crime, tied with their hands behind them, and exposed to the heat of the sun, the fury of the elements, or the still more distressing outrages of the hordes of revolutionary banditti, who loaded them with every disgusting insult language can supply. The inhabitants of Paris were daily shocked with the sight of cart-loads of persons similarly bound, going to the guillotine; this infernal object took away the pleasure of their best walk; reddened their streets with the gore which

adhered

adhered to the shoes of those who had directed their steps near the place where it was erected, and shed human blood in such profusion, that the earth being incapable of absorbing it all, it ran to discolour the waters of the Seine. The night was no less terrible than the day, for besides the dread of domiciliary visits, of plunder and assassination, those whom illness or accident kept awake were alarmed with the noise of carts carrying people to some of the prisons, which were now to be found in every street, and from one to the other of which the prisoners were conveyed in the most outrageous and wanton manner. The guillotine seemed to supersede or preside over every thought; even the women are said to have given to their babes, instead of a coral, a machine which represented the action of that instrument, and the falling of the human head under its stroke. The passage of the condemned through the streets to the guillotine was embittered by every sarcasm and insult brutality and malice could suggest, and it was not uncommon to see children of twelve years old sucking the blood which trickled from the fatal machine [g].

The expences of government were incalculable. The fabrication of assignats was so great, that the daily consumption of paper for them alone amounted to six thousand reams [h]. The committees of surveillance, those abominable hosts of spies and robbers, were maintained at an expence of near *thirty-two millions of pounds sterling a-year* [i]. These were but the least considerable parts of the public expenditure; the convention, the armies, the navy, all other departments were administered with equal prodigality. The people were exposed to all the miseries of famine; commerce was annihilated, and industry suppressed: the possession of wealth was certain de-

Expence of government.

Misery of the people.

[g] Etat de la France, p. 77.
[h] Tench's Correspondence, p. 177.
[i] Idem, p. 189.

struction, as Robespierre had been known to declare, that he did not think it necessary for the richest man in the republic to possess more than three thousand livres (131*l.* 5*s.*) a-year[k]. The holding any of the necessaries of life subjected the citizen to the insults of revolutionary plunderers, and the horrors of a breach of the law of *maximum*. Humanity shudders at hearing the distresses to which the poor were reduced; there was in Paris a general want of bread, meat, milk, eggs, and even fuel. The depreciated paper-money would not afford a sufficiency of these articles to support the wives and families of the labourers, and the difficulties sustained by the poor surpass description and belief. When they complained of distress at home, they were directed to turn their thoughts towards the glories of the armies of the republic, to suffer with patience for the good of the country, and to impose on themselves voluntary fasts, or *civic lents*. Far more harsh treatment awaited them if they uttered a complaint on the subject of their proscribed or imprisoned relatives: a deputation of women, in considerable number, came one day to the convention, to solicit the enlargement of parents, sons, or husbands, snatched from them and buried in dungeons. Their tears, the eloquent language of nature, which softened the tribunes into silence, only increased the fury of Robespierre; he accused them of aristocracy; of a wish to oppose the progress of the revolution, by enervating the measures of the convention. After hearing these, and many more brutalities, they were dismissed to devour their chagrin in retirement.

A party formed against Robespierre.

In the latter part of his life, Robespierre seems gradually to have lost sight of all his cunning, to have forgot the means to which he owed his elevation, and, intoxicated by a plenitude of power, to

[k] Pagès, vol. ii. p. 506.

have

have addicted himself without reserve to his most ferocious propensities, regardless of the public opinion, and indifferent to the censures of his colleagues. An opposition from any of them was, as Freron said, a passport to the scaffold; but on the slightest hint of a contrariety of opinion, he gave way to the violence of his temper, and overwhelmed them with the coarsest abuse. His ingratitude or fear triumphed over his judgment in the destruction of Danton, his constant friend and defender, and the principal engine of his elevation; Camille Desmoulins, and Fabre d'Eglantine, to whom he owed much of his popularity. The execution of these deputies alarmed the rest; Danton had a strong party in his interests, and these reinforced by others, whom fear, jealousy, or honesty united against the tyrant, formed a conspiracy which at last freed their country from the scourge of his existence. This task was attended with difficulty and danger apparently insurmountable; the power of Robespierre exceeded that of any monarch in Europe; the Jacobins were entirely devoted to him, and by means of their affiliated societies, spread their sentiments all over France; the staff and principal officers of the national guard were of his own appointing, and the major part of the artillery of the capital was at his disposal; the *commune* of Paris was servilely devoted to his commands, and many of them were judges of the revolutionary tribunal. That execrable court, together with the revolutionary committees, and his legions of armed ruffians, insured the subjection of Paris, and the influence of that city extended over the remainder of France. The members of the committee of public safety, in their reports to the convention, loaded him with the most exaggerated praises, and the journalists extolled him above all the heroes of antiquity. Wherever he went he was surrounded by a crowd of officious flatterers, who attended to every one of his motions, and seemed to place their whole happiness in his smile. The Jacobins had given him the title of *incorruptible*, and this was generally annexed to his name. He received numerous addresses from the departments, in which all the modes and expressions of adulation were exhausted. He was styled, " the glorious, " incorruptible Robespierre, who covers the republic " by his virtues and talents, as with a shield; who " joins to the self-denial of a Spartan or Roman of " early date, the eloquence of an Athenian. Even " the tenderness and humanity of his disposition " were praised! One man congratulated himself " on a personal resemblance to him; and another, " at the distance of six hundred miles, declared he " was hastening to Paris to feast his eyes with a " sight of him. He was compared, not by an in- " dividual, but by a body of people, to the Mes- " siah, announced by the Supreme Being as the " reformer of all things; and afterwards, he was " said to manifest himself, like the Almighty, by " miracles. On some occasion a *Te Deum* was " performed for him, the burthen of which was " *Vive Robespierre—vive la Republique*[1]!"

23d May 1794. Supposed attempt to assassinate him. The enthusiasm of admiration and servile adulation was carried to its extremest height by a reported plot to assassinate him, entered into by a woman of the name of Cecile Regnaud, and a man named Amiral. The only facts proved against the woman were, that she demanded to see Robespierre with impatience and haughtiness, and said she wished to know how a tyrant was made. Amiral had attempted to pistol Collot d'Herbois. Regnaud[m] was guillotined

---

[1] Tench's Correspondence, p. 194. From Courtois' report of 16 Nivose (5th January).

[m] AIMÉE CECILE REGNAULT or REGNAUD, was daughter of a stationer, living in *rue la Lanterne*, in the section of *la Cité*. From her conduct she appears to have been deranged in her intellects. She went to the house where Robespierre resided, and demanded to see him: being informed he was not at home, she answered, it was very astonishing

guillotined together with her father, mother, and aunt, who, without proof, were adjudged to be accomplices in her plot. This circumstance afforded the sanguinary tyrant a plea for accelerating his course in the race of blood; he was dissatisfied with the tardiness of the revolutionary tribunal, which, though it destroyed fifty or threescore a-day, with no form of trial, or any ceremony save that of call-

ing that, as a public functionary, he was not at home. Possessing such a place as he did, he ought always to be at home and ready to see those who had business with him. The purport of these words alarmed Duplai, the master of the house, who immediately apprehended and carried her before the committee of public safety. In their way she observed that, during the old government, the king was always accessible; and that she would shed the last drop of her blood to have a king again. Being asked by the committee if she had used the above expressions, she readily acknowledged them; and added, that there were then in France fifty thousand tyrants, and she wanted to see how a tyrant was made. On this she was committed to the Conciergerie, together with her father, mother, and aunt. She underwent another examination, during which she repeated her former assertions: her inquisitors wanted her to add that she went to Robespierre's house in consequence of a conspiracy to assassinate him, and threatened that if she did not confess it, all her family should suffer. She persisted, nevertheless, in denying any such intention. A new species of torture for the discovery of truth was invented by these sapient investigators: as Cecile was in the prime of youth, in her twentieth year, very handsome, and dressed with care and neatness, they had her clothes taken from her, and after making her put on squalid rags in their stead, renewed their interrogatory: she persevered in her denial of the conspiracy, and with considerable effect rallied her examiners on the absurdity of their experiment. She was then transferred to the revolutionary tribunal, and put to the bar, together with Amiral, her own relations, and upwards of threescore persons beside, most of whom had been in prison six months before, and had never seen or heard of her. The jury, on hearing their names called over, declared themselves sufficiently instructed, and pronounced sentence of death on the whole party, sixty-nine in number, without hearing evidence or defence; they were all guillotined the 25th of May. Her two brothers, who were fighting on the frontier, were arrested, loaded with chains, and sent to Paris; but before the executioners had time to bestow their attention on them, the revolution of the 27th of July deprived them of their murderous power. There is no doubt but insanity must have been the cause of this unfortunate young woman's proceeding; that she was not emulous of imitating Charlotte Corday appears by her going unprovided with effensive weapons; that she did not expect impunity appears by her having furnished herself with a bundle of linen, expressly because it would be useful to her in prison.

ing

ing over their names, seemed too slow for the rapidity of his destructive desires; it was proposed at the Jacobin club to kill three thousand a-day with grape-shot, till the prisons should be emptied; and orders were actually given for enlarging the court of the revolutionary tribunal, so that two or three hundred persons might be dispatched at once. Whether his fears of assassination were real or affected, he made use of the reports raised on the subject to 25th May. gratify his vanity as well as his cruelty; he made a pompous speech in the convention, wherein he exaggerated the magnitude of his services and dangers, and challenged the gratitude of his cotemporaries, and the admiration of posterity. He also made use of it to a purpose still more detestable; to obtain the decree for giving no quarter to English or Hanoverian prisoners ".

8th June. Feast in honour of the Supreme Being.
In the midst of the horrors he excited, of the executions with which he ensanguined his native land, hardened against the impressions of self-abhorrence, which a consciousness of his unrelenting savageness ought to have inspired, Robespierre had the incredible assurance to propose a festival in honour of the Supreme Being, that creative power, who even in the majesty of offended justice, *desireth not the death of a sinner*, and to propose himself as high-priest on the occasion. In a prepared speech, replete with affectation, he asserted, as if it were a discovery of his own, the existence of a Deity, and the immortality of the soul; and enforced the doctrine with those trite topics which would hardly be thought worthy to fill a page of a school-boy's exercise, expressed in all the florid pomposity of self-conceit, and uttered in the complacent accents of self-applause. This festival actually took place;

" For an account of Cecile Regnault's apprehension and examination, see Jordan's Political State, vol. vi. p. 462.; Miss Williams's Letters in 1794, vol. ii. p. 66.; New Annual Register for 1794, p. 366.; Playfair's History of Jacobinism, p. 637.

David

David the painter arranged the order of the procession, the decorations of the altar, the ornaments of the houses, and the whole *spectacle* of the *Champ de Mars*. The following animated and accurate description of it is taken from the Letters of Miss Williams[o]. " David, ever ready to fulfil the mandates
" of his master, Robespierre, steps forth, marshals
" the procession, and, like the herald in Othello,
" orders every man to put himself into triumph!—
" At this spot, by David's command, the mothers
" are to embrace their daughters—at that, the
" fathers are to clasp their sons—here the old are to
" bless the young, and there the young are to kneel
" to the old—upon this boulevard the people are to
" sing—upon that, they must dance—at noon they
" must listen in silence, and at sun-set they must
" rend the air with acclamations.——The citizens
" of Paris had been invited, and the invitation
" amounted to a command, to decorate their houses
" in honour of the festival. Accordingly Paris on
" that morning, lighted up by brilliant sun-shine,
" presented the most gay and charming spectacle
" imaginable. Woods had been robbed of their
" shade, and gardens, to the extent of some leagues,
" rifled of their sweets, in order to adorn the city.
" The walls of every house were covered with luxu-
" riant wreathes of oak and laurel blended with
" flowers; civic crowns were interwoven with
" national ribbands; three-coloured flags waved
" over every portal; and the whole was arranged
" with that light and airy grace which belongs to
" Parisian fancy. The women wore garlands of
" fresh-blown roses in their hair, and held branches
" of palm or laurel in their hands; the men placed
" oaken boughs in their hats, and children strewed
" the way with violets and myrtle. The repre-
" sentatives of the people had large three-coloured
" plumes in their hats, national scarfs thrown across

[o] Letters in 1794, vol. ii. p. 86.

" their

"their shoulders, and nosegays of blended wheat-ears, fruits, and flowers in their hands, as symbols of their mission. A great amphitheatre was raised on the garden of the Thuilleries immediately before the palace, now the seat of the convention. Upon a tribune in the centre of the theatre, Robespierre, as president of the convention, appeared; and having for a few hours disencumbered the square of the revolution of the guillotine, this high-priest of Moloch, within view of that very spot where his daily sacrifice of human victims was offered up, covered with their blood, invoked the Parent of universal nature, talked of the charms of virtue, and breathed the hope of immortality. When the foul fiend had finished this impious mockery, he descended from the tribune, and walked with great solemnity towards a grotesque kind of monument that was raised upon the bason in the front of the palace, which had been covered over for that purpose. On this monument was placed a mis-shapen and hideous figure, with ass's ears, which for some hours served as an enigma to the gaping crowd, who knew not how to account for this singular appearance; till Robespierre having set fire to this image of deformity, which was declared to be the symbol of atheism, its cumbrous drapery suddenly vanished, and a fair and majestic form was discovered, emblematical of wisdom and philosophy. Atheism being thus happily destroyed, the convention, attended by a numerous procession of people, and preceded by triumphal cars and banners, marched to the *Champ de Mars*, where, with much toil and cost, a rocky mountain had been reared, upon whose lofty summit the tyrant and his attendants climbed, and from whence he once more harangued the people; and the festival closed with hymns and choral songs in honour of the Supreme Being."

While

While this execrable monster, by this sacrilegious ceremony, seemed to place himself point-blank in the very aim of the vengeance of an offended Deity; while making his puerile harangue, he waved in one of his blood-stained hands a nosegay, in the other his hat: doubtless many who had to require of him the blood of parents, children, relations, and friends, lifted up their hands to the God he profaned in ardent and pious ejaculation for an emanation of divine wrath to rid the earth of its greatest pest. Their prayers were heard; from that day he seems to have stood marked as a person on whom the stroke of Death was ready to descend. In the progress of the festival, he gave much offence by affecting to walk at the head, and at some distance from his colleagues. He had put them out of temper by a childish display of vanity in keeping them and the impatient spectators waiting two hours after the appointed time before he made his appearance. A feeble attempt was made by some of his most resolute partisans to raise a cry of "*Vive Robespierre!*" but it was not re-echoed by the multitude. *His improper conduct.*

The motives of Robespierre's conduct during the latter part of his life are involved in a considerable degree of obscurity, they form a riddle which it is not easy to solve. The power he already possessed so extensive, so apparently stable, left him nothing to desire, unless it were a greater name, as that of king, dictator, protector, or perpetual president; but to have attained that end it was necessary to have conciliated the affections of the people, by remitting in some degree the operation of terror. So far was he from doing this, that every day presented an enlarged list of victims to his rage for blood, and measures were in agitation to increase still more the exterminating power of the revolutionary tribunal. If his own safety prompted him to measures so destructive, he ought not to have remained so long as he did indifferent to the move- *Efforts of his opponents.*

ments of the junto he saw forming in the convention against him. It is said that a party, headed by Bentabole, and consisting of Collot d'Herbois, Vadier, and Tallien, had been leagued together for some months, and that these men had resolved, if other means failed, to assassinate Robespierre in the convention [p]; but there is much improbability in the account. Two days after the festival, an abridgment of his power took place, which ought to have convinced him of the decline of his influence, and urged him to its re-establishment by some speedy and effectual stroke. The act alluded to is that which deprived the committees of public safety and of general security, of the power of sending members of the convention to trial before the revolutionary tribunal, till that body should have framed the articles of their accusation. Robespierre's conduct on this occasion shews the littleness of his mind; incapable of preparing, combining, and maturing a conspiracy, but accustomed to lurk in a recess during the hurricane, and afterwards to come forward and assume to himself the credit, that he might derive advantage from the event, he, on this occasion, left the front of the battle to his partisans, and for four decades absented himself from the committees and the convention. His pusillanimity confounded his partisans; the committee of general security was inimical to him, and he meditated their destruction, but had not time to effect it. In the committee of public safety a strong party was formed against him, he knew their intentions, and included their names in one of his lists of proscription; this list was found in the hands of one of the revolutionary jury who had been arrested, and by alarming the fears of those whose names were inscribed in it, accelerated the event of an open rupture. The Jacobins, amongst whom were a great many of the friends of

10th June.

[p] Suite de l'Etat de la France, p. 57.

Danton, and many confidants of the profcribed deputies, were not difpofed to enter into all the views of Robefpierre with fo much ardour as he wifhed. They maintained, on many occafions, a torpid indifference, which drew on them the reproaches of the younger Robefpierre. The ingratitude of Maximilian was now about to be thoroughly and feverely punifhed. The energy and refolution of Danton, the eloquence of Camille Defmoulins, and the addrefs of Fabre d'Eglantine were wanting to him in this emergency, and very ill fupplied by the brutality and inconfideratenefs of Henriot, the vulgarity and heavy ignorance of Couthon and St. Juft, and the negative affiftance and ftudioufly concealed fervices of the abbé Syeyes and la Clos [q]. Yet to triumph over the tyrant was not matter of facility; the habitual deference paid him, the ftrength of his party, united by a guilty fear, and the difunion of his opponents, occafioned by terror, rendered the event of a conteft extremely precarious. He was known to poffefs an unlimited influence over the national guard, and the camps in the vicinity of Paris were devoted to him. The party in oppofition did not know their own ftrength; for many who inwardly hated the tyrant, and faw in his deftruction their only hope of fafety, externally paid him the moft fervile homage, and, as well in his abfence as when he was prefent, made his praifes their favourite theme.

At length, he himfelf threw down the gauntlet of hoftility. He appeared in the tribune of the convention after a long feceffion, and in a prolix, ill-connected fpeech, complained of the treatment he received from intriguers and calumniators, both abroad and at home; at the head of thofe abroad he placed the duke of York and Pitt; thofe at home he would not name, but intimated fo ftrongly certain members of the convention, that feveral rofe to ex-

26th July. Conteft in the convention.

[q] See Etat de la France, p. 15.

culpate

culpate themselves. The other party, thus called upon, were obliged to put themselves in a state of defence; Bourdon de l'Oise moved that the speech might be referred to the committees previous to its being printed; Cambon and Vadier complained of Robespierre's insinuations against them: Couthon defended Robespierre, reprobated the system of calumny which prevailed, insisted that a line of demarcation should be drawn between the patriots and the intriguers, and that the speech should be printed without being referred to the committees. A tumultuous debate ensued, in which Freron demanded the exemption of the members from arrest, adding, that no man could speak freely while influenced by that fear. Billaud de Varennes answered him with a logic altogether singular, that he, whom fear hindered from delivering his opinion, was unworthy the title of representative of the people. Barrere spoke a few words perfectly equivocal; in the end, however, the matter took a favourable turn for the usurper; the printing of his speech was ordered unconditionally. From the convention he hastened to read his speech at the Jacobins, where it excited a general enthusiasm in his favour. Couthon denounced the two committees as traitors; Coffinhal proposed the purification of the convention, which was well understood to import the destruction of all the members except those devoted to his patron; and David, embracing Robespierre, promised if he drank hemlock, to drink it with him.

27th July. Fall of Robespierre. The imminence of the danger could not arouse the opponents of Robespierre to a decisive mode of conduct. The convention met the next day, and business was proceeding in its usual channel, till St. Just, instigated by his evil genius, ascended the tribune, and after stating that the committees of government had directed him to make a report on the state of the country, added, that their remedies were inefficient for the existing grievances, and he would

would speak to the convention from himself.—
Tallien pushed him from the tribune, complained of
the audacity of individuals in attacking government,
and demanded that the veil should be withdrawn.—
He was interrupted by Billaud de Varennes, who,
from his seat, demanded an unequivocal explanation.
He stated that the convention was between two precipices; the public force was in the hands of a man
denounced by the committee, but who was retained in
his command by an individual—that individual had
for more than a month past plotted the dissolution of
the convention: that individual was Robespierre.
He deprecated tyranny, and asked if any members
present would wish to live under it. Robespierre
was, at first, thunderstruck; he afterwards endeavoured to speak, but was prevented by the menaces
of Tallien, who drawing a dagger, and brandishing
it in the eyes of his colleagues, said he would destroy
him with it unless the convention delivered him to
the sword of justice. After some amplification, he
moved that the sitting should be declared permanent.
His efforts were seconded by Delmas and Barrere,
by Billaud and Collot d'Herbois, who was president.
They obtained a decree for the arrestation of Henriot, d'Aubigni, Lavalette, Dufraisse, all the staff
of the national guard, and a man of the name
of Sijas; but they had not yet the courage to
arrest the tyrant himself. While the president was
arranging these decrees, Robespierre got possession
of the tribune, but they would not permit him to
utter a word: " Down with him! down with
" Cromwell!" resounded from every quarter. As
he persevered in his efforts to obtain a hearing, a
member said to him; " Robespierre, you shall not
" speak; the blood of Danton is upon your head,
" it flows into your throat, it choaks you!" " Ah,
" ah! (exclaimed he grinding his teeth and foaming with rage,) Ah, ah! robbers, it is Danton,
" then."—He was heard no more; Vadier interrupted

rupted him, and made a speech wherein he unfolded his tyranny and all his iniquities: this blow completely overpowered him; he cast a look of piercing indignation towards the Mountain, and reproached their desertion; he is even said, in his extremity, to have turned to the *right side*, to solicit their protection, but in vain. Tallien and Billaud poured fresh accusations on his head with unceasing assiduity. He perceived the world sliding from under him, and that he would be speedily precipitated into the abyss of destruction: " Well! (exclaimed he in a tone of " desperation,) lead me, then, to instant death." " Execrable monster! (exclaimed Dumont, with a " threatening gesture,) thou hast deserved it an " hundred times!" The decree for his accusation was then put and carried unanimously, and Couthon and St. Just were added. The younger Robespierre and Lebas, indignant at what was passing, insulted the convention, and threatened some of the members in such a manner as to get included in the decree of accusation. The officer who was ordered to take them into custody, and lead them to the committee of public safety, impressed with the habitual respect and fear excited by the presence of Robespierre, hesitated to obey the repeated commands of the president, and would not receive the prisoners, till the chief of them made a sign expressive of his obedience to the law, when they were all led out.

Opposition and destruction of his party.

Meantime the rumour of what was doing in the convention spread all over Paris; Robespierre's partisans lost no time in endeavouring to oppose the rising storm. The Jacobins assembled in their hall, and sent to put the sections of Paris in a state of insurrection. The *tocsin* was sounded, the *gréve* covered with armed men, and several pieces of artillery planted on the Quai Pelletier, threatening the hall of the convention; the barriers were shut, and Henriot, who had been arrested and had escaped, was indefatigable in collecting an armed force to resist the execution

execution of the decree. The keepers of the various prisons, participating in the general dread excited by his name, had refused to receive Robespierre and the other deputies, who were speedily rescued from their guard, and having opened a sitting at the *hotel-de-ville*, outlawed the national convention. After spending much time in debate, which conspirators of only moderate talents would have employed much more effectually, they sent a part of the armed force, and Henriot at their head, to dissolve the convention. But that body, convinced that they were struggling for their lives, had in the time so foolishly wasted by their opponents, concerted measures against them; Legendre had dispersed the Jacobin club, seven deputies were sent into the various parts of the city with a proclamation, explaining the true state of things; a decree of outlawry was passed against the commune, and when Henriot, at the head of his troop, made his appearance in the court-yard of the Tuilleries, they put him *out of the law* also. The effect operated like electricity; his soldiers, panic-struck, refused to obey his orders, and the people demanded his arrestation; confused and abashed, he hastened to the *hotel-de-ville*, and informed his comrades of his ill-success. The convention, seeing the operation of their new engine, proclaimed sentence of outlawry against Robespierre and all his associates, and set a price on their heads. The seven deputies had suc- 28th July. ceeded in raising a party of the armed inhabitants of Paris in their favour, and with these, reinforced by some soldiers, who remained faithful to the national representation, they found themselves able, at about three o'clock in the morning, to march against the commune, having first persuaded the cannoneers at the Quai Pelletier to resist the commands of Henriot, who was now *out of the law*, and to join them. The *hotel-de-ville* might have made a powerful resistance, and perhaps have turned the tide of success; but

but the soldiers of the national guard, hearing that the commune and the deputies there assembled were outlawed, refused obedience; the cannoneers were differently disposed, but the curious mob had obtained possession of the gun-carriages, and used them as ladders to enable them to look into the windows of the *hotel-de-ville*, to see how the conspirators behaved in this emergency. Bourdon de l'Oise, having read to the people the proclamation of outlawry, rushed into the *hotel-de-ville*, armed with a sabre and pistols, and followed by a considerable force. The discomfited confederates were most of them taken on the spot, a few escaped, but were speedily brought to justice.

His second arrestation. Robespierre was found in one of the apartments of the *hotel-de-ville*, sitting squat against a wall with a knife in his hand, apparently intended for the purpose of self-destruction, but which he durst not use. A soldier who found him, apprehending some resistance, fired two pistols at him, one of which wounded him on the head, the other broke his under jaw; he was taken and conducted before the committee of general security in a Morocco-covered arm-chair, his broken jaw bound up with a cloth, passed under his chin, and tied at the top of his head. As he was carried along in this condition, he rested his chin on a handkerchief which he held in his right hand, while the elbow was supported by his left. A message was sent to the convention to know if he should be brought to the bar, but the members unanimously exclaimed that they would no more suffer their hall to be polluted by the presence of such a monster. He lay for some hours in an anti-chamber of the committee of general security stretched on a table, motionless, apparently insensible of corporeal anguish, though the blood flowed in streams from his eyes, mouth, and nostrils, but torn with racking recollections, and abandoned to remorse, he pinched his thighs with convulsive agony,

agony, and scowled gloomily around the room, when he fancied himself unobserved. After enduring, in this situation, the taunts of all who beheld him, he was replaced in the arm-chair, and carried to the hospital, called the *hotel-de-Dieu*, where his wounds were dressed, merely to prolong his existence, and from thence was sent to the prison of the Conciergerie. He was brought before the revolutionary tribunal the same day, together with his accomplices, in number twenty-one; as they were all out of the law, the identification of their persons alone was necessary, and sentence of death was demanded against them by their former friend and creature Fouquier Tainville, the public accuser. In the evening of the same day, at about five o'clock, they were conducted to the place of execution, amidst the acclamations of numerous spectators, who considered the procession before them as the earnest of future happiness. The streets, the windows, and the roofs of the houses were crowded; even the guard who escorted them partook of the general transport; and, which they were never before known to do, joined the cry of *Vive la convention!* A group of women stopped the carts and danced around them to testify their joy.

During this fatal progress, Robespierre, pale and disfigured, held down his head on his breast, and never looked up except once, when a woman, decently dressed, approached the cart and uttered those heart-piercing exclamations, and deep-drawn maledictions, which put it almost beyond conjecture that she was a mother whom his cruelty had deprived of a son, or a widow from whom he had snatched her husband; at hearing her horrible denunciations, Robespierre turned his eyes languidly towards her, and shrugged up his shoulders. He suffered last but one; when he was about to be tied to the fatal plank, the executioner snatched the dressing from his broken jaw, which immediately fell, and a profusion of blood gushed

gushed out; the horrible chasm occasioned by the width of his mouth, owing to this accident, rendered his head, when held up by the executioner, the most terrible and disgusting spectacle which can be imagined '.

Remarks on his fall. Thus perished Maximilian Robespierre, in the thirty-sixth year of his age. His life had been for some time past a perpetual provocation of the thunder of the Omnipotent; and his death afforded, in all its circumstances, a most ample vindication of eternal justice. He was cut off in the prime of life, and at the height of unexpected exaltation meditating new crimes, and unrepentant of those he had already committed. He who had shed blood with unexampled profusion, went to the scaffold covered with his own blood; he who had banished from France the sentiment of humanity, was in his last hour overwhelmed with insult, reproach, scorn, and cruelty; he whose life had been a scene of the most atrocious perfidy and ingratitude, died renounced by all mankind, and his death was called for by a man he himself had put into office, and on whom he relied as a friend; he who had abrogated every form of jurisprudential proceeding, was led to execution without the ceremony of a trial. Even the minuter circumstances of his fate were not without a moral. In the prison of the Conciergerie, could he avoid thinking of the persecuted queen whom he had so long shut up there? Must not the sight of the guillotine have conjured up to his imagination an immense crowd of innocent victims, with his murdered sovereigns at their head, clamouring to heaven for vengeance? It is even worthy of observation, that the coat he wore when he was thus called before his

---

' For the account of Robespierre's decline and fall, with all the antecedent and attendant circumstances, see Conspiracy of Robespierre; Debates; Miss Williams's Letters in 1794, vol. iii. p. 158. 168, et seq.; Page, vol. ii. p. 201 to 223; New Annual Register for 1794, p. 369 to 381; Necker on the Revolution, vol. ii. p. 35 to 44.; Playfair's History of Jacobinism, p. 680 to 699.

Maker,

Maker, with "his crimes full blown, and all his imperfections on his head," was the same he had worn when wantonly and sacrilegiously he obtruded himself into his sacred presence, and profaned the land where christianity had been professed, with a mock-festival.

The person of Robespierre was short and puny, and he was of a tender constitution. His complexion was livid and cadaverous, his features harsh and forbidding. The smile of confidence never rested on his lips, but they were almost always contracted by the sour grin of envy aiming to appear disdain. His eye was dead and sunk, except when his irascible propensities were aroused by opposition or the desire of vengeance, and then his look assumed a ferocity so singular, as to lead an accurate observer to compare his general aspect to that of the cat-tyger. Reserved in his temper, and rarely addicted to excess, he never was betrayed into any of those weak efforts of confidence which arise from an unreserved indulgence in love and friendship, and very seldom into those which result from conviviality. His dissimulation was excessive; and he was so apprehensive of the sentiments of his mind being read in his eyes, that he commonly wore green spectacles, and, on some occasions, covered his eyes with his hands. Ever desirous of admiration, he would not, even when the rage of equality was at its greatest pitch, degrade himself by assuming the blue pantaloon, red cap, and dirty linen; on the contrary, though the word *muscadin* was a term of proscription, he was always well dressed, and sometimes elegantly. Though forbid by nature to riot in the excesses of sensual enjoyment, he was ambitious, even to coquetry, of being admired by the fair sex; and succeeded so far that they were amongst his most zealous partisans. In the earlier part of his life he was supple, insinuating, and complaisant, but latterly uncontrolled power had carried the ferocity of his temper

His person, manners, and abilities.

temper to the excess of unrestrained violence in speech. Whoever contradicted or displeased him was assailed with the coarest invective; an indecorum which, acting on Gallic sensibility, probably increased the rage of his enemies, and accelerated his fall. Of the extent and nature of his abilities, his life affords a sufficient display. Condorcet estimated them justly when he said, "The French revolution is a religion, in which Robespierre is the leader of a sect; he has all the characteristics, not of the founder of a religion, but the leader of a schism." He possessed considerable vigour of mind, though not sufficient to entitle him to a comparison with Cromwell. His eloquence has been already noticed; its characteristic is elegance rather than closeness of reasoning; he had improved very much from the time of his coming to Paris as a deputy; his enemies, therefore, chose to characterise him by his earlier efforts, rather than those made at a more advanced period. He is described, in the New Annual Register, as being more a statesman than an orator*; I think exactly the reverse: his ideas on negro emancipation, on the penalty of death, on subsistence, and in almost every other particular where he affected to legislate, will sufficiently prove that his rhetoric was superior to his judgment. His ingratitude, and the facility and indifference with which he abandoned, and even sacrificed his friends and former coadjutors, were his constant characteristics. His want of personal courage was remarkable, and bore an exact proportion to his savage and unrelenting cruelty. He was disinterested to a certain degree; that is to say, without children, without affections, he took no pleasure in the sordid folly of amassing unnecessary wealth; but in his life he maintained much more splendor and elegance than a man without patrimony or employment could derive

* For 1794, p. 283.

from

from the salary allowed to a deputy; and though he did not outrage decency by a display of inordinate luxury, he lived in a style equal to his exaltation in other respects. His self-denial in matters of sensuality, arising from the formation of his person, and made conspicuous by an affectation of austerity, procured him the name of Cato; after his fall he was denominated Catiline, and has been compared to Cromwell; but he is not worthy to associate with either character[t]. He owed his elevation to accident rather than design, and lost it through his vanity, treachery, and cowardice. His vanity and treachery made him, thinking himself all-sufficient, destroy his only friends; his cowardice rendered him incapable of those exertions which might have turned the impending storm on the heads of his adversaries. His conduct in the great crisis which decided his fate was astonishingly weak and imprudent. When he went to the convention on the 26th of July, he was well apprised of the party which was formed against him, yet he omitted his customary precautions; he had not prepared the tribunes to applaud his speech; he had appointed no clamorous *sans-culottes* to drown the voices of his opponents; no armed ruffians to terrify them in their approach to and passage from the hall. On the 27th, though he must have known that the manner in which his cause was taken up at the Jacobins would bring the contest to an issue, no preparations were made; even his own party were uninstructed how to act. St. Just, uncalled, began a speech in the tribune, which rendered the opposing party furious; Robespierre's adherents out of doors were unprepared; the voice of ru-

[t] For descriptions of his person and manners, and remarks on his character, see Roland's Appeal, vol. i. p. 58.; Moore's Journal, vol. i. p. 338. vol. ii. p. 239; Pagès, vol. ii. p. 17. 21, 22.; New Annual Register for 1794, p. 381, 382, 383.; Necker on the Revolution, vol. ii. p. 37. 39.; Etat de la France, p. 11. 15, 16.; Garat's Memoirs, p. 226.

mour

mour was the alarm-bell of the Jacobins; and, when they were affembled, the armed force was yet to provide, and yet to feduce. This furprifing want of forefight proves that Robefpierre owed his elevation to accident and the operations of others, and that he was deficient in the genius, courage, and conduct requifite to form an illuftrious chief of a party.

APPENDIX.

No. I.

The KING's LETTER *to the* NATIONAL ASSEMBLY, *when required to sanction certain Articles of the Constitution; read the 5th October 1789.*

Gentlemen,

NEW constitutional laws can only be properly judged of by being acquainted with the whole of them; for in so great and important a work, every part is connected intimately with the whole. It appears, however, to me natural that, at a time when we invite the nation to come to the assistance of the state by a signal act of its confidence and patriotism, we should assure it of our attention to the principal object of its interest. So on the persuasion that the first articles of the constitution which you have presented to me, when added to the rest of your labours, will fulfil the desire of the people, and insure the happiness and prosperity of the kingdom, I grant, according to your desire, my consent to these articles; but under the express condition, from which I mean never to depart, that by the general result of your deliberations, the executive power shall be wholly lodged in the hands of the monarch. A series of facts and observations, a particular account of which shall be presented to you, will convince you that, in the present state of affairs, I cannot insure either the raising of the legal imposts, or the free communication of provision, or the individual safety of the citizens. It is my wish to fulfil these essential duties of royalty. The happiness of my subjects, the public tranquillity, and the

maintenance

maintenance of social order depend upon it: I therefore demand that we should, in common, level all the obstacles that may cross the execution of so desirable and necessary an end.

You cannot but be sensible that the existing institutions and judicial forms ought to undergo no change till they are replaced by the new order of things; I have therefore no need to make any observations on this head.

It remains that I should frankly assure you, that though I consent to the different articles of the constitution which you have offered, it is not that all of them without distinction present to me the idea of perfection, but because I do not think it advisable to delay acceding to the present wish of the national deputies, and to the pressure of those alarming circumstances which so powerfully invites us to wish, above all, for the immediate re-establishment of peace, order, and confidence. I make no remarks on your declaration of the rights of man and a citizen; it contains some excellent maxims, very proper to regulate your labours; but principles susceptible of different applications, and even interpretations, cannot be justly appreciated, neither do they require being so, till their true meaning is fixed by those laws to which they serve as the base.

No. II.

Letter from M. BERTRAND DE MOLEVILLE *to the* PRESIDENT OF THE NATIONAL CONVENTION, *containing a Defence of* THE KING.

Mr. President,

I HAD the honour of announcing, in my last letter, that I should, without delay, address to you an exact declaration of all the important and unknown facts with which I am acquainted, and which have any relation to the present circumstances. I am the more eager to fulfil this engagement, since I learn, from the public papers, that the great question, Whether Louis the Sixteenth ought to be tried?

tried? is at prefent open for difcuffion; and that the national convention are difpofed to receive lights and proofs from every quarter on that momentous fubject. I flatter myfelf it will receive with fatisfaction thofe I now have the honour of addreffing to you, becaufe I am firmly convinced that it feeks nothing but truth, and defires nothing but juftice. This conviction alone is fufficient to allay the inquietudes of good citizens, and to keep up the hopes of thofe who, having had opportunities of nearly obferving the conduct of Lewis the Sixteenth, and of knowing his virtues, cannot help taking a great intereft in his misfortunes.

The following then are the facts, the truth of which I atteft, and of which I can either give or point out proofs.

On the pretended favours and affiftance given to the emigrants.

It is publifhed in all the journals and all the pamphlets, and has been repeated a thoufand times from the tribune, that the *king* always approved of and favoured emigration. This opinion, unfupported by proof, has become general in the kingdom, and is the principal motive of the regicide addreffes daily received.

Towards the end of October 1791, one of the minifters having informed the king, in full council, of a report generally circulated, that the emigrants in arms againft France, and particularly the body guards, were in the pay of the civil lift; " This (replied the king, in the firmeft tone) is " an egregious calumny; for I have, on the contrary, " given the moft exprefs orders to M. de la Porte, that " none fhould receive pay but thofe who were able to " fhew the certificate required by the decree of laft July " (1791). I am certain this order is put in execution. " It was propofed to me to make an exception in favour " of the *gardes du corps*, but I refufed."

Notwithftanding this order, the exiftence of which can be attefted by many deputies to whom it was originally communicated, and which muft have been found among the papers of M. de Septeuil, they have continued to give out that the emigrated *gardes du corps* were paid by the civil lift: and this is affirmed as certain, in the 10th and 11th pages of the report made to the affembly at the fitting of the 27th of September laft. The reporter was not aware, that the only writings cited by him in fupport of his affertion, clearly demouftrate its falfehood. The firft is a memorial

memorial found in the king's writing-desk, in which M. de Poix proposed the paying the whole corps of *gardes du corps* up to the 1st of January 1792. If the king had approved this proposal, he would have affixed his assent to the memorial, and sent it to the intendant of the civil list. Thus from the circumstance alone of this memorial being found in the king's writing-desk, without any mark of his approbation, is a complete proof that the payment proposed by M. de Poix had not been ordered by the king. As to those orders of payment signed by the king at the bottom of the general lists of the four companies of his guards, it is sufficient to compare those lists with the registers of payments, to be convinced that in reality only those of the *gardes du corps*, who proved their residence according to the form prescribed by the decree, were paid; and that if the ordinance lists contained all the names, it proceeded entirely from an ignorance of who had and who had not emigrated. For the same reason, the ministers of war and marine, in their respective departments, regulated in a similar manner the general lists of the officers of the different corps, without violating the decree concerning the certificates of residence, because its execution was always guaranteed by the vigilance and personal responsibility of the treasurers, conformably to the regulations of this decree. It is also proved by a letter of M. de Poix, in the 16th page of the thirteenth collection of papers found in the house of M. de la Porte, that the execution of these orders for payment of the *gardes du corps* was so much retarded, that on the 28th of last January there had been nothing paid of the arrears due for the first six months of 1791.

Were I now to cite the letters written by the king, in the beginning of October 1791, to the officers of the army and of the corps of marines, to induce those who had left the kingdom to return, and to retain those who had intended to emigrate, I should undoubtedly be told, that these letters being the works of the ministers, no conclusion could be drawn from them: but I declare, that the minute written to the officers of marine remained two days in the king's possession, who with his own hand made many corrections in it, some in the margin, others interlined; and this minute, with many other important papers, must have been found in a red port-folio, which the commissioners of the committee of *surveillance de la commune* carried away from my house with my other papers.

pers. I must presume that this writing has been suppressed, since there is no mention made of it in the report made to the assembly the 6th of this month. It would, however, be of the more importance to produce this paper, because the corrections in it being the king's own, the free and pure expression of his sentiments may there be found. I have no doubt, therefore, but the national convention feels the necessity of ordering that paper to be searched for and produced.

The king expressly commanded me to employ, in his name, every method of persuasion and authority to prevent the emigration of the officers of marine; and if the execution of this order had not all the success I could have desired, I at least used every exertion in my power, and am not afraid on this point to call upon the testimony of the chief clerks of my office. I cannot indeed quote many written proofs, but shall mention one of sufficient weight to render any other unnecessary from me.

A superior officer of the most distinguished merit, having been forced by frequent outrages to give up his command, came to Paris last February with the intention of leaving the kingdom. After having in vain attempted by my advice and exhortations to dissuade him from his purpose, I mentioned the affair to the king, who authorised me to send him an order, couched almost in similar terms with the old *lettres de cachet*. The words follow:

"Sir,
"Being informed that your knowledge and experience
"enable you to give important information concerning
"the marine service, my pleasure is, that you hold your-
"self in readiness to furnish the minister of that depart-
"ment with the informations he may require from you.
"On this account I prohibit you from leaving Paris until
"further order, under pain of disobedience.
                    (Signed)   "Louis.
           (And under,)   " De Bertrand."

The minutes of this order, addressed to M. de Marigni, should be found in my office, (*bureau des officiers,*) amongst the minutes of the month of February. If it has been accidentally withdrawn, M. de Marigni, who has not left Paris, will produce the original.

I must here declare, that amongst the officers whom I persuaded to stay at Paris to insure their not leaving the kingdom

kingdom, there were some unable to support themselves; to whom the king ordered different sums of money to be paid, sometimes by me, at other times by M. de la Pore' The last which was sent to me by the king for this purpose was the sum of 12,000 livres, in the beginning of March 1792. If the national convention be desirous minutely to examine this matter, I can point out to whom the money was given.

How then is it possible to reconcile the reproaches which are thrown out against the king, relative to the emigrants, with all these facts, none of which can be disputed?

On the treasons and conspiracies in which it is pretended the king had a share.

These names certainly cannot be given to the measures, always weak and insufficient, taken for the personal security of the king; and of which he never failed to prevent the effect, when he observed the avowed assassins accompanied by a party of the people; because while surrounded by them he was always confident that he had no danger to fear. We saw him, on the 20th of June, remove from his person those faithful servants who were ready to spill the last drop of their blood in his defence, and present himself, accompanied by four national guards, to the armed multitude who had come to force open the gates of the palace.

It is impossible at this day to doubt that a formidable conspiracy was formed against the court. The deputies *Louvet* and *Barbaroux* arrived, and attested this important fact in the tribune, in the sitting of the 30th of October. " It was at Charenton (said they) that the conspiracy " against the court was fixed to be executed, on the 29th " of July, but which did not take place until the 10th of " August." (Moniteur of the 1st of November, p. 1298, col. 3.) The king having been informed of this, did undoubtedly take some precautions to defend the palace from the impending attack: but as soon as he knew, from the members of the directory of the department, that thousands of the citizens and national guards had joined the conspirators who surrounded the palace, he did not hesitate to deliver himself and family to the national assembly, leaving orders for the Swiss not to fire*. It is indeed certain,

* When the king had determined to deliver himself up to the assembly, he spoke to the ministers and others who were around him

these

tain, that the gates of the court royal were forced without any resistance on the part of the Swifs, who did not fire until five of their companions had been massacred at the bottom of the great stairs. The events of the 10th of August can, no more than those of the 20th of June, furnish the slightest cause of accusation against the king. It is therefore necessary to look for proofs in his conduct prior to these periods. But it is impossible, with any share of candour, to form conclusions against him from letters, memorials, or plans, addressed to him, and which were found, or said to be found, either in the palace or the house of M. de la Porte. If treasonable or criminal writings could involve the persons to whom they are addressed, the lives of the most innocent and most virtuous of mankind would always be in the power of the most wicked.

With regard to the numerous writings, the impressions of which were paid out of the civil list, and which are quoted as so many proofs of treason, it is sufficient to remark, that before the abolition of royalty, the anti-republican writings were so much the less reprehensible, that at the memorable sitting of the 7th of July last, the assembly decreed unanimously, and by acclamation, that those who should propose a republican government, or the establishment of two chambers, should be devoted to public execration. The violent writers on both sides were indeed equally distant from the spirit and principles of the con-

---

these memorable, though too little known words: "Let us depart, gentlemen; there is nothing for us to do here." This was certainly giving the clearest and most positive order to stay no longer at the palace, since nothing was to be done there. And if this order had (as it ought) been officially conveyed to the Swifs officers and guards, they would have all retired; the entry to the palace would have been left open; and though perhaps it might have been demolished, yet not a musket would have been fired, or a drop of blood shed. Unfortunately this order was not conveyed to the Swifs. From thence it followed, on the one hand, that the Swifs, the national guards, and all those who had repaired to the palace to defend the king, believed he was only anxious about his personal safety, and complained that he had abandoned them; while, on the other, the people believed that the king, at his departure, had ordered the resistance and firing which happened. Such is the origin of the suspicions and clamours against the pretended treasons of the king, and the conspiracies of the court. These details are corroborated by so many ocular witnesses, that it is impossible I can ever call their truth in question. They prove that the reproaches against the king are not better founded on one side than on the other.

stitution,

stitution; and their incendiary productions supported and maintained the agitation of the people. It was incumbent on the king to turn his attention to the serious inconveniences which must have resulted from hence. Obliged by his oath to maintain the constitution by every possible means, his authority and his duty prompted him to choose as one of those means, the instructing of the people by prudent constitutional writings, which might operate as antidotes to the dangerous pamphlets daily published. It is, however certain, that both my colleagues and myself considered it as our duty to give this advice to the king, and accordingly we did often give it. Thus it is very possible such an order was given to the intendant of the civil list. As to the method in which it was executed, every body must be sensible the king could not possibly enter into all the detail of the business. Besides, it is an established principle, that the most culpable execution of a lawful order can never involve the person who gives that order, but only him who executes it. An order to distribute prudent and constitutional writings was certainly legal. The king had the right of giving such an order, and he assuredly gave no other. But the following facts personally concern the king, and from them we can judge of his true sentiments.

First Fact.

I shewed the greatest reluctance to accept the ministry, and I cannot deny that my principal reason for this reluctance was my uncertainty of the real sentiments of the king relative to the constitution. He was informed of this; and when I was presented to him on the 3d of October, by the minister of the home department, he addressed me in his presence, in the very words which follow:

" I know your uneasiness, and do not blame your desiring
" to know how it is expected that you should conduct
" yourself. I now inform you, that I do not pretend to
" consider the constitution as unexceptionable. I am even
" convinced, that had not the assembly prohibited the
" receiving my observations, it would have adopted the
" principal alterations which I would have proposed. But
" that is now over. I have accepted the constitution in
" its present form. The general opinion is in its favour;
" we can, therefore, no longer think of changes until ex-
" perience shall make us feel the necessity of them; for
" force

" force can do nothing againſt opinion. The ſucceſs of
" this experience depends upon the fidelity with which
" the conſtitution is carried into execution ; and it is my
" intention to execute it as completely and as well as
" poſſible. Such, then, is the line of conduct I have
" marked out for *myſelf*, and I require my miniſters not
" to depart from it. If the means for carrying it into
" execution may appear inſufficient, or if they experience
" embarraſſments, let them appeal to the aſſembly."

The queen, to whom I was preſented the ſame day, ſpoke to the ſame purpoſe; and concluded with ſaying, " Obſerve the plan the king has adopted ; I think it is " the only reaſonable one, and hope you will not make " him change it."

I affirm this fact upon my honour and conſcience, and will ſupport the affirmation with my oath, which I offer to renew before whatever perſon, and in whatever form the aſſembly ſhall think proper to preſcribe. Upon my return home, I immediately made a memorandum of what the king and queen had ſaid. The memorandum dated the 3d of October, was in the ſame red port-folio which the commiſſioners of the committee *de ſurveillance de la commune* carried away. If the national convention think proper to order that it ſhould be ſearched for, it will not be difficult to have it laid before them.

SECOND FACT.

Towards the end of December laſt, or the beginning of January, an old officer, retired from the ſervice, came to conſult me, at the office of marine, upon a propoſal which had been made to him the evening before, to enter into an aſſociation with ſome gentlemen to eſcort the king, who intended, as they ſaid, ſoon to leave the kingdom. The perſon who made this propoſal to him, introduced himſelf at his houſe under the title of a marechal-de-camp, and gave him twenty-four hours to reflect on the ſubject. I adviſed the perſon who gave me this information to ſhew a diſpoſition to join the aſſociation, provided they would explain to him the whole of their plan, their means of executing it, and inform him of the perſons who were engaged in it. I expreſsly enjoined him to forget nothing they might tell him, and particularly to make himſelf acquainted with the name and reſidence of this marechal-decamp. He promiſed ſoon to acquaint me with the reſult of his second conversation. He accordingly gave me, the very next day, a detached account of what passed. I took an exact memorandum of it, which I read the same night at the council. The king was full of indignation, and ordered the minister of the home department immediately to denounce the association to the directory of the department, and to enjoin him to make every possible search after this pretended marechal-de-camp, to watch him narrowly, and even to seize his person, if there should be occasion. As this letter was instantly written by M. Cahier de Gerville, and sent directly after the council, it is possible that he did not keep a memorandum of it; but the original may be easily found among the papers of the directory of the department. The inquiries ordered by the king were carefully made. They discovered the usual residence of this man, but he had concealed himself in such a manner, that it was not possible to seize him. It appeared, moreover, by the accounts obtained at the police office concerning him, that he was a worthless, wrongheaded fellow. But whatever truth there is in this, the conduct of the king in this affair proves, at least, that he did not favour associations formed under pretence of consulting his personal safety.

THIRD FACT.

In January last, M. Cahier de Gerville, reading in the council a rough draught of a proclamation, the *king* interrupted him at the expression " *the love of my people*," and desired him to correct it by inserting the words " the " love of the *French people*. I can no longer," added he, with emotion, and his eyes swelled with tears, " I can no " longer say *my* people! but they cannot prevent that " from being the expression of my heart."

This interesting fact can be attested by the ministers who then composed the council; and I require all those who have been in it, either before or since, to declare whether they did not observe, in many instances, that one of the most prevailing sentiments with the king, was that of a most tender and affectionate attachment to the French people. It is not yet forgotten, that on the day of his arrival from Varennes, one of the principal officers of his houshold, expressing his regret at the ill success of that expedition, and particularly at the increase of credit and power which it would give to the assembly, the king immediately

diately made this remarkable anfwer, " So much the
" better, a thoufand times; fo much the better, provided
" it conduces to the happinefs of my people."

Fourth Fact.

At the fitting of the 6th of this month, the reporter
Valazé read a note found in my houfe, concerning a new
order of knighthood, called that of the *queen*; and in
order to give this writing (which juftly excited the rifi-
bility of the affembly) more importance, he faid it was
found in my port-folio. The reporter Valazé is miftaken;
and if the affembly will order the verbal proeefs, which
took place at the examination of my papers, to be looked
into, it will appear that this writing was not found in any
of my port-folios, but in a different place, which I fhall
not name. It would have been difficult to have read it,
had they not feparated it from a letter which was inclofed
under the fame feal. This letter, dated the beginning of
September or October 1790, was nearly in the following
terms:

" I fend you the note which I mentioned the day
" before yefterday. I muft forewarn you, that I had it
" from one whofe fancy is a little exalted; fo you may
" believe what you pleafe of it."

The place in which it was found proves that I had
formed the fame judgment concerning it with the national convention.

The members of the committee *de Surveillance de la
commune*, who fpent nine hours in examining thefe papers,
found alfo a lift of an Auftrian committee, compofed of
about thirty fictitious names. They were eager to feize
that writing, which they at firft confidered as a moft important difcovery. Fortunately, however, the key to thofe
names was written in the fecond column of the fame page,
and contained the names of M. M. Syéyes, Condorcet,
Briffot, Robefpierre, &c. &c. But had this key been
written upon a different fheet, and could they have as
eafily feparated it from this lift as they did the note concerning the order of *Chevalier de la Reine*, from the letter
above mentioned, they might then have employed the lift
as a ftrong proof of the exiftence of an Auftrian committee.

Such then are the facts which I thought it incumbent
on me to make known to the affembly. Their accuracy

will be established by the proofs which I cite, which can be verified by the witnesses whom I point out. I should have had a much greater number to present, if the catastrophe of the month of September had not driven from France, or destroyed, the persons who could have attested the truth.

(Signed)   De Bertrand.

No. III.

Denunciation of Prevarications committed in the Trial of Louis XVI. *addressed to the* National Convention, *by* M. Bertrand de Moleville, *Minister of State in France.*

M. President,

I denounce to the national convention, to the people of France, and to all Europe, the odious prevarications which have taken place in the trial of Louis XVI. of which I shall here point out the proofs, in order to have justice administered against the guilty.

In the course of last month, I sent papers for the defence of Louis XVI. to the *garde du sçeau*, with formal requisition to have them delivered to the king. I thought that the surest means of having them conveyed to their sacred destination, was to address them to that minister of justice. I accordingly wrote the following letter to him:

" Sir,

" As it is one of the most sacred duties of a minister of
" justice to protect those who are under accusation, and to
" secure to them every means of clearing their innocence,
" I address these papers to you, solemnly requesting that
" they may be delivered into the hands of Louis XVI.
" As the king's ancient minister, I feel not only autho-
" rized, but obliged in duty to point out those circum-
" stances during my administration, that tend to overset
" the principal articles of the accusation brought against
" him. Such is the object of my demand; and you must
" be

APPENDIX, No. III.

"be fenfible, Sir, that you cannot reject it, without fhew-
"ing yourfelf the accomplice of one of the moſt atrocious
"crimes of which there is any example."

A few days afterwards, I fent under cover to the fame miniſter a packet for M. de Maleſherbes, intitled, "Papers for the juſtification of Louis XVI." I wrote at the fame time to advertife M. de Maleſherbes of my fending them as above mentioned to the *garde du fçeau*, and requiring that he fhould afk them from that miniſter.

I am this day informed, that when, in confequence of that letter, M. de Maleſherbes went himfelf to claim thefe packets, he was anfwered by the miniſter of juſtice, that, on finding they contained papers for the juſtification of Louis XVI. he had thought himfelf obliged to fend them to the national convention.

I muſt obferve here, that the conduct of the miniſter of juſtice upon this occafion is of a piece with the barbarous practice of the keepers and jailors of prifons under the ancient government, in fending all letters or papers addreſſed to the prifoner, to the magiſtrate fuperintending the prifons. There was then, however, one fure means of having letters, &c. remitted to the prifoner, namely, by addreſſing them directly to that magiſtrate. Nevertheleſs the conſtituent aſſembly, juſtly indignant at the flowneſs of this means, and the inhumanity of thefe precautions, formally abolifhed this cuſtom by the new criminal code. It decreed, that the prifoner fhould not only receive all papers and memorials which might aſſiſt in their defence, but that a copy of their indictment, and of the procedure, fhould be given them in twenty-four hours after it was demanded, either by themfelves or their counfel. But when I folemnly addrefs myfelf to the miniſter fpecially appointed to maintain the execution of this law, he does not fcruple to infringe it, under pretence that he has no communication with the prifoner.

If fuch a pretext is admitted, every law made for the protection of the accufed may be equally violated by his judges themfelves, as there is not one of them who has any communication with the prifoner.

The conduct of the miniſter of juſtice is ſtill more unjuſtifiable with regard to M. de Maleſherbes. Could he poſſibly imagine it was his duty to deprive the defender of Louis XVI. of papers fent for his client's juſtification? So that the fuperfcription which I wrote upon the packet, as a security for its being delivered, was exactly what determined the minister of justice not only to keep it up from M. de Malesherbes, but to send it to the very committee which conducted the process against the king.

Could we suppose a legal court of assassins, what conduct could more naturally be expected from the principal agent of such a court, than to deliver the papers transmitted to him for the defence of the accused, into the hands of the accusers?

I submit the above considerations to the justice of the national convention, and shall proceed in my statement of facts.

M. de Malesherbes went to the committee, and claimed the packets. He found that both had been opened; they contained printed and written papers. The printed papers were delivered to him; but he was informed that he could not have the others without an order from the convention. A member of the committee went with the papers to the convention to demand this order. He returned, and told M. de Malesherbes, that, upon his demand, the assembly had passed to the order of the day. The member did not bring back the papers, he left them on the bureau.

M. de Malesherbes asked what means he could take to obtain these papers? The members of the committee looked at each other, but nobody answered him.

The striking injustice of refusing to allow M. de Malesherbes so much as to read those papers, must be imputed to the ignorance or guilt of some inferior agent of the committee; for certainly none of its members would have been accessory to such illegal conduct.

I am equally convinced that the assembly would not have passed to the order of the day, on the demand of M. de Malesherbes, had the nature of the request been clearly represented. The fact however is, that those intrusted with the king's defence were obliged to make it without the assistance of these papers. Unfortunately they were not the only papers which were kept up; for it is known, that when the papers in the king's cabinet were seized and carried away, none of the formalities which the law exacts, and the particulars can loudly called for, were used to prevent subtraction, alteration, or substitution; of course none of those papers can, with the least colour of law or justice, be produced against the king; yet they are produced

duced and urged against him, as if all those formalities had been observed; and besides, a collection, falsely called complete, of the papers found in his majesty's cabinet, was, by orders of the committee, printed, and profusely distributed over the kingdom; but this collection, so far from being complete, consisted only of such papers as admitted of malignant interpretations, which were with much assiduity given to them, enforced and illustrated by calumnious notes. It is to be hoped, that, the authors of these notes are not of the number of the king's judges, no more than those deputies who have betrayed such a thirst for the king's blood, that they have anticipated their votes for his death by printing and publishing their opinions. According to the laws of all civilised countries, a judge who condemns a person accused, without having heard his defence, thereby loses the right of finally judging him, and is considered as on the same footing with the accusers. Were it possible to suppose that this law could be violated in the case of Louis XVI. the French nation, fired with indignation against such flagrant injustice, would undoubtedly rise like one man, and pour vengeance on the base infringers of a principle so self-evident and sacred. Trusting to the justice of the national convention, I demand that the papers for the justification of Louis XVI. which I send under cover to the minister of justice, may be remitted to the king's defenders; and as to the papers found in the king's cabinet, but which the authors of the printed collection thought it expedient to suppress, I can, from my own certain knowledge, only point out the following:

1st, A copy of a letter to the king from three deputies of the legislative assembly, of great influence, dated in the month of July last. This letter contained a prediction of the 10th of August; and the recall of Servan, Claviere, and Roland, was proposed as the only means of preventing that catastrophe. As I saw the king in public only after my retreat from the ministry, I had not an opportunity of reading the letter myself, but I was informed of its contents by persons who have read it. I shall name these persons, and likewise the deputies, as soon as the proofs shall be taken into consideration, and the witnesses in favour of the king are to be heard, according to the indispensable form in all criminal causes.

The letter of those three deputies may at least serve to prove, that the torrents of blood shed on the 10th of August

gust ought not to be attributed to Louis XVI. but to the faction who wished to dethrone him, in order that Servan, Claviere, and Roland might be recalled to administration. Thyerry, the king's first *valet de chambre*, who received the letter from them, and delivered it to the king, was afterwards assassinated, though he was absent from the palace on the 10th of August.

2d, A copy of a plan, consisting of twenty one articles, secretly agreed on at Mantua, in the month of May 1791, by the emperor Leopold; the object of which was the re-establishment of the king's ancient and legal authority. For this end the emperor proposed to enter France with his army, in the beginning of the month of July following, a period in which neither our armies nor frontiers were in a state of defence.

The king alone could have prevented the execution of this plan, and he did prevent it. All exacted from him was his consent, which was to be kept secret. He refused this, without consulting any body; he needed no advice when the tranquillity of his people was at stake; and he saw that this plan could not be executed without bloodshed.

The two only ministers who had knowledge of these facts, and of an infinity of others equally important for the king's justification, were Messrs. Montmorin and de Lessart, who unfortunately have both perished. It is difficult to attribute to chance either the selection of the victims sacrificed on the 2d of September, or that of the king's papers which have been suppressed. However that may be, if Leopold's plan is not found, I shall, as soon as the king's process is commenced, name three persons who had a complete knowledge of all the particulars of that plan, and can ascertain the contents in as satisfactory a manner as if the original plan itself were laid before the convention.

3d, A journal written by the king himself for his own private use, containing every thing of consequence he has done since he ascended the throne; his projects, views, and even the faults he has to reproach himself with, are there inserted. This journal, which may be considered as a faithful picture of Louis XVI. drawn by himself only, would be a most interesting part of the intended process. Even in the faults with which he reproaches himself, his virtues, and uniform attachment to his people, would evidently appear.

That

That this journal was amongst the king's papers, is proved by a letter which M. de Malesherbes has just received from M. de Liancourt.

These, Sir, are the facts on which I call for the animadversion of the national convention, and the attention of all Europe; and for this purpose I have thought it my duty to render this application as public as possible, by confiding it in the hands of the lord mayor of London, and directing it to be published in the newspapers. And I now solemnly call on you, Sir, as president, to communicate it to the convention, otherwise you become personally answerable for the consequences of those important facts remaining unknown to them.

(Signed) De Bertrand.

No. IV.

Jean Silvain Bailly, *to his Fellow-citizens.*

I was summoned as a witness on the trial of Marie Antoinette; I found myself named and inculpated in the act of accusation directed against her. In the course of my deposition, I was interrogated respecting the events of the 17th of July at the *Champ de Mars*; I was also questioned respecting my connections with la Fayette and la Rochefoucault. It was suggested that I had had criminal relations with the *ci-devant* court; and I was asked concerning certain secret meetings said to have been held at the castle. My answers, satisfactory as they were, could only be heard by the citizens present at the trial.

He who has occupied an important post owes to the people an account of his conduct in the exercise of those functions with which they have intrusted him. I am going, therefore, at present to discharge the duty.

The act of accusation against Marie Antoinette contained the following passage: " It is manifest, from the " declarations of Louis Charles Capet, and of the girl
" Capet,

APPENDIX, No. IV.

"Capet, that la Fayette, a favourite, *in every sense of the word* *, of the widow Capet, and Bailly, then mayor, were present at the flight from the palace of the Thuilleries; and that they favoured it with all their power." It is false, that I was at the Thuilleries on the day of the 20th of June. It is false, that I in any manner facilitated the flight of Louis's family. It is true, on the contrary, that I did every thing in my power to prevent it.

Upon being informed of the declaration made by young Louis and his sister, I requested the president of the tribunal to demand of the accused, 1st, At what hour she and Louis left the Thuilleries on the 20th of June? 2dly, If I were present? The president replied, that the accused had in her examination anticipated my questions, by declaring, 1st, That they had set off between eleven and twelve o'clock at night; and 2dly, That I was not present. Thus the testimony of the mother overthrew that of the children.

For several months it had been rumoured, that the flight of Louis was at hand. I had constantly transmitted to the committee of research all the information that I received. These rumours were renewed on the 19th and 20th. I had been for seventeen days ill of a quinsey, from which I was beginning to recover. On the evening of Monday I received fresh information, which induced me to send for three of the nearest municipal officers to my house, that I might not have to decide alone on the exigencies of the moment.

I sent for the commander in chief of the national guards; and in the meanwhile dressed myself at all events. The citizen Cochon de l'Apparent, at that time member of the constituent assembly and of the committee of research, came to communicate to me what he knew: he was witness to what passed at my house, and can give testimony of my conduct. Upon the arrival of the commander in chief, we communicated to him the information which we had received, and the apprehension which we

---

* Any one would conclude from this expression, that la Fayette was very much in the queen's good graces. She could not endure him, and often used to say to her friends, "Must I always have that coxcomb before my eyes?" I have this anecdote from persons of veracity. Recourse was had to la Fayette only because he was commander of the national guard, and might have disconcerted their projects.

had entertained. We reminded him that it was his duty to guard the Thuilleries. He answered, that he was going to the palace; that he would give the strictest orders; and that, though he thought the supposed project very improbable, he would take care to prevent the possibility of its execution. La Fayette went in fact to the palace, and returned a little after twelve o'clock to my house. He assured us that all the gates were fast; and that he had himself renewed the watch-word at all the entrances; he added (an expression which I very well remember), that a mouse could not get out of the palace. He further said, that Gouvion, the major-general, would pass the night at the gate of Villequier. These are the facts which are in the knowledge of the persons before-mentioned; besides which, the steward and porter of the house, Jean Baptiste Mousson, my present servant, my former coachman (named Bellanger), François the inspector of the lights, and all those who were in my service on the 20th of June, can attest that I did not leave my house on that day.

Louis and his family, it is well known, travelled with a passport given by Montmorin, for a person named, if I recollect right, the baroness de Kroff. Some days before the flight in looking over my letters, I found that M. Simolin, the Russian ambassador, had applied to me for a passport for the baroness de Kroff. I had some passports ready signed, which were delivered to me by the minister. After a moment's reflection, I said, "But why does the "Russian ambassador desire a passport for a foreigner? "He ought to apply to the minister for foreign affairs." I referred him, therefore, to that minister, and thus escaped, by good fortune, the snare which was laid for me. Montmorin, it is known, declared that he gave two passports, on an assurance that the first was burnt.

It is, therefore, false that I was present at the flight of Louis, and that I favoured with all my power the liberticide project. It is, on the contrary, most indisputable, that I did every thing in my power to prevent it.

I was interrogated respecting certain private meetings said to have been held at the Thuilleries, and composed, as it was asserted, of intriguers and members of the constituent assembly, Mirabeau, Barnave, Lameth, &c.: it seemed that I was supposed to have assisted at them. I affirm that I never had any knowledge of such meetings; that I never assisted at them; that I never was connected with any of those who were considered as party-leaders, such as Mirabeau, Barnave, and the two Lameths; that my connections with la Fayette necessarily resulted from the mutual relation of our offices; that the confidence which I had in him, especially during the first year, was dictated by the whole nation; but that those connections were only official, and that I never possessed his peculiar confidence.

It was asserted that some of their meetings were held at la Rochefoucault's. I answered, that I knew several deputies, and amongst others la Fayette, often met in the evening at the house of la Rochefoucault; but that I was never there myself.

The unfortunate day of the Champ de Mars was mentioned; and it was termed a conspiracy to assassinate the true patriots. The national assembly being informed that mobs were collecting to resist the decree passed the preceding evening, and judging that every appearance of resistance against the law was criminal, ordered the department and the municipality to restrain those mobs by all the means with which the constitution had invested them. The official accounts, which are preserved among the archives of the national assembly, and of the municipality, prove that the municipal body had in the morning employed all the means of persuasion to disperse the multitude.

When the municipality in a body afterwards entered the Champ de la Federation, every one knows the magistrates had not time to make the summonses prescribed by the law; but that the municipality and the national guard were assailed with a shower of stones; that one of the rioters fired a pistol-shot against the municipality; and that the ball, after passing by me, struck the thigh of a dragoon of the troops of the line who had joined the national guards, and who afterwards died of the wound.

It has been said that the authors of these disorders, and of this murder, were not at all connected with the citizens assembled round the altar of their country. But, in fact, the national guard only fired upon the bank from whence the stones and the pistol-shots had proceeded. It is added, that the men who occupied this bank had been sent by la Fayette and me. This accusation is without proof; and it is absolutely false. I make this affirmation as far as regards myself. It is, moreover, evident that if these men had

had been our agents they would doubtlefs have avoided firing on me or on the municipality.

But it is faid, la Fayette was reconciled, in June 1791, with Lameth and the others, and they altogether plotted the downfal of liberty. I know not what plots may have been formed by men with whom I never had any connection. I remarked indeed that reconciliation, and I was furprifed at it; but it cannot be faid that I was reconciled with the Lameths, fince I had neither any quarrel or connection with them. I do not recollect that I have fpoken with either of them for two minutes together fince the revolution. I have never had a continued intercourfe with any of the deputies, unlefs it was what the affairs of the city gave me in the different committees. If la Fayette engaged in any intrigues, he was too well acquainted with my patriotifm to make me his confidant.

With regard to my connections with the court, a circumftance which fully proves my innocence, is, that among the numerous papers belonging to Louis, which were found both at the houfe of la Porte and in the iron clofet, papers in which a great number of perfons are implicated in affairs more or lefs culpable, there is not one which can draw on me the fmalleft reproach. What is more, I am named in fome of thofe papers, but it is as an enemy. Some attack me by farcafm, and endeavour to place me in a ridiculous point of view (fee Cazotte's letters); others, fuch as Talon, fay, " Sire, if you make " fuch facrifices, Bailly will come and make you a fine " harangue." Others fay, and that of the date of 1791, " the mayor of Paris will be managed, fo as to prevent " him from giving us any further trouble." Finally, fome of them talk of the neceffity of taking off my head.

I have gained nothing in the revolution; on the contrary, it has caufed me to lofe fome valuable places; and it has almoft entirely deftroyed my fortune. I have need, my dear fellow-citizens, of your efteem; I am fure that you will fooner or later do me juftice, but I have need of that juftice whilft I am alive and in the midft of you. I had previoufly deferved it by fifty years of continued probity; and my claim cannot but be augmented and confirmed by nearly three years of entire devotion to your interefts, with no other recompence than your efteem.

(Signed)   BAILLY.

No. V.

Letter from CHARLOTTE CORDAY *to* BARBAROUX.

> In the prison of the Abhaye, from the room formerly occupied by Briſſot, the second day of my preparation for peace.

YOU requeſted, citizen, an account of my journey; I will not excuſe you from a detail of the ſlighteſt anecdote. I travelled with good mountaineers, whom I ſuffered to talk as much as they pleaſed, and their diſcourſe, which was as abſurd as their perſons were diſagreeable, contributed not a little to lull me to ſleep. I was not perfectly awake till I came to Paris. One of my fellow-travellers, who undoubtedly is an admirer of ſleepy women, took me for the daughter of one of his old friends, ſuppoſed me poſſeſſed of a fortune which I have not, gave me a name which I had never heard, and in concluſion, offered me his fortune and his hand. When I was tired of his converſation, I ſaid, "We are admirable comedians, "what a pity, that with ſuch talents, we have no ſpecta-"tors: I will go and fetch our fellow-travellers, that "they may have their ſhare of amuſement." I left him in a very ill humour; all night he ſung plaintive ſongs, excellent provocatives of ſleep. At length I parted with him at Paris, refuſing to give him my addreſs or that of my father, of whom he wiſhed to aſk me in marriage. He left me evidently diſpleaſed.

I did not know that the people here had interrogated my fellow-travellers, and I maintained that I knew none of them, that I might ſpare them the diſagreeable taſk of undergoing interrogatories reſpecting me. In this, I followed my oracle, Raynal, who ſays, it is not our duty to tell truth to our tyrants. The lady who travelled with me, gave them the information that I was acquainted with you, and had ſpoke to Duperret.

You know the firmneſs of Duperret's mind; in his anſwers he told them the exact truth, and his depoſition was corroborated by mine, nothing appears againſt him, but his courage is a crime. I confeſs, I was apprehenſive that my having ſpoke to him would be diſcovered, and repented

pented it when too late. I wished to repair my fault by inducing him to go and join you, but he was too resolute to take my advice. Sure of his innocence, and of the innocence of every one else, I resolved to execute my project. Would you believe it? Fauchet is in prison as my accomplice; he who did not even know of my existence.

But the people are not content to have only an unimportant woman sacrificed to the manes of that *great man*. Pardon me, my fellow-creatures! for such an use of this word as dishonours your species; he was a ferocious beast, who intended to destroy the rest of France by the flames of civil war. Now, peace for ever!

Four members were present at my first interrogatory. Chabot looked like a madman; Legendre insisted that he had seen me in the morning at his house; I who never thought of the man; I do not consider him possessed of sufficient abilities to be the tyrant of his country, and it was not my design to punish every body. All who see me pretend that they have known me a long while, though, in fact, they never saw me before.

I believe that the *dying words* of Marat have been printed. I doubt whether he uttered any, but these are the last he said to me. After having written down all your names, and those of the administration of Calvados who are at Evreux, he said, for my comfort, " In a few " days, I will have them all guillotined at Paris." If the department places his bust opposite to that of St. Fargeau, they may have these words engraven on it in letters of gold.

I will give you no details of this great event, the journals will be sufficiently explicit. I confess that my resolution was rendered complete, by my observing the courageous manner in which our volunteers inrolled themselves on the seventh of July; you may recollect the delight I felt, and I promised myself that I would make Petion repent of the suspicions he had manifested respecting my sentiments. In short, I reflected that all those brave fellows were setting out to obtain the head of one single man, that they would be disappointed, or that his destruction would have occasioned the death of many good citizens. He did not deserve so distinguished a fate; the hand of a woman was sufficient.

I acknowledge that I used a treacherous artifice to induce him to admit me: all expedients are justifiable in such

such a cause. I intended, when I left Calvados, to have sacrificed him on the summit of the Mountain, but he no longer attended the convention.

I wish I had kept your letter, it would have proved that I had no accomplices; but time will elucidate that point.

We are such good republicans at Paris, that it is not conceived how an useless woman, who, if she lived her longest possible term, would do no good, could, in cold blood, sacrifice herself to save her country. I expected to have been instantly put to death, but some men, truly courageous, and superior to all commendation, preserved me from the excusable rage of those whom I had rendered unhappy. As I really retained my presence of mind, I felt hurt at the exclamations of some women, but those who save their country think nothing of the price it costs them. May peace be established as soon as I wish it! This, however, is a grand preliminary, without which it would never have been obtained. For these two days I have enjoyed a delicious state of peace. The happiness of my country constitutes mine; there is no act of self-devotion which does not over-pay in pleasure, the pain of resolving to adopt it.

I have no doubt that my father will be tormented on my account: the loss of me will be a sufficient affliction. If my letters are found in his possession, the greater part of them are portraits of you; if they contain any pleasantries reflecting on you, I beg you to forgive me, and impute them to my levity. In my last letter I led my father to believe that, apprehensive of the horrors of a civil war, I intended retiring to England. My project then was to remain *incognita*, to kill Marat publicly, and, by an immediate death, leave the people of Paris to an unavailing inquiry after my name.

I beg, citizen, that you and your colleagues will take care to defend my relations and friends, if they are molested; I say nothing of my dear friends the aristocrats, the remembrance of whom I preserve in my heart; I never hated but one single being, and I have demonstrated how violent that hatred was; but there are thousands whom I love with still more warmth than I hated him. A lively imagination and a feeling heart promise but a stormy life; I beg those who may regret my fate to think of this, and they will rejoice at seeing me enjoy repose in the Elysian fields with Brutus and a few of the ancients.

As

APPENDIX, No. V.

As for the moderns, there are few real patriots, who know how to die for their country; they are almoſt all ſelfiſh. What a diſmal people to form a republic!

It is neceſſary, in the firſt place, to eſtabliſh peace, and a government will afterwards come as it can: at leaſt, if my advice may be taken, the Mountain would not be permitted to reign.

I am exceedingly well accommodated in my priſon; the jailors are the beſt kind of people in the world; to keep away *ennui* they have placed military men in my room. I like that very well by day, and very ill by night. I have complained of the indecency, but no one has thought fit to pay any attention to my remonſtrance: I believe this muſt be an invention of Chabot; none but a Capuchin could have ſuch ideas.

I paſs my time in writing ſongs; I give the laſt ſtanza of one written by Validi to all who will accept of it; I aſſure all the Pariſians that we only take up arms againſt anarchy, which is the exact truth.

* * * * * * * * *

[At the time of writing this part of her letter, Charlotte Corday had undergone her firſt examination; when ſhe had proceeded thus far, ſhe was interrogated a ſecond time, and committed to the Conciergerie, from which priſon ſhe continued her epiſtle to Barbaroux in theſe words:]

Here am I, committed to the Conciergerie, and the gentlemen of the jury having promiſed to ſend you my letter, I proceed.

I have undergone a long interrogatory, which, if it is publiſhed, I beg you will obtain. I had in my poſſeſſion, when arreſted, an addreſs to the friends of peace; I cannot ſend it to you, and it would be in vain for me to demand that it ſhould be publiſhed. I had thought yeſterday of making a preſent of my portrait to the department of Calvados; but the committee of public ſafety, of whom I demanded it, returned no anſwer, and it is now too late.

I deſire, citizen, that you will communicate this letter to citizen Bougon, *procureur-general ſyndic* of the department. I do not write to him for ſeveral reaſons; I am not certain, in the firſt place, that he is now at Evreux. I fear, moreover, that being naturally compaſſionate, he will be affected at my death, yet I believe him good citizen enough to console himself in the hope of peace; I know how sincerely he desires it, and hope that in facilitating its return I have fulfilled his wishes. If any of my friends desire to see this letter, I hope you will not refuse them.

I must have a defender, for it is a rule; I have chosen one from the Mountain, Gustavus Doulcet; I suppose he will refuse me the honour, it would, however, cost him but little trouble. I thought of asking Robespierre or Chabot. I shall require leave to dispose of the remainder of my money, which, if I obtain, I will devote it to the wives and children of the brave inhabitants of Caen who have marched to the deliverance of Paris.

It is astonishing, that the people suffered me to be conducted from the Abbaye to the Conciergerie, it is another proof of their moderation; mention the circumstance to the good inhabitants of Caen. They indulge themselves with occasional insurrections, and are not so easily restrained.

My trial comes on to-morrow at eight; probably at noon, according to the Roman phrase *I shall have lived.* I cannot say how I shall encounter my last moments: I have no need to affect insensibility, for I never yet knew the fear of death, I never loved life but in proportion to its possible utility.

I hope Duperret and Fauchet will be set at liberty tomorrow; they assert that Fauchet conducted me to the convention, and placed me in the gallery. What business could he have to take women there? As a deputy he ought not to have been in the galleries, and as a bishop, he ought not to have been with a woman; thus there is somewhat of a charge against him, but Duperret is totally exempt.

Marat will not be placed in the Pantheon, yet he was highly deserving of it. I beg you will collect the proper documents to make his funeral eulogy.

I hope you will not lose sight of madame Forbin's interest; this is her address in case you should wish to write —To Alexandrine Forbin, Mandrefie, near Zurich, Switzerland. I beg you will inform her that I love her with all my heart. I am going to write a line to papa; I say nothing to the rest of my friends, I ask nothing of them but a speedy forgetfulness; grief would disgrace my memory.

memory. Tell general Wimpfen that I think I have helped him to gain more than one battle by facilitating peace.

Adieu, citizen. I recommend myself to the memory of all true friends of peace.

The prisoners in the Conciergerie, far from insulting me like the people in the streets, looked as if they pitied me: misfortune ever renders men compassionate; this is my last reflection.

M. C. CORDAY.

Tuesday the 16th, at 8 o'clock at night.

No. VI.

FORM *of Admission in a* LODGE *of* FREE-MASONS *in Palermo.*

ALL' Oriente di Palermo luogo Illuminato ove regna il Silenzio & la pace & l'unione & l'amicizia l'anno del lume 5766, & li 17 del sesto mese
A' tutti le R. R. LL. sparse su la superficie della terra.

(S. S. S.)

Noj. V. M. della R. L. di S. Gio: di Scozia di Palermo, figlia della R. L. di S. Gio: di Scozia di Marsiglia assistito da tutti li nostri fili regolarmente associati pelli numeri misteriosi & sacri certifichiamo, ed attestiamo che il carisᵛ slloͤ. A. B. è stato per noi ricevuto al grado d'apprendente di cui egli ha sofferto li prove necessarie, in testimonio di che la R. L. li ha accordato il presente certifichato fatto p͞ma controsignare per lui stesso pregando & ricercando le R. R. L. L. regolari ove egli si presentera d'ammetterlo in questa qualita nel loro Oriente offerendo loro in simile caso l'itesso. Dato all Oriente di Palᵒ in Loggia & col sigello generale.

C. D.
E. F.
G. H.

L. S.
A. B.

No. VII.

Translation of the Introduction, and a general Account of Mirabeau's Essay *on the Sect of* Illuminati.

Introduction.

WHEN I wrote this book, I did not flatter myself with the hope of obtaining belief, and, consequently, did not flatter myself that I should impart conviction. The man who discloses facts so extraordinary must be resigned, and expect to pass for a mere declaimer. When that character is once given of an author, no person troubles himself to examine his work. But if the importance of the subject alone has inflamed his imagination, if the knowledge of iniquity has soured his judgment, if the noble desire of saving his fellow-creatures has armed him with those sublime powers of eloquence which overwhelm error with the force of thunder, if he has only stepped beyond the line of his character from a conviction of imminent danger, the impartial reader ought at least to obey that salutary impulse of fear which disturbs a treacherous security, and judge for himself, whether the evils pointed out are merely chimerical, or whether prudence demands that they should be attended to.

The simple are alarmed, the lukewarm doubt, the guilty deny, the wise reflect; these then I invoke on the present occasion, these are the men whose zeal I wish to stimulate.

This mystical machination would be sufficiently detected; but its existence is not believed. To obtain general belief, it would be necessary to specify facts, to afford means of proof, to name agents, accuse impostors, produce witnesses, publish writings, commence a regular suit, and follow it to conviction. All this might be done; but the *Coriphies* of the sect stifle every voice which raises itself in those countries where the sovereign is the pontiff of this new church.

I know

APPENDIX, No. VII.

I know not by what magic it happens that princes, who in general are divided between the love of pleasure and the desire of a brilliant reputation, have been the first to accede to a confederacy by which they must infallibly be losers. In Europe there are no less than thirty, reigning and not reigning, so imbued with these absurdities, that they are inaccessible to reason however recommended by moderation If an attempt is made to compromise differences of opinion, and the reasoner proceeds by most obvious modes of argumentation, they soon mistrust, and finally avoid him. Some of them, who would be the outcasts of mankind but for the respect attached to the names they bear, turn preachers, and diffuse the dogmas of the *illuminati*, in an insipid jargon. Others constitute themselves fanatical protectors of a religion they do not understand, and open their dominions (which they call states) to all the adventurers employed by the sect for the furtherance of their views. The greater part of them court with a fanatical eagerness every one who wears the livery of Swedenburg or Schrœpffer.

The court of France is unacquainted with the elements of this theosophy. The rapidity of those motions by which their minds are agitated does not afford leisure for any religious system to unfold itself. The literary bodies deride it; the middle class, fully employed, and (fortunately) little informed, are as yet inaccessible to this kind of seduction: but there exists a number of little antiphilosophical parties, composed of learned ladies, theological *abbés*, and a few pretended wise men. Each of these parties has its creed, its prodigies, its *hierophantes*, its missionaries, its adepts, its detractors. Thus Paris, the centre of all deception, as well as of all knowledge, affords a specimen of every class of visionaries. Every one affects to explain the Bible in favour of his own system, to found his own religion, to fill his temple, and increase his cathecumens. Here Jesus Christ acts a conspicuous part; there 'tis the Devil; in another place it is Nature; a little farther it is Faith. They all agree that reason is a nullity, knowledge useless, and experience chimerical. Barbarin somnambulizes, Cagliostro performs cures, Lavater administers consolation, Saint Martin affords instruction, d'E****†,—*res sacra miser*. All of them use deceit to

---

† He was, at the time this was written, suffering the horrors of exile in the isles of Saint Marguerite.

acquire a profitable reputation; and, if we except Lavater, who, by means of a medley of genius and simplicity, makes his dupes with the utmost sincerity, their visions are to the others a spring, the movements of which they regulate with the greatest address.

In Germany, the courts give an impulse to the public mind. The people are characterised by solidity rather than by refinement, and are therefore convinced by untruths put into the form of syllogisms. When their simplicity has once received a bias towards their idol, called philanthropy, there are few paradoxes which they are not ready to adopt. The petty princes who are infected with the mania of being praised, and whose names would easily be forgotten amidst the important discussions by which Europe is continually agitated, suffer themselves to be gained by the sweet incense with which the priests of the *illuminati*, men prodigal of eulogium even to satiety, are ever ready to regale them in books which every body begins, but nobody peruses. The ladies also encourage this mystic illusion, in the hope of recalling the happy days of their original innocency; the courtiers embrace the interests of the new sect, because, between the protectors and the adepts, there is a constant commerce kept up in pensions, presents, and titles, which are given in exchange for initiations, revelation of mysteries, and consolatory predictions; this accounts for their great fidelity to these remuneratory dogmas.

In Poland and Russia they gain many proselytes; especially in Russia, where the established religion affords countenance to mystic systems, and to every thing tending to excite enthusiasm. There many great personages become apostles, and though the empress rejects every thing which can enfeeble the human mind, there are theosophers under her very eye, who evade detection, or brave scrutiny. May her successor inherit her philosophy! May her vast dominions never experience any other slavery than that to which they were doomed by their original masters!

Will it be believed that England, *the country where men think,* is not totally free from this degrading superstition? There is not a complete system as in Germany, but there are certain confraternities, where the adepts dogmatise, and keep up the zeal of the initiated by the charm of secrets. Their progress, however, is not so rapid as in

other

other countries, becaufe the Englifh travel a great deal; and though the greater part of them travel to very little purpofe, yet they learn to appreciate the mafs of mankind, and at leaft acquire this knowledge, that, in all countries, the vileft and moft contemptible of the fpecies are thofe who make a trade of deceiving and degrading their fellow creatures.

We were long undecided on the fubject of publifhing this work. We fhall be told that it is founding an alarm, and giving confiftency to a fect juft ftruggling into life, and which is compofed of a hundred times more dupes than impoftors. None of the great bodies, the depofitaries of knowledge, have as yet embraced thefe new dogmas; and if the fect were diftinguifhed but by one juft man, yet for his fake favour ought to be fhewn to fo great a number of individuals, whofe only crime is that of not being endowed by nature with a fortunate and uncommon perfpicacity, which forms an effectual barrier againft deceit.

Far from us be fuch a principle! It is pufillanimity, under the mafk of commiferation. What! muft we be filent for fear of being exclaimed at for calumny, libelling, and malignity?—Calumny!—But there are men whom it is not poffible to calumniate. The atrocity of their projects forms a mephitic abyfs into which vulgar mortals are unable to penetrate, and which would have remained ftill undifcovered, but for its treacherous exhalations, which, unhappily for mankind, fpread themfelves far and wide. —A libel!—Yes, undoubtedly, thofe parts of the work wherein they are mentioned may be fo denominated, for they will be occupied in the detection of vice, the difplay of guilt, and the expofure of hypocrify.—Malignity!— Who is moft obvious to the charge?—He who coolly beholds the deftruction of his fellow-citizens, or he who places centinels in the path which leads to the precipice? No delicacy, confideration, or politenefs, can be claimed by an iron-hearted race, who with the dagger in their hands are marking out their victims.

Follow, follow this bafe principle, you whofe trade it is to offer adulation to kings, to excufe their failings, to extol the flighteft indications of beneficence, and to immortalize a few equivocal virtues. Purchafe, at this price, I will not even fay diftinctions, vain as they are, but a fmall quantity of gold, a prefent worthy of your fordid fouls,

and

and do not come to us with declarations of your love of truth, of your philanthropy, and your attachment to virtue; take back your insulting esteem for these daughters of heaven, and reserve it for the divinities of your sect.

When they are addressed in this style, they cannot reply, much less confute. Then they commence persecutors, and substitute a tyrannical use of the authority lodged in their hands, for the force of reason, which would but feebly assist them. To escape the stigma attached to persecutors, they divert the stream of favour, nay of justice; for the employment of modest men of ability is no more than the discharge of a debt. They divert, I say, the stream of favour from their adversaries, and suffer them to vegetate in that disgraceful obscurity which amounts to a persecution, and which is perhaps the only persecution capable of putting genius to the torture. Stung with contempt, she goes in search of climes less unjust; or if she remains inflexibly attached to her penates, she stays to maintain the combat, and display the standard of reason. Then parties are formed, quarrels arise, plans of defence are combined, discontent becomes general, ambitious neighbours take advantages, visionary commanders are placed at the head of a neglected army, more interested about the money with which they are to be paid, than the defence of a country from which they are completely alienated. The highest posts are occupied by men without vigour, without genius, or by some men of ability, but who have been studiously subdued, and subjected to the insignificant junto in favour. Freedom of thought is annihilated by an inquisitorial watchfulness; the enslaved press keeps back every kind of truth, or persecutes religion, now a fugitive, and compelled to yield her pulpits and her altars to fantastic divinities; the lyceums are converted into extensive solitudes, for, where all the branches of science are subjected to *illuminati*, the boxes, and not the universities, ought to be frequented.

However charming it may be to avenge the cause of integrity, it was not the contemptible pleasure of railing which induced us to take up the pen. The hope, faint as it is, yes, the hope of rescuing a few virtuous men from the fascinations of the *illuminati*, has animated me in this attempt. For some years I have presented myself in the Arena under various shapes. Sometimes enveloped in the veil of fiction, sometimes in the restricted line of academical disputation,

APPENDIX, No. VII.

disputation, but more frequently in discussions of greater profundity, I have disclosed extraordinary secrets. I now come to place the subject in a most important point of view, and to present a train of ideas, which by degrees will lead to conviction.

Seeking the source of the evil in the fatal predilection of all mankind for the marvellous, a rapid view of the ages of our æra will demonstrate that all ages have reason to blush for incredible errors by which mankind has been continually harassed, errors which have been exposed, but never eradicated.

Men receive these errors with joy, and seem in yielding to them to shield themselves from the austere lessons of truth. Some privileged countries naturalize them, and give themselves up to their deceitful influence; all nations respect, at least, if they do not embrace them.

With what warmth has all Europe defended the Jesuits, a sect which has supplied so many resources to the theosophic system. They were formed under the diadem and under the tiara, under the helmet and under the mitre, under the president's cap and under the doctor's. The same fanaticism which preserved them has revived, within these thirty years, the languishing order of freemasons, who find no difficulty in keeping a secret, which nobody is anxious to discover.

A philosophical inquiry into the system of free-masonry has led to a still more elaborate investigation of the mysteries of the illuminati. Was it not indispensably necessary to distinguish vulgar and precipitate notions, from the judgment which ought really to prevail, respecting an inscrutable association, the mysteries of which are carefully hid from profane inspection.

It was necessary to traverse those famous circles, the true secret of the order, the grand instrument of their frauds, those laboratories of iniquity, where chains are forged for kings, and poisons distilled for mankind, and then to disclose the dreadful probations which precede those oaths, of which the wretches themselves possess no written forms, and which they would not dare to adopt for the consolidation of their plots, oaths which realize the sanguinary fable of Atreus, and would cover the whole face of the earth with a nation of assassins.

Granting these alarms to be exaggerated, yet certainly it ought to be believed that the sect of *illuminati* will necessarily

cessarily destroy every kingdom in which they find protection, and will not even respect the institutions of society. This double truth is as clearly proved as one immediately consequent to it, namely, that kings themselves have the greatest interest in hewing down this poisonous tree, the roots of which descend even to hell, while the branches cast a gloom over their thrones.

After the woful spectacle on which our eyes had dwelt too long, we sought for a pleasant illusion in the means of effacing those fatal impressions, and adverted to the notions entertained of them in ages anterior to our own. This idea alone, developed by a more able pen, would leave the mind in a state of profound reflection very unfavourable to the sectaries, a state which must be strengthened by a faithful delineation of their founder, and an impartial review of the condition of those nations who have protected these modern errors.

The last division of the work concludes with an offer of some means adapted to diminish their credit. We have thrown together, at the end, historical annotations. There are, amongst them, some pieces translated from the German, and entirely unknown in France and Italy. The greater part of the remainder is original. We might have made them more numerous, but have said enough for those who really wish to be instructed.

We will not affect to conceal that most of our ideas are directed against Germany, and that we have drawn most of our portraits from the life. But does not even that prove the necessity of this book? If there do exist such men as we have pourtrayed, we are threatened with an imminent peril. If we have only displayed imaginary beings, these sheets will soon float on the tide of oblivion, and will fail to excite even that momentary curiosity which is very far from success.

But the same act of sincerity which puts the public in possession of our intentions, will also guarantee the purity of our judgment with a great number of persons of the first ability, constantly animated, like ourselves, with a sacred horror against visionaries.

Yes, Germany, in almost every class, presents to us men with honest hearts, who sigh over the projects of these mystical innovators. They feel astonished that a people, whose national character is frankness, can be so altered as to give themselves up to a set of pretended apostles

apoſtles, whoſe principal reſource is impoſture. They lament that a nation, whoſe favourite idol is reaſon, ſhould ſubmit to a few madmen, whoſe profeſſion is abſurdity, whoſe doctrine is a chimera. They uſe the two reſources committed by Heaven to the hands of the wiſe, contempt and retirement. They encourage and animate thoſe who enter the liſts.

They are ſenſible, like ourſelves, that the efficacious remedy would be, perhaps, one of thoſe mighty convulſions which are produced by the chain of events, and which it is not in the power of kings to prevent. Involved in one of thoſe ſanguinary diſputes which agitate all Europe, a nation does not invoke the aid of ſpeculiſts, judgment and experience then become the tutelary deities of the univerſe; precepts are regenerated, the aſcendancy of valour is exerciſed, every one appears at his proper ſtation, the uſurpers of celebrity are unmaſked, men of ſtrong minds govern the country, and men whom fate had deſtined "*to the limited honours of one ſingle legion,*" fly and diſappear before them, to grow old in the ſubaltern labours of ſome obſcure chanceries. What a deſtiny! by what incredible fatality are we reduced to beg of heaven as a boon, that which is the laſt effect of its wrath? To what an exceſs do our woes amount, when our only hope is in one of the moſt dreadful ſcourges? Yet nothing is more true. The evil would be tranſitory, and might, perhaps, rid the world of a cruel error which will laſt for ſeveral ages.

As to France, we may hope that in the verſatility of principle, which ſeldom permits any object to take a deep root, her theatres, her ballads, and her faſhions, will come to her aid. Occupied as ſhe is with various fermentations, theoſophy will hardly become a complete religion. It is in itſelf too heavy, too inſignificant to act on a people who ſtill preſerve ſome remains of gaiety, and who have reſiſted the dull diſputes of Janſeniſm, the diſcuſſions of their parliaments, the tedious invectives of the economiſts, and the mania of thinking, all gifts of the modern philoſophy. Beſides, that philoſophy does not afford ſo unſteady a light as ſome of her detractors would wiſh. A month ſeldom elapſes in which there is not a ſucceſsful re-production of eternal truths. It would not be difficult to demonſtrate that philoſophy has only loſt her enthuſiaſm, her ſarcaſtic bitterneſs, and her deſpotic ſtyle, while

while she has strengthened her proofs, and increased her perspicuity.

It remains to be examined how far it is proper to be explicit with respect to great men, and those to whom they intrust the cares of administration. They are, almost every where, like the ark of the Lord. Whoever touches them, is struck in the moment of his presumption. It seems to me, however, that a prudent warning is a duty rather than an intrusion, an homage rather than an insult. The offer of truth to any man, implies a supposition that he is a friend of truth; not to dare to point out error, is to act as if he were an accomplice in it. So far from its being a crime to write with a courageous freedom, it would be criminal to palsy energetic pens. They weaken the vapours of that incense which intoxicates men in power and esteem; they snatch the one from torpor, the other from thoughtlessness; they plead the cause of the people, of virtue, of wisdom—three strangers at court, and who are treated there as impertinent intruders. If revenge dips these pens in the gall of satire, if they are degraded by being employed in the cause of selfishness, they then become unavailing arms, but seldom dangerous; for abuse reflects dishonour only on those who have recourse to it.

Ah! why are there no means of eradicating from mankind the mania of flattery! A prince sends ten thousand men to be butchered, he is praised; he overwhelms his subjects with ill-contrived taxes, the day of his accession to the throne is hailed as a festival; he makes an useless and expensive voyage, at his return he passes under triumphal arches; listlessness sends him on a periodical tour through his provinces, crowds assemble to lavish on him acclamations to which he has no claim. The idol, accustomed to this perfidious concert of praise, is irritated at the voice of the sage who tenders wholesome instruction, and only appeased by the flattering sounds which efface the sombre traces left on his mind by austere truth.

O sacred truth! In spite of this ungracious reception, do not abandon the throne of kings! Protect them, in spite of their irritability, against the illusions with which they are surrounded. Restore to us the courage which disarms persecution, impress on our writings thy celestial stamp, and compel man to acknowledge thine empire.

APPENDIX, No. VII.

All others difappear under the fcythe of time, thine alone receives additional vigour from his trembling hand.

CHAP. I.
On the Predilection of Mankind for the Wonderful.

In this chapter the author, taking a review of the new fects which every age has produced fince the firft eftablifhment of Chriftianity, refers the propenfity of mankind to adopt the vifions of the illuminati to the fame difpofition which induced them to give credit to religious fchifmatics and impoftors.

CHAP. II.
On the moral Difpofitions of the European Nations.

Mirabeau makes a rapid and incorrect eftimate of the progrefs of learning and liberty in different countries, and attributes the fuccefs of the illuminati to the want of freedom in various governments, and concludes that Germany will be the theatre of theofophifm, whence it will fpread to the north, and make fome progrefs in France.

CHAP. III.
On Jefuitifm, as the firft Source of the Theofophic Syftem.

In treating of the Jefuits, Mirabeau refcues them from many imputed crimes and immoralities, but he charges them with the moft extenfive views of ambition, and defcribes them as the bafis on which the illuminati have founded themfelves.

CHAP. IV.
On Free-mafonry, confidering it as the moft ufeful Eftablifhment to the Illuminati.

This inftitution is treated with refpect on account of its fundamental principles, equality and charity; but he adds, "Whatever may be the operations of the free-
"mafons, they give rife to an affociation, the affociation
"produces meetings, thefe meetings are filled with elo-
"quent orators, the progrefs from religious eloquence
"to fanaticifm is but fhort, and the difcourfes of thefe
"orators excite the defire of attempting it. Inftructions
"are

"are imparted on the attainment of new degrees, degrees are the reward of zeal, zeal leads to the formation of engagements, engagements to oaths, oaths to every thing."

CHAP. V.

Account of the Sect of Illuminati.

They are described as conspirators " in favour of despotism against liberty, of incapacity against genius, of vice against virtue, of ignorance against knowledge. Formed in the recesses of impenetrable darkness, this society constitutes a new race of beings: they are acquainted without seeing each other, understand without the aid of expression, and assist each other without friendship. The aim of this society is to govern the world, to appropriate to itself the authority of sovereigns, to usurp their place, leaving them only the barren honour of wearing the crown. From the Jesuits they have adopted the principles of blind obedience, and the regicide system of the seventeeth century; from free-masonry, probations, and exterior ceremonies; from the templars, subterranean incantations, and an incredible boldness. They make use of physical discoveries to impose on the unlettered multitude; the fashionable fables to awaken curiosity, and encourage proselytism; and the opinions of antiquity to familiarize mankind with the commerce of intermediate spirits. Every kind of error which afflicted mankind, every experiment, every invention, is rendered subservient to the views of the illuminati."

Speaking of their artifices to gain esteem and prevent suspicion, he says, " The illuminati have also the address to load with honours, simple masons of acknowledged probity. The vulgar (and by this word I do not mean the mere mob, but men of every class who reflect but little), the vulgar I say, confound objects, and guarantee the integrity of Orontes and Cleon. Well! there is no doubt that Orontes and Cleon are men of honour, zealous citizens, and warm friends; but they themselves are dupes to their leaders, and thus become the first springs of a machine, the uses of which they do not understand, and people more artful than themselves exhibit to the world, the integrity of

" Orontes

" Orontes and Cleon, as an assurance of the purity of
" their mysteries, and thus give an effectual contradic-
" tion to any one who entertains a doubt of the inno-
" cency of their occult sittings."

CHAP. VI.
Of the Circles.

The circles are described as the administrative committees of the sect, scattered in different provinces, and composed of nine persons each. Their mysterious operations and local connection are described with affected minuteness, and a mixture of truth and falsehood.

CHAP. VII.
Of the Probation which must be undergone to constitute one of the Illuminati Member of a Circle.

This chapter, written with great affected exactness, and no inconsiderable share of invention, displays a series of probations at once disgusting, impious, and obscene, and gives the form of an abjuration, which releases the party who makes it from all previous ties, however sacred and binding, and delivers him over entirely to the illuminati. The account is curious, and even, if totally untrue, becomes interesting by the surprise and horror which it excites.

CHAP. VIII.
That the Sect of Illaminati must necessarily destroy any Kingdom where they are encouraged.

This is proved by a variety of positions and inductions, and by a review of the different professions and public bodies which affect government.

CHAP. IX.
That Kings are peculiarly interested to destroy the new Sect.

In this chapter a distinction is made between the dignity of the crown, and the general interests of the kingdom, and the topic is inforced by a variety of arguments and instances.

CHAP. X.

That the Sect of Illuminati would, if it were possible, destroy Society itself.

CHAP. XI.

On the Means of destroying the Sect of Illuminati.

This Mirabeau proposes to effect by means of a combination of men of letters who shall expose their principles, secrets, and exertions to the abhorrence of society.

CHAP. XII.

The degree of Estimation bestowed on the Illuminati in former, and in the present Times.

After relating the principles and fates of several ancient impostors, Mirabeau describes the hatred and jealousy which prevail among the visionaries and magnetists of these times, and the contempt with which Swedenborg and Lavater treat all sectaries but their own.

CHAP. XIII.

The Degree of Estimation in which the Founders of the Modern Sect are held.

In this chapter, the author derides and ridicules several noted visionaries and founders of sects, as Saint Germain, le Grand, Schrœpfer, together with their adherents.

CHAP. XIV.

Of the State of those Countries which are considered as protecting the Sect.

This chapter contains a severe satire against many modern governments and social institutions.

CHAP. XV.

Different Methods of diminishing the Estimation of the Sect.

The subject begun in the eleventh chapter is here resumed and extended. The means proposed are, 1st, The productions of men of letters. 2d, To inspire a taste

taste for literature. 3d, A new system of education. 4th, A reform in the order of free-masons. 5th, Ridicule, and principally dramatic satire. The treachery of these suggestions is remarkable, as every one of the means adverted to, except the fourth, which is a mere absurdity, has been used or referred to by the members or favourers of the sect. They have had a ready and determined band of literary assistants prepared to aid their cause by every possible effort. They have established book-societies and reading-rooms for the mere purpose of extending their pernicious systems. They have been constant advocates for and projectors of new systems of education. And the drama in Germany and France! as been almost entirely devoted to the celebration of their heroes, to the enforcement of their dogmas both moral and political, and to the ridicule both of persons and establishments which they were desirous to destroy.

The notes, which are twenty-one in number, are many of them extracted from scarce publications, and are in general curious and interesting.

No. VIII.

Letter from Thomas Pain *to Sir* Archibald Macdonald, *then Attorney-General; read at Guildhall on Pain's Trial; the Hand-writing being proved by* Thomas Chapman, *Printer, and* John Purdue *Esq. of the Excise Office. Extracted from* Gurney's *Edition of his Trial, p.* 92.

Paris, 11th of Nov.
1st Year of the Republic.

Sir,

As there can be no personal resentment between two strangers, I write this letter to you, as to a man against whom I have no animosity.

You have, as attorney-general, commenced a prosecution against me, as the author of the Rights of Man.

Had not my duty, in confequence of my being elected a member of the national convention of France, called me from England, I fhould have ftayed to have contefted the injuftice of that profecution; not upon my own account, for I cared not about the profecution, but to have defended the principles I had advanced in the work.

The duty I am now engaged in is of too much importance to permit me to trouble myfelf about your profecution: when I have leifure, I fhall have no objection to meet you on that ground; but as I now ftand, whether you go on with the profecution, or whether you do not, or whether you obtain a verdict, or not, is a matter of the moft perfect indifference to me as an individual. If you obtain one (which you are welcome to if you can get it), it cannot affect me either in perfon, property, or reputation, otherwife than to increafe the latter; and with refpect to yourfelf, it is as confiftent that you obtain a verdict againft the man in the moon as againft me; neither do I fee how you can continue the profecution againft me as you would have done againft one of *your own people* who had abfented himfelf becaufe he was profecuted: what paffed at Dover proves that my departure from England was no fecret.

My neceffary abfence from your country now, in confequence of my duty here, affords the opportunity of knowing whether the profecution was intended againft Thomas Paine, or againft the rights of the people of England to inveftigate fyftems and principles of government; for as I cannot now be the object of the profecution, the going on with the profecution will fhew that fomething elfe was the object, and that fomething elfe can be no other than the people of England, for it is againft *their rights* and not againft me, that a verdict or fentence can operate, if it can operate at all. Be then fo candid as to tell the jury (if you choofe to continue the procefs) whom it is you are profecuting, and on whom it is that the verdict is to fall.

But I have other reafons than thofe I have mentioned for writing you this letter, and, however you may choofe to interpret them, they proceed from a good heart. The time, Sir, is becoming too ferious to play with court profecutions, and fport with national rights. The terrible examples that have taken place here, upon men who lefs than a year ago thought themfelves as fecure as any pro-

fecuting

APPENDIX, No. VIII.

secuting judge, jury, or attorney-general, can now do in England, ought to have some weight with men in your situation. That the government of England is as great, if not the greatest, perfection of fraud and corruption that ever took place since governments began, is what you cannot be a stranger to, unless the constant habit of seeing it has blinded your senses; but though you may not choose to see it, the people are seeing it very fast, and the progress is beyond what you may choose to believe. Is it possible that you or I can believe, or that reason can make any other man believe, that the capacity of such a man as Mr. Guelph, or any of his profligate sons, is necessary to the government of a nation. I speak to you as one man ought to speak to another; and I know also, that I speak what other people are beginning to think.

That you cannot obtain a verdict (and if you do it will sign'fy nothing) without packing a jury, (and we both know that such tricks are practised,) is what I have very good reason to believe. I have gone into coffee-houses, and places where I was unknown, on purpose to learn the currency of opinion, and I never yet saw any company of twelve men that condemned the book, but I have often found a greater number than twelve approving it, and this is I think a fair way of collecting the natural currency of opinion. Do not then, Sir, be the instrument of drawing twelve men into a situation that may be injurious to them afterwards. I do not speak this from policy, but from benevolence; but if you choose to go on with the process, I make it my request to you that you will read this letter in court, after which the judge and the jury may do as they please. As I do not consider myself the object of the prosecution, neither can I be affected by the issue, one way or the other, I shall, though a foreigner in your country, subscribe as much money as any other man towards supporting the right of the nation against the prosecution; and it is for this purpose only that I shall do it.

THOMAS PAINE.

To ARCHIBALD MACDONALD,
  Attorney-General.

No. IX.

Abstract of Petion's *Speech, intended to have been delivered in Reply to* Robespierre's *Answer to* Louvet's *Accusation; and* Petion's *Letter to the Jacobin Club.* Extracted from the Mercure François, No. du 17 Novembre 1792.

The inferences drawn from Petion's publication are these:

1. That the men who have assumed to themselves the glory of the 10th of August, are those to whom it least belongs; that it is due to those who prepared the event, to the imperious nature of things, to the brave federates, and their secret directors.

2. That the *commune*, instead of putting an end to the revolutionary effort when its object was attained, thought it more dignified to enter into a state of rivalship with the legislative assembly; whose decrees they obeyed or resisted, just as they found them favourable or contradictory to their views.

3. That from that epoch, Petion retained only a shadow of power, and that he was unwilling that his name should be annexed to a multitude of irregular acts.

4. That Robespierre assumed the greatest ascendancy in the council; that subsequently to the decree for opening the barriers, he saw nothing but precipices and conspiracies, and was continually denouncing supposed conspirators; that he inflamed the people by the most animated declamations; that the sections were influenced by these impressions, communicated them to others.

5. That the committee of inspection filled the prisons; that a man, whose very name is become odious, and inspires terror in the minds of peaceable citizens, Marat, had assumed the direction of the police.

6. That the crimes of the 2d of September and the following days would not have taken place, or would have been stopped, if those who had in their hands the direction of the armed force had beheld them with horror; that

those who committed the massacres in the prisons were very few in number; that Petion was only informed of the event in a vague and indirect manner; that he immediately wrote to the commandant-general, from whom he received no answer; that he wrote again, and the commandant-general replied, that he had given orders, but they were not obeyed.

7. That the committee of inspection of the *commune* had, in fact, issued a decree of arrest against the minister, Roland, on the 4th of September, a period when the massacres were still continued.

8. That the electoral assembly was influenced, commanded, by a small number of men; and that the elections were regulated by lists which were exactly followed.

9. That fresh massacres were announced for the 20th of September; that several representatives of the people, the most ardent defenders of liberty, were pointed out as victims; that Petion had often severely reproached Robespierre for the suspicions he entertained of several deputies, and particularly Brissot, and that Robespierre had assured him that Brissot was sold to Brunswick.

Finally, That he did not believe that Robespierre had aspired to the dictatorship, but that Marat had solicited it on his behalf. If ferocity were not the characteristic of folly, Petion added, there would be nothing so ridiculous as that being whom nature seems expressly to have marked with the seal of reprobation.

JEROME PETION's *Letter to the Jacobin Club.*

For some time past attacks, more or less direct, more or less violent, have been levelled at me in this society. Till now, I never thought it necessary to answer, but it is time to stop this system of intrigue and calumny. I do not love to speak of myself; I never permitted myself in public to say a single word of the services I had rendered; at this day it becomes a duty, and I shall perform it, without affecting a false delicacy.

I loved and cultivated liberty before her birth in my country.

I gave myself up to the study of laws and governments, and, before the revolution, was the author of several works, which breathe the love of equality and liberty.

In

In the constituent assembly, I defended the rights of the people with courage and constancy.

At the period of the famous secession, I saved this society. I remember a period when it was composed only of three members of the national assembly, and twenty or thirty other citizens. Terror had dispersed the rest. It had driven away many who, at this day, act the most conspicuous parts in the club. Of the three members of the assembly, one was little known. Robespierre, though he enjoyed a high reputation for patriotism, had not acquired that estimation which is derived from wisdom and temperance in the conduct of public affairs. I have seen Robespierre trembling; Robespierre proposing flight; Robespierre not daring to shew himself in the assembly.—Ask him if I trembled.

I saved Robespierre himself from persecution, by attaching myself to his lot, when he was deserted by the rest of the world.

I have more than once saved Paris, and spared the blood of the people.

I contributed, in no slight degree, to bring on the events of the 10th of August.

I have, since that period, found my influence considerably reduced; the public will judge whether that reduction has been beneficial or injurious to the welfare of this city, and the tranquillity of the inhabitants.

I still retain hopes of serving my country.

I declare that I do not, nor ever will belong to any party.

I declare that I know not of a *Brissotine faction*; that in spite of the general blindness and warmth on this subject, this faction is a mere chimera, and that there is no man so little qualified to be the head of a party as Brissot.

I declare that the Jacobin club has rendered most important services to the country, that it may still continue to do so, and that I will defend the society with all my strength, but without prejudice; that I will adopt their opinions when I think them reasonable, but will combat them when I think them erroneous.

When we contemplate some of those men who affect an appearance of such ardent patriotism; those boasters in the cause of liberty, who but lately were slaves, and who would to-morrow relapse into the same condition under a king; those men who have the presumption to assert that no one elſe is capable of attaining their height: it is ſufficient to excite a difguſt againſt patriotiſm, in every heart where that virtue is not deeply engraved.

As for myſelf, I am, at this day, what I have ever been. Immovable in my principles, I ſay that whatever may happen, I will die free.

No. X.

ROBESPIERRE's *Letter to* JEROME PETION, *occaſioned by the preceding Publications.*

How great, my dear Petion, is the inſtability of human affairs, when you, heretofore my brother in arms, and at the ſame time the moſt gentle of mankind, on a ſudden declare yourſelf the moſt violent of my accuſers! Do not ſuppoſe from this exordium that it is my intention to ſpeak either of you or of myſelf. We are but two atoms, loſt in the immenſity of the moral and political world. I am not going to anſwer your inculpations; (I am accuſed of having already ſhewn too much condeſcenſion in that reſpect;) but your preſent political doctrines. It would now, perhaps, be rather too late to refute your ſpeech; but it is always time to defend truth and principles. Our quarrels are but topics of a day; principles are eternal.

It is on this condition only, my dear Petion, that I will take up the gauntlet you have thrown. You will even recognize, in my manner of combating, the friendſhip or the weakneſs I formerly felt for you. If in this difpute, which is entirely philanthropic, you ſhould be expoſed to ſome ſlight blows, they will be aimed only at your vanity; and you have, beforehand, put me quite at eaſe on that head, by declaring that you have none. Beſides, the right of cenſure is reciprocal; it is the ſhield of liberty; and you are ſo ſincerely attached to principles, that you will, I am ſure, feel more pleaſure in being yourſelf the object of it, than you experienced in exerciſing it againſt me.

I will

APPENDIX, No. X.

I will not diffemble that one of the moſt powerful of the motives which induce me to enter into the liſts againſt you is the deſire of ſeeing thoſe heroic actions which do honour to the French nation, and to the human race, and which you, undoubtedly from not knowing them, have miſrepreſented, faithfully tranſmitted to poſterity. I will remind you of circumſtances known to ſix hundred thouſand perſons; and I ſhall not be expoſed to ſuſpicion; for I was, almoſt as much as yourſelf, a ſtranger to the glorious events of our laſt revolution; we have only the ſatisfaction of knowing, that at that memorable period the country had many defenders, more uſeful than either of us.

In the firſt place, it ſeems to me that you do not ſpeak of the revolution which has broken our fetters with all the reſpect that it deſerves. Whence ariſes the acrimony with which you expreſs yourſelf reſpecting every tranſaction, and every individual at all connected with that event?

When you ſay that the event is principally to be aſcribed to thoſe who prepared it, it is evident that you allude to thoſe who did not accompliſh it. And if it is to yourſelf that you mean principally to advert, you muſt ſhare that merit with all thoſe who have defended the cauſe of liberty. You are willing to yield a ſmall portion to the federates, to whom you never ceaſed to recommend inaction; whom you gave yourſelf no trouble to procure the means of remaining at Paris;—to their ſecret directors, of whom you never ſpoke but with uneaſineſs and miſtruſt, men whom you and your aſſociates now claſs in the rank of agitators. Do you know that member of the legiſlative aſſembly who on the 9th of Auguſt ſaid to one of his friends, "If the people " are timid, or heſitate, blow my brains out with a piſtol, " and let my bloody corpſe be dragged about Paris, that " revenge may lead the people to liberty!" This is one of the men whom your friends inceſſantly calumniate.

But why do you not, with equal readineſs, do juſtice to the people of Paris?

Why do you not, at leaſt among thoſe who prepared the revolution, enumerate the ſections of Paris, ſo much ſlandered ſince that period by your aſſociates? Inſtead of aiding their pernicious deſigns, why do you not remind the departments, deceived by their impoſtures, that, for more than a month, they had declared themſelves permanent,

nent, that they had fignalized their ufeful activity by immortal decrees, the infallible precurfors of the revolution? Why did you not fay that it was they who folemnly difcuffed the facred neceffity of infurrection, who rallied all the foldiers of liberty, and who, in the night of the 9th of Auguft, at length gave the fignal of battle againft a rebellious and confpiring court? Do you not perceive that this politic and courageous proceeding was abfolutely neceffary, to unite and direct the popular force againft the anti-revolutionary army affembled by the tyrants in Paris?

This was not all; it was neceffary to create a central authority, to fubftitute for thofe who had loft the confidence of the people. This authority could not be vefted in the department, notorioufly fold to the court; or in your old department, which had juft refufed the requeft of the citizens to throw down the bufts of la Fayette and Bailly, where the moft zealous reprefentatives of the people had been infulted with impunity, by fatellites, and even by their colleagues, while you prefided, and even in your prefence. You might, then, have praifed the prudence of the fections who named commiffioners to replace the old council-general of the *commune*, and who invefted them with full powers to fave the *commune* of Paris, and all France. By what fatality, my dear Petion, does it happen that this new council-general is the principal object of the libellous publication on which we are now engaged? You have permitted an important avowal to efcape you, under the form of a qualification of your reproaches. "Thefe "commiffioners, *neverthelefs*, (you fay,) conceived a grand "idea, and took a bold ftep, in poffeffing themfelves of "all the municipal powers, in putting themfelves in the "place of the council-general, whofe weaknefs or cor"ruption they dreaded; they courageoufly rifked their "lives, if fuccefs had not crowned their enterprife." What was this enterprife? The deftruction of tyranny: then they expofed themfelves in the caufe of liberty. Add, if you pleafe, that in the firft days of September they fhook Paris, and all France, to crufh the armies of defpotifm; and you will be compelled to own, that they have twice faved the country. Do you then affume the pen to join their detractors? When fublime actions prefent themfelves for admiration, whence arifes this mania of feeking for a few defects to cenfure? If a nation is ungrateful, it has fome fort of right to be fo. Citizens owe every thing to their country, and the country owes nothing to them; or at least it is their duty to pardon her injustice: but you, citizen, by what right do you speak of the destroyers of tyranny in the same terms as tyrants themselves? You even go the length of attempting to wrest from them the merit of those services you have so recently acknowledged, by saying that *the revolution of the 10th of August would have been effected without them*. Strange manner of appreciating those who so powerfully contributed to it! Had you been at the house of the *commune* you would have known where was the rallying point for the people; that it was with the new magistrates that the defenders of liberty maintained a constant communication; you would have known how great were their exertions to procure for the citizens ammunition and arms, and to stifle the conspiracy of the court. You would have seen the calm and tranquil courage with which, among other things, they performed, in that dreadful crisis, a decisive action. I allude to the treachery of the commandant of the national guard, who, in confederacy with the conspirators of the Tuilleries, had given orders to the officers of the *corps-de-reserve* to let the people advance, and then fire upon them in the rear, at the same time that the cannon of the castle should mow them down in front. The council-general discovered this plot in the middle of the night; they sent twice for the commandant-general, who did not obey till the second summons; they presented to him the fatal order, signed with his hand, and which still remains in the archives of the *commune*; the council-general caused the traitor to be arrested, and adopted measures equally prompt and vigorous to disconcert his treasonable designs. Without this, liberty was at an end; and yet you do not deign to give this circumstance a place among those which decided the victory in favor of the people! What are the enormous crimes which, in your contemplation, have effaced the merit of these services*?

---

* Robespierre displays consummate art in giving this false account of the circumstances attending the murder of Mandat. He knew that Petion, who himself had signed the order to repel force by force, would not dare to contradict, or challenge a proof of these facts; and the insinuation that some written document was preserved in the archives of the *commune* is well calculated to intimidate the treacherous Petion.

Who would believe it? You reproach the council-general for not having abdicated, on the morrow of the combat at the Tuilleries, the authority with which they had been intrusted by the people, and which the legislative assembly had sanctioned, in order to recall the old municipality, and, consequently, the old directory. *You attribute this conduct to the love of power!*

You reproach the council-general with having prolonged the revolutionary effort beyond the necessary period. What was this effort? You do not describe it: it is probable that the necessary period to which you allude, was the same you had fixed as the time for abdication. So that, according to you, the revolutionary effort ought to have lasted four-and-twenty hours precisely; you measure political revolutions by those of the sun. But as you found yourself possessed of that infinite wisdom, which regulates by certain laws the most irregular phenomena of the moral world, why did not you say to the people, as the Almighty says to the ocean, " Thus far shalt thou " come, and here shall thy proud waves be stayed?" Why did you not come, and create in one day a new political world, as the Creator formed the world in three days. You did not appear at the *commune* till the third day after the capture of the Tuilleries. You came to announce to us, that the committee of twenty-one in the legislative assembly was willing to sanction the revolution, *and confirm all the acts of the commune*. This was but a preamble to the further information that the committee of twenty-one in the legislative assembly had a report ready, the effect of which was to recall the old municipality. This idea, with which you seemed infinitely delighted, was unanimously rejected by the council-general, as the infallible means of knitting up the threads of those conspiracies which ought to be broken for ever. The same day you made a long speech to prove that Louis XVI. ought not to be shut up in the tower of the Temple, and that if he was not lodged in a magnificent hotel, all France would rise against the *commune*; your opinion was over-ruled. You appeared alarmed; you seemed to think that the council-general was actuated by madness. You spoke of it in the most unqualified terms; *you thought its style and disposition both reprehensible*. You were continually sighing for the return of your semi-aristocratic municipality. You thought to punish the council-general by absenting yourself;

VOL. II.   K K

self; and continually held councils with your friends, either at the committee of twenty-one, or at your own house, to concert measures for its dissolution. You were, like Achilles, sulky with the Greeks. You see how much your reproaches against the *commune* are disfigured by passion, and, I will not say how unjust, but how childish they are. You *were terrified*, you say, at the disorder, the tumult, *the spirit which prevailed in that assembly*. The spirit which animated the defenders of liberty terrified you! You discuss the necessity of silence, not like a statesman, but like the regent of a college. You wonder that the council general, *instead of confining itself to the affairs of the* commune, *rather resembled a political assembly*. The public liberty occupied a part of their deliberations on the 12th and 13th of August! They were wrong, undoubtedly, they should have debated only on the duties of *scavengers and lamp-lighters!* For what besides had the people appointed them? *They discoursed of plots against the public liberty.* What folly to think of plots! Did any ever exist? or if they did, was it the business of the council-general to counteract them? *Citizens were denounced before them.* Was it not enough, on the 10th of August, to have conquered the Swiss soldiers, and have lost a great number of patriots? Could they think the following days properly spent in arresting conspirators! in denouncing Montmorin, Depoix, Duport, Lamballe, and so many other worthy people! These crimes must be punished. *They cited them to their bar.* They ought, at least, to have waited on them, at their own houses, to have paid them a visit in a body! *They heard them in public.* It would have been better to subject them to a private interrogatory. *They dismissed them if acquitted, or else detained them.* They ought neither to have been dismissed or detained! *The customary rules were totally dispensed with.* Hang me up these municipal officers! what, violate customary rules during a revolution! You do not tell us what rules these were, but with such guilty magistrates, it is not worth while to descend to particulars. Was it any business of theirs to adopt precautions to render the event of the battle of the Tuilleries favourable to liberty? Prudent Petion, the *commune* of Paris had raised the standard of insurrection, in the name of the country; the cause of the *commune* interested all France.

The

The effervescence of the public mind was so great, that it was impossible to restrain the torrent. What ravages were occasioned by this torrent of effervescent minds! *All their deliberations were inflamed with the impetuosity of enthusiasm.* Rouse up your choler against the enthusiasm of liberty; never stop to inquire whether these deliberations were good or bad. *They succeeded each other with a terrifying rapidity.* You are always *terrified:* take courage; in an urgent crisis, when all people animated with the same spirit, rapidity of discussion is rather a consolatory, than an alarming phenomenon. *Day and night the council-general continued their sittings.* Scoundrels! to consecrate their days and nights to the public weal!

I would not suffer my name to be annexed to a multitude of acts, no less irregular than contrary to principle. What principles? Not those by which tyranny was destroyed. What are we to conclude but that your slumbers were less interrupted, and that the revolution is a nullity, because not sanctioned by the signature of Jerome Petion?

I was equally sensible that prudence required me not to approve, or strengthen by my presence, the transactions then passing.—Exactly so; the council-general was without authority; in vain the people had created it; in vain the people approved it; you refused your approbation. Take care of yourself, my dear Petion, this language excites a suspicion of dictatorship.

Those whom my presence incommoded were very solicitous to make the people believe that I presided at all their operations; and that nothing was done but in concert with me.—Whom did your presence incommode? Were you not a good citizen? and the delegates whom the people, in the night of the 9th of August, had judged worthy to defend their cause, were they of less importance than yourself? Had the people forbid them to fulfil the object of their mission without the consent of Jerome Petion? Do you believe that citizens armed for the overthrow of despotism are so idolatrous, so cowardly, so stupid as you would insinuate?

I seldom made my appearance: if at that time I had loudly declared my sentiments of opposition, it would have occasioned a schism which might have been productive of unhappy consequences; there is in every thing a moment of maturity, which ought prudently to be turned to advantage.—I firmly believe you to be a man eminently endowed with the gift of *pru-*

dently

dently turning to advantage the moment of maturity. Yet, whether you had declared in favor of the old municipality, difmiffed by the public voice, or for the new council of the *commune*, or for or againft the revolution; I much doubt whether you would have been fo unfortunate as to have occafioned a fatal fchifm.

It muft be acknowledged that this ftyle of reafoning appears extraordinary; but your imagination, though generally quiet enough, is fo much ftruck with every thing relating to our laft revolution, that you fee monfters and crimes where other men difcern only ordinary events, or virtuous actions. Thus you confefs yourfelf to be fhocked that the council-general of the *commune* fhould have thought it neceffary to prolong the fhutting of the barriers four-and-twenty hours beyond the moment you had fixed for their being thrown open; and becaufe I was accidentally of their opinion, you fpeak of my propofal in terms like thofe you would ufe to defcribe an eruption of Mount Vefuvius. You indulge yourfelf in declamations, and draw portraits, but you prefent no facts; and ftill lefs reafons. You are compaffionate towards thofe traitors who were adverfarious to liberty, and inexorable only towards the moft zealous patriots.

You even renew the reproaches which Louvet has vented againft the *commune*, for having prefented too violent petitions to the legiflative affembly; but in terms much more vague, and infignificant, though not lefs rafh. I can only refer you to my anfwer to Louvet. But how could you fo far forget every principle of liberty, as to fubmit to this abfurd and procraftinated inquiry into words uttered during the moft ftormy days of the revolution? How could you forget in what manner the conftituted authorities were then compofed, and what were the rights of the people? I am particularly grieved to fee you tranfgrefs the fidelity of hiftory, to transfer to the phantom of a conftituted power, which now no longer exifts, the glory of thofe illuftrious acts, which belongs to the people. In the legiflative affembly we can only praife a few individuals who were worthy of the public confidence; but who does not know that the majority was bafe and corrupt? that it deified la Fayette, acquitted all confifcators, and was in league with the court againft the nation? Who does not know that the affembly favored, as much as poffible, all thofe treafons, which, but for the

infur-

insurrection of the 10th of August, would have yielded France into the hands of the foreign armies, and to the rage of tyrants; who does not know the servile baseness with which Louis XVI. was received in the bosom of the assembly, at the moment when victory was yet wavering between liberty and despotism! Who does not know that when all parties rose with a sudden motion, and saluted the nation, with an unanimous exclamation, the thunder of the people had already pealed in their ears? Who does not know, that it was at the roar of cannon, the cry of victory, and even on the petition of the triumphant people, that the assembly took the oath of equality; that when it abolished the distinctions between active and passive citizens, the sections, then permanent, had already received them without discrimination; that the people were already overturning the statues of kings, when the assembly decreed their destruction; that the people were masters of the king's fate when the assembly decreed his suspension; that the people were masters of their own lot, and had resumed the exercise of their right, when, on the formal demand of the people, the assembly decreed the convocation of a national convention; in fine, that the people were abandoned or betrayed by all their delegates, when they were obliged to effect their own deliverance: what do you mean, then, by *that dignified character of the legislative body, which saved the empire*, and that indirect reproach against the city of Paris, for having restrained the liberty of the assembly, when it is obvious that all the decrees which you extol were produced by those imperious circumstances which the people had created by the insurrection of the 10th of August? What right have you to impute as a crime to the *commune* of Paris certain petitions which the public interest required, which were adopted, almost without exception, by the assembly itself; petitions which united with the language of free men, the rules of decorum, and a respect even for the shadow of an expiring representation.

It was not *the* commune *that entered into a state of rivalship with the assembly;* but certain members of the assembly, your Mentors, who were desirous to destroy the *commune;* who, on the very morrow of the 10th of August, began to rally all the enemies of the revolution, who, from that moment, calumniated the people of Paris in all the departments, who laboured incessantly to lull or to deceive the

the legiflative body, that it might become the inftrument of their pitiful intrigues. In a fortnight afterwards, when the Pruffians were advancing towards Paris, when the *commune*, to the found of the tocfin and the alarm gun, affembled in the *Champ-de-Mars* the innumerable inhabitants of this great city, what were Briffot and his allies about? Caballing, and telling lies. What was Roland doing? Pofting up bills againft the Parifians: he wanted to take flight, with the executive council, the king, and the affembly. To flatter thofe who have endangered the people, to defame thofe who have ferved them, what can we call this conduct, but doubly to betray the public caufe?

Here, I confefs, you embarrafs me extremely. How does it happen, I fhall be afked, that a man fo praiseworthy in the republic, as Jerome Petion, can have reafoned and written in fuch a manner? I believe, however, that I can explain the matter, by means which you yourfelf have furnifhed.

The mayor of Paris, you fay, in your fpeech, fpeaking of this difaftrous epoch, the 10th of Auguft, *was no longer a centre of union. I was continued in my place; but had only an empty title. I feldom appeared at the* commune. *I was not informed of any thing.* That is the fact; you were not there. You were the Crillon of the laft revolution. But the whole truth muft be told: it will, at firft, aftonifh thofe who, far from the fcene of action, learn the hiftory of France in Roland's pamphlets, and in the journals of Rœderer, Gorfas, and other writers of that ftamp. You will not, however, deny the facts I am about to unfold. You will ingenuoufly confefs that you did all in your power to impede the revolution of the 10th of Auguft. Not that you are inimical to liberty, far from it: but, in the firft place, you are naturally unfufpicious, and could not believe in the confpiracies of the court, with which we were begirt. You had a pitying fmile for thofe who mentioned them to you; fo that you feparated yourfelf from the patriots of the committee of police, who did believe in them, and they were obliged to difpenfe with your fignature, in giving orders for the diftribution of ammunition to the federates.

You had already, feveral times, rendered the incipient infurrection abortive, by running through the fections and the fuburbs, preaching order and tranquillity. You had

had fettered the courage both of the people and the federates.—Nothing could be more dangerous than this conduct, an attempt of the kind, if relinquished, delivered up the people to the sword of tyranny. Mean time the danger became more urgent, and proofs of the project framed by the court to murder the patriots, were universal. The revolutionary directory of the citizen federates had fixed on the night of the 9th of August for suppressing it. Your usual prudence led you to exert every means to oppose their intention. You spoke to all men of the necessity of remaining calm and peaceful. The 7th of August, I was surprised by a visit from the Mayor of Paris; it was the first time of my being so honoured, though formerly extremely intimate. I concluded that some great motive had brought you: you harangued to me, for a whole hour, on the dangers of insurrection. I had no particular influence over events: but, as I often went to the society of friends of the constitution, where the members of the directory of the federates habitually went, you earnestly pressed me to preach your doctrine in that society. You told me it would be necessary to defer resistance to oppression, until the assembly should have pronounced the king's forfeiture of the crown: but, at the same time, leisure must be allowed for the discussion of this great question, will all possible premeditation. You could, however, offer no security that the court would adjourn their project of cutting our throats, for so long a time as it might please the national assembly to adjourn the king's forfeiture; and it was well known that at that time, the royalist party predominated in the assembly; your own Brissot, himself, and his friends had pronounced several long speeches, the only object of which was to prove, that the discussion ought to be deferred, and deferred without end. You even know how much their equivocal conduct had disgusted the public; who perceived that their project was to alarm the court with the fear of an insurrection, in order to secure the return to office the ministers of their own choosing. I myself might have developed these mysteries; but such was my confidence in you, and such, to speak the truth, the sentiments of friendship, which your unexpected condescension revived in my heart, that I, to a certain degree, thought you in the right; but the people and the federates judged differently, and there was a general preparation for insurrection. Your opinions still

KK 4   biassed

biassed your conduct, and even in the night of the 9th of August, at the moment when the sections were all ready to march, they received from you a pressing circular letter, in which you conjured them to remain quiet. What a moment to give such advice! Some appeared inclined to follow it, and a general consultation was held. The section *du Theâtre François*, where the Marseillois battalion resided, had acquired a great ascendency, by the courage which it had constantly displayed. Danton, who was president of that section, rejected your letter with the energy which he always has exhibited in moments of great danger to the country; the tocsin was rung in all quarters. But all those who were going to devote themselves in the cause of liberty were sensible that their efforts would be unavailing, if his honor the mayor came, according to custom, to thwart their operations, and to relax and divide the effect of the popular force. Citizens of Paris and federates, all were agreed on the necessity of one preliminary step of infinite prudence, which you do not mention, the object of which was to put it out of your power to renew your pacific operations and sermons: you were confined by order of the people, in your own house, under the honourable pretence of insuring your safety. You must recollect, that on the morrow of the 11th or 12th of August, when the victory was gained, Brissot and Guadet, in despair at the turn things had taken, loudly vented their choler at your table, in presence of many witnesses; they openly reprimanded you for the facility with which you obeyed the will of the people; Brissot even carried his familiarity so far as to accuse you of cowardice; he charged you, at least, to put a spoke in the wheel of the revolution, which you had been unable to keep inactive; and you, like a docile pupil, appeared the next day at the *commune*, to announce that project of a committee of twenty-one, suggested by them, and which I have already mentioned.

I do not mean to assert that you have an invincible antipathy for popular commotions, or that your zeal for the public tranquillity admits of no exception; but you are always guided by the same impulse. You shewed as much complaisance for the riot of the 20th of June, as you displayed repugnance to the insurrection of the 10th of August. What could occasion this contradiction of conduct. I will explain it. The revolution in August was

expected

APPENDIX, No. X.

expected to produce public liberty; the armed proceſſion in June, the recall of the miniſters Claviere and Roland. The event in Auguſt was provoked by the neceſſity of the public welfare; that in June by the artifices of intrigue. On both occaſions, the citizens were guided by the pureſt motives, but on the 20th of June they were deceived. They were not appriſed that the petition preſented in their name would be ſurreptitiouſly altered, and that, to the grand objects of national welfare which formed its baſis, a dexterous hand would ſubjoin a demand of the recall of Meſſrs. Claviere and Roland. While the throne yet continued to ſtand, I was cautious of publiſhing my opinion on this point; it was enough for patriots to know that the court attempted to turn this event to the diſadvantage of liberty, to attempt juſtifying it, and no one ſtept forward with more zeal and frankneſs than myſelf to defend you againſt all the perſecutions to which it gave riſe. But at this day it is of uſe that I ſhould freely publiſh my real opinion. Beſides, the intriguers who ſurrounded you preferred the kind of inſurrection which took place in the 20th of June, as tending to reſtore them to office. Thus, though it was publicly announced for eight days, though their emiſſaries publicly ran about the ſuburbs, and even complained of the ill ſucceſs of their efforts, you took no ſtep to prevent them. You might have done it with much more facility than you retarded the general iuſurrection againſt tyranny. Even the court was not diſpleaſed, as your party furniſhed a pretence for calumniating the popular cauſe; good citizens, only, publicly oppoſed the inſurrection. The day before it took place I met Chabot, who, like myſelf ſaw with uneaſineſs the miſerable manœuvre which was in preparation. I adviſed him to repair to the fauxbourg St. Antoine, where the petitioners were aſſembled, to enlighten them with reſpect to the nature of this proceeding; he harangued the people in the church of the *Quinze-Vingts*. He was too late, and his civic homily was cut ſhort by theſe words, pronounced in the preſence of three thouſand perſons: " We are ſecure of Petion: It is " Petion's order: Petion is on our ſide." It was fortunate for you on this occaſion that you were attacked by the enemies of the people, and defended by thoſe very patriots, who internally blamed your conduct; for you had ſeriouſly endangered your reputation for prudence and integrity; and however wrong the directory who perſecuted

you

you might be in their motives and means, it is certain they were but too much in the right as to certain facts ; and however conftitutional Camus might seem, in an opinion which he publifhed againft you, which I was far from approving, at leaft he was not in the wrong when he accufed you, very ungenteely to be fure, of having *lied* to the public, and to the legiflative affembly, in the account you gave them of your conduct in this particular. The people alone was in the right. Neither you nor your adverfaries were exempt from blame: yet this was one of the principal fources of your popularity.

The court daily laboured to augment it by their abfurd attacks, and by their plots. The intriguers, calling themfelves patriots, who looked on your popularity as their patrimony, fwelled it by all the great means then at their difpofal. The real friends of the country fupported it with all their powers. The thick-headed Louis XVI. thought he faw a rival in the Jacobin mayor of Paris; but Cæfar, on contemplating, your countenance, dilated with an eternal fmile, would have faid, " This is not the " man who will tear the empire from me." The day of the federation arrived, and the armed citizens came from all parts of the country to offer to you the homage of public efteem. You were the hero of the federation in 1792, as la Fayette was in 1790, but la Fayette's adorers were flaves; your partifans were free men; the applaufes they were pleafed to lavifh on you, turned to execrations which they levelled againft the tyrant. Your glory was pure as the heart of patriotifm, or as the love of liberty. How eafy would it have been to you to affure for ever the happinefs of your country, and with the fame blow to deftroy both defpotifm and intrigue. But, far from fuffering yourfelf, even for a moment, to be led away by the glorious deftiny of France, you employed yourfelf only in arrefting its progrefs. From that day you have been continually retreating towards that miferable fyftem of intrigue, in which you were girt by that petty ambitious faction which befet you.

Such are the unfortunate circumftances which have foured you, my dear Petion, even without your knowledge, againft the laft revolution, and even againft the city of Paris. Anger, fometimes, entered into celeftial minds; and anger has placed in your hands the arrows which you let fly againft the electoral affembly of the department of Paris.

You perfuaded yourfelf that you had grounds of complaint againſt that affembly, becaufe you were only nominated as a deputy to the convention on the fecond fcrutiny. O human weaknefs! you could not even for a moment difguife your chagrin; and rather than be affronted by the priority of another citizen, you preferred being chofen third at Chartres, to being fecond at Paris; and on the very next day, at the opening of the fitting, you eagerly declared to the electoral affembly, that you would not be deputy for the department of Paris; you fhunned the affembly from that moment, as before you had fhunned the *commune*. Yet you repeat all the calumnious abfurdities heaped on that body by difappointed ſtupid intriguers. I am again obliged to refer you to my anfwer to Louvet, whom you have weakly and imperfectly copied.

But what have the Jacobins done to you? What could be your inducement to poſt that ſtrange *placard?* Was it the fervices they have rendered their country, and the great influence they alfo had in bringing about the laſt revolution? Does this fingle crime efface, in your judgment, all the benefits for which you were yourfelf indebted to the patriots who people this immortal city?

I no longer retain the fame influence over events, you continually exclaim in a plaintive tone; *time will fhew whether that circumſtance has been beneficial or injurious to Paris and the welfare of its inhabitants.* Is this meant as a threat? Are you determined to punifh us? Does only a remnant of pity plead in your breaſt in favor of Paris? Why then do you not undertake her defence againſt the bafe perfecutions of her daſtardly enemies?

I have more than once faved Paris; and I have fpared the blood of the people.

Who is the man that can deliberately rank among the fervices which he has rendered to the people, that of not ordering them to be affaffinated? If a general boaſts, that by ordering a ceffation of carnage, he has fpared human blood, I can conceive him: but what affinity is there between the functions of a mayor, and the maffacre of citizens? Are the friends of humanity to eſtimate their civil virtues by a contraſt with the monſtrous exceffes of tyranny? But by what right could Petion command the murder of the people who protected him; of the people who, on the 20th of June, might have exclaimed, " It is you and " your party who have led us to flaughter."

I have

APPENDIX, No. X.

I have more than once saved Paris;—(before the 10th of August,) It is certain that many heroic actions are still shrouded in darkness, but pray inform us exactly *how many times* you saved the country, and we will erect to you, at least, an equal number of statues. The gratitude of the whole human race has confecrated the names of those who have only once saved liberty, what should we do for the man to whom this fort of tranfactions is fo familiar that he does not even condefcend to enumerate them?

I have faved Robefpierre himfelf from perfecution, by attacking myfelf to his lot. What a combination! After fo great an action, what need can there be to recite one fo indifferent? It would not claim difcuflion but for the importance you annex to it. You are defirous to recur to that honorable period of your life, when, during the revifion of the conftitution, you, with a few of your colleagues, fulfilled the duties of a faithful reprefentative. By whom was I then perfecuted? By la Fayette and his faction, as I now am by the factions which fucceeded them. For what caufe was I perfecuted, but the caufe of liberty? And why were you not alfo perfecuted, yourfelf? Why do you affume that you attached yourfelf to *my* lot, rather than that I attached myfelf to yours? What do I fay? Why is it faid that you were attached to me, rather than to the country, or, at leaft, to your own honor? And how could you imagine that your protection availed me more than the public intereft, and the facred caufe which I had efpoufed?

But admitting that you have faved us all; would this great kindnefs give you a right to deftroy us, or even to calumniate a fingle individual? The vileft infect revolts againft the man who attempts to crufh him; and I againft Jerome Petion, as well in my own name, as in the name of all good citizens againft whom he declares war. What a moment have you felected for your attack? I had, in oppofition to calumny, juft gained a victory, an eafy victory, in which I was far from exulting. You fecretly came to the field, armed cap-a-pie, but the rapidity of the combat was fuch, that you had not time to draw your fword, and at the moment when I was peaceably retreating from the field of battle, you came and affaulted me in the rear.

You could not then refolve to return into your port-folio your difmal fpeech. The directors of your political confcience science gave you to understand that the credit of the party was too cruelly endangered, by so shameful a check, that your civic *chef-d'œuvre* alone could repair it, and you delivered it to the printer. But as it undoubtedly forms one of the principles of the coterie *, that all means are legitimate which tend to promote the good cause, you thought it your duty to prepare for the success of this sagacious manœuvre, by a posting-bill against the Jacobins, in which you send forth a sharpened arrow against me. The result was, a decree from the directory of mayoralty, confirmed by that of the minister of the interior, importing that the above-mentioned posting-bill shall be printed at the end of Jerome Petion's speech; that most honorable mention shall be made of both by all the public news-writers, and that they shall be distributed to all the administrative bodies, to all the municipalities throughout the republic, to all rectors, and clergymen. The virtuous Roland ought honestly to inform the committee of finance, how much this new distribution will cost the republic: he might also tell us, whether those who stop the justificatory publications at the post-office, when they are sent to the departments by order of the *commune*, and franked by the mayor, are more cautious with respect to covers franked by the minister. Can it be just, my dear Petion, to attack us with such unequal arms? Your want of generosity is the more conspicuous in this respect, that you are emboldened to the combat by an opinion which you entertain, that your name alone will give to your assertions the authority of a demonstrative proof, as you yourself insinuate in your preface. Thus am I, without appeal, attainted and convicted, before the tribunal of the eighty-three departments, of all the absurdities and all the vices which you impute to me. For I have not even a right to answer you. Did I ever dispute your right of printing every day, and even of posting your virtues, when no man was employed in discussing them? And against me, who never justified myself, but in defence of my life, you have passed a law, by which I cannot repel your calumnies, without proving, by that single act, an excess of vanity. Suffer at least, a word of animadversion on the abuse you make of this strange privilege. In fact, it is too much to arrogate a right of loudly accusing me of

---

* Alluding to the meetings held by the Brissotines at madame Roland's.

cowardice,

cowardice, of posting that you saw me trembling. And when? At the very time when la Fayette was proscribing the patriots; the day when with thirty individuals, among whom you were not, I remained at the Jacobin club, surrounded by satellites, while the blood of patriots, which he had recently shed, was still streaming; at that time when I obstinately defended that tutelary institution of liberty against the formidable faction which governed the constituent assembly. They trembled then, in your opinion, all those who denounced that faction, in the midst of its guilty success, and who never ceased their struggle for the rights of the people, which that faction had proscribed.

But for what purpose do you thus cavil at my conduct in the constituent assembly? You pretend to explain yourself on the accusation against me for aspiring to the dictatorship, which you acknowledge to be a calumny. What then was left for you to say? You were precisely employed to come to the relief of Louvet, whose defeat was foreseen, though it was not expected to be so speedy. Your commission was to make a digression on my general character; and as it is well known that, in the eyes of frivolous men, absurdities and errors are more degrading than vices, you have depicted me captious, morose, and atrabilious. Those who directed you knew, by instinct, that the only resource of intrigue was to hold up, beforehand, to the public opinion, those who might unmask them, as *suspicious, visionary beings, ever ready to denounce rashly; men of gloomy imaginations, who every where see chimeras, precipices, plots, and monsters; and moreover, vain, ambitious, and desirous of making court to the people.*——Very well, my dear Petion, nothing can be better conceived than to compare the people to kings, and the friends of liberty to courtiers; for if this opinion prevails, a vast field lies open to those political sharpers, who do not flatter the people, but who plunder them, and cut their throats. And, in fact, so many pay their court to kings or to ministers, the depositaries of the public power and wealth, that they may easily hope for pardon who court the people, by defending the cause of justice and humanity; for I call you yourself to witness that such are the only means by which they can be flattered.

As for men of gloomy imaginations, I must do you the justice to acknowledge, that you were ever exempt from that

that fault. I am a witness that you never believed in any plot against the state, till after it was executed. I am a witness, that till the day of the *Champ-de-Mars*, you cast an eye of pity on those who spoke ill of la Fayette ; that, even after that period, you never ceased to put a favourable interpretation on his intentions. I am a witness, that when the faction, of which he was at the head, named, in the constituent assembly, commissioners to go and meet Louis XVI. in his return from Varennes, they cast their eyes on you, as the least dangerous of all the patriots, and as a proper person to be joined with Barnave, and la Tour Maubourg. I am witness, that after la Fayette had assumed the command of the armies, you, on an hundred occasions, guaranteed his innocence, and said to every one who would give you a hearing ; " La Fayette is on our " side." I further attest, that you spoke of the *Patriot Narbonne*, and of the *Patriot Montesquieu*, with peculiar veneration, precisely in the same terms as the *Chronique*, and the *Patriote François*. In a word, I attest, that there is hardly a man at this day accused as a traitor to the country, to whom you have not delivered a similar brevet of patriotism.

I will pass my word for you, that far from being troublesome, mistrustful, and melancholy, you are the man of all others whose blood flows most placidly, whose heart is least agitated by the spectacle of human perfidy, and whose philosophy most patiently endures the miseries of others.

For myself, I acknowledge my faults ; and though, according to the opinions of those who have the best means of judging, I am no less easy, and unsuspicious in private life than you think me mistrustful in public affairs ; though you have long experienced this truth, and my friendship for you existed long after the date of those proceedings which were most offensive to my principles, I own, to my shame, that I have the weakness still to believe in the existence of fatal intrigues, which you perhaps will guess at, when all France is sacrificed to them.

But you, who but a fortnight before the revolution of the 10th of August, of your own spontaneous motion, had the turpitude to go to the king ; we know not whether it was to convert him or to justify yourself ; you who, on the very eve of the insurrection, went, in all simplicity, to range in that royal forest, to expose Jerome Petion to

the

the derision of Herod's court, you who could not believe that there was so much wickedness, even in a court, how can you still be so unrelenting towards those who, on certain occasions, have proved that their folly was more reasonable than your wisdom ? Does your kind-heartedness extend only to mountebanks and tyrants ? Is it a law in nature that minds distinguished by apathy hate those possessed of ardour and energy ? This is certain, that I always thought I perceived in you less kindness for the ebullitions of patriotism, than for the excesses of aristocracy. For example, I have seen you less prepossessed against la Fayette, than against Danton ; less angry with the court at Coblentz, than with the Jacobin club.

You indemnify yourself, however, for the pain you experience in accusing so many persons; you lay down the censor's rod, to assume the panegyrist's censer. It is not necessary for me to say in whose favour; your remnant of popularity was not to be expended for the sole purpose of defaming Paris and the Jacobins; it was also to revive the credit of a faction trembling for itself.

You dogmatically assure us that you know not of a Brissotine faction ; that Brissot, of all men in the world, is the least proper to be the head of a party. You assert it in your posting-bill, you repeat it in your speech. And what does it signify ? It is not my intention here to enter into a discussion of Brissot's character. Who ever said that he was the head of a party ?

I have not yet seen among us a real head of a party; even la Fayette was not to be considered in that light; he was an agent for the king ; his only aim was, to be the most powerful man in the court of Louis XVI. In France, and in a revolution, the object of which is not to substitute one tyranny for another, but to restore the reign of justice and equality, heads of parties can only be petty knaves, without either courage or genius. Now, these kind of men can easily plunder, ruin, and tear the state to pieces : that is the most easy of all trades, but they can never enslave us. Two powerful obstacles will always oppose that undertaking, their mediocrity, and the good sense of the people.

As for your Brissot, since you will return to the subject, does it follow, because his name is become the root of a new conjugation, that the public look up to him as the head of a party ? Escobar possessed the same honour, and

yet

yet he was nothing but a Jesuit. If father Briſſot was acknowledged generaliſſimo of all the Briſſotines in the republic, he would certainly be the moſt formidable power in Europe. You have repeated to me twenty times, that Briſſot was a mere child, and that is a cant word of the coterie, when they wiſh to ſoften down certain frauds, ſomewhat too glaring, with which he is reproached: they even pretend that he is not diſpleaſed at being thus exhibited, juſt as Sixtus Quintus ſometimes affected ſimplicity, ſometimes pretended to be ill. You will however give me leave to conſider him as a perverſe child; but as I am unwilling to undertake the taſk of correcting him, permit me to leave him to the public. Clootz, who judges him with great forbearance, ſays, in his ingenious and inſtructive opinion, *To contemplate his indirect proceedings, his lies,* &c. &c. *one would think he was in the pay of the enemies of France, and of the human race;* and I, ſtill more forbearing, conſider him only as one of the moſt extenſive mercantile agents in Europe. If the public form a more uncharitable opinion, make your complaint to them: and as you complain of *the general blindneſs on that ſubject,* be you the operator to remove the cataract which deprives them of the ſight of ſo many virtues. Do not diſdain to enlighten thoſe whom you have ſaved. Briſſot, you ſay, *has knowledge and genius.* Be it ſo. We are even credibly informed, that he has written ſome large books: he is, at leaſt, a revolutionary Dacier, and a political Scudery. Clootz alſo pretends, that he does not carry his head a jot higher than he did ten years ago. Now, I cannot ſay whether, ten years ago, he held his head very high. But again, what does all this ſignify? We might both of us have avoided this diſcuſſion. You yourſelf ought not to have begun it. Briſſot, extolled by you, ſeems to be praiſing himſelf. The pupil is not conſulted reſpecting the capacity of his maſter, or the lover on the charms of his miſtreſs. Was Orgon a competent judge of the character of Tartuffe? How many were the proofs requiſite for the diſenchanting of the credulous man? and proof of what a nature! Nothing leſs than *an Elmira* can effect ſuch a prodigy. *Le pauvre homme,* is the conſtant anſwer he gives to every argument: and ſimilarly at your houſe, every one continually repeated *Le pauvre Warville* *.

In

---

* Robeſpierre alludes to Moliere's comedy called Tartuffe, ou l'Impoſteur. The endearing tenderneſs of the French exclamation, *Le pauvre*

In vain you deny this difgraceful fubjection, the very efforts you make to repel the fufpicion only confirm it. Why do you always begin your fpeeches with this exordium: *Never did man in place think and act for himfelf fo much as I?* Why, in the preface to the fpeech we are difcuffing, are you fo folicitous to inform your readers, that *in order to compofe it you retired within yourfelf; you were deaf to the voice of friendfhip; and had no communication with any perfon whomfoever.* Is an author obliged to prove that he put himfelf in clofe confinement to compofe his books? And are not fuch oratorical precautions fomewhat fufpicious?

Befides, your whole fpeech proves, that nothing in it belongs to you, except perhaps, the colouring, and the ftyle: but the thoughts, the principles, the moral, the aim, the moment of publication, the vague accufations, the declamations unfupported by proof, the malignant infinuations, the equivocal tone, the crafty windings, grofs contradictions, even the political abfurdities, the mixture of fimplicity and art, of moderation, and rooted malice; thofe exhortations to peace, immediately followed by thofe infidious reflections which revive dormant prejudices, thofe farcafms by which that difcord is renewed which feemed at an end, and the pofting-bill pafted on our walls; all thefe things are not your own. You calumniate yourfelf when you pretend that you are led by nobody. Perhaps you even believe it; but I will take my oath you are quite miftaken. Do people know when they are led? Only obferve what paffes on our theatres: when a dexterous chambermaid, or an intriguing valet, leads a Geronte, or an Orgon, as it were in leading-ftrings: don't you fee with what art the rogues extol the wonderful wifdom and incredible firmnefs of the poor man, while he, in the midft of their noify joy, cries, " Oh I am very certain that I am not a man to be led, and if there is a fteady head in France, I warrant it is this on my fhoulders."

Make proper allowances for the exaggeration neceffary in the dramatic art, and above all for your great merits, and I would almoft venture to affirm that there is in this portrait fome refemblance of yourfelf. For example, in the month of January laft, when a new adminiftration was

pauvre homme, is not adequately conveyed by the Englifh expreffion, *poor man!*

formed, I saw that you were in the firm conviction that it was you who had chosen them. When I asked you, if that measure of the court did not strike you as a little suspicious; you answered, with an air of extraordinary satisfaction, "Oh if you did but know what I know! If you knew who it was that pointed them out." I perceived your meaning, and laughing at your credulity, said "it was you, perhaps;" on which, rubbing your hands together, you gave an assenting hem! hem! It was in vain that you persisted in assuring me the fact was so. I had too sincere an esteem for you to suppose that you had sufficient credit with Louis XVI. and his courtiers, to form a ministry. But I will inform you by what means you persuaded yourself that you had created these ministers. When Brissot, and certain patriots of the same stamp in the legislative assembly, in concert with Narbonne, by the consent of la Fayette, and the intervention of certain women, such as the baroness de Stael, and the marchioness de Condorcet, had made all the arrangements, and the whole transaction was settled, Brissot came to you and said, " Whom shall we appoint ministers? Roland, Cla-
" viere,—they are good men! do you approve of them?—
" Eh—egad, yes!—Roland, Claviere—Oh that would be
" charming! let them be appointed by all means;"—and then you thought you had formed the administration.

When these ministers were thrust out by another faction, the same men dexterously availed themselves of your popularity to obtain their recall. Thus originated the transactions of the 20th of June; you persevered with firmness towards that object, but you carried your views no farther, because your leaders did not wish that you should go farther. The torrent which subverted the throne, deranged their real projects; and their only consolation for the events of the 10th of August was, that they were enabled to recall Roland and Claviere. They wish, under the name of these two ministers, to reign for ever; to effect which, they must enslave the people; divide the convention, in order to govern it, and persecute the friends of liberty. Hence arise all their intrigues, all their calumnies, all their crimes, their alliance with the old partisans of royalty and aristocracy. You suspect nothing of this, and you still remain with them, because you are accustomed to follow wherever they lead you. They have already led you far enough, and I am afraid they will lead you still farther

astray.

astray. Reflect on yourself, if it be possible, and examine how heavy the conditions, by which you are bound to them, hang on you.

I own that you are, in some degree, obliged to them; they have materially accelerated the maturity of your reputation; cried up in all the journals which were at their disposal, you were a deity to all who took those journals for oracles. In a distant view spots are not discerned, the springs of political events are not perceived; and you perhaps are the only instance among the defenders of liberty, throughout the world, of a man who has enjoyed the plenitude of his glory. You ought, however, to mistrust your good fortune, Rousseau will inform you, that a real statesman sows in one century, and reaps in the succeeding ages. Read history, and you will find that the benefactors of the human race were its martyrs. Agis was condemned by the Ephori, for his attempt to revive the laws of Lycurgus; Cato plunged the dagger in his own entrails; the younger Brutus was obliged to destroy himself, after having killed the tyrant; the son of Marius expired under the sword of tyranny; Socrates drank hemlock; Sydney died on a scaffold; but Petion, in an instant, found himself loaded with the honors recently lavished on la Fayette. Had you sought to fathom the causes of this phenomenon, you might have discovered that a detached intrigue lent its support to your patriotism. You would have reflected that the Guadets of Athens were not the friends of Socrates; that Brutus and Cato were not deified by the Brissotines of Rome: and you would have discovered that you were the hero of June 1792, because you were not destined to be the hero of future ages. But these services of your friends are abundantly compensated by the advantages you have procured for them. Reflect, in the first place, that you furnished the most precious article of their whole stock in trade, I mean the reputation for integrity which you brought from the constituent assembly; for in the eyes of judicious observers, that was your real title to glory. Your new partners have increased it by their industry, but for their own benefit. It has served as a veil to their manœuvres, as an instrument of their ambition. It is your reputation that has furnished them the means of privately undermining the edifice of liberty, and of converting the first days of the republic into days of discord, disorder, and tyranny. To them you have sacrificed your glory. Please

Heaven

Heaven that you may, at least, have preserved your virtue! Observe how they already dare to place you in the front as a forlorn hope, on desperate occasions; how they place you in the same line as their Barbaroux's and their Birotteau's. Why is it not in my power to counteract the effects of their pernicious councils by austere and useful truth? They alone to whom nature has imparted greatness can love equality. Others require stilts or triumphal cars; when once they descend from them, they seem to enter the tomb. Many men appeared republicans before there was a republic, and ceased to be so when once it was established. They wished to degrade those who were above them, but would not descend from the eminence to which they themselves were elevated. They only love those revolutions of which they are the heroes; if they do not govern, they think all is anarchy and confusion; if the people conquer without their aid, they are in a state of revolt; they do not even forgive the people for reducing the importance of individuals by elevating its own majestic head.

Such is the melancholy secret of human vanity which explains so many wonderful metamorphoses. Such too is the only clue which can guide the public opinion in the maze of modern political events. As for us, my dear Petion, let us divest ourselves of these shameful weaknesses, let us not be compared to that tyrant who wished to reduce the size of man to a determinate standard; let us not require that fortune should find a full compensation for our merit; let us be content with the destiny which nature has reserved for us, and let the lot of the human race be accomplished.

To conclude, I repeat your own phrase, *let us occupy ourselves in the important concerns of the republic.* But, above all, let us endeavour, if possible, to acquire the morals and principles of true republicans.

THE END.

www.ingramcontent.com/pod-product-compliance
Lightning Source LLC
Chambersburg PA
CBHW020858020526
44116CB00029B/345